Pro LINQ Object Relational Mapping with C# 2008

Vijay P. Mehta

Apress®

Pro LINQ Object Relational Mapping with C# 2008

ISBN-13 (pbk): 978-1-59059-965-5

ISBN-10 (pbk): 1-59059-965-9

ISBN-13 (electronic): 978-1-4302-0597-5

9 8 7 6 5 4 3 2 1

Lead Editor: Ewan Buckingham
Technical Reviewer: Fabio Ferracchiati
Editorial Board: Clay Andres, Steve Anglin, Ewan Buckingham, Tony Campbell, Gary Cornell, Jonathan Gennick, Matthew Moodie, Joseph Ottinger, Jeffrey Pepper, Frank Pohlmann, Ben Renow-Clarke, Dominic Shakeshaft, Matt Wade, Tom Welsh
Project Manager: Sofia Marchant
Copy Editor: Sharon Wilkey
Associate Production Director: Kari Brooks-Copony
Production Editor: Kelly Gunther
Compositor: Susan Glinert Stevens
Proofreader: Elizabeth Berry
Indexer: Carol Burbo
Artist: April Milne
Cover Designer: Kurt Krames
Manufacturing Director: Tom Debolski

Distributed to the book trade worldwide by Springer-Verlag New York, Inc., 233 Spring Street, 6th Floor, New York, NY 10013. Phone 1-800-SPRINGER, fax 201-348-4505, e-mail `orders-ny@springer-sbm.com`, or visit `http://www.springeronline.com`.

For information on translations, please contact Apress directly at 2855 Telegraph Avenue, Suite 600, Berkeley, CA 94705. Phone 510-549-5930, fax 510-549-5939, e-mail `info@apress.com`, or visit `http://www.apress.com`.

Apress and friends of ED books may be purchased in bulk for academic, corporate, or promotional use. eBook versions and licenses are also available for most titles. For more information, reference our Special Bulk Sales–eBook Licensing web page at `http://www.apress.com/info/bulksales`.

For my wife and family

Contents at a Glance

PART 4 ■■■ The Bank of Pluto Case Study

PART 5 ■■■ Building on the Bank of Pluto Foundation

Contents

PART 2 LINQ to SQL Examined

PART 3 ■■■ Entity Framework Examined

PART 4 ■■■ The Bank of Pluto Case Study

PART 5 ■■■ Building on the Bank of Pluto Foundation

About the Author

VIJAY P. MEHTA is a software architect and author. He has provided creative and insightful leadership throughout his career as a *Fortune* 500 company enterprise architect and consultant as well as through published articles on software development patterns and practices. Starting off in the VC++/ATL, MFC, Win32, and VB6 worlds, Vijay later moved on to Java and .NET development. Currently working as a technology strategist, Vijay spends the bulk of his time involved in the design and implementation of large, cutting-edge software systems.

About the Technical Reviewer

FABIO CLAUDIO FERRACCHIATI, a prolific writer on cutting-edge technologies, has contributed to more than a dozen books on .NET, C#, Visual Basic, and ASP.NET. He is a .NET MCSD and lives in Milan, Italy. You can read his blog at `www.ferracchiati.com`.

Acknowledgments

Writing a book is a difficult task, one that cannot be done without the help of a supporting cast. *Pro LINQ Object Relational Mapping with C# 2008* is not an exception; many people have contributed and made this project possible. First, I need to thank the wonderful people at Apress who were immeasurably helpful along the way. In particular, I would like to thank my excellent tech editor Fabio Ferracchiati, my project manager Sofia Marchant, my copy editor Sharon Wilkey, and my production editor Kelly Gunther. Thanks, team—this would not have been possible without you.

There are a number of people who have mentored and guided me over the years on the ins and outs of enterprise software development. First are two of my early mentors, Matt Crouch and George McCoy; you two taught me the fundamentals that school couldn't, and for that I am very grateful. Next, the two Java guys who taught me to really appreciate object-relational mapping, Michael Kinnaird and Umesh Manocha, thank you for opening my eyes. Finally, the people who taught me to think about software architecture, in particular Paul Logston and Charles Hurley, thank you for influencing the way I think about software.

The last group of people who made this book possible is my family. First, I need to thank my parents and sisters for always supporting me over the years. Last but definitely not least is my wonderful wife, Alia, without whom this book would not have been possible. Thank you for putting up with me during this process and helping to keep me sane.

Introduction

It is nearly impossible today to write enterprise software without the use of one or more relational databases. Granted, in some cases the data is transient and not stored in a database, but for the most part software needs to consume and manipulate the data in a database. Easy enough, right? You put the lime in the coconut and you've got yourself a data-aware software application. Wrong! There are hundreds of ways to connect software systems to databases and thousands of people who think they have the skeleton key for data access layers. I can't say that I have the end-all pattern for data access, but I do have an efficient, repeatable way to apply industry design patterns to build scalable object-oriented persistence layers.

Object-relational mapping (ORM) has been a gray area in Microsoft development for many years. It's not that Microsoft language developers didn't understand ORM; in fact, the opposite is true, as is exemplified by the glut of third-party .NET ORM tools on the market. The struggle has come more from the lack of native tools with the object-oriented and object-persistence capacity to effectively work in this arena. With the inception of .NET, Microsoft overcame the first obstacle by developing an object-oriented environment and framework. The second obstacle, the native object persistence layer, is only now being realized with the introduction of the upcoming data access enhancements in Visual Studio 2008. The gray area is no longer gray, and the .NET developers of the world finally have the native tools required to build modular, reusable data access layers.

Working as an architect and consultant, I have noticed a severe dearth in the .NET community when it comes to the finer points of using design patterns to build data access layers. The Java camp has followed the *patterns = reuse* mantra for a long time, but the .NET side of the house is just starting to move in that direction. After scouring the Internet and bookstores, I have been shocked at how few books address using object-relational mapping patterns with .NET. The idea for this book has been in the back of my mind for a while, but I was always hesitant because of the deficiency in the native Microsoft tools. Now, with the Language-Integrated Query (LINQ) suite and the ADO.NET Entity Framework (EF), the object-relational mapping pattern can finally be realized in the .NET space. Although there are numerous books about LINQ, this book goes further and ties together the use of ORM design patterns with LINQ and Visual Studio 2008.

Before the naysayers start in on me for not writing this entire book about the ADO.NET EF, the "true" ORM tool that Microsoft is developing, let me say that I understand that EF is expected to be a far more sophisticated ORM tool than LINQ to SQL, the .NET Language-Integrated Query for Relational Databases, a subset of the LINQ suite. I also understand that some people are cursing my name right now because I'm calling EF an ORM, but a cat is a cat even if you shave off its hair and call it a dog. Bottom line, with VS 2008 there are two ORM tools: LINQ to SQL, which is not getting the recognition it deserves, and EF, which might be getting too much attention. The focus of this book is ORM with LINQ and C# 2008. This includes EF and LINQ to SQL, and therefore this text covers both.

This text can be utilized as a practical guide for ORM with the .NET Framework. Although some of this book is based on theory and design patterns, the focus is not an academic or theoretical discussion. However, it is important for everyone who is using an ORM tool to understand that certain principles and patterns lay the foundation of what you are doing. After reading this text, you will have knowledge of ORM and LINQ, and knowledge of the patterns you need to write robust software applications. Additionally, by walking through some real-world examples, you will have the tools you need to move forward in developing ORM solutions in .NET.

PART 1

Object-Relational Mapping Concepts

CHAPTER 1

Getting Started with Object-Relational Mapping

In the introduction, I stated that the purpose of this book is to explore object-relational mapping (ORM) by examining the new tools, LINQ to SQL and EF, as well as tried-and-true design patterns. Unfortunately, to become a "professional" at ORM development, you have to start with the basics. This chapter introduces you, largely in a technology-independent manner, to some of the essential concepts of ORM. In addition to a basic examination of the "what and why" of ORM, you will also be exploring the qualities that make up a good ORM tool and learning whether LINQ to SQL and EF make use of them.

Introduction to Object-Relational Mapping

Developing software is a complicated task. Sure, developing software has come a long way from the assembler days, and we have all sorts of managed, interpreted, Fisher-Price languages and tools to make things easier for us; even so, things don't always work as intended. This is especially evident when a software application has to connect to a relational database management system (RDBMS). Anyone with experience in this area knows it is rare in modern enterprise architecture for a piece of software to live in a silo, without needing to connect to some sort of database.

Although some might disagree, relational database systems are really considered the lifeline of every enterprise application and, in many cases, of the enterprise itself. These remarkable systems store information in logical tables containing rows and columns, allowing data access and manipulation through Structured Query Language (SQL) calls and data manipulation languages (DMLs). Relational databases are unique in the enterprise because they form the foundation from which all applications are born. In addition, unlike other software applications, databases are often shared across many functional areas of a business. One question that I've been asked in the past is this: if databases have all the data, why don't we just write all our software in the database? After I controlled my laughter, I began to really think about this question. From the eyes of a business *user*, it makes perfect sense to have a single layer in the architecture of the system, rather than multiple layers. You would have fewer servers and moving parts—and to paraphrase Mark Twain, as long as you watch that basket closely, it's fine to put all your eggs in a single basket. It makes perfect sense.

But wait a second. That sounds a lot like a mainframe: a single monolithic environment in which you write procedural code to access data and use a nonintuitive user interface (UI) for interacting with that data. Now don't get me wrong—the mainframe has its place in the world (yes, still), but not if you plan to write distributed applications, with rich user interfaces (that is, web, thick client, mobile, and so forth), that are easy to customize and adapt, in a rapid application development environment; these aspects instead require an object-oriented language such as C#, VB.NET, Java, or C++.

If you've decided that you're not going to write an entire application in Transact-SQL (T-SQL), and you've decided to use an object-oriented programming language, what are your next steps? Obviously, you need to go through some sort of process to gather requirements, create a design, develop the software, and test (some people unwisely skip this step). However, during the design phase, how do you plan out your data access layer? Will you use stored procedures for your create, read, update, and delete (CRUD) transactions? Maybe you have built a custom data access layer based on ADO.NET and COM+, or perhaps you have purchased some widget to do this or that. In my experience at Microsoft shops, ORM rarely comes up in the discussion. Why would it? ORM fundamentally goes against the direction that Microsoft pursued for years. Although many Microsoft shops have turned to third-party tools for ORM support, the norm has always been to use `DataSets` and ADO.NET objects. True object-oriented programming techniques, like business objects, were hardly ever discussed, and when they were, they were discussed only as an offshoot of ADO.NET. I suppose you could say the de facto stance of Microsoft and most Microsoft developers has always been that the power of the `DataSet` and `DataTable` was good enough for any enterprise application and any discerning developer.

What Is ORM?

ORM is an automated way of connecting an object model, sometimes referred to as a *domain model* (more on this in the coming chapters), to a relational database by using metadata as the descriptor of the object and data.

■ **Note** I use the word *automated* in the sense that the ORM tool that you are using is neither homegrown nor a manual process of connecting objects to a database. Most people with some basic knowledge of ADO.NET can create a data access layer and populate a business object. In this context, an ORM tool is a third-party tool (for example, LINQ to SQL) that provides you with commercial off-the-shelf mapping functionality.

According to Wikipedia, "Object-relational mapping (a.k.a. O/RM, ORM, and O/R mapping) is a programming technique for converting data between incompatible type systems in relational databases and object-oriented programming languages." Frankly, this definition is good enough for me because it is simple enough for everyone to understand and detailed enough to tell the full story. Over the coming chapters, the semantics of ORM are further refined, but this definition is a good place to start.

Benefits of ORM

It is important to understand that there are many benefits to using ORM rather than other data access techniques. These benefits will become more evident as you work through examples, but the following are ones that most stick out in my mind. First, ORM automates the object-to-table and table-to-object conversion, which simplifies development. This simplified development leads to quicker time to market and reduced development and maintenance costs. Next, ORM requires less code as compared to embedded SQL, handwritten stored procedures, or any other interface calls with relational databases. Same functionality, less code—this one is a no-brainer. Last but not least, ORM provides transparent caching of objects on the client (that is, the application tier), thereby improving system performance. A good ORM is a highly optimized solution that will make your application faster and easier to support.

Those points are important, but let's talk about a real-world situation that I have seen at various companies. Company X has developed a piece of software for a dog food producer and has followed the mantra that stored procedures are the fastest solution, and all CRUD operations should be handled by using stored procedures. The developers at this company have followed this approach to the point that they have individual stored procedures for each CRUD transaction—more than 3,000 stored procedures in all. This approach is a common scenario in the .NET world, with ADO.NET and SQL Server. This software has ballooned so much over the past couple of years because of customizations, a lack of standardization, and novice developers that development costs have doubled.

■ **Note** Writing stored procedures does not equate to bad design. On the contrary, stored procedures if managed correctly are an excellent alternative to dynamic SQL. If you use a code generator to create your CRUD stored procedures, or if you develop them by hand and have good oversight, in many cases you will be able to use them in conjunction with an ORM tool.

Company X has a major dilemma now because it has an opportunity to sell its software to a cat food producer, but the software needs to change to meet the business needs of the cat food company. With the increased development costs, Company X won't be making enough money to justify this deal. But company officials like the idea of selling their software, so they hire a consulting company to help reduce their overhead. The consulting company wants to use an ORM tool to help improve the situation. This consulting company builds an object model to represent the business and to optimize and normalize the company database. In short order, Company X is able to eliminate the thousands of stored procedures and instead use "automagic" mapping features to generate its SQL. Development costs go down, profits go up, and everyone is happy. Clearly this is an oversimplified example, but you can change Company X's name to that of any number of organizations around the world. The point is simple: ORM tools can't make coffee, but they can provide a proven method for handling database access from object-oriented code.

Qualities of a Good ORM Tool

I have often been asked what criteria I like to use when evaluating an ORM tool. Because the primary focus of this text is VS 2008, I've decided to outline all the features I look for, and then discuss if and how LINQ to SQL and EF implement them. In Chapter 12, I present some non-Microsoft commercial ORM tools and use the items in this list to help evaluate their usability.

Object-to-database mapping: This is the single most important aspect of an ORM tool. An ORM tool must have the ability to map business objects to back-end database tables via some sort of metadata mapping. This is fundamentally the core of object-relational mapping (and yes, LINQ to SQL and EF support mapping business objects to database tables with metadata).

Object caching: As the name indicates, this functionality enables object/data caching to improve performance in the persistence layer. Although query and object caching are available in LINQ to SQL and EF, both require some additional code to take advantage of this functionality. You will examine this topic throughout the text as you look at how LINQ to SQL and EF control object and state management. At this time, it is important that you understand only that both tools support caching in some form or another.

GUI mapping: Like so many other topics in the IT world, this is a debated topic. I'm of the mind that software with a graphical user interface (GUI) is a good thing, and the simpler the interface, the better. However, there are still purists in the ORM world who say mappings should be done by hand because this is the only way to ensure that the fine-grained objects are connected correctly. I believe that if an ORM tool has everything else you need, yet no GUI, you should still use it. If the GUI is included, consider it the icing on the cake. After all, if the framework is in place, you can always write your own GUI. In the case of LINQ to SQL and EF, GUI designers are provided with Visual Studio 2008.

Multiple database-platform support: This is pretty self-explanatory: a decent ORM offers portability from one RDBMS provider to another. At the time that I'm writing this, though, I am sad to say that LINQ to SQL supports only SQL Server 2000 and up. However, this is the first version of this tool. EF, on the other hand, uses the provider framework and supposedly will support multiple database platforms. It's unclear whether these providers will be available for release to manufacturing (RTM), but again the provider model is part of the strategy. Although I consider this a critical piece of functionality for an ORM tool, providing examples in anything other than SQL Server is outside the scope of this book.

Dynamic querying: Another important aspect of ORM, and the bane of database administrators (DBAs) everywhere, is dynamic query support. This means that the ORM tool offers projections and classless querying, or dynamic SQL based on user input. This functionality is supported natively in LINQ to SQL and EF, allowing users to specify a filter or criteria, and the framework automagically generates the query based on the input.

Lazy loading: The purpose of lazy loading is to optimize memory utilization of database servers by prioritizing components that need to be loaded into memory when a program is started. Chapter 2 details the lazy-loading pattern, so for now just know that lazy loading typically improves performance. LINQ to SQL has a built-in functionality that allows you to specify whether properties on entities should be prefetched or lazy-loaded on first access. This is actually built right into the VS 2008 designer as a property on the entity. EF also supports lazy loading by default; however, there are a few caveats with the object context and concurrency, which you will look at in more depth in upcoming chapters.

Nonintrusive persistence: This is an important one, and it is discussed in depth in Chapter 2. Nonintrusive persistence means that there is no need to extend or inherit from any function, class, interface, or anything else provider-specific. LINQ to SQL supports this concept, because you can use a custom class that does not have any provider-specific technology, and still have it participate in the ORM process. It's not as black-and-white with the Entity Framework because EF does not support nonintrusive persistence. EF does support the use of the IPOCO pattern, which you will explore later, but natively you are required to inherit from and extend EF-specific technology to use this ORM.

Code generation: This is another gray area of ORM. The purists will insist that there is no place for code generation in ORM, because a well-thought-out object model should be coded by hand. It should, in fact, be based on the conceptual model of the business domain, not on the metadata of the database. There is room for code generation when using an abstract data object layer, which extends your object model, but that is a different situation that I discuss in the next chapter. I think that code generation can be useful when working on a project in which the database schema is static, and the customer understands the ramifications of using this approach (see the Bottom Up approach). However, even though LINQ to SQL and EF support code generation, I'm not a big proponent of it. I think that the semantics of the object model get lost along the way and the database schema becomes the focus, thus making the application rigid and inflexible. Nonetheless, code generation is an important aspect of these tools, so the text does present some examples.

Multiple object-oriented framework support: This is blue sky. You would be hard-pressed to find an ORM product offering compatibility with multiple object-oriented languages and development environments. I'm not talking about Visual Basic (VB) and C#; rather I'm referencing .NET and Java. This may sound far-fetched, but at some point in the future I envision the persistence layer becoming language agnostic. You say CLR, I say JVM . . . can't we all just get along? This ranks very low on the determining factors for choosing an ORM vendor; however, I like to keep it on the list just to keep everyone on their toes.

Stored procedure support: The object purists are going to read this and say that stored procedures serve no purpose in an ORM tool. Why on earth would you defile your decoupled model and data layer with the integration of stored procedures? The fact of the matter is, in many large organizations you can't get away with using dynamic SQL. The DBA group may have had a bad experience with ORM, or they may enjoy holding all the cards, or may just not like what you have to say. Additionally, because Microsoft has been pushing stored procedures on developers and DBAs for years, it may be difficult for you to change the stored procedure culture overnight. Along with the possibility that the DBA group is standing in your path, at times stored procedures are really the only viable option because of performance problems with long-running or complex queries in the ORM tool (for example, reporting). Regardless of the situation, you're not out of luck because many ORM tools, including LINQ to SQL and EF, support stored procedures.

Miscellaneous: I once worked for a guy who said to never put *miscellaneous* in a list because it showed a lack of completeness. Well, I think miscellaneous is a good way to describe the following items that aren't worth a subheading, but still need to be mentioned for completeness. The miscellaneous criteria are as follows: price, ease of use, documentation, market penetration, performance, and support. I would include all these criteria in an ORM tool analysis, but they are not really relevant to the heart of this text.

The most important thing for you to remember when choosing and using an ORM tool is that it is not going to solve world hunger. It is important that you familiarize yourself with ORM and the tool before making any significant changes to your architecture. ORM tools can increase productivity and decrease time to market, but they can also do the opposite if not fully understood by the stakeholders involved.

Impedance Mismatch

It would be utterly irresponsible of me not to include a section about the *impedance mismatch* that occurs between object code and relational databases. This is probably the single most common explanation that people give for using ORM tools. The object-oriented archetype is founded on the principle that applications are built by using a collection of reusable components called objects. On the other hand, the relational database pattern is one in which the database stores data in tabular form. Whereas the database is largely based on a purely mathematical algorithm, the object-oriented model is based on a representation of life and one's surroundings. Therefore, to overcome the disparities between the two paradigms, it is necessary to map the object model to the data model.

Let's look at an example of the paradigm mismatch. In this example, we begin with a simple class model and slowly expand the model to illuminate the mismatch problem. Here we have the start of a retail banking application, with a `Customer` class and an `Account` class. As seen in Figure 1-1, the `Customer` class has one or more `Account` classes, similar to a customer at a bank.

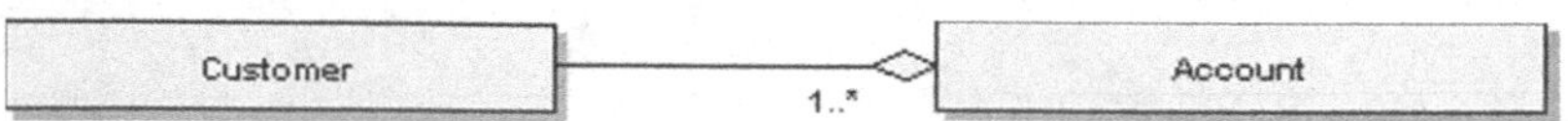

Figure 1-1. *An example of a Customer class with one or more Account classes*

The source code associated with Figure 1-1 resembles the following:

```
public class Customer
{
    private string _firstName;
    private string _lastName;
    private string _fullName;
    private List<Account> _accounts = new List<Account>();
    private int _id;

    // Get and Set Properties for each of our member variables
}

public class Account
{
    private int _id;
    private int _accountNumber;
    private int _customerID;

    // Get and Set Properties for each of our member variables

}
```

The Data Definition Language (DDL) for Figure 1-1 looks similar to this:

```
CREATE TABLE [Customer](
    CustomerID] [int] IDENTITY(1,1) NOT NULL,
    FirstName] [nvarchar](50) NULL,
    LastName][nvarchar](50) NULL,
    MiddleName] [nvarchar](50) NULL,
    FullName] [nchar](10) NULL,
    CONSTRAINT PK_Customer PRIMARY KEY ([CustomerID])
)

CREATE TABLE [dbo].[Account](
    AccountID] [int] IDENTITY(1,1) NOT NULL,
    AccountNumber] [int] NULL,
    CustomerID] [int] NOT NULL,
      CONSTRAINT PK_Account PRIMARY KEY ([AccountID]),
      CONSTRAINT FK_Account_Customer FOREIGN KEY (CustomerID)
         REFERENCES [Customer]([CustomerID])
)
```

In this scenario, we have a pretty vanilla example: we have one class for one table, and we have a foreign-key relationship of the account table containing the ID of the customer table—if only every database and application were this easy to design. I guess I would probably be out of a job, so maybe it's a good thing that ORM, software engineers, and design patterns are needed.

Let's expand this case so it is based more on a system that you might see in the real world. In the preceding case, you have a `Customer` class that uses strings for the first and last name.

Suppose after speaking with the business, you realize that the banking software will be used in various countries and regions around the world. You know from reading a white paper on internationalization and localization that you are going to need *finer-grained* control of the names in the system because not all cultures use first and last names in the same way. Additionally, after looking at the object model, you realize that it is lacking abstraction, which is really just a nice way of saying that your object model is lacking flexibility and extensibility. Therefore, as illustrated in Figure 1-2, you should refactor your model to add inheritance and abstraction and to make your model a closer representation of the business domain.

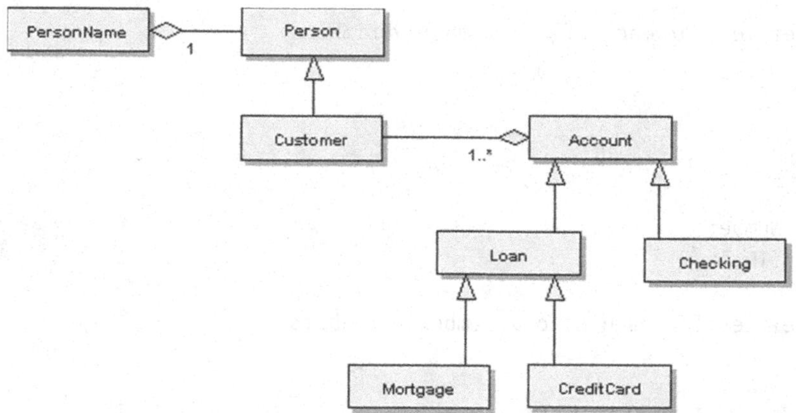

Figure 1-2. *A more realistic representation of an object model for a banking application*

As represented in Figure 1-2, we have expanded our object model to better represent the banking domain. We have modified the `Customer` class so it inherits from a `Person` base class, and we have created a relationship between the `Person` class and the `PersonName` class to account for complex naming situations in foreign countries. In addition, we have expanded the taxonomy of `Account` so that it includes classes for `Loan`, `Checking`, `Mortgage`, and `CreditCard`—all realistic examples of how you would use inheritance for an object model in the banking industry.

In Listing 1-1, you have the diagram from Figure 1-2 enumerated into C#. In this example, you have a better representation of an object model that would be used in the banking industry.

Listing 1-1. *A More Realistic Object Model for the Banking Industry*

```
{
    public int Id {get; set;}
    public PersonName Name {get; set;}
}

public class PersonName
{
    public string FirstName {get;set;}
    public string LastName {get;set;}
    public string FullName{get;set;}
}
```

```
public class Customer:Person
{
    private List<Account> _accounts = new List<Account>();
    public List<Account> Accounts
    {
        get
        {
            return this._accounts;
        }
        set
        {
            this._accounts = value;
        }
    }

}

public class Account
{
    public int Id {get;set;}
    public int AccountNumber{get;set;}
}
```

How does this more-accurate object model in Listing 1-1 relate back to our database schema? If you start with Person and PersonName, you already can see the mismatch between the data model and object model. In the database schema, it is perfectly acceptable to have a Customer table contain all the information for Person and PersonName. This variance has to do with the difference between fine-grained objects and coarse-grained objects, and the database's inability to handle these common object-oriented relationships and associations.

Let's talk about what I mean here when I say *fine-grained* and *coarse-grained* objects: the analogy comes from any particulate matter (for example, sand) consisting of small or large particles. Like particles, a *coarse-grained object* is one that semantically is large and contains many aspects—for example, the Account class in Figure 1-1. Alternatively, *fine-grained objects* are much smaller and detailed, like the refactored version seen in Figure 1-2. The fine-grained approach is almost always preferred when building an object model.

There are several reasons to prefer a group of smaller objects to one giant object, but some of the most important reasons are performance, maintainability, and scalability. Why would you retrieve all the data for a single large object when you can easily retrieve the data you need from a smaller object? Why remote a large object when all you need is a subset of the data? Why make maintenance more complex by putting everything in a single class when you can break it up? These are all questions you should ask the next time you find yourself building an object model.

■ **Tip** In Listing 1-1, I am taking advantage of one of the new C# 3.0 language features, *automatic properties*. As you can see, the code is much cleaner because you do not have to explicitly declare a private field for the property; the compiler does it for you. I use the new language features throughout the text, and they are called out in Tip boxes like this one.

Continuing with the comparison between the object model and the data model, notice that there is significantly more inheritance in the object model in Figure 1-2 as compared to Figure 1-1. This is a common scenario in today's object-oriented world, with applications designed with multiple layers of inheritance for extensibility and abstraction. After all, inheritance is one of the core tenets of object-oriented programming and accordingly is extremely useful when it comes to building flexibility and scalability into your application. Unfortunately, my relational database doesn't come with an inheritance button, and if you think yours does, as they say, I've got a bridge you might be interested in purchasing. Every developer who has worked with a relational database knows that there is no good way to connect multilevel or single-level inheritance relationships in a database. Sure, you can create various relationships and extension tables, and yes, with SQL Server 2005 you can use the Common Language Runtime (CLR); nonetheless, you will still never be able to create an inheritance model in a relational database as cleanly (if at all) as you will in your object model.

Along with inheritance, another core aspect of object-oriented programming rears its head in Figure 1-2; specifically, polymorphism and polymorphic associations are apparent. As you are likely aware, this was bound to happen because anytime you introduce inheritance, there is the possibility of polymorphism. Obviously, this polymorphism depends on your hierarchy and implementation of your concrete classes, but it's safe to say that polymorphism is a possibility when you have inheritance in your object model. A good example of this is seen in the `Customer` class, in which a one-to-many association with the `Account` class exists, and the `Account` class in turn has subclasses of `Loan`, `Checking`, and so forth. Figure 1-2 tells us that the `Customer` object may be associated with any instance of `Account`, including its subtypes at runtime. What this means for you as the developer is that there is a good possibility that you will want to write a query to return instances of the `Account` subclasses. This, of course, is one of the great features of object-oriented programming and one of the drawbacks to relational databases.

As seen in the previous examples, without manipulating the object model with Adapters and other SQL data access code, there is no straightforward way to connect the object-oriented model to a relational database model. The term *Adapters* is taken from *Design Patterns: Elements of Reusable Object-Oriented Software* by Erich Gamma, Richard Helm, Ralph Johnson, and John Vlissides (Addison-Wesley Professional, 1994) and is defined as the conversion of the interface of a class into another interface that clients expect. Although the examples simply portrayed the inherent mismatch between fine- and coarse-grained objects, inheritance, and polymorphism, I can tell you that encapsulation, abstraction, and the other fundamentals of object-oriented programming don't fare much better. The bottom line: vendors or languages and databases have never addressed the impedance mismatch between object and data, and so ORM continues to thrive.

Object Persistence

Object *persistence* is at the heart of ORM. To quote Obi-Wan: "It surrounds us and penetrates us. It binds the galaxy together." I'm not going to write extensively about persistence because it has been covered exhaustively elsewhere (and if you have picked up this book, I believe you already have a basic understanding of persistence as it relates to object-oriented development). I think it's important, however, to provide a brief refresher and give you my two cents on the subject.

The essence of persistence is the act of saving and restoring data. These objectives are not specific to ORM or object-oriented programming; rather, persistence is a concept that transects software engineering as a whole. Persistence is apparent every time you turn on your computer, whether you are saving a document, an e-mail, or any other data. The minute you turn on your computer, persistence occurs, from the lowest-level circuit all the way up to the web browser you use to log in to your bank.

In the ORM world, persistence relates to the act of dehydrating and rehydrating (or vice versa) an object model complete with the object's current state. Everyone knows that application data can be persisted to relational database systems for permanent storage, but who wants to always make a round-trip call to the database to retrieve our object data? Additionally, I have already shown that there is an inherent mismatch between an object model and the data model. We need a mechanism to save and restore our object hierarchy, complete with state, in our data access layer: hence, object persistence and ORM.

The primary way to handle object persistence is to utilize object serialization. *Object serialization* is the act of converting a binary object, in its current state, to some sort of data stream that can be used at a later date or moved to an alternate location. The concept isn't new; object persistence has been around a long time. In classic ActiveX Data Objects (ADO), it is possible to serialize a recordset; in Java, you can use Enterprise JavaBeans (EJB) or Plain Old Java Objects (POJOs); and in .NET, you can use ADO.NET or Plain Old CLR Objects (POCOs). Of course, in .NET (and Java), your objects must implement `ISerializable`, allowing the language interpreter to do the serialization work for you. But back to the heart of the matter: when trying to persist an object, serialization is imperative.

This truth was known and embraced by the ORM gurus and developers of yesteryear, and it has carried into the designs of all modern-day ORM tools. Fortunately for us, LINQ to SQL and EF both make good use of object persistence and serialization, making our lives simpler and eliminating the need to spend endless hours designing a persistence mechanism in our data access layer. As you progress deeper into LINQ to SQL and EF, you will explore caching and object persistence in more detail.

Basic ORM Approach

Similar to much of this chapter, the ORM approach is discussed throughout the text; however, I want to set the stage for detailed discussions in the coming chapters. Fundamentally, there are three key approaches when it comes to ORM: the Bottom Up, the Top Down, and the Meet in the Middle approaches. Each approach has its benefits and problems, and no approach should be considered the panacea. It is critical when designing an application to understand that the "one size fits all" mentality never works. Although a chunk of this book looks favorably at the domain-driven design (DDD) model, and the patterns that Martin Fowler and others have produced, the fact is that those patterns and practices are still fallible. A more-holistic view of the environment, requirements, and needs of the customer is vital when designing software.

The Bottom Up approach is as it sounds: you start at the bottom, or in this case the database, and work your way up to the object model. In the LINQ to SQL designer, this is the most supported approach. That isn't to say that you can't use the other approaches with LINQ to SQL (because you can), but the quickest and easiest way is to start with the database and generate your object model from your schema. EF, like LINQ to SQL, supports this approach; however, unlike LINQ to SQL, this is not the primary approach for the EF designer.

Although the DDD people are going to strongly disagree with me, in some situations the Bottom Up approach is as sound as any other development technique. However, it does lend itself better to situations where you have a normalized, well-thought-out data model, or are designing the entire system from scratch. Nonetheless, in these cases it can be the fastest approach, and if you follow some common design patterns (which are presented in Chapter 2), you can get a pretty good bang for your buck.

Unfortunately, I have to say that it is rare that an organization has an existing well-designed database. My experience over the years puts the estimate of companies with normalized, well-thought-out data models somewhere around 10 percent. The other 90 percent fall somewhere between "Oh boy, they have no referential integrity and are using a single table to store all their data" and "Not too bad—just needs a little normalizing." In these cases, I tend to focus more on the Top Down and the Meet in the Middle approaches.

The Top Down approach, the preferred method of DDD people everywhere, is simply put, modeling your domain on business or conceptual needs rather than the database. This definition is a bit basic and thus is expanded further in later chapters. However, the Top Down approach is the core of DDD. The main drawback to this approach is that it presents a strong learning challenge for people who are not familiar with it and can take some time to implement correctly. However, this approach does allow you to truly model the domain based on specific business needs, thus providing the most flexible design approach.

The Meet in the Middle approach is most applicable to situations in which a database and object model already exist, and your goal is to determine the mappings between the two. This is one of those situations that rarely, if ever, happens because no matter how hard you try, the chances that you have a domain model that orthogonally transects multiple database models is unlikely. Most likely, you will end up refactoring, so this approach really morphs into the Top Down or Bottom Up approach.

In both the Top Down and the Meet in the Middle approaches, LINQ to SQL comes up short. Although the mapping support and the entity support are available, the designer doesn't add much to the equation. Yes, you can drag "classes" from the toolbox, but the functionality is underdeveloped at best. Nevertheless, the designers of LINQ to SQL had the foresight to keep the application programming interface (API) and the internals open enough for us to use the engine with both of these approaches. The Entity Framework designer does a very good job in both of these scenarios; it supports robustly building your conceptual domain model first and supplying the model and the database to build the mappings.

Summary

In this chapter, I have introduced you to some of the basic concepts surrounding ORM, EF, and LINQ to SQL. ORM is the act of connecting object code, whether it is in C#, Java, or any other object-oriented language, to a relational database. This act of mapping is an efficient way to overcome the mismatch that exists between object-oriented development languages and relational databases. Such a mismatch can be classified as an inequality between the native object-oriented language operations and functions and those of a relational database. For example, it is impossible to take an object model and save it directly into a database without some manipulation. This occurs because the database doesn't have the ability to handle inheritance or polymorphism, two basic tenets of object-oriented development. An ORM tool is an excellent solution to overcome the inherent difference between object code and relational databases.

The ORM tool you choose to use in your software should be evaluated based on a set of criteria that meets your goals; however, the following are good starting points: object-to-database mapping, object caching, GUI mapping, portability (multiple DB support), dynamic querying, lazy loading, nonintrusive persistence, code generation, and stored procedure support. Additionally, along with the criteria and the process direction you use to choose your ORM tool, you should also think about the approach that you envision yourself using. There are three key approaches that you may find useful in your development: the Top Down, Meet in the Middle, and the Bottom Up approaches. Knowing your requirements and your business needs (and wants) will help you choose an appropriate approach and long-term ORM solution.

Chapter 2 more extensively explores the patterns and practices used to create a modular and scalable data access layer using ORM. Chapter 2 does not reinvent these architectural patterns but instead draws upon and simplifies the plethora of existing patterns out there and consolidates them into a single grouping of ORM categories.

CHAPTER 2

ORM Patterns and Domain-Driven Design

As I pointed out in the first chapter, it is impossible to discuss ORM without talking about patterns and best practices for building persistence layers. Then again, it is also impossible to discuss ORM patterns without calling out the gurus in the industry, namely Martin Fowler, Eric Evans, Jimmy Nilsson, Erich Gamma, Richard Helm, Ralph Johnson, and John Vlissides, the last four of whom are known in the industry as the Gang of Four (GoF). The purposes of this chapter are to explain and expand some of the patterns created by these gurus and to provide concrete examples using language that every developer can understand.

Domain-Driven Design

For as long as I can remember, there have been heated debates about the process used when developing software. Domain-driven design (DDD) is one of a handful of software-development philosophies that have emerged in the last ten years that provides us with a precedence of knowledge and a direction to overcome the complexities of a problem. At the heart of DDD lies the domain, which according to Merriam-Webster Online (`www.meriam-webster.com`) is "a sphere of knowledge, influence, or activity." Although semantically correct, the essence of what the domain is in DDD is not adequately captured by this definition.

Let me tell you what I consider the domain and DDD to be. First, the *domain* is the business of a business. It is fundamentally the problem that you are trying to solve with the software. For example, in a banking originations engine, you need to determine how to create a loan application and how that application will be processed through the system. The domain in this case is the whole of the banking and originations process. You need to *model* the domain in order to solve the problem at hand. Thus, *DDD* in simple terms is the act of focusing your development efforts on the model and the domain, using proven design patterns and practices.

In *Patterns of Enterprise Application Architecture* (Addison-Wesley Professional, 2002), Martin Fowler describes the domain model as "an object model of the domain that incorporates both behavior and data." At the highest level, this is an accurate definition. The domain model is a common conceptual model that is used to represent the realm. Additionally, the domain model defines a common vocabulary and interactions that can and should be used by everyone in the software life cycle. This is not to say that a business analyst needs to become an object-oriented expert. However, it is important that everyone involved in the life cycle have a basic understanding of object-oriented expression and design principles.

Let's face it: the stakeholders in your software development life cycle all seem to speak different languages. It's not that everyone except the engineers in the life cycle is incompetent; the problem has to do with the thought process and the lexicon used for expression by the different stakeholders. For example, an engineer might say that software success is all about code, whereas the quality assurance (QA) tester believes that software success is all about the testing, and the DBA may say that software success is all about the data structure. Like the impedance mismatch between object code and relational databases, the same can be said of the mismatch in communication between stakeholders in the software development life cycle. This mismatch is the primary reason for modeling and for the development of modeling languages. I'm not going to devote too much time on modeling because entire volumes of work have been written on model-driven architecture (MDA) and development, but I think it is important that you understand the main points because it is impossible (yes, I said *impossible*) to build a decent domain model without going through the exercise of modeling your domain.

UML

The *Unified Modeling Language (UML)* is the most common vocabulary used for modeling in the industry today. The UML specification is nothing if it isn't robust. According to the Object Management Group (OMG), considered the innovators and policemen for MDA, UML 2.0 contains approximately thirteen diagrams (reference). In my opinion, this is about ten more diagrams than most people need, but I really can't fault them for having too much functionality because the opposite is far worse.

Of the thirteen diagrams, the two that I find most useful are the class and object diagrams, or some combination of the two. You will be exposed to both of these diagrams throughout this book because they provide an adequate mechanism for displaying object-relational patterns and relationships.

The object diagram and the class diagram are similar in their construction and makeup. The *class diagram* (see Figure 2-1) is used to depict and capture the logical structures in a system, such as classes and the other items in the model. It displays the static model with all its attributes and relationships between classes and interfaces. This can include inheritance structures, aggregations, associations, and compositions. The *object diagram* is a simplified version of the class diagram, which at a high level depicts the role an object plays when instantiated, and its multiplicity. Both of these diagrams are classified under the category of *structural diagrams*, which simply means that they are used to represent the structural elements of the system, such as classes and relationships.

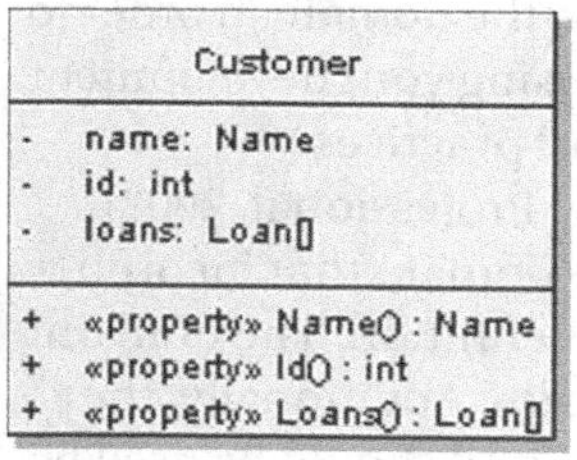

```
Customer
- name: Name
- id: int
- loans: Loan[]
+ «property» Name() : Name
+ «property» Id() : int
+ «property» Loans() : Loan[]
```

Figure 2-1. *Class diagram*

An alternative to a structural diagram is the *behavioral diagram*, which, as its name suggests, is a diagram that represents the interactions (that is, the business logic) that take place in a given system. Of the seven diagrams that fall under the behavioral category, I find only one useful enough to deem it a necessity when modeling a domain: the sequence diagram. The *sequence diagram*, which falls under another subcategory of behavioral diagrams called *interaction diagrams*, is a useful form for displaying structured sequences of steps between functional and behavioral artifacts in the system. You can think of a sequence diagram as a workflow or a business process diagram that outlines the interactions in your system. Structurally, you can see in Figure 2-2 that a sequence diagram consists of vertical swim lanes, and has *lifelines*, which are dotted stem lines that depict the involvement of a particular element. Additionally, a sequence diagram can represent stereotyped elements, such as screens, controllers, entities, and database items.

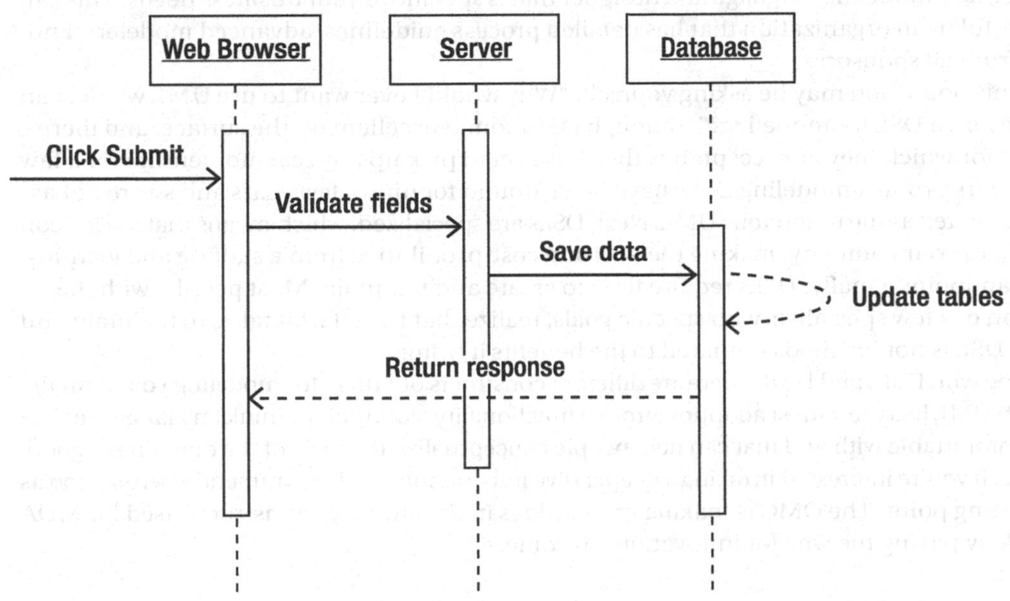

Figure 2-2. *Sequence diagram*

In a nutshell, UML is an excellent tool for encouraging and enabling a common vocabulary among the stakeholders in your development life cycle. However, as evidenced by my comment that I really use only two of the thirteen diagrams afforded by the UML 2.0 specification, UML can also be the crux of a poorly managed project. I've seen many situations firsthand in which the development process in an organization requires a ridiculous number of UML artifacts and everyone hates the language. This is typically found when an unqualified "methodology expert" has come in and made a mess of things, or when the Rational Unified Process (RUP) has become irrational after years of "process improvements." Although I think it is safe to say that any good methodology could go bad along the way, if you find that UML has become a nuisance and is despised throughout the life cycle, do yourself a favor and find out why and how to fix the problem(s). The purpose of UML, as in all modeling, is to make your life easier and provide you with the means to an end. Don't get hung up with the bends in your connectors; focus on the model, and you should be fine.

Domain-Specific Languages and More

Another area that is picking up some steam in the modeling arena is domain-specific language (DSL) tools. Although they have been around for years in the form of macros and problem-oriented languages, DSL tools have only recently matured into a viable modeling solution. Microsoft's first foray into a robust DSL for modeling was with Visual Studio 2005.

DSL tools provide you with the ability to create a custom modeling language and designer to manipulate that language. Specialization is becoming an important aspect of every facet of information technology. It makes sense that the next logical step would be customized languages for your domain. This is pretty close to what is seen in modern enterprise workflow systems with their UI designer. These workflow systems provide a series of widgets that you can customize for your specific domain. You can in turn use these custom widgets to expand upon and ultimately build your process and system. Like a workflow solution, DSL gives you the ability to easily define a modeling language and designer that is specific to your business needs. This can be powerful in an organization that has detailed process guidelines, advanced modelers, and buy-in from all sponsors.

At this point, you may be asking yourself, "Why would I ever want to use UML when I can create my own DSL for modeling?" Although DSLs sound excellent on the surface, and there are tasks for which they are acceptable, they have yet to pick up any real momentum for a few reasons. First, robust modeling DSLs have been around for only a few years and so are not as widely accepted as the ubiquitous UML. Next, DSLs are specialized, which means that the lexicon is limited to your company, making the decision cost-prohibitive from a staffing and learning-curve standpoint. Finally, DSLs require time to create and maintain. Most people, with the exception of a few specialists with specific goals, realize that the effort it takes to maintain and create a DSL is not justified compared to the benefits it brings.

Along with DSLs and UML, there are different constructs out there for modeling your domain. Although UML has the widest adoption, from a functionality standpoint I think any language that you're comfortable with and that can help people conceptualize the logic of the domain is a good language. If you're interested in taking a deeper dive into the subject, I recommend `www.omg.com` as your starting point. The OMG is making great strides in the language constructs used for MDA and is likely paving the way for innovations to come.

Domain Model Structure

Before I dive into the patterns of ORM, it is important that you understand the architectural structure of an efficient domain model. As Eric Evans points out in his popular book *Domain-Driven Design* (Addison-Wesley Professional, 2003), the domain model can be broken into the following pieces:

- Entities
- Value objects
- Services
- Aggregates
- Factories
- Repositories

All of these concepts are presented in this section, with the exception of factories and repositories, which are discussed in the "Object-Relational Patterns" section.

Entities

The word *entity* is thrown around quite often in software and database development, but what does it really mean? In the context of a relational database, an entity is a table. It is also sometimes a database object such as a view, but in most cases a database entity is a table. I can't say that I know the genesis of the word *entity* in database development, but it is most often associated with relationships or entity-relationship diagrams (ERDs). On the software side, the word *entity* is typically used as an extension of the database entity. This implicitly relates back to the Bottom Up approach, in which the structure of the object model is based on the database model. As you may have gathered already, I am a firm believer that this is not the best way to structure your domain, and therefore I think of an entity in the context of software development as something different from what exists in my database.

To expand on the entity concept, let's first look at the word and remove the techie side from the equation. According to Merriam-Webster Online, *entity* is defined as an "independent, separate, or self-contained existence." Now, you obviously can't create a sentient being from your code (cue the Frankenstein music), but as an object-oriented programmer you can create a representation of a particular being. How, however, can one define *real existence* in terms of software development? Well, I like to start with the concept of identity.

Identity in the real world is what gives us uniqueness and differentiates us from everyone else. This is typically a set of characteristics or traits that defines who we are. In the software world, the concept is similar. In the context of a database, identity is your primary key; it may consist of a single field such as a globally unique identifier (GUID) or an integer, or, alternatively, as a combination of multiple fields (that is, a composite key—yuck). On the software, or domain, side, I like to think of an entity in terms of *real existence*. This feeds right into the modeling aspect of creating a conceptual set of objects to represent the domain. Here is where it gets tricky: defining an entity in your domain model is not a static exercise but rather a relative notion of what your domain experts define as needing identity in your sphere of development. An entity is not a business object, regardless of the tendency to call it that. According to Evans, an entity is an object that is defined by a "thread of identity that runs through time and often across distinct representations."

Consider your automobile as a metaphor. Your car has a vehicle identification number (VIN) that is used to uniquely identify it and track its existence. However, you don't refer to your car as 3M8RDK9A9KP042788 (or if you do, you have a serious problem). No, you call it *my car*, or you may have a name for it such as *Betsy* or *Old Blue* or *piece of junk*. How do you know it's your car, though? Well, besides the fact that you make a monthly payment for it, you have given the car an identity. This identity might be made up of attributes such as color, model, engine, and fuzzy dice, but the fact remains that you have still given this object identity and so it has become an entity.

■ **Tip** When building your domain model, try to keep your class definitions as simple as possible. By taking a minimalist approach, you can enhance ease of use and maintainability of your framework.

You may be wondering how a tangible concept such as an entity translates into source code. Well, in Chapter 8 you will be building out a domain model for the First Bank of Pluto so you will see entities in action. However, there are a few technical items that you should understand now. First, realize that not every object in your domain model is an entity, and therefore your framework must have the capability to evaluate the identity of multiple different objects. This is typically done through comparison operations and by overriding *equals*, and it is necessary to promote a healthy existence. Next, ensure that your entity objects have stability throughout their life cycle. This is largely controlled by the ORM tool; however, it is important to keep stability in mind when using transactions and developing your model. Finally, focus on identity by building each entity with some mechanism for defining uniqueness.

Value Objects

As discussed in the previous section, your domain model will consist of other objects in addition to entities. The next major area for your consideration when building your domain model is the creation of value objects. Every system you build is going to need some sort of reference data in order for it to function correctly. A *value object* is where this data is stored and manipulated in your model.

■ Note Don't get the term *value objects* confused with CLR *value types*, because they are not the same. Value objects are an architectural concept and do not have any knowledge of the programming language or the constructs used. Just because a structure or enumeration is a value type doesn't mean that it is a value object.

Evans probably describes the value object best by saying, "When you care only about the attributes of an element of the model, classify it as a value object." I like to think of a value object as an object that cannot exist on its own—that is to say, an object that has no identity by itself. For all intents and purposes, value objects are the parasites of your model because there is no reason for their existence except to describe and associate themselves with your entities.

For example, to continue with the automobile referenced in the preceding "Entities" section, your automobile has attributes including color, tint, and stereo type. Each of these items cannot exist by itself in the system—that is, each of these attributes lacks identity. Thus, a value object is typically an immutable object with no identity, containing values used to describe entities. Figure 2-3 illustrates our automobile example.

From a design standpoint, several techniques exist to build value objects into your model. The purists say that you should create a separate class for each value object in the system. I don't think that there is one correct way to create value objects. However, Chapter 8 demonstrates my preferred method, which uses generics, reflection, and caching. The important thing to remember about value objects is that in 99.9 percent of cases, you shouldn't assign or track their identity or you will likely impair system performance. Additionally, never lose sight that these objects are used to describe aspects of the system and so they should, in most cases, be treated as immutable.

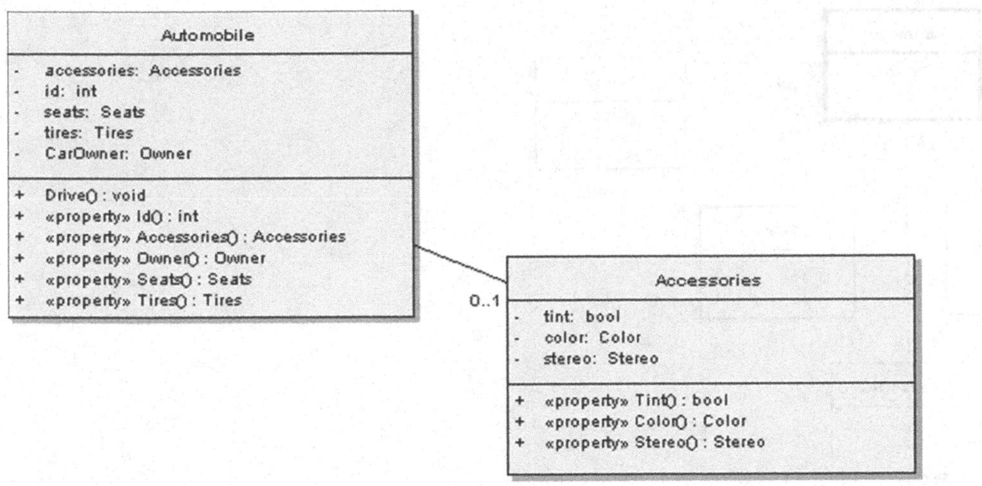

Figure 2-3. *Automobile value object*

Aggregates

According to Merriam-Webster Online, an aggregate is "formed by the collection of units or particles into a body, mass, or amount." *Aggregates*, in terms of the domain model, are just that: a logical grouping of entities and value objects into a collection. The reason for aggregation in your model is that complex relationships can lead to data inconsistencies in your application and database. This concept is simple: the more moving parts in your model, the more likely you are to end up with problems.

A case in point is the cleanup of orphaned data and objects. Say, for example, that you have an account record in your database. If you delete the account, you can use a cascading delete to ensure that you don't have any orphaned data hanging out in other related tables. In the object world, however, you don't have this luxury and therefore need to use aggregation to ensure that you don't end up leaking memory or corrupting your data store.

Our `Automobile` entity, as seen in Figure 2-4, is the perfect example of an aggregate. The automobile has value objects such as `Seats` and `Tires`, and can also have other entity objects such as the `Owner` object. By this account, the `Automobile` object becomes the source of the aggregate and for all intents the owner of the group.

You may be asking yourself how this helps to enforce referential integrity in your model. The answer actually lies in the structure of your domain model and the objects you expose to consumers. By controlling what objects a consumer can create and by exposing the aggregate, you can ensure integrity in your model. The most common way to enforce this technique is to use the factory pattern discussed later in this chapter and demonstrated in detail in Chapter 8. However, a solid understanding of accessibility modifiers and a well-laid-out hierarchy will also be critical to ensure integrity.

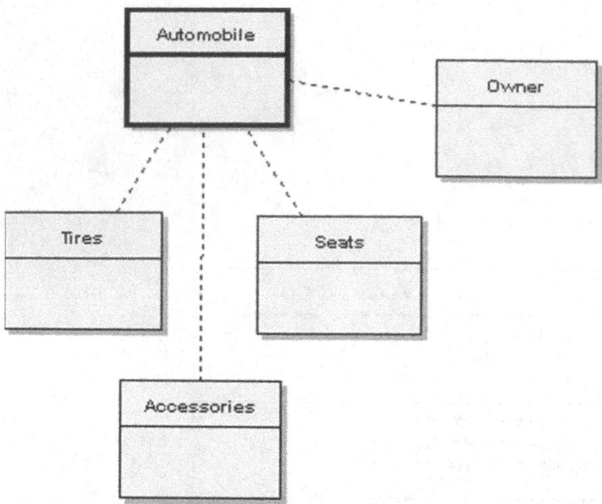

Figure 2-4. *Car aggregate*

Services

With all of the service-oriented architecture (SOA) hype and hope, the word *services* is probably the most overused and abused word in computing today. Nonetheless, the fact remains that not everything in your model can be classified as an entity or a value object. Typically in your domain model, a service will be developed as an action or an activity, which doesn't make sense to build into your entities or value objects.

> *Some concepts from the domain aren't natural to model as objects. Forcing the required domain functionality to be the responsibility of an Entity or Value either distorts the definition of a model-based object or adds meaningless artificial objects.*
>
> —Eric Evans

One thing that I should point out here, because of all of the SOA hype, is that a service in this context may or may not have anything to do with a web service. Again, the point here is a higher-level architectural concept as opposed to an implementation-specific detail. Continuing with the automobile example, suppose your automobile informs you when it is time to change your oil. This service requires the evaluation of a series of domain objects and thresholds to determine that it is time for an oil change. Although the service is expressed by using your `Automobile` entity (technically an aggregate), it wouldn't make sense to encapsulate it as that object. This service interface needs to be outside the entity and value to keep it reusable. After all, you need the ability to evaluate your spouse's automobile, because he or she may forget to change the oil or perform maintenance.

I don't plan to spend too much time on service design and development because some excellent books on service orientation are currently available (see "Further Reading" at the end of this chapter). However, it is important for you to understand that there are different implementation layers of services (for example, application, domain, infrastructure) in your architecture. I like to think of these layers as front, middle, and back, but you can throw whatever tier names you want on them. The point is to make sure that you understand what you are trying to achieve, build in as much reusability as possible, and encapsulate outside the implementation of your value and entity objects.

Object-Relational Patterns

Before you embark on any ORM endeavor in your application, it is important that you first understand a handful of basic design patterns required for successful implementation. This section by no means provides a comprehensive list of patterns. However, it is a good starting point for building a solid understanding of pattern-based development. For those of you who read this and still want to know more, at the end of this chapter I provide a list of additional reading that I have found beneficial.

Domain Model

To this point, I have been talking about the domain and the domain model pattern, but have yet to define it in any significant manner.

> *At its worst, business logic can be very complex. Rules and logic describe many different cases and slants of behavior, and it's this complexity that objects were designed to work with. A Domain Model creates a web of interconnected objects, where each object represents some meaningful individual, whether as large as a corporation or as small as a single line on an order form.*
>
> —Martin Fowler

This quote defines the domain model as an object model in which each entity represents something meaningful in the domain. Although I mostly agree with Fowler's definition, I tend to think about it a little differently. From my perspective, the *domain model* is much more than just an object model because its creation is rooted in the collaboration among the experts in the organization. Specifically, the domain model is the conceptual layer that can be used to represent the process as a whole and is fundamentally a mechanism that can bring the people in the software life cycle closer together. Similar to UML acting as a common vocabulary, a completed domain model can also be a catalyst for enhanced cross-process and cross-functional communication.

As an example, take Company X, comprising a handful of new developers, a few senior developers, some quality control people, a couple of business analysts, and a project manager (in other words, a rather typical development team). Suppose that the developer and business analysts have a hard time getting anything done because the developers don't really understand the nuances of banking and likewise the business analysts can't explain things effectively to the technical personnel. To overcome these communication problems, Company X has implemented a Software Development Life Cycle (SDLC) process, involving reams of paper defining specific problems and development needs for the current system. The quality control (QC) people resent the developers because the developers have never adequately explained the situation from an impact standpoint, and the project manager is frustrated because the communication issues are reducing the time he is able to spend on the golf course. Now, give this team a robust domain model that conceptualizes the realm of interactions in the software, and many of these communication issues disappear. The UML (or any common modeling language) used to diagram the domain is a common way for everyone to communicate. The domain model itself can be used to explain complex interactions from a functional and a technical perspective.

One of the biggest problems with trying to explain what a domain model is and how it can be used is that any short-term example I give you will be too simplistic to truly demonstrate the power of this model. Therefore, the example of the First Bank of Pluto that we will create in the coming chapters with LINQ to SQL and EF is designed and built based on the domain model pattern. Unlike some of the other patterns discussed in the coming pages, with the domain model pattern I do not provide a code example. The core of the rest of this book is based on this pattern, and so the cumulative effect of the text should be an understanding of the domain model as a whole.

Figure 2-5 gives you a simple overview of the domain model as an interaction between objects in the domain. However, remember that it *doesn't* include the GoF patterns and the interaction strategies that you will see after we create the First Bank of Pluto.

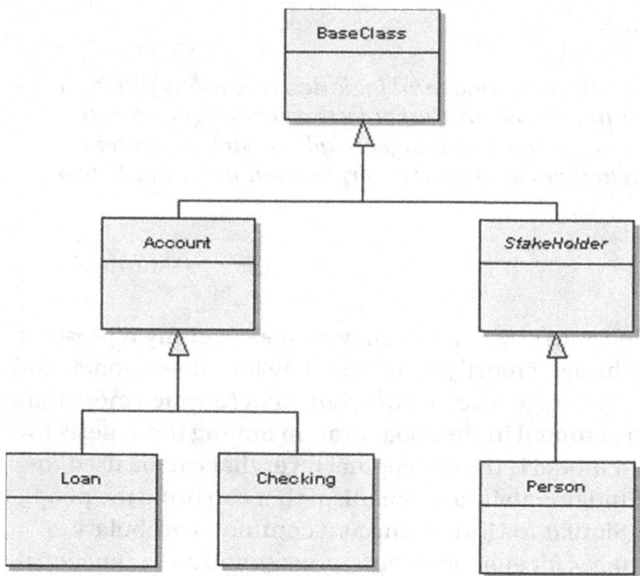

Figure 2-5. *Simple domain model*

It is important not to lose sight of the purpose of the domain model, that is, to provide a logical model that can be used to map to external data. Although the domain model is a robust representation of the business and is in simple terms your middle tier, it is really a bunch of meaningless objects without a mapper and some strategies to move the data in and out. I will be talking about this more as you look at the mapper pattern in this chapter and begin to examine the application of ORM to real situations.

■Tip When you are working on modeling a business domain, don't get hung up on formalized UML in meetings with the domain experts. The UML should not become an obstacle in development. Instead, it should help people communicate by using a common lexicon. I find the easiest way to build a good domain model is with paper and pencil or a whiteboard. I use rudimentary notation that everyone can understand, demonstrating the relationships and behavior within the model. After the initial meetings, I take the whiteboard drawing and use a formal modeling tool and add any formal notation that I may have glossed over in the meeting.

Table Module

One of the most common methods for creating an object model that can be used with ORM tools is the *table module*. Code generators and most ORM tools throughout the .NET Framework utilize this technique. The purpose of the table module is to create a class per table, and in many cases when not using a mapper, you create or use some sort of disconnected container to hold the tables and build relationships. The obvious example here is the ADO.NET `DataSet` and `DataTable` infrastructure; however, this example can also effectively be used with an ORM tool.

As seen in Figure 2-6, the classes you create by using this pattern have a one-to-one relationship with the tables in your database. As I explained in Chapter 1, this creates problems in terms of the impedance mismatch. To reiterate the point, object-oriented programming has flexibility and scalability that the tabular forms of relational databases don't have. Your database can't have inheritance or polymorphism among its entities, and therefore it is a poor solution to handle complex business logic. Don't get me wrong: the table module *is* a quick and easy way to get data in and out of a relational database. The emphasis here, however, is on the *relational database*, because the table module is really good only for data sources built in tabular form (for example, SQL Server or Oracle)—unlike the domain model, which can be used for any form of data because it is rooted in the conceptual paradigm.

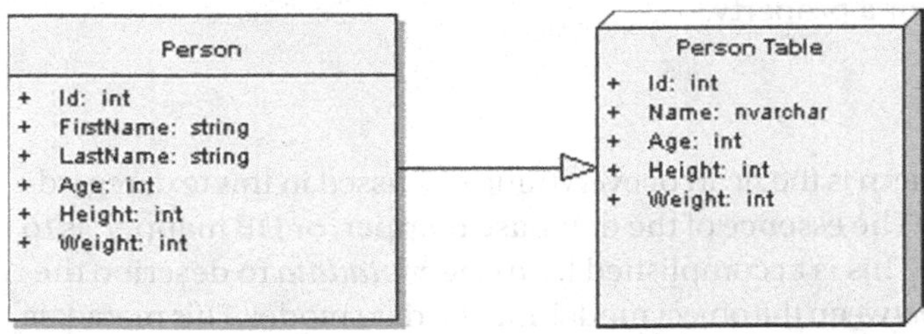

Figure 2-6. *Table module*

Although the table module pattern is deficient compared to a rich domain model, it does have a place in software development when the object model can closely resemble the database. Additionally, in the majority of situations, the overhead and complexity required to develop a rich domain model is not justified. A good example of this is a software application used internally in your organization for any number of rudimentary tasks, such as an internal auction web site to sell off old equipment or a simple tracking system to monitor vacation days.

Another important item to remember (because many people get confused when they hear *table module* and assume that they can use only a database table) is that a view or a query that returns a table is appropriate to the pattern as well. As Fowler points out, "the table module doesn't really depend on the structure of tables in the database but more on the virtual tables perceived by the application, including views and queries."

Active Record

An *active record* is similar to the table module except that the table module is an architectural design principle, whereas an active record falls under the data access pattern category (like database mapper). However, the implementation is similar in that a class is created to represent a table in the database, but unlike the table module, the active record pattern also encapsulates database access functionality.

As you can see in Figure 2-7, the `Person` class has database access methods alongside domain-specific logic.

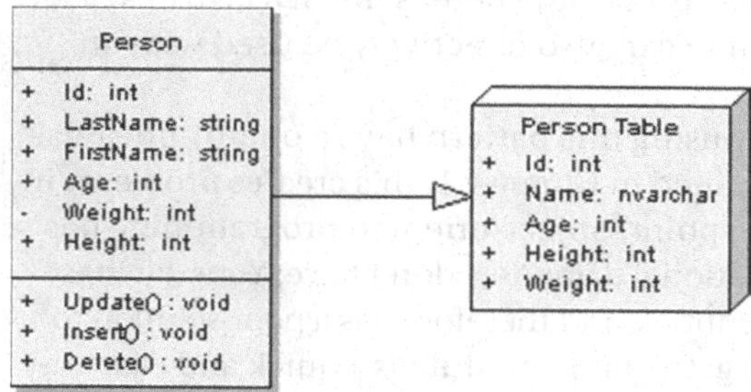

Figure 2-7. *Active record*

You may be asking why I'm even including this pattern in a section on ORM patterns. The fact is, this is a common pattern to see with ORM tools, where a foreign-key relationship is exposed as an object via an attribute or a property.

Database Mapper

The *database mapper* (a.k.a. ORM) pattern is the heart of everything discussed in this text, regardless of the tool that you choose to use. The essence of the database mapper, or DB mapper, is to map objects to a relational database. This is accomplished by using *metadata* to describe the attributes and relationships that exist between the object model and the data model. This metadata can come in many forms, but for the most part Extensible Markup Language (XML) is a consistent option for the metadata mappings that the ORM uses. Along with the metadata, a mapping engine of some sort is needed to translate the metadata into something useable, handle transactions and caching, and control the underlying access to the data source. EF and LINQ to SQL are both examples of DB mappers.

In general, a DB mapper is a complicated piece of logic, and most people look to third parties (for example, Microsoft) to develop one. As you can imagine, writing a flexible mapping program is a tedious endeavor. That is not to say that hard-coding the mapping between object and data model is not a valid form of this pattern, because it is, but it is not the recommended approach for ORM. In general, the DB mapper should meet the criteria identified in Chapter 1 for ORM tools.

As is evident in Figure 2-8, the DB mapper acts as an intermediary between your domain model and your database. This layer of abstraction is probably the most critical aspect of this pattern. The mapper allows the domain model to remain completely decoupled from the database and provides you with a remarkable amount of flexibility.

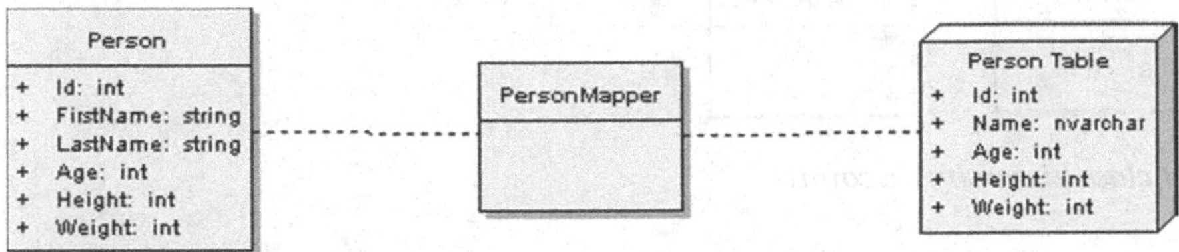

Figure 2-8. *Mapper UML*

Inheritance

It is impossible to discuss the DB mapper pattern without including a subsection about inheritance and the DB mapping engine. In "Mapping Objects to Relational Databases: O/R Mapping in Detail" (`www.ambysoft.com`, 2006), Scott Ambler identifies four approaches to mapping an inheritance structure with an ORM tool. Although briefly discussed in Chapter 1, it is essential to understand three of these approaches in more depth because they are critical aspects of ORM. The fourth approach is mentioned but not explored to any great length because it is a pattern that I don't recommend in a typical application development. The three key inheritance-mapping approaches are as follows:

- A single table per class hierarchy
- A table per concrete class
- A table class to its own table

■ Note One thing worth mentioning here is that not all of these approaches are fully supported by LINQ to SQL and EF—yet. Chapters 9 and 10 present LINQ to SQL and EF (respectively) in depth, but it is worthwhile for you to understand all the inheritance patterns so you have a foundation to work from.

Table per Class Hierarchy

In the table per class hierarchy technique, you map your entire class structure to a single table. As you can see in Figure 2-9, the technique is to create a table in a way that a discriminator column can be used to determine the type of class being mapped. Additionally, the primary key is the identity for the mapped classes, and the table contains all attributes in the class hierarchy.

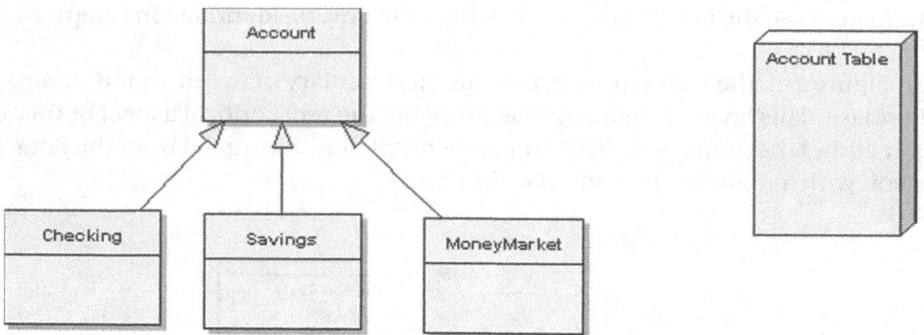

Figure 2-9. *Table per class hierarchy (accounts)*

Although many people write the table per class hierarchy technique off as simplistic and lacking scalability, it is one of the fastest approaches when it comes to inheritance structures and ORM. The reasons are simple: you don't have to write a lot of complex joins or queries to get your data out of the database, and everything is stored in a single location, making polymorphism a snap.

Unfortunately, this approach also has significant drawbacks. First, if you have more than a couple of types in your class model, this approach can become very complex very quickly because of the single-table structure and lack of foreign-key relationships. Second, as your schema expands, your database has the potential to become nothing more than a glorified flat file and your table size can grow very large. Finally, did I mention that this approach has the possibility of creating a single data structure? I'm all for building robust object models and removing much of the onus from the database, but relational databases are meant to store relational data. This means multiple tables with indexes, keys, Declarative Referential Integrity (DRI), and all those other functions that relational databases are specifically designed and tuned to handle. The bottom line: this approach works great in simple applications and can be beneficial to enterprise applications that have tight control over their object model and database schema, yet it also has several drawbacks, so it is not ideal for every situation.

Table per Concrete Class

The table per concrete class is probably the most common approach to handling inheritance with an ORM, mostly because it is the easiest to build into the ORM engine. In this technique, you map each nonabstract class to its own table in the database.

In Figure 2-10, you can see that our accounts data model from Figure 2-9 has changed to include a distinct table per nonabstract class. In this case, the abstract classes are not involved in the mapping, but their attributes are represented by the concrete classes.

This approach's biggest advantage is its simplicity and ease of implementation. However, this technique has issues with regard to polymorphism and data redundancy. Typically in the database, a foreign-key association is used to create a pseudo-polymorphic structure. Unfortunately, if all classes are defined as their own entities with no foreign-key relationship to the base table, this mapping becomes difficult, if not impossible. Another problem with the shortage of foreign-key associations in this approach is that data can become redundant quickly. For example, if you add a new field to the `Account` class, you potentially have to add that same field to all the subtype database tables of `Account`. In general, the table per concrete class pattern is useful when your relationships are not complex and you are looking for a quick solution.

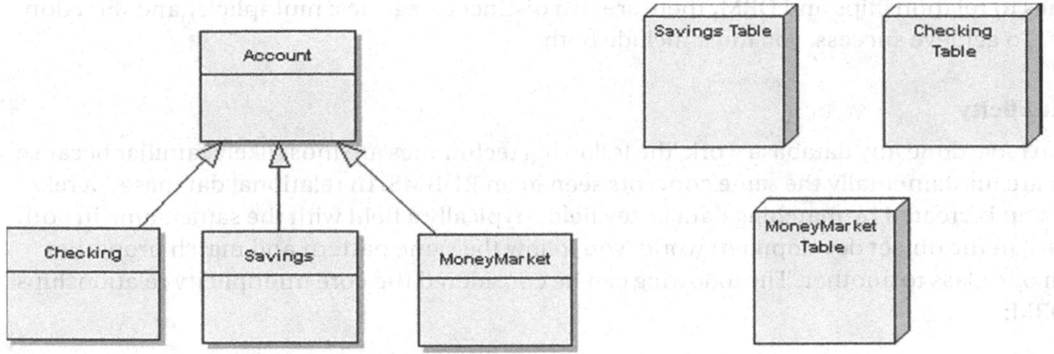

Figure 2-10. *Table per concrete class (accounts)*

Table per Class

As you have probably already guessed, the table per class approach is similar to the table per concrete class approach, with the addition of tables representing the base class. This is the most typical approach to building an inheritance structure into your application.

As evidenced in Figure 2-11, the table per class approach has expanded again in our model. However, this time you are adding more tables and foreign-key relationships to represent the class hierarchy in your domain model.

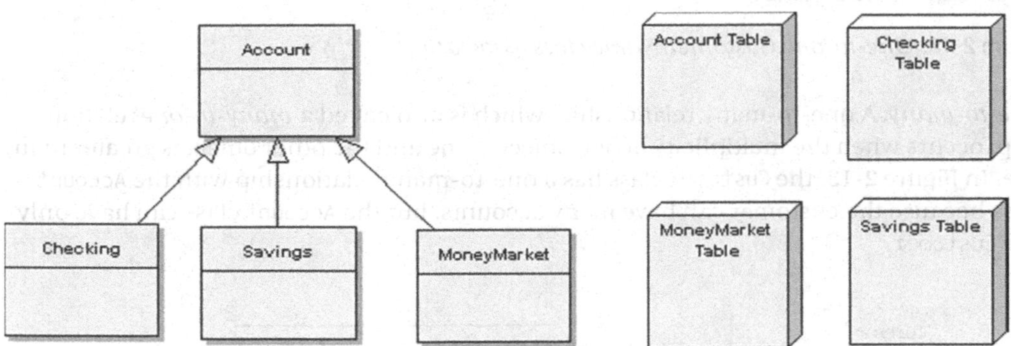

Figure 2-11. *Table per class*

This approach is quite powerful because it provides polymorphism, since the abstract class has a relationship in the database schema. Additionally, unlike the table per concrete class approach, there is little or no issue with adding additional fields to the database or object model because of the separation and abstraction in your code.

Relationships

Handling relationships in your domain model with an ORM can be a tricky task because of the inherent mismatch between the relational database and your object code. Nonetheless, if you plan to use ORM, it is imperative that you develop the appropriate relationships in your domain model and accurately represent the business and efficiently map to your database. When it comes to relationships and ORM, there are two distinct categories: multiplicity and directionality. To achieve success, you must include both.

Multiplicity

If you have done any database work, the following techniques are most likely familiar because they are fundamentally the same concepts seen in an RDBMS. In relational databases, a relationship is created by matching data in key fields, typically a field with the same name in both tables. In the object development world, you follow the same pattern and match properties from one class to another. The following can be considered the core multiplicity relationships in ORM:

One-to-one: A one-to-one relationship is the simplest ORM relationship. The maximum of each object's multiplicity is one. In Figure 2-12, you can see that the `Customer` can have only one `Name` class association.

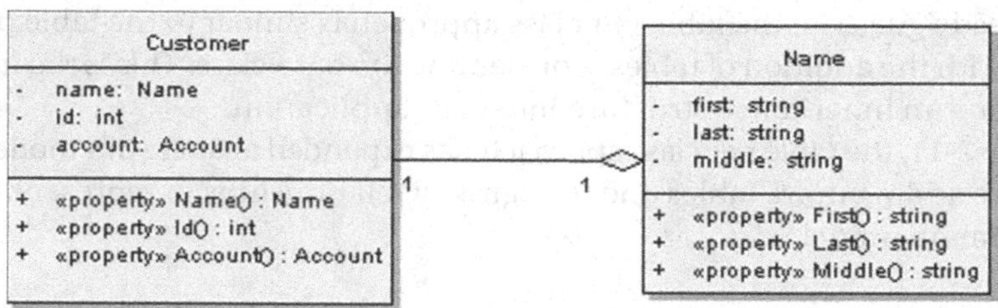

Figure 2-12. *One-to-one Customer/Name class association*

One-to-many: A one-to-many relationship, which is also called a *many-to-one* relationship, occurs when the multiplicity of one object is one and the other object is greater than one. In Figure 2-13, the `Customer` class has a one-to-many relationship with the `Account` class because the customer can have many accounts, but the `Account` class can have only one `Customer`.

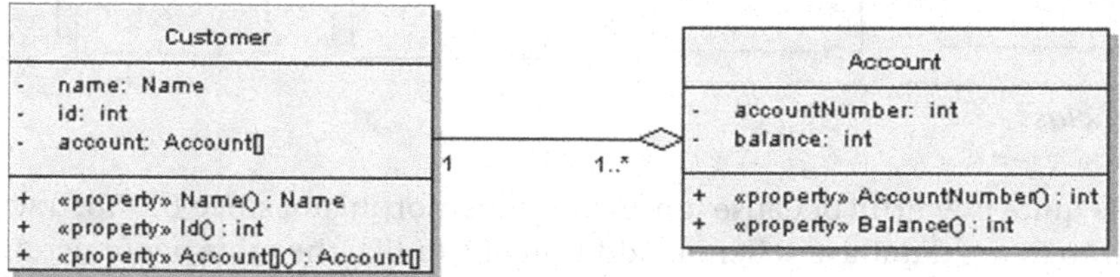

Figure 2-13. *One-to-many Customer/Account classes*

Many-to-many: The many-to-many relationship is the most complex multiplicity relationship, because the multiplicities of both objects are greater than one. As seen in Figure 2-14, the `Account` class can have multiple pieces of `Collateral`, and the `Collateral` class can be associated with multiple `Accounts`.

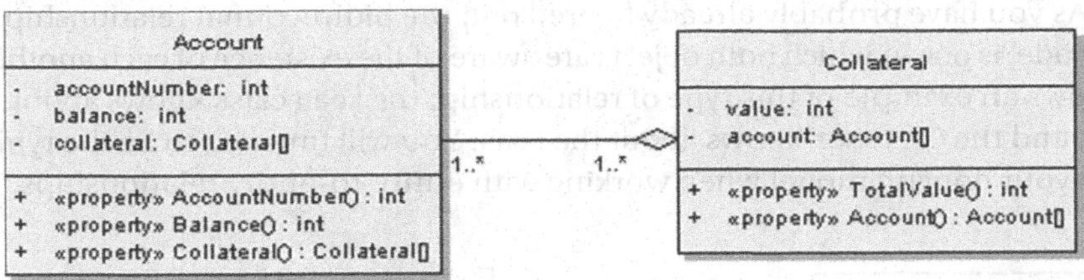

Figure 2-14. *Many-to-many Account/Collateral*

In the relational model, multiplicity is most often implemented as a foreign-key relationship. However (and I don't recommend this), I have also seen this relationship enforced with triggers. The reason why triggers are not typically recommended to enforce referential integrity has to do with the performance gains received when using the native, declarative, referential-integrity functions in modern database servers. In Chapter 8, as you build out your domain model and database model, you will see the relationship implementations unfold.

■ **Note** The multiplicity and directionality relationships identified in this section are not all necessarily supported by LINQ to SQL or EF. The purpose of this section is to illuminate all possible ORM relationships from an architectural perspective. In Chapters 9 and 10, when we start to map the domain model by using LINQ to SQL and EF (respectively), the implementation of these relationships will be examined in detail.

Directionality

Along with object multiplicity, another important aspect in defining and understanding relationships in ORM is directionality. *Directionality*, as the name implies, indicates the direction of the relationship between objects. You have two choices here: unidirectional and bidirectional, and, as I previously mentioned, both work in conjunction with multiplicity relationships, and thus should not be considered as stand-alone patterns.

Unidirectional: The unidirectional relationship is defined as one object knowing about the existence of another, but the second not knowing about the first. This can be seen in Figure 2-15: the `Loan` class knows about `Currency`, but `Currency` doesn't know about `Loan`. This type of relationship is typically seen in domain models between entities and value objects.

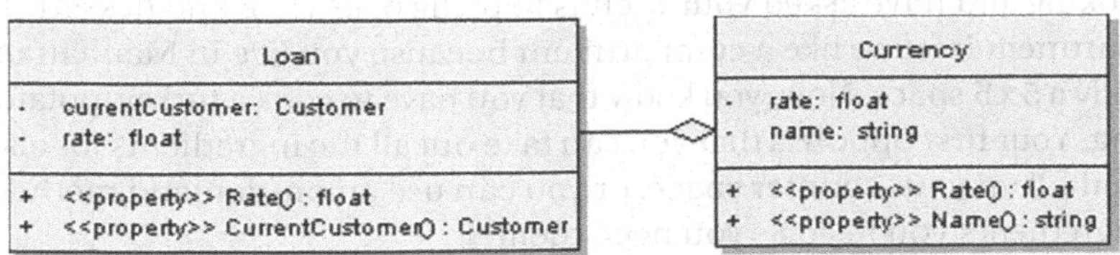

Figure 2-15. *Unidirectional relationship of Loan/Currency*

Bidirectional: As you have probably already figured out, the bidirectional relationship in your domain model is one in which both objects are aware of the existence of each another. Figure 2-16 shows an example of this type of relationship: the `Loan` class knows about the `Customer` class, and the `Customer` knows about the `Loan`. You will find this to be the typical relationship in your domain model when working with entity-to-entity relationships.

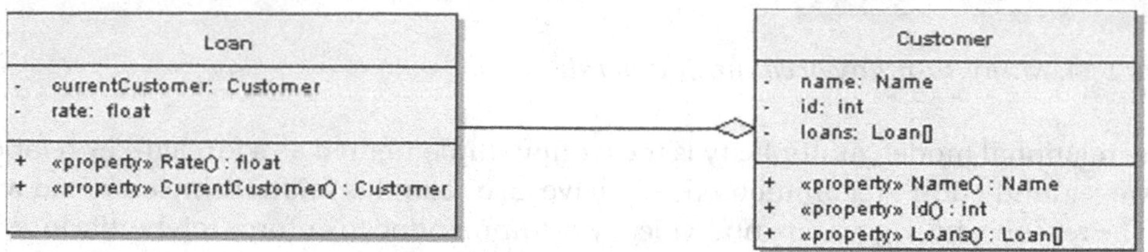

Figure 2-16. *Bidirectional relationship of Loan/Customer*

The unidirectional relationship is unique to object-oriented development because it does not exist in relational databases. In the relational database, all relationships are considered bidirectional because of the traversal options when using foreign keys. Specifically, Table A knows about Table B, and vice versa, because of their foreign-key relationship, and so it is possible to traverse in either direction.

Now that you have reviewed multiplicity and directionality and the concepts related to the database mapper pattern, you can move to the wide-ranging topics of laziness, factories, and repositories.

Laziness

Laziness (a.k.a. *lazy initialization, lazy loading, lazy reads,* and *deferred reads*) is a wide-ranging topic with regard to ORM. *Patterns of Enterprise Application Architecture* includes 15 pages on laziness and deconstructs the pattern in detail. I don't think that level of detail is necessary for this text. However, there are a few fundamental concepts that you need to understand in order to build a decent domain model.

Chapter 1 briefly describes lazy loading as a way "to optimize memory utilization of database servers by prioritizing components that need to be loaded into memory when a program is started." Although this definition is accurate, it doesn't provide sufficient background to enable you to determine when and how to use lazy loading in your domain model. To expand on this definition, let's think about a real-world situation. You have invited a group of your closest friends over to your Manhattan apartment for Thanksgiving dinner. As a good host, you've decided to do all the cooking and have asked your friends to bring over wine and dessert. The problem is that your apartment is more like a compartment because you live in Manhattan, and your kitchen is literally a 5 x 5 space. Now, you know that you have to cook a turkey, potatoes, green beans, and stuffing. Your first option is that you can take out all the ingredients for all the dishes you're making and fill up your counter space, or you can use an on-demand method, and take out only the ingredients you need as you need them.

In a nutshell, this is laziness as it relates to ORM: delaying the loading of data from a database, the creation of an object, or a calculation until the time it is needed. This can be accomplished in various ways, but the technique used most often is a flag or a marker to identify the property or field that should be considered lazy. This flag tells the ORM engine that this particular field should not be loaded, because it is an expensive transaction, until it is needed. The concept should be familiar to you as a programmer because it is frequently employed when checking whether an object is null prior to loading. Figure 2-17 shows the sequence of events involved in the lazy-loading process.

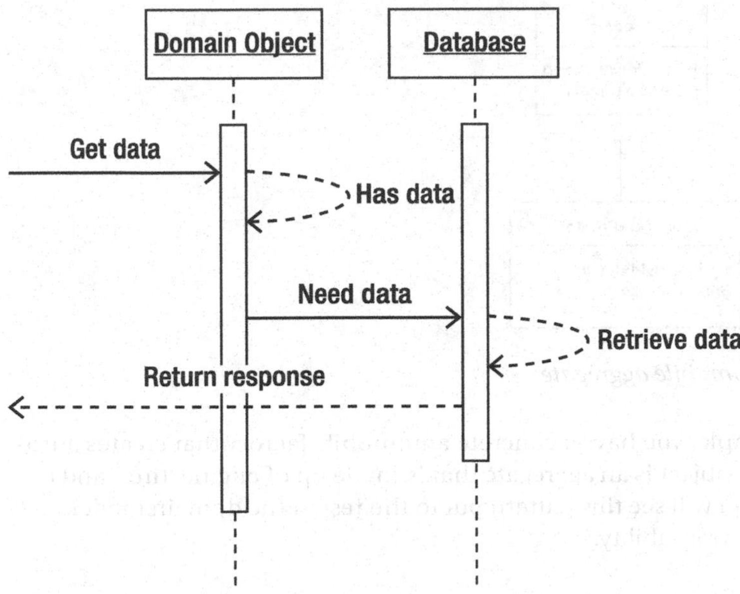

Figure 2-17. *Lazy-load sequence diagram*

One thing to keep in mind when using laziness in your model is to determine ahead of time which fields are candidates for this loading technique. It can be extremely detrimental to performance if you go overboard with laziness because this functionality is fundamentally synchronous, meaning the consumer of your model will be waiting for a return response.

Factories

The factory pattern was originally documented by the GoF in their famous book *Design Patterns: Elements of Reusable Object-Oriented Software* (Addison-Wesley Professional, 1994). The *factory pattern* is a creational pattern, and every developer should be familiar with it regardless of whether the context is ORM or another approach. At the heart of the factory pattern is encapsulation. As I mentioned in the "Aggregates" section earlier in this chapter, it is always a best practice to limit creation of objects in your domain. The factory pattern provides a standard technique for controlling the creation of objects and aggregates in your domain model. By using this technique in your domain model, you can decouple the creation of objects, thereby increasing flexibility and reusability. In addition, by using encapsulation, you can enforce any constraints in your aggregates and reduce the risk of corruption.

As you may have realized, if at all possible I like to think of all patterns and object-oriented design in terms of real-world, nontechnical examples. The factory pattern is an easy one to think about in this manner. Similar to a factory producing potato chips, an object-oriented "factory" assembles all the pieces to create a final product for your consumption. Additionally, with minor modifications to your factory, you can change the flavor of your potato chips to barbeque or nacho cheese, and the same holds true in the object world. With abstraction and interfaces, you can create a generic blueprint for your factory and change the aggregate object that is created. Figure 2-18 shows a diagram of the factory pattern.

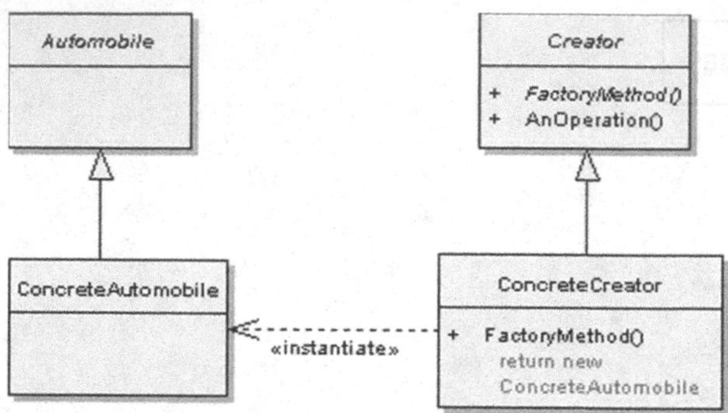

Figure 2-18. *Factory pattern automobile aggregate*

As you can see in this example, you have a concrete automobile factory that creates automobile objects. The `Automobile` object is an aggregate that is made up of engine, tires, and a steering wheel. In Chapter 8, you will see this pattern put to the test in the domain model, where it is abstracted for greater reusability.

Repository/Data Access Objects (DAOs)

The *repository pattern*, which is fundamentally the same as the Data Access Object (DAO) pattern often seen in the Java world, is a proven technique for decoupling your domain model from your database. As you will see in detail in the "Persistence Ignorance" section later in this chapter, and in Chapter 8 during implementation, keeping your model independent from the ORM, database, and provider- or vendor-specific technologies is paramount to a reusable domain model. Using this pattern is a proven method for accomplishing this decoupling. Additionally, by building in this layer between your domain model and your ORM, the backing data store becomes irrelevant. Granted, in this text you will be exploring only relational database access. However, by using the DAO pattern, you can more easily change the backing data store without having to adjust the model itself.

Unlike many of the other examples in this chapter, there really isn't a good nontechnical example for this pattern because this pattern is inherently technical. Figure 2-19 demonstrates the basic sequence involved in utilizing the DAO. As you can see in this example, our domain object interacts with our DAO, which in turn communicates through the ORM engine to the database.

We have already decided that you should never directly instantiate an object, and the same holds true for our DAO. As you can see in Figure 2-20, we have expanded our example to include a DAO factory that will be used for creation of our DAOs to provide greater encapsulation and control.

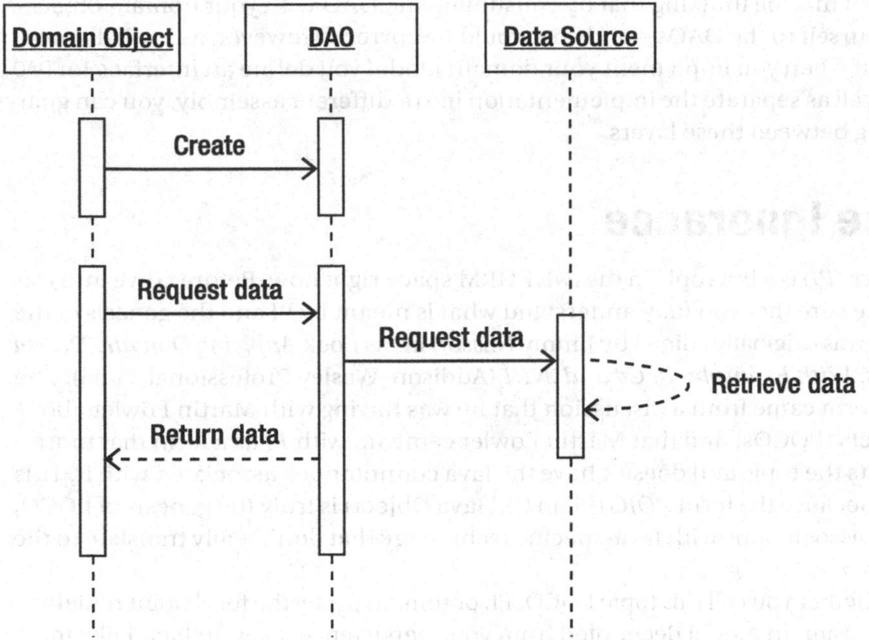

Figure 2-19. *DAO sequence*

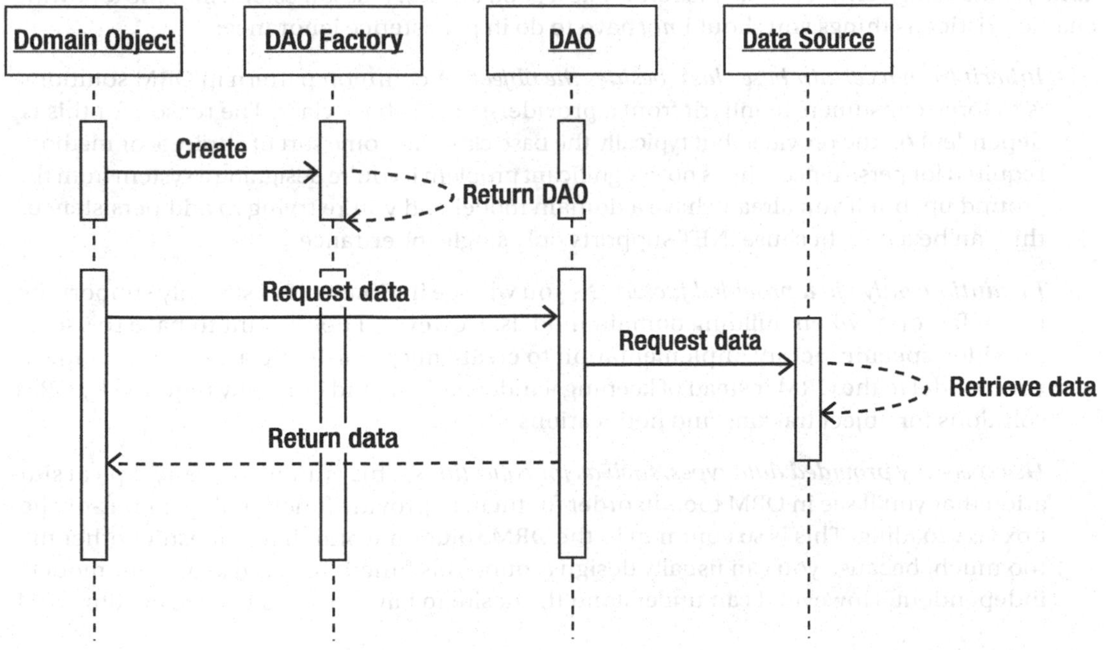

Figure 2-20. *DAO with factory*

At this point, you may be thinking that by consuming the DAO with your domain object, you are coupling yourself to the DAOs—and you would be correct. However, as I will demonstrate in Chapter 8, if when you implement your domain model you define an interface for `DAO` and `DAOFactory` as well as separate the implementation into a different assembly, you can guarantee loose coupling between these layers.

Persistence Ignorance

Persistence ignorance (PI) is a hot topic in the .NET ORM space right now. Before I dive into this topic, I want to make sure that you fully understand what is meant by PI and the genesis of the subject. The term *PI* was originally coined by Jimmy Nilsson in his book *Applying Domain-Driven Design and Patterns: With Examples in C# and .NET* (Addison-Wesley Professional, 2006). The story goes that the term came from a discussion that he was having with Martin Fowler about Plain Old CLR Objects (POCOs) and that Martin Fowler came up with *PI* as a term that more accurately represents the topic and doesn't have the Java connotations associated with it. This makes sense to me because the term *POJO* (Plain Old Java Object) is truly the genesis of POCO, and POJO has other associations with Java-specific technology that don't really translate to the generic term *persistence*.

Regardless of whether you call this topic POCO, PI, or tomato paste, the focal point remains the same: keep your domain model decoupled from your persistence layer. In fact, I like to expand on that and say, keep your domain model as decoupled from any provider-specific technology as humanly possible. Only when your model is decoupled can you truly have portability, reusability, and scalability (sounds like a good tattoo). Nilsson establishes the following characteristics as things you should *not* have to do in persistence ignorance:

Inherit from a certain base class (besides the object): A common pattern in ORM solutions is to force consumers to inherit from a provider-specific base class. The reason for this is dependent on the provider, but typically the base class has some sort of attribute or method required for persistence. This is not a significant problem if you're designing a system from the ground up, but if you already have a domain model and you're trying to add persistence, this can be a pain because .NET supports only single inheritance.

Instantiate only via a provided factory: As you will see in Chapter 8, I strongly support the use of factories when building domain models. However, I don't want to have to use a provider-specific factory implementation to create my persistent classes. This couples your model to the ORM instead of keeping it independent, and is usually required by ORM solutions for object tracking and notifications.

Use specially provided data types, such as for collections: This is another pretty typical situation that you'll see in ORM tools in order for them to provide functionality for out-of-the-box lazy loading. This is so common in the ORM solution world that it doesn't bother me too much, because you can usually design around this functionality to keep your model independent. However, I can understand the desire to have this as a feature of your ORM.

Implement a specific interface: Similar to base class inheritance, this is another situation in which the ORM engine needs a specific implementation in the persistent classes to do its job. This is obviously a better design—to have to implement an interface instead of having to use up your only class inheritance option in .NET—but you are still tightly coupling your domain model to the ORM, making it less portable.

Provide specific constructors: This is common in ORM solutions so the engine can create instances of your domain model type or reconstitute a particular value. My personal opinion is that having to implement a default constructor doesn't really violate any major design law. However (and I have yet to see an example this), anything beyond the default constructor implementation would be a significant irritation.

Provide mandatory specific fields: Providing specific types on fields (for example, a GUID for an ID) is sometimes mandatory in ORM frameworks. This is often part of an interface or a base class implementation, and is required in many cases for handling associations and relationships.

Avoid certain constructs and forced usage of certain constructs: This criterion can consist of a forced access modifier on a field or method or can be the metadata used for mapping. A good example of this is using get and set functions as you might in Java versus a property in C#. Additionally, as you will see later, this can also be the use of .NET attributes in your model. Attributes, extraneous methods, base classes, and so forth are a big concern of mine when developing a domain model because I don't like having to change my well-thought-out access modifiers or pollute my model with some garbage in order for the persistence engine to work.

I believe that the criteria that Nilsson established are accurate measures of PI in an ORM solution. However, my opinion on the necessity to have complete PI in your solution is not as fervent as many DDD purists in the industry. I believe that with the current state of .NET and ORM in the .NET space, it is unrealistic to believe that true PI is 100 percent achievable all the time. Even in the Java space, where ORM has been used and embraced for many years, many solutions don't support true PI. The fact is, the purpose of PI is to enforce complete portability of your domain model, which in itself is a difficult task. On the other hand, just because it is difficult—and with the current technology, nearly impossible—to have complete PI, I strongly believe in the concept and do everything I can in my design to achieve decoupling (which I demonstrate in Chapter 8). On that note, the following is an analysis of LINQ to SQL and EF and their ability to achieve PI.

■ **Tip** Don't get too caught up with all the POCO and PI hype. If you follow good design patterns and practices and avoid tight coupling, you're going to be fine if you have some instances in your domain model that break the PI rules.

PI and LINQ to SQL

LINQ to SQL does an excellent job of enabling the PI approach to development by achieving almost all of Nilsson's criteria. Let's take a closer look:

Inherit from a certain base class (besides the object): You do not have to inherit from any base class other than the object to enable persistence with LINQ to SQL.

Instantiate only via a provided factory: There is no requirement when using LINQ to SQL that a provider-specific factory be used for instantiation. With LINQ and LINQ to SQL, as you will see in later chapters, the entities can be disconnected or connected, and added or attached at any time.

Use specially provided data types, such as for collections: Here's the first aspect of PI that LINQ to SQL falls short on. For LINQ to SQL to support lazy loading, you need to use LINQ-specific types, `EntityRef` and `EntitySet`, for associations. Although it would be nice if we could use a standard collection or something provider agnostic, this is one of those areas that I feel comfortable giving in to. With a good design, we can use encapsulation techniques to avoid tight coupling.

Implement a specific interface: With LINQ (and not LINQ to SQL), when working with collection classes you have to implement `IEnumberable<T>` or `IQueryable<T>`. Because this implementation is LINQ specific (not LINQ to SQL specific) I consider this a fairly moot point, and although this still means that LINQ to SQL fails this point, I consider it a minor issue.

Provide specific constructors: With LINQ to SQL, you are required to have default constructors for the persistence engine to do its job. Again, this is one of those cases that I don't consider to be a significant deficiency because only a default constructor is required.

Provide mandatory specific fields: As mentioned earlier, this is typically used for object tracking and notification in the persistence life cycle. LINQ to SQL meets this requirement of PI, because the engine tracks the state of the object and compares before and after to determine what SQL to generate.

Avoid certain constructs and forced usage of certain constructs: LINQ to SQL does not force any construct on consumers. LINQ to SQL supports two mechanisms for creating the metadata to describe a persistent object: .NET attributes and XML mappings. The purists may say that the attributes break PI and that an external XML file is the only way to go (I will be discussing this more in the PI and EF section). Additionally, you do not have to use a particular accessibility modifier in order for the engine to do its job, unlike some other ORM solutions.

Overall, LINQ to SQL does an excellent job at enabling PI development. The biggest failure is that you have to use `EntityRef` and `EntitySet` for lazy loading. However, this should not disqualify LINQ to SQL as a viable ORM solution because its many other desirable features make up for this deficiency.

PI and EF

Unlike LINQ to SQL, EF doesn't do the greatest job at enabling PI in your model. However, you shouldn't fret, because this is a topic that Microsoft is putting a lot of time into and it is also on the minds of all EF developers. So, even though you won't see true PI in the first version, it has already been announced that EF will support PI in a future release. Let's take a look at the current PI state of EF:

Inherit from a certain base class (besides object): EF does not require you to inherit from a specific base class other than `Object`. However, as will be explained shortly, EF does require some interface implementations.

Instantiate only via a provided factory: When using EF, there is no requirement that a provider-specific factory be used for instantiation.

Use specially provided data types, such as for collections: Supporting relationships in your model EF requires you to use the `IEntityWithRelationships` interface.

Implement a specific interface: Unfortunately, in order for the EF engine to perform with acceptable results, you must at a minimum implement the `IEntityWithChangeTracker` and `IEntityWithKey` interfaces in your model. These interfaces are used for optimized object tracking and state management. If you choose not to implement the interfaces, the engine will not function correctly. In addition, as previously stated, in order to have any relationships in your model, you also need to implement `IEntityWithRelationships`.

Provide specific constructors: Unlike LINQ to SQL and many ORM solutions, EF does not require you to have a default constructor in your classes for the persistence engine to do its job.

Provide mandatory specific fields: Another aspect of the EF tracking system requires you to store a copy of an `EntityKey`. Although this breaks the PI rule, this is one of those situations that I don't consider to be significant because with good design you can avoid the coupling in this situation.

Avoid certain constructs and forced usage of certain constructs: One of the biggest problems with EF and its lack of PI comes in the way that it handles metadata mappings. Unlike LINQ to SQL, EF requires that you use attributes in your persistent objects as the mapping language. I'm really not the biggest fan of attributes because I see them becoming a container of metadata, which makes your code sloppy and much more difficult to transport. It's not that I dislike the concept of attributes, because I love their declarative and cross-cutting nature, but I strongly believe that developers are using an excessive number of them. Another problem with EF is that in order for change tracking to perform well, you need to modify each your setter properties to notify the change-tracking mechanism that the property has changed. You will see more on this topic in Chapters 5, 6, and 7, but keep this in mind when choosing an ORM.

As you can see, EF is far from PI compliant in this first release. Does that mean that you shouldn't use EF as your ORM tool? The answer is a resounding *no*. The EF has many excellent features and is one of the first ORM tools to really embrace the idea of the conceptual model (more on this in later chapters). Additionally, the roadmap for EF looks appealing and will support PI, so there are advantages in moving to EF now.

PI and NHibernate

This is the first time that I've mentioned NHibernate in the text, but not the last. For those who have been living in a box, *NHibernate* is a port of the popular Java ORM Hibernate. As a port from Java, NHibernate comes into the .NET space with one strong advantage: conceptual maturity. Because Hibernate is one of the most popular ORM tools in Java, NHibernate brings with it many lessons learned. However, as a port from Java, it also has some disadvantages, such as being a port from Java. Unlike .NET ORM tools written from the ground up, NHibernate is bound to some of the language constructs and design structures from the Java world. I digress; the NHibernate topic is explored more in Chapter 12, but I wanted to set the stage for the topic of this section: PI and NHibernate.

I'm not going to go through the same exercise that I did with LINQ to SQL and EF, to analyze NHibernate's PI success, because Nilsson's book does that already. However, I do want to point out some of the main points because NHibernate is the de facto standard in the ORM world. For the most part, NHibernate is PI compliant. However, there are a couple of items that keep it from being truly PI. NHibernate requires a default constructor, like most other ORM solutions. In addition, you can't give identity fields a default. The infrastructure of NHibernate uses your identity fields to determine whether the transaction should be an insert or an update. Finally, you can't use read-only fields in your model because NHibernate can't reflect on those fields.

Overall, from a pure PI perspective, NHibernate is far more advanced than EF or LINQ to SQL. This has a lot to do with its maturity from its Java roots. However, now that Microsoft has thrown its hat in the ORM ring, it is likely that NHibernate's following will level off and people will begin to embrace LINQ to SQL and EF more.

Further Reading

To be honest with you, I have only scratched the surface of DDD and pattern-based development in this chapter. As previously stated, most of the contents of this chapter are extensions or examples of the patterns that the gurus of the industry have defined and developed. If you have read this chapter and are feeling like you want to know more, I recommend the following books and web sites:

- *Patterns of Enterprise Application Architecture* by Martin Fowler (Addison-Wesley Professional, 2002). This book is the blueprint for the development of pattern-based enterprise-class software.
- *Domain-Driven Design: Tackling Complexity in the Heart of Software* by Eric Evans (Addison-Wesley Professional, 2003). Evans is the father of DDD, and his book is the outline for the philosophy and methodologies involved.
- *Applying Domain-Driven Design and Patterns: With Examples in C# and .NET* by Jimmy Nilsson (Addison-Wesley Professional, 2006). In this book, Nilsson creates a modern-day guide for implementing DDD. Although the focus of this book is NHibernate, it is a vital read for anyone using ORM.

- Ambysoft (`www.ambysoft.com`). Scott Ambler has written a stack of books on modeling, agile development, and ORM. I would recommend any of his essays or books on these subjects, which can be accessed from his web site.
- *Design Patterns: Elements of Reusable Object-Oriented Software* by Erich Gamma, Richard Helm, Ralph Johnson, and John Vlissides (Addison-Wesley Professional, 1994). If there is a bible for software engineers, this is it. The Gang of Four has laid out structural, creational, and behavioral patterns that every developer needs to know.

Summary

In this chapter, you have learned the basics of DDD and the patterns involved in successfully using ORM, and have been introduced to the concept of PI. At the heart of DDD is the domain, which is fundamentally the solution you are trying to develop. Using a domain model to enumerate the needs of the business is the best way to create a flexible object model for working with an ORM tool. However, remember that you must model the domain before you write any code for the domain model.

UML is the de facto industry standard for modeling your domain. Of the 13 diagram types that UML provides, I recommend becoming an expert in class diagrams and sequence diagrams. However, it is important for you to realize that developing a good domain model has little to do with UML, but rather a deep-seated involvement between yourself (the modeler) and the domain experts.

Gathering requirements by working with your domain experts is critical for success, but understanding the core development patterns is equally important. The patterns you were introduced to in this chapter, such as factories, laziness, and PI, are critical for your success when working with an ORM solution.

Now that you have been exposed to the basic theoretical aspects of ORM, you will start to apply this knowledge in the coming chapters. However, in Chapter 3 you are going to switch gears and begin to learn the fundamentals of LINQ to SQL and how to apply the technology to common development situations. Don't fret, though; the knowledge that you have learned in this chapter is critical and will be applied later in the book and will be used to build the foundation of the Bank of Pluto case study.

PART 2

LINQ to SQL Examined

CHAPTER 3

■ ■ ■

Introduction to LINQ to SQL

In Chapter 2, you learned the fundamentals of ORM and the patterns and practices needed to work with ORM—but forget about them for the time being, because you won't be using those patterns in this chapter. Instead, this chapter introduces you to LINQ to SQL (LTS) through simple examples that highlight the features of ORM. To keep this chapter concise and focused on LTS, the Bottom Up approach is used because it is natively the most supported technique in LTS. Alternatively, when you map the FBP domain model by using LTS in Chapter 9, you will use the Top Down approach because it is the preferred method of building enterprise applications.

Before you can jump into the functionality of LTS by using the Bottom Up approach, it is critical that you have a data model in place. For simplicity, you will be working with the ubiquitous `AdventureWorks` database in the examples in this chapter. Because `AdventureWorks` is probably the most common sample database for SQL Server 2005, it is a good place for you to start your development with LTS and good common ground for most people. However, before you write any code, I want to introduce you to the origins of LTS and some of the fundamentals behind LINQ.

What Is LINQ to SQL?

Prior to answering this question, you must first understand what LINQ is. *LINQ* stands for the .NET *Language Integrated Query* and is a new framework extension in .NET 3.5. As the name suggests, LINQ is a language construct that enables the user to write data access queries natively in .NET languages.

In days of yore, you had to write inline T-SQL or use a third-party tool to be able to write queries in your .NET code. With LINQ, your inline queries natively use the metadata from your project, so you have syntax checking, IntelliSense, and type-checking functionality. In addition, you also benefit from a single declarative language construct for all your data sources (for example, XML or a database). LINQ defines a set of standard query operators that allow your queries to be applied to any `IEnumerable<T>` interface.

LINQ is the foundation for many native substructures in .NET that enable you to query disparate data sources. For example, LINQ to XML gives you the ability to write LINQ to query XML stores; LINQ to DataSets allows you to use `DataSets` as your data source; LINQ to Objects provides you with the means to query over collections of objects; and, finally, LINQ to SQL gives you the ability to work with relational databases.

LTS is the focus of the current and next few chapters and is Microsoft's first attempt at ORM. LTS allows you to model a database and gives you the ability to query the database by using native .NET classes, such as LINQ. Additionally, LTS supports transactional processing, views, and stored procedures, and provides a centralized structure for business validation.

Understanding the Basics

LTS is a robust framework that ships with tools that will make your development easier. In this section, you will learn about the basics of the LTS designer, Database Mapping Language and mapping, data context, entities, SqlMetal, and CRUD operations.

LINQ to SQL Designer

The first aspect of LTS that you should familiarize yourself with is the designer. This section walks you through the LTS user interface that comes with Visual Studio 2008. Instead of contaminating your `BoP` solution with a bunch of one-off examples, let's create a new Windows Forms solution in VS 2008 called `LTS_Harness`. You may be asking yourself why you are creating a Windows Forms application. To keep things focused on LTS, using a Win Forms or console application is much faster than building a full-blown web application.

Now that you have created a new Forms application, you need to add a new data connection to `AdventureWorks` to your Server Explorer. Next, add a LINQ to SQL Classes file, which is a new template under the Add New Item, Data section in VS 2008 (see Figure 3-1). Name the file `AdventureWorks` and add it to your solution. The LINQ to SQL Classes file is actually a new file format called Database Mapping Language (DBML), which is the core of the LTS visual designer, the data context, the mappings, and the generated code.

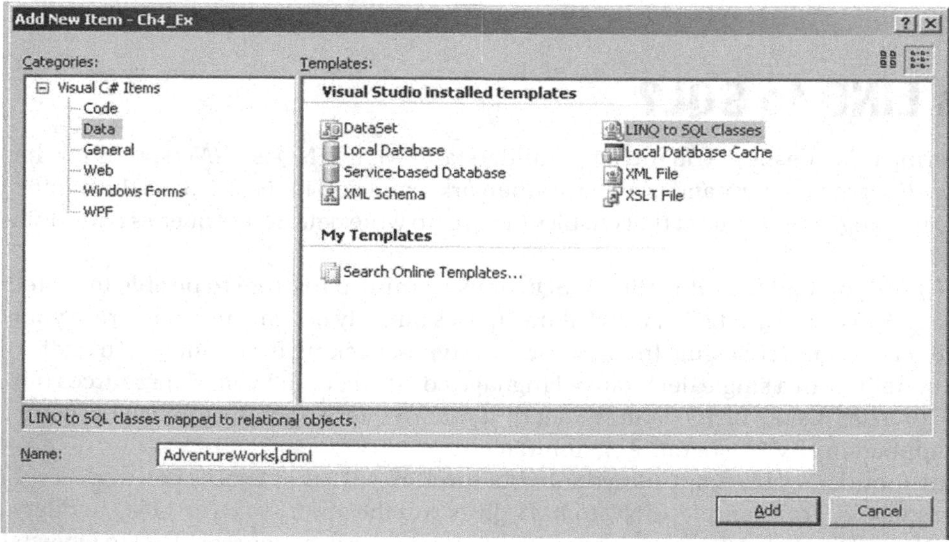

Figure 3-1. *The new DBML file template ships with Visual Studio 2008.*

AdventureWorks.dbml is divided into three separate files: AdventureWorks.dbml.layout, AdventureWorks.designer.cs, and AdventureWorks.dbml. In Figure 3-2, you can see that I have dragged the Department table from my AdventureWorks connection in Server Explorer. The table is now represented on the DBML design surface.

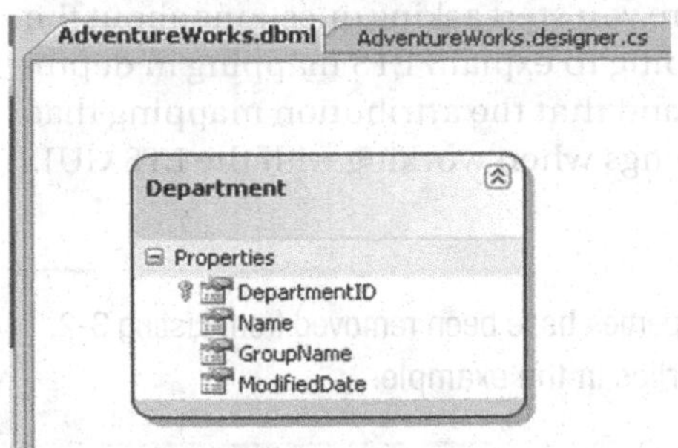

Figure 3-2. *The Department table is represented in the LTS designer.*

Examining the AdventureWorks.dbml.layout file, you can see in Listing 3-1 that it contains the XML and metadata to create the visual representation in the GUI designer. In this example, you have the Department table that is associated with the AdventureWorksDataContext and the coordinates that the GUI needs to display the object.

Listing 3-1. *The LTS DesignerXMLl (dbml.layout)*

```
<?xml version="1.0" encoding="utf-8"?>
<ordesignerObjectsDiagram dslVersion="1.0.0.0" absoluteBounds="0, 0, 11, 8.5"
    name="AdventureWorks">
    <DataContextMoniker Name="/AdventureWorksDataContext" />
    <nestedChildShapes>
           <classShape Id="b65c43ed-b63e-4a9d-b4f4-a7a12ed1f9b7"
                   absoluteBounds="0.5, 0.5, 2, 1.4248478190104168">
                  <DataClassMoniker Name="/AdventureWorksDataContext/Department" />
                  <nestedChildShapes>
                         <elementListCompartment
                             Id="449984a2-44a5-40b5-afb5-34dfc9086605"
                             absoluteBounds="0.51500000000000012, 0.96,
                             1.9700000000000002, 0.86484781901041674"
                             name="DataPropertiesCompartment"
                             titleTextColor="Black"
                             itemTextColor="Black" />
                  </nestedChildShapes>
           </classShape>
    </nestedChildShapes>
</ordesignerObjectsDiagram>
```

The next file in the list is AdventureWorks.designer.cs. As you may suspect, this is a C# file that contains the code to interact with the LTS. When using the designer, this file is 100 percent code generated and contains partial classes and mappings of what is represented in the GUI.

In Listing 3-2, you can see a portion of the generated partial class Department, which maps back to the HumanResource.Department table in the AdventureWorks database by exposing properties that represent the columns in the Department table. Before you start asking questions about the mapping attributes in this partial class, know that I'm going to explain LTS mapping in depth later in this chapter; however, it is important to understand that the attribution mapping that you see in Listing 3-2 is not the only way to create mappings when working with the LTS GUI.

Note For readability, the GroupName and ModifiedDate properties have been removed from Listing 3-2. These properties follow the same pattern as the rest of the properties in the example.

Another important aspect of Listing 3-2 is that the Department class inherits from INotifyPropertyChanging and INotifyPropertyChanged. These two interfaces contain the contract for the PropertyChangingEventHandler and the PropertyChangedEventHandler, respectively. These events are used by the DataContext for data tracking to determine when something is "dirty" or needs to be refreshed.

The last thing to mention about Listing 3-2 has to do with the region labeled Extensibility Method Definitions. This region contains *partial methods* that allow for extensions to the partial class. Partial methods were introduced in .NET 3.0 to provide you with the means to create extension points in a partial class without having a separate interface or base class. They are unique because they are typically used only by code-generation tools and cannot have an access modifier. As you move into advanced topics in later chapters, you will be writing some extensions to these partial methods, so keep them in the back of your mind.

Listing 3-2. *The Autogenerated Department Partial Class*

```
[Table(Name="HumanResources.Department")]
public partial class Department : INotifyPropertyChanging,
   INotifyPropertyChanged
{

    private static PropertyChangingEventArgs
              emptyChangingEventArgs = new
              PropertyChangingEventArgs(String.Empty);
    private short _DepartmentID;
    private string _Name;

#region Extensibility Method Definitions
```

```
    partial void OnLoaded();
    partial void OnValidate();
    partial void OnCreated();
    partial void OnDepartmentIDChanging(short value);
    partial void OnDepartmentIDChanged();
    partial void OnNameChanging(string value);
    partial void OnNameChanged();

#endregion

    public Department()
    { OnCreated(); }

    [Column(Storage="_DepartmentID", AutoSync=AutoSync.OnInsert,
        DbType="SmallInt NOT NULL IDENTITY", IsPrimaryKey=true,
        IsDbGenerated=true)]

    public short DepartmentID
    {
        get
        { return this._DepartmentID; }
        set
        {
            if ((this._DepartmentID != value))
            {
                this.OnDepartmentIDChanging(value);
                this.SendPropertyChanging();
                this._DepartmentID = value;
                this.SendPropertyChanged("DepartmentID");
                this.OnDepartmentIDChanged();
            }
        }
    }

    [Column(Storage="_Name", DbType="NVarChar(50) NOT NULL",
        CanBeNull=false)]
    public string Name
    {
        get
        { return this._Name; }
        set
        {
```

```
                if ((this._Name != value))
                {
                    this.OnNameChanging(value);
                    this.SendPropertyChanging();
                    this._Name = value;
                    this.SendPropertyChanged("Name");
                    this.OnNameChanged();
                }
            }
        }

        public event PropertyChangingEventHandler PropertyChanging;

        public event PropertyChangedEventHandler PropertyChanged;

        protected virtual void SendPropertyChanging()
        {
            if ((this.PropertyChanging != null))
            { this.PropertyChanging(this, emptyChangingEventArgs); }
        }

        protected virtual void SendPropertyChanged(String propertyName)
        {
            if ((this.PropertyChanged != null))
            { this.PropertyChanged(this,
                     new PropertyChangedEventArgs(propertyName)); }
        }
    }
```

DataContext Class

I have mentioned the DataContext class several times thus far, but I have yet to provide a good explanation. The DataContext class is the core channel that you use to work with (for example, to query or update) your database. For each LTS DBML file you add to your solution, a new DataContext will be created.

The DataContext class is a generated partial class that exists in your AdventureWorks.designer.cs file. In this example, your partial class is called AdventureWorksDataContext, which is based on the name that you gave the DBML file. As you can see in Listing 3-3, the DataContext class contains the properties and methods for interacting with the table(s) that have been added to the designer.

In addition to the properties and methods in the AdventureWorksDataContext class, you can also see in Listing 3-3 that the System.Data.Linq.DataContext is used as the base class. This base class is part of the LINQ framework and contains the contract and implementation logic to work with the database and the entities in the database. Some examples of what is in the DataContext class include Refresh, CreateDatabase, GetTable, and SubmitChanges.

Note Like the generated `Department` partial class, the `AdventureWorksDataContext` partial class implements partial methods that can be used to extend the generated `DataContext` for increased functionality.

Listing 3-3. *The DataContext Class: The Main Channel for Interacting with the Database*

```
using System.Data.Linq;
using System.Data.Linq.Mapping;
using System.Data;
using System.Collections.Generic;
using System.Reflection;
using System.Linq;
using System.Linq.Expressions;
using System.ComponentModel;
using System;

[System.Data.Linq.Mapping.DatabaseAttribute(Name="AdventureWorks")]
public partial class AdventureWorksDataContext : System.Data.Linq.DataContext
{

    private static System.Data.Linq.Mapping.MappingSource
         mappingSource = new AttributeMappingSource ();

#region Extensibility Method Definitions
partial void OnCreated();
partial void InsertDepartment(Department instance);
partial void UpdateDepartment(Department instance);
partial void DeleteDepartment(Department instance);
#endregion

    static AdventureWorksDataContext()
    {
    }

    public AdventureWorksDataContext(string connection) :
            base(connection, mappingSource)
    {
        OnCreated();
    }

    public AdventureWorksDataContext(System.Data.IDbConnection connection) :
            base(connection, mappingSource)
    {
        OnCreated();
    }
```

```
        public AdventureWorksDataContext(string connection,
                    System.Data.Linq.Mapping.MappingSource mappingSource) :
                base(connection, mappingSource)
        {
            OnCreated();
        }

        public AdventureWorksDataContext(System.Data.IDbConnection connection,
                    System.Data.Linq.Mapping.MappingSource mappingSource) :
                base(connection, mappingSource)
        {
            OnCreated();
        }

        public AdventureWorksDataContext() :
                base(global::
                  LTS_Harness.Properties.Settings.Default.
                      AdventureWorksConnectionString, mappingSource)
        {
            OnCreated();
        }

        public System.Data.Linq.Table<Department> Departments
        {
            get
            {
                return this.GetTable<Department>();
            }
        }
    }
```

DBML and Mapping Fundamentals

The final aspect to round off your basic understanding of the LTS file structure is the actual DBML and the mapping that is done with LTS. Looking first at the AdventureWorks.dbml file in Listing 3-4, you can see that you have an XML file that has your connection string, provider information, and metadata mapping to the Department table. The DBML file represents the database schema and is used by the designer to show the mapping information in the GUI.

As you can see in Listing 3-4, the DBML file is very intuitive. Along with having a Database and Connection node, you also have a Table node that contains the mappings from the type Department to the table HumanResources.Department. The child nodes of Table, the Column nodes, contain the Type attribute (which is the .NET type) along with the DbType (which is the database type). In addition, the Column nodes contain other attributes such as CanBeNull to help with the mappings.

Listing 3-4. *The DBML File Contains Some of the Mapping Information Used by LTS*

```
<?xml version="1.0" encoding="utf-16"?>
<Database Name="AdventureWorks" Class="AdventureWorksDataContext"
   xmlns="http://schemas.microsoft.com/linqtosql/dbml/2007">

    <Connection Mode="AppSettings"
      ConnectionString="Data Source=ORCASBETA2_TFSV\SQLEXPRESS;
      Initial Catalog=AdventureWorks;Integrated Security=True"
      SettingsObjectName="LTS_Harness.Properties.Settings"
      SettingsPropertyName="AdventureWorksConnectionString"
      Provider="System.Data.SqlClient" />

   <Table Name="HumanResources.Department" Member="Departments">

       <Type Name="Department">

           <Column Name="DepartmentID" Type="System.Int16"
               DbType="SmallInt NOT NULL IDENTITY" IsPrimaryKey="true"
               IsDbGenerated="true" CanBeNull="false" />

           <Column Name="Name" Type="System.String"
                         DbType="NVarChar(50) NOT NULL" CanBeNull="false" />

           <Column Name="GroupName" Type="System.String"
                         DbType="NVarChar(50) NOT NULL" CanBeNull="false" />

           <Column Name="ModifiedDate" Type="System.DateTime"
                         DbType="DateTime NOT NULL" CanBeNull="false" />

       </Type>
   </Table>
</Database>
```

■ **Note** The DBML file is *not* the file used for object mapping. The mapping in the DBML file is used only for the designer, not for any type of persistence.

You have two options for object mapping when using LTS: XML mapping and attribute-based mapping. Unfortunately, when using the VS 2008 designer (as you have been), you are stuck with attribute-based mapping. As you may recall from Chapter 2, I consider using attributes in your domain model an action that breaks PI and corrupts your model; however, because LTS is generating the code for you in the Bottom Up approach, it is less of a problem.

Attribute mapping, like XML mapping, is similar to the DBML file you reviewed in Listing 3-4, as they all use the same schema (DBMLSchema.xsd) for construction. In Table 3-1, you can see the enumeration of the DBMLSchema.xsd file that defines the mapping construct in LTS. Although the table does not go through every attribute in the schema, it does identify the most important elements and attributes.

Table 3-1. *DBML Mapping Options*

Element	Attribute	Type	Description
Database			The Database element is used to store the default database mapping details; this information is optional because the Connection can also supply these details. The Database element is the parent of the Connection, Table, and Function elements.
	Name	String	The Name attribute specifies the name of the database.
	Class	String	The name of the DataContext class.
	EntityNamespace	String	Default namespace of your Entity classes.
	ContextNamespace	String	Default namespace of your DataContext class.
	AccessModifier	AccessModifier	The accessibility level of the DataContext class. Valid values are Public, Protected, Internal, and Private.
	BaseType	String	The BaseType of the DataContext class.
	Provider	String	The Provider of the DataContext class. SQL Server is the only supported database at this time.
	ExternalMapping	Boolean	Specifies whether the DBML is used for external mapping.
	Serialization	SerializationMode	Specifies whether the DataContext and Entity classes are serializeable.
Table			The Table element is used to specify that your class is an Entity class and provides the class-to-table association details. The Table element is the parent of Type, InsertFunction, UpdateFunction, and DeleteFunction elements.
	Name	String	The name of the table, which defaults to the class name if left blank.
	AccessModifier	AccessModifier	The accessibility level of the Table<T> class in the DataContext. Valid values are Public, Protected, Internal, and Private.

Table 3-1. *DBML Mapping Options (Continued)*

Element	Attribute	Type	Description
Type			The Type element contains the details about your class, and is the parent node for the Column and Association elements.
	Name	String	The name of your entity class.
	InheritanceCode	String	Use this attribute to tell the framework the hierarchy of inheritance in your model. Although this is a String, you supply an integer for this attribute.
	IsInheritanceDefault	Boolean	This attribute, which is required if you are using inheritance, is used in combination with the InheritanceCode attribute to specify the default or root class in your hierarchy.
	AccessModifier	AccessModifier	The accessibility level of the CLR type being created. Valid values are Public, Protected, Internal, and Private.
	Id	String	A unique ID that can be used by other tables or functions and that appears only in DBML, not in the object model.
	IdRef	String	An attribute that is used to refer to another type's ID and is stored only in DBML, not in the object model.
Column			The Column element is used to indicate that a member of your Entity class is mapped to a database field. This element is required for the LTS persistence framework to function.
	Name	String	The name of the column in a database table or view. If you don't supply a value, it defaults to the name of the class member.
	Member	String	The name of the property to be generated on the containing type.
	Storage	String	The Storage attribute can be used as an override of the underlying class storage mechanism. By default, LTS is the public property accessor; this attribute gives you a way to change that binding.
	DBType	String	The type of the database column. This is the same type that you would use when in T-SQL.

Table 3-1. *DBML Mapping Options (Continued)*

Element	Attribute	Type	Description
	IsPrimaryKey	Boolean	Defines the column that is the primary key in the table. You can set multiple columns to be primary in your mappings to create a composite key association.
	IsDbGenerated	Boolean	Used to identify the fields that have generated values, such as an identity field.
	IsVersion	Boolean	Identifies the column that is a time-stamp or version in the database. This tells LTS that this field needs to be updated when changes occur.
	UpdateCheck	UpdateCheck	To override the default handling of optimistic concurrency conflict detection in LTS, use the UpdateCheck attribute. The enums for this attribute are Always, Never, and WhenChanged.
	IsDiscriminator	Boolean	Use this attribute to tell LTS which columns are discriminators in your inheritance hierarchy.
	CanBeNull	Boolean	You can use the CanBeNull attribute to specify whether a field can be null in the database.
	AutoSync	AutoSync	Tells LTS to automatically synchronize the value when an insert or update occurs. The values for this attribute are OnInsert, Always, and Never.
	AccessModifier	AccessModifier	The accessibility level of the property being created. Valid values are Public, Protected, Internal, and Private.
Association			The Association element is used to specify the relationships (for example, foreign key) in the model.
	Name	String	The name of the association, which is typically the same name that you see in the database (that is, the foreign-key constraint name).
	Storage	String	The name of the underlying class storage member. By default this is your public property accessor, but you can change that by supplying a value in this attribute.
	ThisKey	String	This attribute is a list of comma-separated member names that represent the keys on the left side of the association.

Table 3-1. *DBML Mapping Options (Continued)*

Element	Attribute	Type	Description
	OtherKey	String	This attribute is a list of comma-separated member names that represent the keys on the right side of the association.
	IsUnique	Boolean	Used to specify whether the field has a unique constraint in the database.
	IsForeignKey	Boolean	Used to designate a field as a foreign key.
	DeleteRule	String	The DeleteRule attribute tells LTS how to handle cascading deletes or other special referential integrity constraints around deletions.
	IsDelayLoaded	Boolean	Specifies whether the column should be immediately loaded or delayed until used. The default is false.
	AccessModifier	AccessModifier	The accessibility level of the property being created. Valid values are Public, Protected, Internal, and Private.
Function			The Function element is used to indicate that a method call is used to call a user-defined scalar or table-valued function. This element also has the Parameter and Return child elements.
	Name	String	The name of the function that is being called in the database.
	AccessModifier	AccessModifier	The accessibility level of the property being created. Valid values are Public, Protected, Internal, and Private.
	Method	String	The name of the CLR method to generate that allows invocation of the stored procedure.
	HasMultipleResults	Boolean	Specifies whether the stored procedure used by this function has multiple results returned.
	IsComposable	Boolean	Indicates whether the function can be composed of LINQ to SQL queries.
Parameter			This element represents a parameter in a stored procedure or function when using the Function element.
	Name	String	The database name of the parameter.
	Parameter	String	The CLR name of the parameter.
	DbType	String	The database type of the stored procedure or function parameter.

Table 3-1. *DBML Mapping Options (Continued)*

Element	Attribute	Type	Description
	Direction	ParameterDirection	The direction that the parameter flows. Can be In, Out, or InOut.
Return			This element represents the return type of a function.
	Type	String	The CLR type of the function or stored procedure.
	DbType	String	The database type of the stored procedure or function parameter.

Entity Classes

In Listing 3-2, you saw the `Department` class that was generated by the LTS designer, and the mapping attributes that decorate the class. After reviewing Table 3-1, you should see that there are many more attributes and options for mapping than just the generation of a single class.

To understand more of the mapping functionality that LTS has to offer, you need to add some more entities to your design surface to expand on this example. Add the `Employee`, `Contact`, and `EmployeeDepartmentHistory` tables to your project, as seen in Figure 3-3.

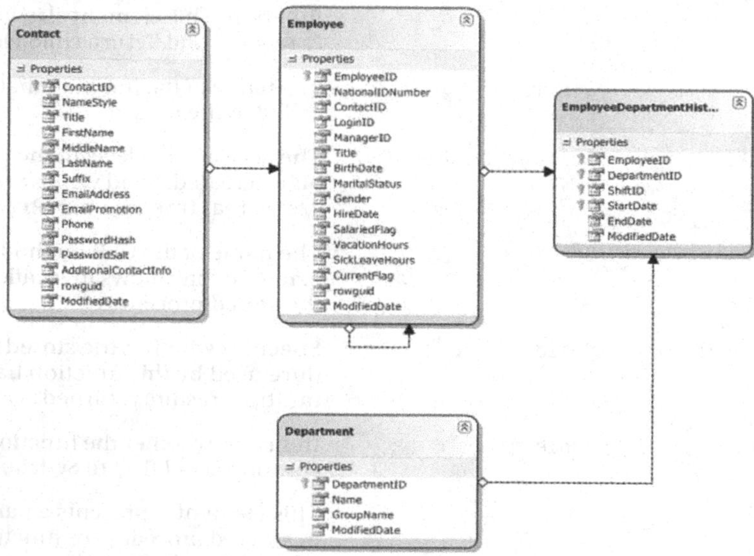

Figure 3-3. *The Department, Employee, Contact, and EmployeeDepartmentHistory entities*

As you can see, we now have four entities and arrows connecting these entities. These connections represent the associations between the entities, which are the foreign-key relationships between the tables. In Listing 3-5, you can see a condensed version of the AdventureWorks.dbml file, which has grown considerably. We now have some new Association elements in the XML, and there are three new entities represented.

Listing 3-5. *The Expanded DBML with Three New Entities and Their Associations*

```
<?xml version="1.0" encoding="utf-16"?>
<Database Name="AdventureWorks" Class="AdventureWorksDataContext"
    xmlns="http://schemas.microsoft.com/linqtosql/dbml/2007">
  <Connection Mode="AppSettings" ConnectionString="Data
      Source=ORCASBETA2_TFSV\SQLEXPRESS;
      Initial Catalog=AdventureWorks;Integrated Security=True"
      SettingsObjectName="LTS_Harness.Properties.Settings"
      SettingsPropertyName="AdventureWorksConnectionString"
      Provider="System.Data.SqlClient" />

 <Table Name="HumanResources.Department" Member="Departments">
    <Type Name="Department">
      <Column Name="DepartmentID" Type="System.Int16"
          DbType="SmallInt NOT NULL IDENTITY" IsPrimaryKey="true"
          IsDbGenerated="true" CanBeNull="false" />
      <Column Name="Name" Type="System.String"
          DbType="NVarChar(50) NOT NULL" CanBeNull="false" />
      <Column Name="GroupName" Type="System.String"
          DbType="NVarChar(50) NOT NULL" CanBeNull="false" />
      <Column Name="ModifiedDate" Type="System.DateTime"
          DbType="DateTime NOT NULL" CanBeNull="false" />
      <Association Name="Department_EmployeeDepartmentHistory"
          Member="EmployeeDepartmentHistories" OtherKey="DepartmentID"
          Type="EmployeeDepartmentHistory" />
    </Type>
  </Table>

  <-- NOTE: COLUMNS HAVE BEEN REMOVED FOR READABILITY -->
  <Table Name="HumanResources.Employee" Member="Employees">
    <Type Name="Employee">
      <Column Name="EmployeeID" Type="System.Int32"
            DbType="Int NOT NULL IDENTITY" IsPrimaryKey="true"
             IsDbGenerated="true" CanBeNull="false" />
      <Association Name="Employee_Employee" Member="Employees"
             OtherKey="ManagerID" Type="Employee" />
      <Association Name="Employee_EmployeeDepartmentHistory"
             Member="EmployeeDepartmentHistories" OtherKey="EmployeeID"
             Type="EmployeeDepartmentHistory" />
      <Association Name="Employee_Employee" Member="Employee1"
             ThisKey="ManagerID" Type="Employee" IsForeignKey="true" />
```

```
    <Association Name="Contact_Employee" Member="Contact"
            ThisKey="ContactID" Type="Contact" IsForeignKey="true" />
  </Type>
</Table>

<-- NOTE: COLUMNS HAVE BEEN REMOVED FOR READABILITY -->
<Table Name="HumanResources.EmployeeDepartmentHistory"
    Member="EmployeeDepartmentHistories">
  <Type Name="EmployeeDepartmentHistory">
    <Column Name="EmployeeID" Type="System.Int32"
            DbType="Int NOT NULL" IsPrimaryKey="true" CanBeNull="false" />
    <Column Name="DepartmentID" Type="System.Int16"
            DbType="SmallInt NOT NULL" IsPrimaryKey="true" CanBeNull="false" />
    <Column Name="ShiftID" Type="System.Byte"
            DbType="TinyInt NOT NULL" IsPrimaryKey="true" CanBeNull="false" />
    <Column Name="StartDate" Type="System.DateTime"
            DbType="DateTime NOT NULL" IsPrimaryKey="true" CanBeNull="false" />
    <Association Name="Department_EmployeeDepartmentHistory"
            Member="Department" ThisKey="DepartmentID"
            Type="Department" IsForeignKey="true" />
    <Association Name="Employee_EmployeeDepartmentHistory"
            Member="Employee" ThisKey="EmployeeID"
            Type="Employee" IsForeignKey="true" />
  </Type>
</Table>

<-- NOTE: COLUMNS HAVE BEEN REMOVED FOR READABILITY -->
<Table Name="Person.Contact" Member="Contacts">
  <Type Name="Contact">
    <Column Name="ContactID" Type="System.Int32"
            DbType="Int NOT NULL IDENTITY" IsPrimaryKey="true"
                IsDbGenerated="true" CanBeNull="false" />
    <Column Name="ModifiedDate" Type="System.DateTime"
            DbType="DateTime NOT NULL" CanBeNull="false" />
    <Association Name="Contact_Employee" Member="Employees"
            OtherKey="ContactID" Type="Employee" />
  </Type>
</Table>
</Database>
```

In addition to the DBML growing exponentially, our generated Entity classes have multiplied as well. As you may have expected, there are now four separate classes for each of the entities (not shown) you added to the designer. Additionally, new association properties and attributes have been added to the classes, and a few examples can be seen in Listing 3-6.

The property EmployeeDepartmentHistories, seen in Listing 3-6, is on the *many* side of the one-to-many association, and so it uses an EntitySet<EmployeeDepartmentHistory> collection as its return type. Alternatively, the properties on the *one* side in Listing 3-6 (that is, Department and Employee) both return only a single entity instance. Another interesting facet is that the Association attribute decorates each of your new properties to provide the mapping metadata that LTS needs to handle persistence. In the properties that are on the *one* side of the one-to-many association, there is validation as well as the standard events being fired when the value of the property changes.

Listing 3-6. *The Updated Entity Classes with Association Properties and Attributes*

```
// This property is in the Department class
[Association(Name="Department_EmployeeDepartmentHistory",
Storage="_EmployeeDepartmentHistories",
OtherKey="DepartmentID")]
public EntitySet<EmployeeDepartmentHistory> EmployeeDepartmentHistories
{
    get
    {
        return this._EmployeeDepartmentHistories;
    }
    set
    {
        this._EmployeeDepartmentHistories.Assign(value);
    }
}

// This propety is in the EmployeeDepartmentHistory class
[Association(Name="Department_EmployeeDepartmentHistory",
Storage="_Department", ThisKey="DepartmentID",
IsForeignKey=true)]
public Department Department
{
    get
    {
        return this._Department.Entity;
    }
    set
    {
        Department previousValue = this._Department.Entity;
        if (((previousValue != value)
            || (this._Department.HasLoadedOrAssignedValue == false)))
        {
            this.SendPropertyChanging();
            if ((previousValue != null))
            {
                this._Department.Entity = null;
                previousValue.EmployeeDepartmentHistories.Remove(this);
            }
            this._Department.Entity = value;
            if ((value != null))
            {
                value.EmployeeDepartmentHistories.Add(this);
```

```
                this._DepartmentID = value.DepartmentID;
            }
            else
            {
                this._DepartmentID = default(short);
            }
            this.SendPropertyChanged("Department");
        }
    }
}
// This property is also in the EmployeeDepartmentHistory class
[Association(Name="Employee_EmployeeDepartmentHistory",
Storage="_Employee", ThisKey="EmployeeID",
IsForeignKey=true)]
public Employee Employee
{
    get
    {
        return this._Employee.Entity;
    }
    set
    {
        Employee previousValue = this._Employee.Entity;
        if (((previousValue != value)
            || (this._Employee.HasLoadedOrAssignedValue == false)))
        {
            this.SendPropertyChanging();
            if ((previousValue != null))
            {
                this._Employee.Entity = null;
                previousValue.EmployeeDepartmentHistories.Remove(this);
            }
            this._Employee.Entity = value;
            if ((value != null))
            {
                value.EmployeeDepartmentHistories.Add(this);
                this._EmployeeID = value.EmployeeID;
            }
            else
            {
                this._EmployeeID = default(int);
            }
            this.SendPropertyChanged("Employee");
        }
    }
}
```

SqlMetal

Now that you understand the LTS designer and the basics behind the metadata needed to map an entity to the database, let's take a look at SqlMetal. *SqlMetal* is a command-line executable that ships with VS 2008 and can be used to generate LTS classes and mapping metadata. The best way for you to understand what SqlMetal can do is to drop to the VS 2008 command prompt and type **sqlmetal /?**. Because this is printed text and there is no embedded Windows kernel in paperback books yet, the following is a subsection of what you would see:

```
sqlmetal [options] [<input file>]

Generate source code and mapping attributes or a mapping file from a database.
Generate an intermediate dbml file for customization from the database.
Generate code and mapping attributes or mapping file from a dbml file.

options:
  /server:<name>      database server name
  /database:<name>    database catalog on server
  /user:<name>        login user id
  /password:<name>    login password
  /views              extract database views
  /functions          extract database functions
  /sprocs             extract stored procedures
  /xml[:file]         output as xml
  /code[:file]        output as source code
  /map[:file]         generate xml mapping file instead of attributes
  /language:xxx       language for source code (vb,csharp)
  /namespace:<name>   namespace used for source code
  /pluralize          auto-pluralize table names
  /dataAttributes     auto-generate DataObjectField and Precision attributes
  /timeout:<seconds>  timeout value in seconds to use for database commands

examples:
Create code from SqlServer:
  SqlMetal /server:myserver /database:northwind /code:nwind.cs /namespace:nwind

Generate intermediate dbml file from SqlServer:
  SqlMetal /server:myserver /database:northwind /dbml:northwind.dbml /namespace:
nwind

Generate code with external mapping from dbml:
  SqlMetal /code:nwind.cs /map:nwind.map northwind.dbml

Generate dbml from a SqlCE sdf file:
  SqlMetal /dbml:northwind.dbml northwind.sdf

Generate dbml from SqlExpress local server:
  SqlMetal /server:.\sqlexpress /database:northwind /dbml:northwind.dbml
```

```
Generate dbml by using a connection string in the command line:
  SqlMetal /conn:"server='myserver'; database='northwind'" /dbml:northwind.dbml
```

As you can see from this output, the command-line tool is powerful and can be used to create the same files as the designer. Additionally, because it is a command-line tool, it is easy to integrate into an automated build process (such as NAnt or MSBuild), and it can be utilized directly from your project in prebuild events. Furthermore, it provides the functionality to generate external XML mapping files instead of forcing you to use attribute-based mapping as the designer does.

For all the positives (for example, easy integration and external XML mappings), the fact remains that SqlMetal is still a command-line tool; thus you lose as much as you gain. Not to say that command-line tools don't have their place in development, because they do, but I personally prefer to use my overpriced graphics card. The GUI gives you ease of use, IntelliSense, and What You See Is What You Get (WYSIWYG) capabilities, not to mention it's a lot easier on the eyes.

■ **Tip** It is usually easiest to use the `/conn` flag and pass in a connection string with SqlMetal instead of trying to pass in all the parameters to connect to your database. Remember that this is a command line, so if your string has spaces in it, you will need to surround it with quotation marks.

When generating an external mapping file, all you have to do is use the `map` flag and you will end up with an XML file that looks nearly identical to the DBML file created in the designer. In fact, I used the DBML generated by the designer and executed this command:

```
sqlmetal /code:adven_gen_sqlmetal.cs/map:adven_gend_sqlmetal.map AdventureWorks.dbml
```

The result was a code file that was identical to the `AdventureWorks.designer.cs` file, sans the mapping attributes, and a map file that was identical to `AdventureWorks.dbml`, sans the connection element. Furthermore, the `adven_gen_sqlmetal.cs` file contained the `AdventureWorksDataContext` partial class just as the `AdventureWorks.designer.cs` did, as well as the `Entity` classes you would expect.

■ **Caution** If using the DBML from the Visual Studio designer with SqlMetal, you may have to change the encoding from `<?xml version="1.0" encoding="utf-16"?>` to `<?xml version="1.0" encoding="utf-8"?>`, or you may receive an error from the executable.

You are probably wondering at this point how this external mapping file can be utilized by LTS. It would be ideal to have this functionality native in the designer. However, even without it, it is quite easy to use. When you instantiate your `DataContext` object, there are multiple constructor overloads, and one of them is for an external mapping file. In Listing 3-7, you can see the various constructor overloads for the `DataContext` class, including an example of the code to load an external mapping file.

Listing 3-7. *DataContext Constructor Overloads*

```
// Default Constructor
AdventureWorksDataContext db = new AdventureWorksDataContext();

// Pass in a connection interface
AdventureWorksDataContext db = new AdventureWorksDataContext(IDbConnection);

// Pass in a file source such as an external mapping file
AdventureWorksDataContext db = new AdventureWorksDataContext(string);

// Pass in a connection interface and a Linq.Data.Mapping.MappingSource class
AdventureWorksDataContext db = new AdventureWorksDataContext(IDbConnection,
   MappingSource);

// Pass in a file source external mapping file and a MappingSource class
AdventureWorksDataContext db = new AdventureWorksDataContext(String,
  MappingSource);
```

Querying

It's time to connect the dots and build out our `LTS_Harness` solution so it does something useful. At this point, you should have a Windows Forms solution with the `AdventureWorks.dbml` files and four entities: `Department`, `Employee`, `Contact`, and `EmployeeDepartmentHistory`. Let's imagine for a second that you are asked to write an application for the Human Resources (HR) department that gives HR the ability to query by an employee's last name, and then spits out the names of the departments the employee has worked in.

You start the process by dropping a list box and a button on your form, naming them `lstResults` and `btnQuery`, respectively, and you update the text property of the button so it reads Query. Next you need to add a text box and a label to the form, rename them `txtLastName` and `lblLastName`, respectively, and update the label so it reads Last Name (see Figure 3-4).

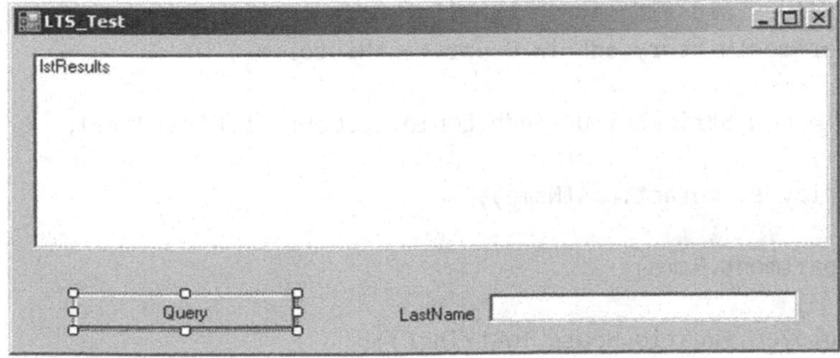

Figure 3-4. *The user interface for your simple HR application*

Now that you have a user interface, you can start writing some code in the button click event. Listing 3-8 shows the code to make this query engine go. In this example, you are creating a new `AdventureWorksDataContext` by using one of the new features in .NET 3.0: the `var` keyword. The `var` keyword defines a strongly typed compile-time variable reference; simply stated, the type casting is handled by the CLR instead of by you, so it is inferred at compile time.

Along with using the new `var` keyword, you are also querying the database by using LINQ. In this example, we are taking advantage of the powerful query functionality in LTS by using the associations from each table. What this means to you is that you don't have to handwrite join statements because the association is a representation of an entity object. For example, the `EmployeeDepartmentHistories` entity has an association to `Employee`, which in turn has an association to `Contact`, which contains the `LastName` property that you want to query against. This type of iteration over association is as easy as typing the dot on your entity and finding the appropriate object.

Listing 3-8. *Basic Query Using LTS*

```
// Validate there is something to query with
if(txtLastName.Text.Trim().Length == 0)
{
    MessageBox.Show("Enter a last name!");
}
else
{
    try
    {
        // Create new database context
        AdventureWorksDataContext db = new AdventureWorksDataContext();

        // Use a variant to hold the EmployeeDepartmentHistories
        //      Use LINQ to query the database, passing in the last name
        var DepartmentHistories = from dep in db.EmployeeDepartmentHistories
                    where dep.Employee.Contact.LastName == txtLastName.Text
                    select dep;

        // Loop through the values and display in the list box
        foreach (EmployeeDepartmentHistory edh in DepartmentHistories)
        {
            StringBuilder sb = new StringBuilder(edh.Employee.Contact.FirstName);
            sb.Append("\t");
            sb.Append(edh.Employee.Contact.LastName);
            sb.Append("\t");
            sb.Append(edh.Department.Name);
            sb.Append("\t");
            sb.Append(edh.Employee.VacationHours.ToString());
            lstResults.Items.Add(sb.ToString());

     }
}
```

```
    catch(Exception ex)
    {
        throw ex;
    }

}
```

In this example, you are using a `where` clause to return all the columns, and then using `foreach` against `IEnumerable` to iterate over the `DepartmentHistories` collection. The results are then pulled from the properties of the entities (that is, `FirstName`, `LastName`, `Department.Name`, and `VacationHours`) and concatenated into a string. The results are then output to the `ListBox` control, as seen in Figure 3-5.

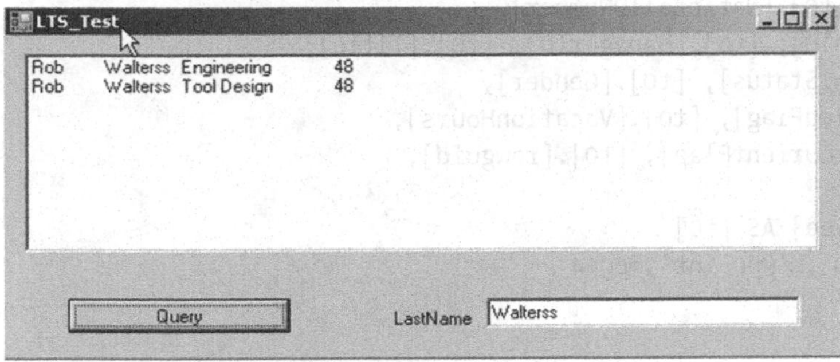

Figure 3-5. *Output of a simple query*

I know that the first time I saw an ORM simplify my query as shown in Listing 3-8, I was concerned about the SQL code being generated. There are ways to debug or review this SQL code. In Chapter 4, you will be looking at the LTS Visualizer, which makes this a snap, but for now let's just use the SQL Profiler to monitor what is being executed.

Listing 3-9 shows the T-SQL code being executed from the LINQ query that you wrote in Listing 3-8. As you can see, the SQL being emitted is parameterized and efficient. However, there are multiple queries where you might expect only one. The first query is the base query and is basically equal to what you wrote in LINQ. As you iterate over the collection and access other properties such as `edh.Employee.Contact.Name`, other queries will be executed to traverse the table structure and populate the LTS entities.

The reason for this is twofold. First, by default all queries that return `IEnumerable<T>` are deferred until you iterate over the collection, and by using the `select dep` statement, you are returning `IEnumerable<EmployeeDepartmentHistories>`. Second, with this LINQ query, you are returning all the rows in the result set; thus multiple queries are needed to meet the requirements. Obviously, this is not the most efficient or productive way to query a database, but there is hope.

Listing 3-9. *SQL Code Generated from the Simple Query*

```
exec sp_executesql
N'SELECT [t0].[EmployeeID], [t0].[DepartmentID], [t0].[ShiftID],
[t0].[StartDate], [t0].[EndDate], [t0].[ModifiedDate]
FROM [HumanResources].[EmployeeDepartmentHistory] AS [t0]
INNER JOIN [HumanResources].[Employee] AS [t1]
ON [t1].[EmployeeID] = [t0].[EmployeeID]
INNER JOIN [Person].[Contact] AS [t2]
ON [t2].[ContactID] = [t1].[ContactID]
WHERE [t2].[LastName] = @p0',N'@p0 nvarchar(8)',@p0=N'Walterss'

exec sp_executesql
N'SELECT [t0].[EmployeeID], [t0].[NationalIDNumber],
[t0].[ContactID], [t0].[LoginID], [t0].[ManagerID], [t0].[Title],
[t0].[BirthDate],[t0].[MaritalStatus], [t0].[Gender],
[t0].[HireDate], [t0].[SalariedFlag], [t0].[VacationHours],
[t0].[SickLeaveHours], [t0].[CurrentFlag], [t0].[rowguid],
[t0].[ModifiedDate]
FROM [HumanResources].[Employee] AS [t0]
WHERE [t0].[EmployeeID] = @p0',N'@p0 int',@p0=4

exec sp_executesql
N'SELECT [t0].[ContactID], [t0].[NameStyle], [t0].[Title],
[t0].[FirstName], [t0].[MiddleName], [t0].[LastName], [t0].[Suffix],
[t0].[EmailAddress], [t0].[EmailPromotion], [t0].[Phone],
[t0].[PasswordHash], [t0].[PasswordSalt],
[t0].[AdditionalContactInfo], [t0].[rowguid],
[t0].[ModifiedDate]
FROM [Person].[Contact] AS [t0]
WHERE [t0].[ContactID] = @p0',N'@p0 int',@p0=1290

exec sp_executesql
N'SELECT [t0].[DepartmentID], [t0].[Name], [t0].[GroupName], [t0].[ModifiedDate]
FROM [HumanResources].[Department] AS [t0]
WHERE [t0].[DepartmentID] = @p0',N'@p0 smallint',@p0=1

exec sp_executesql
N'SELECT [t0].[DepartmentID], [t0].[Name], [t0].[GroupName], [t0].[ModifiedDate]
FROM [HumanResources].[Department] AS [t0]
WHERE [t0].[DepartmentID] = @p0',N'@p0 smallint',@p0=2
```

Rather than having the `where` clause return a collection and having multiple SQL statements execute, we can use some of the new data-shaping features in .NET 3.5 to return only the results that are needed. In Listing 3-10, you can see that I have changed the query to return only the fields that are needed. In this example, I am using the new .NET 3.5 language features, anonymous type and object initialization, to return a subset of the data.

■ **Tip** By default, when you return an `IEnumerable<T>` from your LINQ query, your SQL query is deferred until you iterate over the collection. To execute a SQL query immediately from LINQ, use the native `ToList()` or `ToArray()` in your query.

Anonymous types and object initializations are powerful new language features in .NET 3.5 and warrant a few sentences. *Anonymous types* allow you to define an inline class without having to explicitly declare it. This new functionality is seen in Listing 3-10, where the `new` keyword is being used. *Object initializers* transfer more of the work to the compiler and allow you to set properties in a more concise way. In Listing 3-10, you can see that we are setting properties on our anonymous type without declaring them.

Along with using the anonymous type and object initializers, the iteration code has changed from Listing 3-8. Instead of using an `EmployeeDepartmentHistory` type, you are now using a `var`, and instead of needing to traverse the model to get the needed properties, you can access the new properties directly (that is, `FirstName`, `LastName`, `DepName`, and `VacHours`).

Listing 3-10. *A Shaped LINQ Query*

```
// Create new database context
AdventureWorksDataContext db = new AdventureWorksDataContext();

// Use a variant to hold the DepartmentHistories
//       Use LINQ to query the database passing in the lastname
//       Use an AnonymousType and Object Initializer to shape
//               the results
var DepartmentHistories = from dep in db.EmployeeDepartmentHistories
                          where dep.Employee.Contact.LastName == txtLastName.Text
                          select new
                          {
                                FirstName = dep.Employee.Contact.FirstName,
                                LastName = dep.Employee.Contact.LastName,
                                DepName = dep.Department.Name,
                                VacHours = dep.Employee.VacationHours
                          };

// Loop through the values and display in the list box
foreach (var edh in DepartmentHistories)
{
    StringBuilder sb = new StringBuilder(edh.FirstName);
    sb.Append("\t");
    sb.Append(edh.LastName);
    sb.Append("\t");
    sb.Append(edh.DepName);
    sb.Append("\t");
    sb.Append(edh.VacHours);
    lstResults.Items.Add(sb.ToString());

}
```

Again, you are probably wondering what the SQL code generated by this crazy inline query construct looks like, and I'm sure you're curious about whether you are still executing five separate queries. In Listing 3-11, you have the output of the SQL Profiler trace for the new shaped LINQ query. You can see in this example that there is no funny business going on, and the query being generated is only retrieving the data you need and not executing five separate queries.

Listing 3-11. *SQL Code from Shaped LINQ Query*

```
exec sp_executesql
N'SELECT [t2].[FirstName], [t2].[LastName], [t3].[Name], [t1].[VacationHours]
FROM [HumanResources].[EmployeeDepartmentHistory] AS [t0]
INNER JOIN [HumanResources].[Employee] AS [t1]
ON [t1].[EmployeeID] = [t0].[EmployeeID]
INNER JOIN [Person].[Contact] AS [t2]
ON [t2].[ContactID] = [t1].[ContactID]
INNER JOIN [HumanResources].[Department] AS [t3]
ON [t3].[DepartmentID] = [t0].[DepartmentID]
WHERE [t2].[LastName] = @p0',N'@p0 nvarchar(8)',@p0=N'Walterss'
```

Another important point about queries in this chapter revolves around the `orderby` and `where` clauses. You need to understand that the LINQ `orderby` and `where` clauses are similar to the ones that you write in T-SQL. For example, if you want to order by `Department.Name`, you would add `orderby` inline to the query, as seen in Listing 3-12. You will find that this native query functionality is a huge time- and cost-saver when you start developing with it.

Listing 3-12. *LINQ Queries Are Just Like SQL Queries*

```
var DepartmentHistories = from dep in db.EmployeeDepartmentHistories
                          where dep.Employee.Contact.LastName == txtLastName.Text
                          orderby dep.Department.Name
                          select new
                          {
                               FirstName = dep.Employee.Contact.FirstName,
                               LastName = dep.Employee.Contact.LastName,
                               DepName = dep.Department.Name,
                               VacHours = dep.Employee.VacationHours

                          };
```

The final topic on queries that I want to cover in this chapter (don't worry, we will be covering a lot more throughout the text) is aggregate queries with LTS. LTS natively supports five types of aggregate operations: `SUM`, `COUNT`, `MIN`, `MAX`, and `AVERAGE`. I'm not going to explain what each one means because the keywords are self-explanatory; however, I will demonstrate how you can use these aggregate functions in your code.

Listing 3-13 demonstrates how you can get `SUM` and `AVERAGE` vacation hours from the `Employee` table, without writing a lot of code. In the first part of Listing 3-13, you have a query that is selecting all the `VacationHours` from the `Employees` table, and then using the `Sum()` function at the end of the query to return the results into an integer variable.

In the second part of Listing 3-13, you have a similar query, but this time you are using the Average() function to average all the Employees vacation hours together. In both cases, you have an int cast on the VacationHours property because VacationHours is a short. Additionally, in both cases the results are added to the ListBox you were using earlier.

Listing 3-13. *Aggregate Operations in LTS*

```
//Sum vacation hours
int totalVacHours =
        (from emp in db.Employees
             select (int)emp.VacationHours).Sum();

lstResults.Items.Add(totalVacHours);

//Average vacation hours
int avgVacHours =
       (int)(from emp in db.Employees
            select (int)emp.VacationHours).Average();

lstResults.Items.Add(avgVacHours);
```

Listing 3-14 shows the SQL code generated from the C# in Listing 3-13. As you might expect, the SQL queries generated from Listing 3-13 use the native T-SQL aggregate functions, SUM and AVG. What you might not expect is that the cast you specified translated into a T-SQL CONVERT in the code that is generated.

Listing 3-14. *SQL Generated from Aggregate Operations*

```
SELECT SUM([t1].[value]) AS [value]
FROM (
    SELECT CONVERT(Int,[t0].[VacationHours]) AS [value]
    FROM [HumanResources].[Employee] AS [t0]
    ) AS [t1]

SELECT SUM([t1].[value]) AS [value]
FROM (
    SELECT CONVERT(Int,[t0].[VacationHours]) AS [value]
    FROM [HumanResources].[Employee] AS [t0]
    ) AS [t1]
```

Updating/Inserting/Deleting

In the preceding section, you saw how easy it is to retrieve an entity that is "alive" and associated with your database. Basic updating, inserting, and deleting is as easy as working with an entity and calling SubmitChanges().

Before you write more code in the LTS_Harness test harness, let's talk about change tracking and the fundamentals around how LTS updates the database. LTS tracks all the changes that occur to the entities in your model. This is accomplished through events in the LTS framework and the Entity classes, specifically the INotifyPropertyChanged and INotifyPropertyChanging interfaces that you saw in Listing 3-2.

The LTS framework is keeping an internal object graph of the changes, so as I said, after changing the value of a property, all you have to do is call DataContext.SubmitChanges(), and LTS dynamically generates the necessary SQL UPDATE statements.

To appreciate the simplicity of this, imagine that you have been asked to update the HR application so that an HR employee can first query by employee last name and then update that person's vacation hours based on the current department they work in.

To start, you will need a new button called btnUpdate as well as a new text box and label. The text box should be called txtVactionHours, and the label should read Vacation Hours. In the click event of the button, you are going to add the code seen in Listing 3-15 and update the query functionality so it is more reusable in the application.

In Listing 3-15, you see that the DataContext class declaration has moved from being a local variable to an instance variable, so it can be shared between both button events. Additionally, you can see that you have some new basic validation and a MessageBox that displays Update Was Successful.

Along with the validation, you should notice something new in the LINQ query. Here you are using a new language feature called *lambda expressions* to retrieve a reference to the appropriate entity in the database. Lambda expressions are a succinct way to create an anonymous method. They are a type-safe way to write a function to be passed as an argument, which makes it convenient for LINQ queries.

Listing 3-15. *Update Vacation Hours*

```
// Create new database context
AdventureWorksDataContext db = new AdventureWorksDataContext();

private void btnUpdate_Click(object sender, EventArgs e)
{
    if (txtLastName.Text.Trim().Length == 0
        || txtVacationHours.Text.Trim().Length == 0)
    {
        MessageBox.Show("Please enter values for all text boxes");
    }
    else
    {
        try
        {

            Employee emp =
            db.Employees.Single(r => r.Contact.LastName == txtLastName.Text);
            emp.VacationHours = short.Parse(txtVacationHours.Text);
            db.SubmitChanges();
            MessageBox.Show("Update succcessful");
         }
         catch(Exception ex)
         {
             throw ex;
```

```
        }
    }
}
```

Overall, the update example in Listing 3-15 is pretty straightforward, but it does demonstrate the simplicity of basic updates in LTS. Nonetheless, for the people who still have doubts about the SQL that is being generated, Listing 3-16 shows the dynamic UPDATE statement that was generated.

The SQL code in Listing 3-16 is far from perfect. In fact, in this case it probably appears a bit excessive when all that is trying to be accomplished is an update to the VacationHours field. The real reason behind the large UPDATE statement has to do with the way that optimistic concurrency is handled in LTS. This is a large topic, covered in Chapter 11. For now, understand that there are many ways in LTS to change the way that the generated code looks and performs, and throughout the text you will be exploring these options and honing your skills.

Listing 3-16. *UPDATE SQL*

```
exec sp_executesql
N'UPDATE [HumanResources].[Employee]
SET [VacationHours] = @p14
WHERE ([EmployeeID] = @p0) AND ([NationalIDNumber] = @p1)
AND ([ContactID] = @p2) AND ([LoginID] = @p3) AND ([ManagerID] = @p4)
AND ([Title] = @p5) AND ([BirthDate] = @p6) AND ([MaritalStatus] = @p7) AND
([Gender] = @p8) AND ([HireDate] = @p9) AND (NOT ([SalariedFlag] = 1)) AND
([VacationHours] = @p10) AND
([SickLeaveHours] = @p11) AND ([CurrentFlag] = 1) AND ([rowguid] = @p12) AND
([ModifiedDate] = @p13)',N'@p0 int,@p1 nvarchar(9),@p2 int,@p3 nvarchar(20),@p4
int,@p5 nvarchar(20),@p6 datetime,@p7 nchar(1),@p8 nchar(1),@p9 datetime,@p10
smallint,@p11 smallint,@p12 uniqueidentifier,@p13 datetime,@p14
smallint',@p0=4,@p1=N'112457891',@p2=1290,@p3=N'adventure-
works\rob0',@p4=3,@p5=N'Senior Tool Designer',@p6=''1965-01-23
00:00:00:000'',@p7=N'S',@p8=N'M',@p9=''1998-01-05 00:00:00:000'',@p10=48,@p11=80,
@p12='59747955-87B8-443F-8ED4-F8AD3AFDF3A9',@p13=''2004-07-31
00:00:00:000'',@p14=24
```

At this point, it is important to understand that dynamic SQL generation buys you something that a stored procedure API doesn't: encapsulation of business logic in the middle tier, where it belongs. So often in organizations you see stored procedure APIs that start with good intentions but end up consuming large chunks of business logic. Having your business logic stored in your database is fundamentally an anti-pattern and should be avoided. That's not to say that stored procedures are inherently evil, because they are not—but when using a stored procedure API, you have to enforce some process rules that you don't need when working with a well-built dynamic SQL ORM solution. Nonetheless, you are still going to find yourself in a company at some point where you need to use stored procedures, so in Chapter 4 you will see how to use stored procedures with LTS.

Along with update functionality, LTS obviously also gives you the ability to insert and delete. Imagine, again, that the requirements for your HR application have changed and that management now wants the ability to create a new Department and remove it.

In this example, we are going to create a new form for this functionality. To the new form add two new buttons called `btnInsert` and `btnDelete`, two new text boxes called `txtDepartmentName` and `txtGroupName`, and two new labels called Department Name and Group Name.

Listing 3-17 highlights the syntax for creating a new `Department`. Again, you can see that it is as simple as creating a new `DataContext` class and a `Department` entity class, filling in property information, and calling `Add()` and `SubmitChanges()`.

Listing 3-17. *Creating a New Department*

```
if (txtDepartmentName.Text.Trim().Length == 0
|| txtGroupName.Text.Trim().Length == 0)
{
    MessageBox.Show("Please fill in all of the fields");

}
else
{
    try
    {
        Department dept = new Department();
        dept.Name = txtDepartmentName.Text;
        dept.GroupName = txtGroupName.Text;
        dept.ModifiedDate = DateTime.Now;
        db.Departments.Add(dept);
        db.SubmitChanges();
        MessageBox.Show("Department added");
     }
     catch(Exception ex)
     {
         throw ex;
     }
}
```

So you are assured that this isn't smoke and mirrors, Listing 3-18 is the SQL Profiler output of the create `Department` query in Listing 3-17. As you can see, a single SQL `INSERT` statement is generated and executed for the new `Department` entity.

Listing 3-18. *Creating a New Department SQL*

```
exec sp_executesql N'INSERT INTO [HumanResources].[Department]([Name],
[GroupName],[ModifiedDate]) VALUES (@p0, @p1, @p2)

SELECT [t0].[DepartmentID]
FROM [HumanResources].[Department] AS [t0]
WHERE [t0].[DepartmentID] = (SCOPE_IDENTITY())
',N'@p0 nvarchar(7),@p1 nvarchar(7),@p2
datetime',@p0=N'Testing',@p1=N'Testing',@p2=''2007-10-23 09:55:06:343''
```

To delete a Department, we are going to again use the new lambda expression feature to retrieve a reference to the appropriate entity in the database. In Listing 3-19, you have the click event code for deleting the Department. Like the insert code, it is just a matter of referencing the appropriate entity and then calling the Remove() and SubmitChanges() methods on the DataContext object.

Listing 3-19. *Deleting a Department*

```
if (txtDepartmentName.Text.Trim().Length == 0
|| txtGroupName.Text.Trim().Length == 0)
{
    MessageBox.Show("Please fill in all of the fields");

}
else
{
    try
    {
        Department dept =
        db.Departments.Single(d => d.Name == txtDepartmentName.Text);
        db.Departments.Remove(dept);
        db.SubmitChanges();
        MessageBox.Show("Department removed");
    }
    catch (Exception ex)
    {
        throw ex;
    }
}
```

Listing 3-20 shows the SQL DELETE statement that is generated from LTS. As you can see in this example, the SQL query is parameterized with all the information retrieved to improve performance.

Listing 3-20. *SQL to Delete a Department*

```
exec sp_executesql N'DELETE FROM [HumanResources].[Department] WHERE
([DepartmentID] = @p0) AND ([Name] = @p1) AND ([GroupName] = @p2) AND
([ModifiedDate] = @p3)',N'@p0 smallint,@p1 nvarchar(7),@p2 nvarchar(7),
@p3 datetime',@p0=17,@p1=N'Testing',@p2=N'Testing',@p3=''2007-10-23
09:55:06:343''
```

■ **Note** You may have noticed that transaction support has not been mentioned in this chapter. Don't worry; LTS has full support for transactions, and Chapter 4 covers the ins and outs.

Although the examples in this section haven't really represented a real-world business application, they have introduced you to the essentials of LTS. These examples provide the groundwork you need to move into Chapter 4, where you will start to learn about more-advanced topics.

Summary

In this chapter, you learned the fundamentals of LTS and LINQ by taking a Bottom Up approach to ORM. LINQ is a set of standard query operators that can be valuable in developing a robust, well-architected solution. LINQ provides a framework for querying any data source, not just relational databases.

LTS is one of the products under the LINQ umbrella. LTS uses DBML metadata to handle the mapping of objects to relational databases. LTS ships with two tools, the designer and SqlMetal, that can be used to generate DBML and ORM code.

After creating the entities and data context, it is a simple task to query, insert, update, and delete items in your database. LTS tracks all changes that you make to your entities, thus allowing for a disconnected ORM experience. SQL is dynamically generated and executed against SQL Server with the appropriate statement (for example, `INSERT`, `SELECT`, `UPDATE`, `DELETE`).

In Chapter 4, you will take a much deeper dive into LTS. You will learn about advanced querying, debugging, transactions, functions, stored procedures, and more. You will be building out the HR application so that it is more functional and exploring options for development without code generation.

CHAPTER 4

Advanced LINQ to SQL

This chapter expands on the fundamentals that you learned in Chapter 3 and delves into more-advanced LTS topics. It presents independent examples using the HR Windows Forms application. The examples are considered independent because they do not form a complete application at the end of this chapter; instead the focus is to teach you the inner workings of LTS. The purpose of this chapter to is deepen your understanding of LTS so that in Chapter 8 you can work on the First Bank of Pluto with a solid foundation in LTS. Furthermore, because the focus of this chapter is on mastering LTS, it is approached from a two-tier architecture perspective with significant code samples.

Debugging

Before you write any more LTS code, let's first look at a powerful LTS add-in that can simplify debugging, the debug visualizer. In Chapter 3, I mentioned that LTS has a debug visualizer that can be used natively in Visual Studio 2008. The debug visualizer is not part of the VS 2008 installation; therefore, you need to download it before taking any additional steps. The download for the debug visualizer is free and can be found on the blog of Scott Guthrie, Microsoft's general manager for ASP.NET (`http://weblogs.asp.net/scottgu/archive/2007/07/31/linq-to-sql-debug-visualizer.aspx`).

For those who are not familiar with visualizers in Visual Studio, I'll take this paragraph to explain. The debug visualizer was introduced in Visual Studio 2005 as an add-in component that could be written to improve and extend the debugging capabilities of Visual Studio. A visualizer creates a window, like a dialog box, that can be used to represent a variable in an expanded fashion. The visualizer is represented as a magnifying glass in your code, as you will see shortly. The best aspect about visualizers is that you, the developer, can create your own in .NET. I'm not going to cover how to create visualizers, because that is another book, but understand that the LTS visualizer is just that, a piece of custom code that someone wrote to improve the debugging experience.

After downloading the debug visualizer, you have to install it. The downloaded zip file contains the source code and the assembly. To install the visualizer, all you have to do is move the assembly, in this case `SqlServerQueryVisualizer.dll`, into your `Program Files\Microsoft Visual Studio 9.0\Common7\Packages\Debugger\Visualizers\` directory while Visual Studio is shut down.

Note Many of the examples in this chapter use a module-level variable called `db`. This variable is simply your `DataContext` class, or to be more specific, the `AdventureWorksDataContext` class that you saw in Chapter 3. Additionally, for the sake of simplicity, many of the examples also use `Debug.Print` instead of creating a list box or other output; thus realize that you need to have a `System.Diagnostic` reference for the examples to run correctly.

Now that you have installed the debug visualizer, let's look at an example. In Figure 4-1, I have written a simple LTS query to select the records from the `EmployeeDepartmentHistory` table, where the contact's last name is equal to Walters. I have set a break point in the code and highlighted my variable `edh`. As you can see in this example, I now have the visualizer (that is, magnifying glass) available to me.

```
var edh = from d in db.EmployeeDepartmentHistories
          where d.Employee.Contact.LastName == "Walters"
          select d;

foreach (var p in edh)
⊞ edh  {SELECT [t0].[EmployeeID], [t0].[DepartmentID], [t0].[ShiftID], [t0].[StartDate], [t0]
    lstResults.Items.Add(p.Employee.Contact.FirstName);
}
```

Figure 4-1. *LTS debug visualizer*

By clicking the magnifying glass (shown in Figure 4-1), the SQL code that will ultimately be executed is displayed (see Figure 4-2). Here you can see that you have the T-SQL in the bottom pane, and the core LINQ query in the top pane.

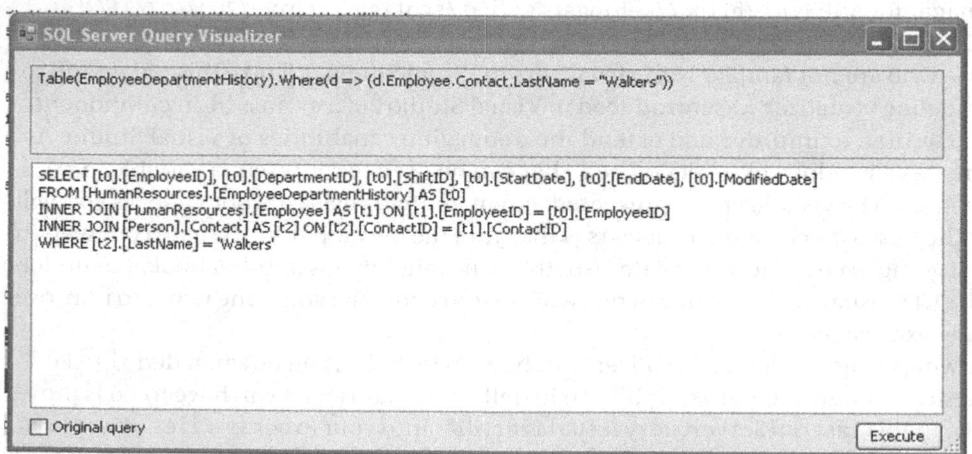

Figure 4-2. *SQL Server query visualizer*

Another useful feature that the debug visualizer provides is a button to execute the SQL code. After you click the Execute button, you end up with the results of the query in a data grid, as shown in Figure 4-3. This is extremely helpful while debugging because it is an integrated environment and thus the number of programs/clicks is simplified.

QueryResult

	EmployeeID	DepartmentID	ShiftID	StartDate	EndDate	ModifiedDate
▸	4	1	1	1/5/1998	6/30/2000	6/28/2000
	4	2	1	7/1/2000		6/30/2000

Figure 4-3. *LTS debug visualizer QueryResult window*

■ **Caution** It is critical that you use a tool such as SQL Profiler to monitor the dynamic SQL code that is being generated. You will see later in this chapter that there are some "undocumented features" in LTS that can cause radical performance problems.

The LTS debug visualizer is an excellent tool for monitoring or debugging a focused area; it does not, however, give you a holistic view of the "chattiness" of your LTS code. SQL Profiler is the only way to see exactly how many SQL queries are being executed from LTS. Nonetheless, having the visualizer capability is convenient and helpful when you are trying to debug a problem area in your code.

Using Stored Procedures

I know that I promised at the end of Chapter 3 to expand on the topic of querying, and I will later in this chapter, but first I want you to look at LTS and stored procedures. Using stored procedures (sprocs) from an ORM tool is something that most purists deem oxymoronic and against the essence of the ORM philosophy. As I have stated before, I believe one should have the option to use sprocs from ORM for long-running or extremely complex queries that would benefit from the horsepower.

LTS provides a simple mechanism for using sprocs from your object model: it is as simple as dragging the sproc (or user-defined function) onto the Methods pane and calling it from your `DataContext` object. Let's take a closer look at the HR application that you have been developing.

In Figure 4-4, you can see that I have dragged the `uspGetEmployeeManagers` stored procedure onto the Methods pane of the LTS designer. Behind the scenes, this is creating the DBML mapping information (see Listing 4-1), and generating the code in the `AdventureWorksDataContext` class to enable direct use of this stored procedure. Simply stated, this drag-and-drop functionality has created the reference and the code to use the stored procedure as you would a function in a class.

Figure 4-4. *Mapping a stored procedure in the designer*

Listing 4-1. *The DBML Stored Procedure Mapping Data*

```
<Function Name="dbo.uspGetEmployeeManagers" Method="uspGetEmployeeManagers">
    <Parameter Name="EmployeeID" Parameter="employeeID"
        Type="System.Int32" DbType="Int" />
    <ElementType Name="uspGetEmployeeManagersResult">
        <Column Name="RecursionLevel" Type="System.Int32"
           DbType="Int" CanBeNull="true" />
        <Column Name="EmployeeID" Type="System.Int32"
           DbType="Int" CanBeNull="true" />
        <Column Name="FirstName" Type="System.String"
           DbType="NVarChar(50)" CanBeNull="true" />
        <Column Name="LastName" Type="System.String"
           DbType="NVarChar(50)" CanBeNull="true" />
        <Column Name="ManagerID" Type="System.Int32" DbType="Int"
           CanBeNull="true" />
        <Column Name="ManagerFirstName" Type="System.String"
           DbType="NVarChar(50) NOT NULL" CanBeNull="false" />
        <Column Name="ManagerLastName" Type="System.String"
           DbType="NVarChar(50) NOT NULL" CanBeNull="false" />
    </ElementType>
  </Function>
```

Listing 4-2 shows the code that was dynamically generated in the `AdventureWorksDataContext` class. You can see that the method, `uspGetEmployeeManagers`, is named the same as the stored procedure. Additionally, the method is decorated with the `Function` mapping attribute and accepts the same type of parameter (`EmployeeID`) as the stored procedure. The method returns a `System.Data.Linq.ISingleResult`, with the type of `uspGetEmployeemanagersResult`. The `uspGetEmployeemanagersResult` is a partial class (a portion is seen in Listing 4-2) that contains the attributes of the sproc. Finally, you can see that the method, `uspGetEmployeeManagers`, calls out to `System.Data.Linq.ExecuteMethodCall` to execute the stored procedure.

Listing 4-2. *The Generated Method in the AdventureWorksDataContext Class*

```
// In this method the uspGetEmployeeManagers
// sproc is called.  The ExecuteMethodCall()
// uses the System.Reflection.MethodInfo class
// to retrieve the metadata needed for the call.
```

```
[Function(Name="dbo.uspGetEmployeeManagers")]
public ISingleResult<uspGetEmployeeManagersResult>
    uspGetEmployeeManagers([Parameter(Name="EmployeeID", DbType="Int")]
     System.Nullable<int> employeeID)
{
     IExecuteResult result =
      this.ExecuteMethodCall(this, ((MethodInfo)
       (MethodInfo.GetCurrentMethod())), employeeID);

     return ((ISingleResult<uspGetEmployeeManagersResult>)
       (result.ReturnValue));
}

// The partial class uspGetEmployeeManagersResults is used
// to expose the structure of the sproc. Each property represents
// a column or field returned in the sproc result set.
public partial class uspGetEmployeeManagersResult
{
    private System.Nullable<int> _RecursionLevel;
    private System.Nullable<int> _EmployeeID;
    private string _FirstName;
    private string _LastName;
    private System.Nullable<int> _ManagerID;
    private string _ManagerFirstName;
    private string _ManagerLastName;

    public uspGetEmployeeManagersResult(){}

    [Column(Storage="_RecursionLevel", DbType="Int")]
    public System.Nullable<int> RecursionLevel
    {
       get
       {   return this._RecursionLevel; }
       set
       {
           if ((this._RecursionLevel != value))
           {
              this._RecursionLevel = value;
           }
       }
     }

     [Column(Storage="_EmployeeID", DbType="Int")]
     public System.Nullable<int> EmployeeID
     {
       get
       { return this._EmployeeID; }
```

```
            set
            {
                if ((this._EmployeeID != value))
                {
                    this._EmployeeID = value;
                }
            }
        }

        // You get the point!  The rest of the sproc attributes are generated in this
        // partial class
}
```

Before looking at how easy it is to use the stored procedure, let's look at what this sproc does. In Listing 4-3, you can see the `uspGetEmployeeManagers` sproc, which lists the employee reporting hierarchy by taking an `EmployeeID` as a parameter and then uses recursion to iterate through the table structure. I chose this stored procedure as an example because it is a good representation of complex logic that you may want to keep in a sproc versus writing it out in a C# or LINQ query.

Listing 4-3 may look a little foreign to you if you are not familiar with Common Table Expressions (CTEs). CTEs were introduced with SQL Server 2005 to provide a simplified method for creating a temporary result set within the execution scope of a single `SELECT`, `INSERT`, `UPDATE`, `DELETE`, or `CREATE VIEW` statement. CTEs are defined with the `WITH` statement, as seen in Listing 4-3, and can be self-referencing and used multiple times in the same query.

Listing 4-3. *Sproc Code to Retrieve Employee Reporting Hierarchy*

```
ALTER PROCEDURE [dbo].[uspGetEmployeeManagers]
    @EmployeeID [int]
AS
BEGIN
    SET NOCOUNT ON;

-- Use recursive query to list out all Employees required for a particular Manager

WITH [EMP_cte]([EmployeeID], [ManagerID], [FirstName], [LastName],
[Title], [RecursionLevel])

-- CTE name and columns

AS (

    SELECT e.[EmployeeID], e.[ManagerID], c.[FirstName], c.[LastName], e.[Title], 0
    -- Get the initial Employee

    FROM [HumanResources].[Employee] e
        INNER JOIN [Person].[Contact] c
        ON e.[ContactID] = c.[ContactID]
```

```
    WHERE e.[EmployeeID] = @EmployeeID
    UNION ALL

    SELECT e.[EmployeeID], e.[ManagerID], c.[FirstName], c.[LastName], e.[Title],
        [RecursionLevel] + 1 -- Join recursive member to anchor
    FROM [HumanResources].[Employee] e
        INNER JOIN [EMP_cte]
        ON e.[EmployeeID] = [EMP_cte].[ManagerID]
        INNER JOIN [Person].[Contact] c
        ON e.[ContactID] = c.[ContactID]
    )

    -- Join back to Employee to return the manager name
    SELECT [EMP_cte].[RecursionLevel], [EMP_cte].[EmployeeID],
        [EMP_cte].[FirstName], [EMP_cte].[LastName],
        [EMP_cte].[ManagerID], c.[FirstName] AS 'ManagerFirstName', c.[LastName] AS
        'ManagerLastName'  -- Outer select from the CTE
    FROM [EMP_cte]
        INNER JOIN [HumanResources].[Employee] e
        ON [EMP_cte].[ManagerID] = e.[EmployeeID]
        INNER JOIN [Person].[Contact] c
        ON e.[ContactID] = c.[ContactID]
    ORDER BY [RecursionLevel], [ManagerID], [EmployeeID]
    OPTION (MAXRECURSION 25)
END;
```

Now that you have the stored procedure mapped and set up in your `DataContext`, it is time to write some code to use it. Instead of giving you an elaborate example, let's just keep it simple and say that your HR people want a button to display the reporting structure. In this example, you are going to create a new form with a `DataGridView` control and you are going to bind the results directly to the grid.

Listing 4-4 has two blocks of code that can be used to populate your `DataGrid`. In the LTS form, I have added a new button that retrieves the `EmployeeID` by the Last Name text box, and then passes it to a new form, `EmployeeHierarchy`, that has a `DataGridView`. The `DataGridView`, called `gridEmpHi`, then calls the `uspGetEmployeeManagers` sproc and binds to a `BindingSource` to populate the grid (see Figure 4-5).

Listing 4-4. *Code to Call a Sproc and Populate a DataGridView*

```
private void btnReporting_Click(object sender, EventArgs e)
{

    Employee emp = db.Employees.Single(d => d.Contact.LastName == txtLastName.Text);
    EmployeeHierarchy eh = new EmployeeHierarchy();
    eh.Show();
    eh.BindGrid(emp.EmployeeID);

}
```

```
public void BindGrid (int employeeID)
{
    AdventureWorksDataContext db = new AdventureWorksDataContext();
    var emps = db.uspGetEmployeeManagers(employeeID);
    BindingSource bs = new BindingSource();
    bs.DataSource = emps;
    gridEmpHi.DataSource = bs;

}
```

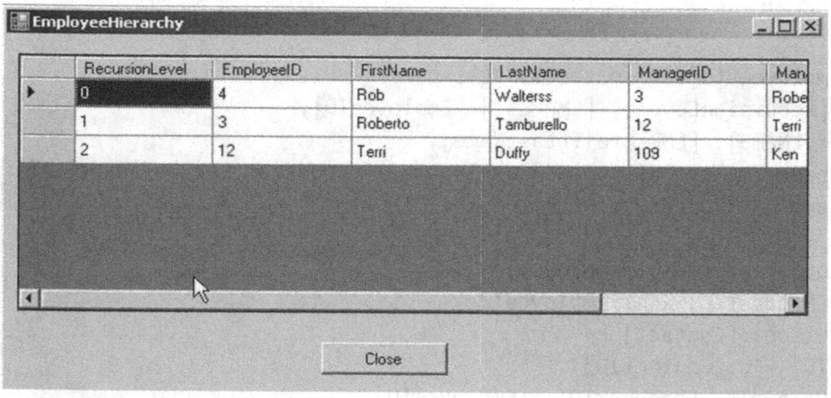

Figure 4-5. *A DataGridView bound to a sproc*

You have now retrieved data from a stored procedure by using LTS; however, the return type of the code does not map to your existing object model. In the example in Listing 4-4, you have used the var keyword to create the return object whose type is inferred by the compiler from the uspGetEmployeeManagers sproc. Fortunately, LTS also allows you to map the output of a sproc directly to an object in your model.

■ **Note** The output of the sproc must match the fields available in the object you are mapping to if you want to use strong typing with sprocs in LTS.

For this example, you can create a new sproc to return a group of employees (see Listing 4-5) based on the managers they report to. In the LTS designer, instead of dragging the sproc from Server Explorer into the Methods pane, you drag it directly onto the object that you want it mapped to. In Listing 4-5, you can drag the sproc directly onto the Employee object, and the mapping will be generated for you. Unlike the code generated in your DataContext in Listing 4-2, which returns ISingleResult<uspGetEmployeeManagersResult>, the code generated in this example (see Listing 4-6) returns ISingleResult<Employee>.

Listing 4-5. *Sproc Code That Can Be Bound Directly to an Employee Object*

```
CREATE PROCEDURE [dbo].[uspGetEmployees]
@ManagerID [int]
AS
    BEGIN

        SELECT * FROM HumanResources.Employee WHERE ManagerID = @ManagerID

    END
```

Listing 4-6. *Generated Code That Returns an Employee*

```
[Function(Name="dbo.uspGetEmployees")]
public ISingleResult<Employee> uspGetEmployees(
    [Parameter(Name="ManagerID", DbType="Int")]
        System.Nullable<int> managerID)
{
    IExecuteResult result = this.ExecuteMethodCall(this,
        ((MethodInfo)(MethodInfo.GetCurrentMethod())), managerID);

    return ((ISingleResult<Employee>)(result.ReturnValue));
}
```

Using the strongly typed return value is as easy as using a weakly typed return value. Listing 4-7 shows some example code using the new functionality. In this example, I'm using a fictitious variable called `managerId`, which is an integer that is being passed into the sproc. Notice that you are using the `ToList()` function to return a list of employees from the stored procedure.

Listing 4-7. *Return a Strongly Typed Value from a Sproc*

```
AdventureWorksDataContext db = new AdventureWorksDataContext();
List<Employee> emps = db.uspGetEmployees(managerId).ToList();
BindingSource bs = new BindingSource();
bs.DataSource = emps;
gridEmpHi.DataSource = bs;
```

After you have a list of employees, the sky is the limit on what you can do with them, because they are now being tracked by LTS. In Listing 4-7, you are just binding the employees to the `DataGridView`, but because the reference is now "alive," you can modify the values of `Employee` and call `SubmitChanges()` to execute dynamically generated SQL code that will update the database. For example, in Listing 4-8, you are iterating through the collection and setting the `ManagerID` to 15. After you have completed the loop, you are calling the `SubmitChanges()` method on the `DataContext` class, and a series of `UPDATE` statements are being generated and executed based on the values that have changed on your entities.

Listing 4-8. *Code to Update an Employee Returned from a Sproc*

```
AdventureWorksDataContext db = new AdventureWorksDataContext();

List<Employee> emps = db.uspGetEmployees(16).ToList();
foreach (Employee emp in emps)
{
    emp.ManagerID = 15;

}
db.SubmitChanges();

BindingSource bs = new BindingSource();
bs.DataSource = emps;
gridEmpHi.DataSource = bs;
```

The last thing you need to be aware of when using sprocs for data retrieval from LTS is the scenario in which your sproc has an output parameter. In Listing 4-9, you have a simple stored procedure that returns an `EmployeeID` as an output parameter. In this example, you follow the same pattern as before, of dragging the sproc onto the LTS designer.

Listing 4-9. *Sproc with Output Parameter*

```
CREATE PROCEDURE [dbo].[uspGetEmployeesOutput]
@ManagerID [int],
@EmployeeID [int] output
AS
    BEGIN

        SELECT @EmployeeID = EmployeeID FROM HumanResources.Employee
        WHERE ManagerID = @ManagerID
    END
```

After you have dragged the sproc onto the LTS designer, a new method is created in your `DataContext` class as expected, but this time you have a reference parameter called `employeeID`. In this example, you are not mapping the sproc to a single entity because the schema doesn't match; however, later in this chapter you will be looking more at shaping results and extending the sproc functionality so you can directly map your sprocs to multiple entities.

In Listing 4-10, the new `uspGetEmployeesOutput` method that was generated in your `DataContext` class can be seen. The `employeeID` is a ref parameter that is equal to the output parameter of the stored procedure. Additionally, the method returns an integer, as you might have expected, because the return type of the sproc is an integer.

Listing 4-10. *Generated Method with Output Parameter*

```
[Function(Name="dbo.uspGetEmployeesOutput")]
public int uspGetEmployeesOutput([Parameter(Name="ManagerID", DbType="Int")]
     System.Nullable<int> managerID,
        [Parameter(Name="EmployeeID", DbType="Int")]
```

```
    ref System.Nullable<int> employeeID)
{
    IExecuteResult result = this.ExecuteMethodCall(this,
        ((MethodInfo)(MethodInfo.GetCurrentMethod())),
            managerID, employeeID);

    employeeID = ((System.Nullable<int>)(result.GetParameterValue(1)));

    return ((int)(result.ReturnValue));
}
```

To call the stored procedure, you use the same pattern as a nonoutput sproc with the exception that you pass in a ref parameter. An example of how you would use this can be seen in Listing 4-11. The managerID parameter is used as the output parameter in this situation, and the employeeID parameter is hard-coded to 16 for this example.

Listing 4-11. *Generated Method with Output Parameter*

```
int? managerID = 0;
int employeeID = 16;
int sprocOutput = db.uspGetEmployeesOutput(employeeID, ref managerID);
```

At this point, you have learned the details of using retrieval sprocs from LTS, but what about using Create, Update, and Delete (CUD) sprocs? CUD sprocs are used in the same manner as the retrieval sprocs, and in a lot of cases are much easier to digest because they have a deeper integration into the designer and LTS.

To use a CUD sproc, you need to first create one that you can map to your model. In Listing 4-12, you can see a new sproc to update the Department table. The DepartmentID column is an identity and should not be updated, so it is not part of the sproc.

Listing 4-12. *Department UPDATE Sproc*

```
CREATE PROCEDURE dbo.uspUpdateDepartment
@Name varchar(50),
@GroupName varchar(50),
@ModifiedDate datetime

AS
        UPDATE HumanResources.Department
        SET [Name] = @Name,
        [GroupName] = @GroupName,
        [ModifiedDate] = @ModifiedDate

        RETURN
```

Now that you have an Update sproc, you can map it to the Department entity. This mapping can be easily done in the designer: drag the sproc onto the designer Methods pane as you did for the retrieval sprocs. View the properties of the Department entity in the designer and click the Update property and the ellipsis button.

Figure 4-5 shows the form that lets you map the parameters of the sproc to the properties of the class. In this window, the sproc parameters are considered method parameters because LTS has already generated the code in the DataContext class to represent this sproc. In addition, the default behavior of LTS is to use the "runtime" for CUD, but in Figure 4-6 you can see that you have the ability to change and override the behavior, class, and method, and you can also override the default mapping.

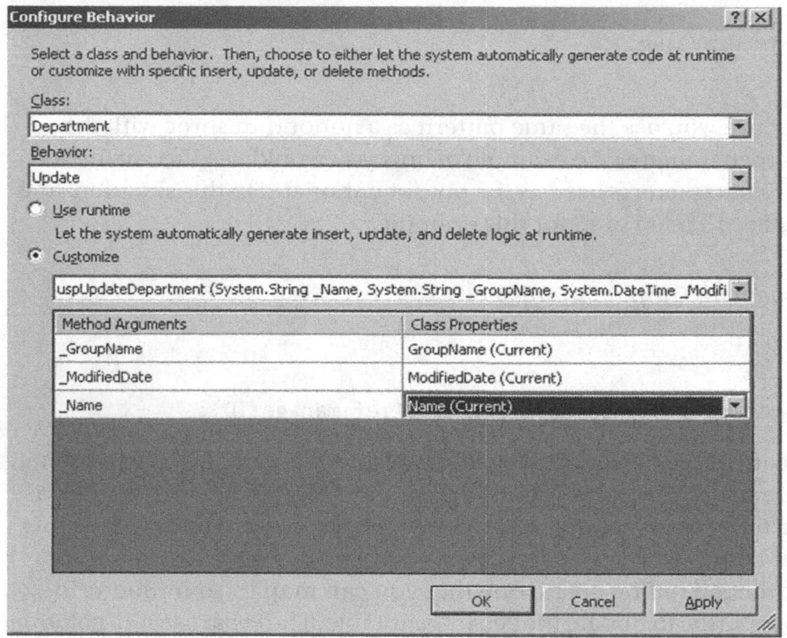

Figure 4-6. *Use CUD sprocs by mapping in the LTS designer.*

Tip LTS CUD sprocs use output parameters the same way that LTS Get sprocs do. Use output or ref parameters when you need finer-grained control over the data coming from the database.

Using the newly mapped sproc is actually easier than using the Get sprocs that you learned earlier in this chapter. Unlike the Get sprocs, all the plumbing code is ready for you after you finish the mapping in the UI for the CUD sprocs. What this means is that you can use the exact same LINQ code with your CUD sprocs as you would with dynamic SQL. For example, you could write something like Listing 4-13 to update the Department table with the new sproc that you wrote in Listing 4-12.

Listing 4-13. *CUD Sproc Code Is the Same as CUD Dynamic SQL in LTS*

```
Department dept = db.Department.Single(r => r.Name == "Blah");
dept.Name = "FooBar";
dept.GroupName = "BarFoo";
```

```
dept.ModifiedDate = DateTime.Now;
db.SubmitChanges();
```

Working with User-Defined Functions

User-defined functions (UDFs) can be used in LTS just as sprocs can. LTS natively supports both scalar-valued and table-valued UDFs. All you need to do is drag the function from your Server Explorer onto the Methods pane, which updates the DataContext and allows you to use the UDF in your code. Let's take a look.

In Listing 4-14, you can see the basic signature of the ufnGetContactInformation UDF that ships with the AdventureWorks database. I have included only the signature of the UDF because it is quite lengthy, but know that it joins and queries many tables to return the details of a particular contact based on that contact's ContactID.

Listing 4-14. *UDF to Get Contact Details*

```
ALTER FUNCTION [dbo].[ufnGetContactInformation](@ContactID int)
RETURNS @retContactInformation TABLE
(
    -- Columns returned by the function
    [ContactID] int PRIMARY KEY NOT NULL,
    [FirstName] [nvarchar](50) NULL,
    [LastName] [nvarchar](50) NULL,
    [JobTitle] [nvarchar](50) NULL,
    [ContactType] [nvarchar](50) NULL
)
```

After dragging the UDF onto the Methods pane in the LTS designer, a new method is generated in your DataContext class. In Listing 4-15, you can see the new ufnGetContactInformationResult method in the AdventureWorksDataContext class. This method returns a System.Linq.IQueryable interface. The IQueryable<T> interface is a powerful LINQ interface that does exactly what its name suggests: it holds a query. According to the summary comments in the code, the IQueryable<T> interface "provides functionality to evaluate queries against a specific data source wherein the type of the data is known."

Listing 4-15. *Generated UDF Code in DataContext*

```
[Function(Name="dbo.ufnGetContactInformation", IsComposable=true)]
public IQueryable<ufnGetContactInformationResult>
    ufnGetContactInformation([Parameter(Name="ContactID", DbType="Int")]
        System.Nullable<int> contactID)
{
    return
        this.CreateMethodCallQuery<ufnGetContactInformationResult>(this,
            ((MethodInfo)(MethodInfo.GetCurrentMethod())), contactID);
}
```

Note `IQueryable` is not a collection, but rather a placeholder for a query. It implements `IEnumerable`, however, thus allowing a `foreach` iteration as if it is a collection.

Using the new `ufnGetContactInformation` function is just like using a sproc in LTS. You can call it directly by using your `DataContext`, and use it directly in your LINQ code. Listing 4-16 shows a simple example of using the `ufnGetContactInformation` UDF from a LINQ query. Because the return type of this UDF is a table, you can use it as you would any other table/entity in LTS. Alternatively, if you have a scalar UDF that returns a nontable type (for example, `varchar`), then you could use it as you would any other method that returns a string or a simple data type.

Listing 4-16. *Using a UDF in a LINQ Query*

```
var contacts = from c in db.ufnGetContactInformation(contactID)
               select c;

foreach (var cont in contacts)
{
    MessageBox.Show(cont.FirstName);
}
```

Constructing Relationships, Joins, and Projections

Now that you have learned about sprocs in LTS, it's time to revisit querying by looking at more-advanced scenarios. In Chapter 3, I discussed some techniques for shaping the results of your LINQ queries in LTS to reduce the amount of SQL that gets executed. There, you used anonymous methods and object initializers to limit the results to what you want, but there are other methods for doing this.

The `System.Data.Linq.DataLoadOptions` is an object that enables you to tell the framework which objects are associated and which objects need to be preloaded. What does this mean? I briefly touched on the default lazy/deferred loading functionality that LTS has, which defers the SQL execution until you iterate through the LINQ query. I mentioned in Chapter 3 that you can change this default functionality so that LTS executes the query immediately by using the `ToList()` or `ToArray()` methods attached to your entity classes, but another indirect way of changing this is to use the `DataLoadOptions` object to specify which types are connected and which types should be loaded in a cascading manner.

Note The word *shape* is used interchangeably with the word *projection* in this text.

Listing 4-17 demonstrates an example of using the `DataLoadOptions.LoadWith<T>` functionality to "tie" entities together. In this example, you are telling the `DataContext` to load the `Contact` entity at the same time you load the `Employee` entity when you query.

Listing 4-17. *Using the DataLoadOptions to Shape the Results*

```
System.Data.Linq.DataLoadOptions options =
    new System.Data.Linq.DataLoadOptions();

options.LoadWith<Employee>(emp => emp.Contact);

db.LoadOptions = options;

Employee x = db.Employees.Single(r => r.EmployeeID == 1);

Debug.Print(x.Contact.FirstName);
```

In Listing 4-18, you can see the SQL from SQL Profiler that is executed from the LINQ query in Listing 4-17. As you can see, you have generated and executed a single SQL query, which was created with an `INNER JOIN` on the `Contact` table to retrieve the `Contact` data to begin with.

Listing 4-18. *Single LTS Query*

```
exec sp_executesql N'SELECT [t0].[EmployeeID], [t0].[NationalIDNumber],
    [t0].[ContactID], [t0].[LoginID], [t0].[ManagerID], [t0].[Title],
    [t0].[BirthDate], [t0].[MaritalStatus], [t0].[Gender], [t0].[HireDate],
    [t0].[SalariedFlag], [t0].[VacationHours], [t0].[SickLeaveHours],
    [t0].[CurrentFlag], [t0].[rowguid], [t0].[ModifiedDate],
    [t1].[ContactID] AS [ContactID2], [t1].[NameStyle],
    [t1].[Title] AS [Title2], [t1].[FirstName], [t1].[MiddleName], [t1].[LastName],
    [t1].[Suffix], [t1].[EmailAddress], [t1].[EmailPromotion], [t1].[Phone],
    [t1].[PasswordHash], [t1].[PasswordSalt], [t1].[AdditionalContactInfo],
    [t1].[rowguid] AS [rowguid2], [t1].[ModifiedDate] AS [ModifiedDate2]
FROM [HumanResources].[Employee] AS [t0]
INNER JOIN [Person].[Contact] AS [t1] ON [t1].[ContactID] = [t0].[ContactID]
WHERE [t0].[EmployeeID] = @p0',N'@p0 int',@p0=1
```

■ **Caution** Although the lazy-loading pattern is a good one, it can be a major performance killer if overused. Because LTS uses lazy loading by default, it is critical that you optimize and shape your queries to enable eager loading and prevent performance problems.

Let's see what happens if you remove `db.LoadOptions` from the code in Listing 4-17. In Listing 4-19, you can see the two SQL queries that get executed when you don't use `DataLoadOptions` in your code. The first query is for retrieving the employee information, and the second query is for retrieving the contact information. This is clearly less efficient then retrieving all your data in a single query, as in Listing 4-18.

Listing 4-19. *Two Queries to Retrieve Employees and Contacts*

```
exec sp_executesql N'SELECT [t0].[EmployeeID], [t0].[NationalIDNumber],
    [t0].[ContactID], [t0].[LoginID], [t0].[ManagerID], [t0].[Title],
    [t0].[BirthDate], [t0].[MaritalStatus], [t0].[Gender], [t0].[HireDate],
    [t0].[SalariedFlag], [t0].[VacationHours], [t0].[SickLeaveHours],
    [t0].[CurrentFlag], [t0].[rowguid],
    [t0].[ModifiedDate]
FROM [HumanResources].[Employee] AS [t0]
WHERE [t0].[EmployeeID] = @p0',N'@p0 int',@p0=1

exec sp_executesql N'SELECT [t0].[ContactID], [t0].[NameStyle], [t0].[Title],
    [t0].[FirstName], [t0].[MiddleName], [t0].[LastName], [t0].[Suffix],
    [t0].[EmailAddress], [t0].[EmailPromotion], [t0].[Phone], [t0].[PasswordHash],
    [t0].[PasswordSalt], [t0].[AdditionalContactInfo], [t0].[rowguid],
    [t0].[ModifiedDate]
FROM [Person].[Contact] AS [t0]
WHERE [t0].[ContactID] = @p0',N'@p0 int',@p0=1209
```

Although the `LoadWith()` functionality in the `DataLoadOptions` class can be powerful, it can also cause you a lot of performance problems in advanced situations. The behavior of the `LoadWith()` method has some unexpected results when you work with multiple 1:n relationships. In Listing 4-19, we have a single n:1 relationship between `Contact` and `Employee`; this is more like a 1:1 relationship because a `Contact` isn't going to represent multiple `Employees` and vice versa, but strictly speaking the referential integrity constraints say that this is an n:1 relationship.

Let's change the LINQ code so you have `Employee` loaded with `Contacts` and `EmployeeDepartmentHistories` loaded with `Employees`. Listing 4-20 demonstrates multiple 1:n relationships in our model. The relationship between `Contacts` and `Employee` is 1:n, and the relationship between `Employee` and `EmployeeDepartmentHistories` is 1:n. Also notice that I am using the `ToList<T>()` method to return an `IEnumerable<Contact>` and to force prefetching of the query.

Listing 4-20. *Multiple 1:n Relationships Using DataLoadOptions*

```
System.Data.Linq.DataLoadOptions options =
    new System.Data.Linq.DataLoadOptions();

options.LoadWith<Contact>(em => em.Employees);
options.LoadWith<Employee>(emdh => emdh.EmployeeDepartmentHistories);

db.LoadOptions = options;

IEnumerable<Contact> contacts = db.Contacts.ToList<Contact>();

MessageBox.Show("done");
```

After executing the code in Listing 4-20, what happened from a query perspective is troubling and also exemplifies the reason that I warned you earlier in the chapter to always monitor the "chattiness" of LTS (or any ORM) with SQL Profiler before releasing to production. Listing 4-21 has two queries. The first query is the retrieval of the `Contact` entity, which looks fine. The second query is the problem: it was executed approximately *20 thousand* times, with a different `EmployeeID` parameter (for example, 629) each time, to retrieve the `Employee` and `EmployeeDepartmentHistory` entities. Obviously, this has the potential to bring down your servers and therefore is a major problem.

Listing 4-21. *Multiple 1:n Queries in LTS*

```
SELECT [t0].[ContactID], [t0].[NameStyle], [t0].[Title],
[t0].[FirstName], [t0].[MiddleName], [t0].[LastName], [t0].[Suffix],
[t0].[EmailAddress],[t0].[EmailPromotion], [t0].[Phone],
[t0].[PasswordHash], [t0].[PasswordSalt], [t0].[AdditionalContactInfo],
[t0].[rowguid], [t0].[ModifiedDate]
FROM [Person].[Contact] AS [t0]

exec sp_executesql N'SELECT [t0].[EmployeeID], [t0].[NationalIDNumber],
[t0].[ContactID], [t0].[LoginID], [t0].[ManagerID], [t0].[Title],
[t0].[BirthDate],[t0].[MaritalStatus], [t0].[Gender], [t0].[HireDate],
[t0].[SalariedFlag], [t0].[VacationHours], [t0].[SickLeaveHours],
[t0].[CurrentFlag], [t0].[rowguid],[t0].[ModifiedDate],
[t1].[EmployeeID] AS [EmployeeID2], [t1].[DepartmentID], [t1].[ShiftID],
[t1].[StartDate], [t1].[EndDate], [t1].[ModifiedDate] AS
[ModifiedDate2], (
    SELECT COUNT(*)
    FROM [HumanResources].[EmployeeDepartmentHistory] AS [t2]
    WHERE [t2].[EmployeeID] = [t0].[EmployeeID]
    ) AS [count]
FROM [HumanResources].[Employee] AS [t0]
LEFT OUTER JOIN [HumanResources].[EmployeeDepartmentHistory]
AS [t1] ON [t1].[EmployeeID] = [t0].[EmployeeID]
WHERE [t0].[ContactID] = @x1
ORDER BY [t0].[EmployeeID], [t1].[DepartmentID], [t1].[ShiftID],
 [t1].[StartDate]',N'@x1 int',@x1=629
```

Why does LTS turn this relationship, which could be defined with a couple of SQL `JOIN`s, into something so horrendous? According to Scott Guthrie (`http://weblogs.asp.net/scottgu/archive/2007/08/23/linq-to-sql-part-7-updating-our-database-using-stored-procedures.aspx#3599383`), this is by design to prevent data explosions happening with 1:n relationships. To say it another way, LTS supports only first-level `JOIN`s in 1:n relationships. For example, if you comment out `options.LoadWith<Employee>(emdh => emdh.EmployeeDepartmentHistories)` in Listing 4-20 and run the query again, you end up with a single query, as seen in Listing 4-22. In Listing 4-22, you have a concise `JOIN` between your `Contact` and `Employee` tables that will populate both entities in your model.

Listing 4-22. *Single 1:n Query with Expected Results*

```
SELECT [t0].[ContactID], [t0].[NameStyle], [t0].[Title], [t0].[FirstName],
[t0].[MiddleName], [t0].[LastName], [t0].[Suffix], [t0].[EmailAddress],
[t0].[EmailPromotion], [t0].[Phone], [t0].[PasswordHash], [t0].[PasswordSalt],
[t0].[AdditionalContactInfo], [t0].[rowguid], [t0].[ModifiedDate],
[t1].[EmployeeID], [t1].[NationalIDNumber], [t1].[ContactID] AS [ContactID2],
[t1].[LoginID], [t1].[ManagerID], [t1].[Title] AS [Title2], [t1].[BirthDate],
[t1].[MaritalStatus], [t1].[Gender], [t1].[HireDate], [t1].[SalariedFlag],
[t1].[VacationHours], [t1].[SickLeaveHours], [t1].[CurrentFlag], [t1].[rowguid] AS
[rowguid2], [t1].[ModifiedDate] AS [ModifiedDate2], (
    SELECT COUNT(*)
    FROM [HumanResources].[Employee] AS [t2]
    WHERE [t2].[ContactID] = [t0].[ContactID]
    ) AS [count]
FROM [Person].[Contact] AS [t0]
LEFT OUTER JOIN [HumanResources].[Employee] AS [t1] ON
[t1].[ContactID] = [t0].[ContactID]
ORDER BY [t0].[ContactID], [t1].[EmployeeID]
```

After I learned about this limitation of LTS, I felt like calling it quits, but there are ways to work around this problem that don't require too much effort. One way is to use n:1 relationships instead of 1:n relationships. In Listing 4-23, I have modified the `DataLoadOptions` to use n:1 relationships instead of the 1:n relationship that you saw in Listing 4-20.

In Listing 4-23, you are loading `EmployeeDepartmentHistories` and `Contact` with the `Employee` entity and then converting the results to an `IQueryable<Employee>` interface that you can query against. This example is also casting from `Employee.Contact` to `Contact`, and then updating the `FirstName` property of `Contact` to prove that this is in fact a tracked (live) reference to the `Contact` entity.

Listing 4-23. *Alternate Way to Retrieve Multiple Relationships*

```
System.Data.Linq.DataLoadOptions options =
    new System.Data.Linq.DataLoadOptions();

options.LoadWith<Employee>(emdh => emdh.EmployeeDepartmentHistories);
options.LoadWith<Employee>(emp => emp.Contact);

db.LoadOptions = options;

IQueryable<Employee> employees = db.Employees.ToList<Employee>().AsQueryable();

var con = from c in employees
          select c.Contact;
```

```
foreach (Contact r in con)
{
    r.FirstName = "Something";
}

db.SubmitChanges();
```

In Listing 4-24, you can see the SQL that is generated by the code in Listing 4-23. This SQL code, although a little ugly with inner and outer JOINs, contains all the relationships that you need to populate your entities. If you are wondering, this is the only retrieval query (although there is an UPDATE) that is executed from the code in Listing 4-23, even with the iteration over the Contact.

Listing 4-24. *The SQL Query with n:1 Relationships*

```
SELECT [t0].[EmployeeID], [t0].[NationalIDNumber], [t0].[ContactID], [t0].[LoginID],
    [t0].[ManagerID], [t0].[Title], [t0].[BirthDate], [t0].[MaritalStatus],
    [t0].[Gender], [t0].[HireDate], [t0].[SalariedFlag], [t0].[VacationHours],
    [t0].[SickLeaveHours], [t0].[CurrentFlag], [t0].[rowguid], [t0].[ModifiedDate],
    [t2].[EmployeeID] AS [EmployeeID2], [t2].[DepartmentID], [t2].[ShiftID],
    [t2].[StartDate], [t2].[EndDate], [t2].[ModifiedDate] AS [ModifiedDate2],
    (
        SELECT COUNT(*)
        FROM [HumanResources].[EmployeeDepartmentHistory] AS [t3]
        WHERE [t3].[EmployeeID] = [t0].[EmployeeID]
    ) AS [count],
    [t1].[ContactID] AS [ContactID2], [t1].[NameStyle], [t1].[Title] AS
    [Title2], [t1].[FirstName], [t1].[MiddleName], [t1].[LastName],
    [t1].[Suffix], [t1].[EmailAddress], [t1].[EmailPromotion], [t1].[Phone],
    [t1].[PasswordHash], [t1].[PasswordSalt], [t1].[AdditionalContactInfo],
    [t1].[rowguid] AS [rowguid2], [t1].[ModifiedDate] AS [ModifiedDate3]
FROM [HumanResources].[Employee] AS [t0]
INNER JOIN [Person].[Contact] AS [t1] ON [t1].[ContactID] = [t0].[ContactID]
LEFT OUTER JOIN [HumanResources].[EmployeeDepartmentHistory] AS [t2]
ON [t2].[EmployeeID] = [t0].[EmployeeID]
ORDER BY [t0].[EmployeeID], [t1].[ContactID], [t2].[DepartmentID],
 [t2].[ShiftID], [t2].[StartDate]
```

■ **Caution** After a DataLoadOption is added to your DataContext, the DataLoadOption cannot be modified.

In the previous examples, you learned one correct way of working with the prefetching functionality in LTS. Other techniques include custom queries, LINQ joins, and extensions, all of which are covered later in this chapter. Before you dive into those topics, let's first look at another piece of native functionality that the DataLoadOptions class gives you: the ability to specify a subquery that can be used for relationship navigation.

Listing 4-25 is an example of a query using the AssociateWith<T> functionality that is part of the DataLoadOptions class. In this example, you are creating a subquery that is associated with Employee. This subquery checks whether EmployeeDepartmentHistory.StartDate is greater than October, 31, 2000. Thus, when you iterate through the collection, the results that you see are based on the original query (db.Employees) and the subquery, which return only start dates greater than October, 31, 2000.

Listing 4-25. *Code to Execute a Subquery Using the AssociateWith Functionality*

```
System.Data.Linq.DataLoadOptions options =
     new System.Data.Linq.DataLoadOptions();

options.AssociateWith<Employee>
    (c => c.EmployeeDepartmentHistories.Where
        (r=>r.StartDate > new  DateTime(2000,10,31)));

db.LoadOptions = options;

foreach (Employee emp in db.Employees)
{
    foreach (EmployeeDepartmentHistory edh in emp.EmployeeDepartmentHistories)
    { }
}
```

The SQL that gets generated from the C# code in Listing 4-25 can be seen in Listing 4-26. In this example, you can see that you have the first query that pulls the Employee information, and the second query that is the subquery you wrote in Listing 4-25.

■ **Note** Although Listing 4-26 shows only two queries, the second query in the series would actually get executed many times with different EmployeeID parameters because of the structure of the foreach loops.

Listing 4-26. *SQL Code Generated from the Subquery*

```
SELECT [t0].[EmployeeID], [t0].[NationalIDNumber],[t0].[ContactID], [t0].[LoginID],
    [t0].[ManagerID], [t0].[Title], [t0].[BirthDate], [t0].[MaritalStatus],
    [t0].[Gender], [t0].[HireDate], [t0].[SalariedFlag], [t0].[VacationHours],
    [t0].[SickLeaveHours], [t0].[CurrentFlag], [t0].[rowguid], [t0].[ModifiedDate]
FROM [HumanResources].[Employee] AS [t0]

exec sp_executesql N'SELECT [t0].[EmployeeID], [t0].[DepartmentID], [t0].[ShiftID],
    [t0].[StartDate], [t0].[EndDate], [t0].[ModifiedDate]
FROM [HumanResources].[EmployeeDepartmentHistory] AS [t0]
WHERE ([t0].[StartDate] > @p0) AND ([t0].[EmployeeID] = ((
```

```
SELECT [t2].[EmployeeID]
FROM (
    SELECT TOP 1 [t1].[EmployeeID]
    FROM [HumanResources].[Employee] AS [t1]
    WHERE [t1].[EmployeeID] = @p1
    ) AS [t2]
))',N'@p0 datetime,@p1 int',@p0=''2000-10-31 00:00:00:000'',@p1=1
```

The next stop on your journey to fully understanding LTS is the wonderful world of joins and custom queries. As you have seen in the previous examples, LTS has native functionality that allows foreign-key relationships to be captured in your object model. This has been seen throughout the examples in the relationships between entities such as `Employee` and `Contact`. However, relationships are not always as cut-and-dry as a foreign-key relationship. One option is to use the shaping (or projection) techniques that you learned earlier in the chapter, and another technique is to use a join to create a relationship between two nonkey fields.

Listing 4-27 shows an example of using a LINQ join query with LTS. In this scenario, imagine that there has been some sort of problem and HR needs to know which employees' hire dates are the same as their start dates. Here you have a simple join on the `Employees.HireDate` and the `EmployeeDepartmentHistories.StartDate`. Additionally, because these are dates and thus have the chance of creating an n:n relationship, I have added the `Distinct()` operator to our `new` anonymous type at the end of the code to ensure that the result set is unique in the returned `var`.

Listing 4-27. *LINQ Join with LTS*

```
var p =
    (from em in db.Employees
        join edh in db.EmployeeDepartmentHistories
        on em.HireDate equals edh.StartDate
        select new
        {
            em.EmployeeID,
            Date = edh.StartDate

        }).ToList().Distinct();
```

Tip As you begin using LTS in a more complex environment, you will find that writing an explicit join will at times improve performance. One way to determine when a join can help is to monitor the chattiness of LTS by using SQL Profiler to see whether LTS is creating underperforming subqueries.

As you are aware, because the Listing in 4-27 uses the `ToList()` operator at the end, it is executed immediately. The SQL code in Listing 4-28 shows the query that is executed against SQL Server. Looking at this code, you should notice that there is no SQL `Distinct` keyword or other operator to ensure the uniqueness of the query. The reason for this is because the `Distinct()` LINQ operator is handling the filtering on the client (that is, C#/framework) versus sending the command to the database. Because the join syntax is being translated into quality SQL, one method of "fixing" the SQL is to add another clause into the LINQ query.

Listing 4-28. *SQL Returned When Using a Join and Distinct ()*

```
SELECT [t0].[EmployeeID], [t1].[StartDate]
FROM [HumanResources].[Employee] AS [t0]
INNER JOIN [HumanResources].[EmployeeDepartmentHistory]
AS [t1] ON [t0].[HireDate] = [t1].[StartDate]
```

Instead of using the `Distinct()` operator, you can just as easily take advantage of the associations that you have and hone the query so it translates into a more efficient result set. For example, in Listing 4-29 you have the same LINQ query, but this time you have a `where` clause added to limit the results to what you need.

Listing 4-29. *Updated LINQ Query to Improve Performance*

```
var p =
     (from em in db.Employees
         join edh in db.EmployeeDepartmentHistories
         on em.HireDate equals edh.StartDate
         where em.EmployeeID == edh.EmployeeID
         select new
         {
             em.EmployeeID,
             Date = edh.StartDate

         }).ToList();
```

■ **Tip** If an entity association (that is, a foreign-key relationship) exists, don't write a LINQ join to do the same thing. These relationships are always the preferred method of querying data.

The SQL results of the code in Listing 4-29 can be seen in Listing 4-30, which shows the original `INNER JOIN` and the `where` clause that you added to the LINQ code. This method is far more efficient because it does not return unnecessary records from the database.

Listing 4-30. *SQL Query Generated by Updated LINQ Query*

```
SELECT [t0].[EmployeeID], [t1].[StartDate]
FROM [HumanResources].[Employee] AS [t0]
INNER JOIN [HumanResources].[EmployeeDepartmentHistory]
AS [t1] ON [t0].[HireDate] =  [t1].[StartDate]
WHERE [t0].[EmployeeID] = [t1].[EmployeeID]
```

Wait a second. What if I want to return all the results from my join? LTS offers you another form of join functionality that is slightly different from your standard join query operations in

SQL. The group join is a technique that can be used to join two sets of sequences, similar to an outer join in SQL. Listing 4-31 shows a group join, which joins into the anonymous type/variable of `totEm` and then returns the results of both sides of the query.

Listing 4-31. *LINQ Query Using a Group Join*

```
var q =
     (from em in db.Employees
         join edh in db.EmployeeDepartmentHistories
         on em.HireDate equals edh.StartDate into totEm
         select new { em, totEm }).ToList();
```

The results of Listing 4-31 are generated into the SQL code in Listing 4-32, which shows the `LEFT OUTER JOIN` that is created. In this query, you are not returning the distinct results; instead, you are asking for all the results in both tables, hence the name *group join*.

Listing 4-32. *SQL Generated by Group Join*

```
SELECT [t0].[EmployeeID], [t0].[NationalIDNumber], [t0].[ContactID], [t0].[LoginID],
    [t0].[ManagerID], [t0].[Title], [t0].[BirthDate], [t0].[MaritalStatus],
    [t0].[Gender], [t0].[HireDate], [t0].[SalariedFlag], [t0].[VacationHours],
    [t0].[SickLeaveHours], [t0].[CurrentFlag], [t0].[rowguid], [t0].[ModifiedDate],
    [t1].[EmployeeID] AS [EmployeeID2],
    [t1].[DepartmentID], [t1].[ShiftID], [t1].[StartDate], [t1].[EndDate],
    [t1].[ModifiedDate] AS [ModifiedDate2], (
        SELECT COUNT(*)
        FROM [HumanResources].[EmployeeDepartmentHistory] AS [t2]
        WHERE [t0].[HireDate] = [t2].[StartDate]
        ) AS [count]
FROM [HumanResources].[Employee] AS [t0]
LEFT OUTER JOIN [HumanResources].[EmployeeDepartmentHistory] AS [t1] ON
    [t0].[HireDate] = [t1].[StartDate]
ORDER BY [t0].[EmployeeID], [t1].[EmployeeID], [t1].[DepartmentID], [t1].[ShiftID],
    [t1].[StartDate]
```

■ Note Although the join examples didn't cover multiple collections, you can in any of your queries add multiple joins across multiple entities.

Now that you have learned about projections, shaping, joins, and sprocs, there is really only one additional core competency that you need to understand about *querying* before you can write some real code: custom queries. Custom queries, which are really an aspect of extending your `DataContext`, can be a useful tool.

At times when working with LTS, you will want to write a custom query to do x, y, or z in your application. Most of these situations arise when you just don't want to write a stored procedure but need to have finer-grained control over the model than LTS provides. In these cases, you have the option to modify the DataContext class to suit your needs by creating helper methods and extending the partial methods available to you.

In Listing 4-33, you have a new helper method called GetEmployeeByManagerID. This method returns an Employee entity by using the ExecuteQuery() method, which is part of the System.Data.Linq.DataContext base class. In this example, you have a simple select query that queries your database for Employee entities by their ManagerID.

Listing 4-33. *ExecuteQuery from your DataContext Class*

```
public IEnumerable<Employee> GetEmployeesByManagerID(int managerID)
{
    return ExecuteQuery<Employee>
       ("select * from HumanResources.Employee where ManagerID = {0}", managerID);

}
```

Using your new DataContext method is as simple as writing LINQ code, but instead of dynamic SQL being generated from LTS, the query is what you have written inline. Listing 4-34 is an example of using the new helper method in AdventureWorksDataContext to query a new Employee entity by ManagerID.

Listing 4-34. *Use the New Helper Method in YourDataContext*

```
foreach (Employee emp in db.GetEmployeesByManagerID(3))
{
    Debug.Print(emp.LoginID);

}
```

As you can see in Listing 4-35, the SQL code that is executed is nearly identical to what you have written in your DataContext helper method. The difference of course is that it has parameterized the query, but the core query remains the same.

Listing 4-35. *SQL Code That Is Executed from the ExecuteQuery() Method*

```
exec sp_executesql N'select * from HumanResources.Employee
    where ManagerID = @p0',N'@p0 int',@p0=3
```

■ **Note** LTS by default escapes the SQL that it generates, thus preventing SQL injection attacks.

One powerful aspect of LTS is that when you query through the LTS plumbing code (for example, in Listing 4-34), you can still take advantage of the object-tracking functionality built into LTS. For example, in Listing 4-36 I have modified the code from the previous example so the word _expired is appended to the LoginID property.

Listing 4-36. *Working with Live Objects from Your Custom Query*

```
foreach (Employee emp in db.GetEmployeesByManagerID(3))
{
    emp.LoginID = emp.LoginID + "_expired";

}

db.SubmitChanges();
```

As you can see in Listing 4-37, by changing the LoginID property and calling SubmitChanges() on your DataContext, an update query is being generated. In this particular example, multiple update queries are executed, but they all look like Listing 4-37, only with different parameters.

Listing 4-37. *Update SQL from the Customer Query*

```
exec sp_executesql N'UPDATE [HumanResources].[Employee]
    SET [LoginID] = @p14 WHERE ([EmployeeID] = @p0) AND ([NationalIDNumber] = @p1)
    AND ([ContactID] = @p2) AND ([LoginID] = @p3) AND ([ManagerID] = @p4)
    AND ([Title] = @p5) AND ([BirthDate] = @p6) AND ([MaritalStatus] = @p7) AND
    ([Gender] = @p8) AND ([HireDate] = @p9) AND (NOT
    ([SalariedFlag] = 1)) AND ([VacationHours] = @p10) AND ([SickLeaveHours] = @p11)
    AND ([CurrentFlag] = 1) AND ([rowguid] = @p12)
    AND ([ModifiedDate] = @p13)',N'@p0 int,@p1 nvarchar(9),@p2 int,@p3
    nvarchar(20),@p4 int,@p5 nvarchar(20),@p6 datetime,@p7
    nchar(1),@p8 nchar(1),@p9 datetime,@p10 smallint,@p11 smallint,@p12
    uniqueidentifier,@p13 datetime,@p14
    nvarchar(28)',@p0=4,@p1=N'112457891',@p2=1290,@p3=N'adventure-
    works\rob0',@p4=3,@p5=N'Senior Tool Designer',@p6=''1965-01-23
    00:00:00:000'',@p7=N'S',@p8=N'M',@p9=''1998-01-05
    00:00:00:000'',@p10=48,@p11=80,@p12='59747955-87B8-443F-8ED4-
    F8AD3AFDF3A9',@p13=''2004-07-31
    00:00:00:000'',@p14=N'adventure-works\rob0_expired'
```

So far, you have seen a simple example of a custom query, but understand that there aren't really too many limits on the inline SQL queries you can write using the ExecuteQuery() method. You can write complex Cartesian join logic, or simple select logic, whatever you think is going to be the best for your application. The one thing you can't do is write CUD operations with the ExecuteQuery() method. This requires another method that is part of the DataContext class, ExecuteCommand().

The ExecuteCommand() method behaves identically to ExecuteQuery(), with the exception that it accepts only the CUD queries (insert, delete, update). For example, if you want to change the default behavior of how LTS inserts a department, you can override the partial method InsertDepartment in the AdventureWorksDataContext class so that it uses the code in Listing 4-38.

■ **Note** You don't have to override the partial methods to use the ExecuteCommand() method; you can create helper methods in the DataContext as you did in Listing 4-33.

PARTIAL METHODS

One of the great features that .NET offers is the ability to split a class, method, interface, or struct over two or more source files. A partial class or struct may contain a partial method, as seen in Listing 4-38. A partial method enables you to define the method signature in one source file, and optionally specify the implementation in the same file or a different one. The really neat aspect is that if the implementation is not specified, the compiler removes the method signature and any calls to it. On the other hand, if the partial method has a body, the compiler does the work of combining the signature and the implementation code together.

The most practical application of partial methods is with code generators, like the one in LTS. The reason that partial methods are so useful with code generation is that they allow for a method name and signature to be assigned and used in the generated code, but also allow for the developer to extend and write the implementation of that partial method.

According to MSDN (`http://msdn2.microsoft.com/en-us/library/wa80x488.aspx`), the following rules apply to partial methods:

- Partial methods must begin with the contextual keyword `partial` and the method must return `void`.
- Partial methods can have ref but not out parameters.
- Partial methods are implicitly private and therefore cannot be virtual.
- Partial methods cannot be external, because the presence of the body determines whether they are defining or implementing.
- Partial methods can have static and unsafe modifiers.
- Partial methods can be generic. Constraints are put on the defining partial method declaration and may optionally be repeated on the implementing one. Parameter and type parameter names do not have to be the same in the implementing declaration as in the defining one.
- You cannot make a delegate to a partial method.

Listing 4-38. *Override of LTS Insert Functionality*

```
partial void InsertDepartment(Department instance)
{
    ExecuteCommand("INSERT INTO HumanResources.Department
        (Name,GroupName,ModifiedDate) VALUES({0},{1},{2})",
                instance.Name, instance.GroupName, DateTime.Now);

}
```

To use the new override code, you do nothing different from what you would normally do to insert a department. Listings 4-39 and 4-40 show the code that you use to insert the department and the SQL code that is generated from the new override. As you can see, the insert statement is sent to the database just as it was created in your code. Furthermore, there is nothing special that needs to be called, just your standard `InsertOnSubmit()` method.

Listing 4-39. *Test the New InsertDepartment Functionality*

```
Department d = new Department();
d.Name = "Dept1";
d.GroupName = "Group1";
db.Departments.InsertOnSubmit(d);
db.SubmitChanges();
```

Listing 4-40. *Custom SQL Code*

```
exec sp_executesql N'INSERT INTO HumanResources.Department
 (Name,GroupName,ModifiedDate) VALUES(@p0,@p1,@p2)',N'@p0
nvarchar(5),@p1 nvarchar(6),@p2 datetime',@p0=N'Dept1',
@p1=N'Group1',@p2=''2007-11-01 09:31:27:837''
```

Validation

In the preceding examples, you have seen the basic pattern that can be used to extend your `DataContext` class. However, your entity classes can also be extended by using similar techniques. In Chapter 3, you saw that LTS generates a series of Extensibility Method Definitions in your entity classes. Examples of these methods include `OnLoaded()` and `OnValidated()`. Although I don't plan on going through all the extension methods and techniques that can be used to extend LTS, I do want to give you at least one example of extending an entity class. I thought I would kill two birds with one stone by throwing in a discussion on validation in LTS.

■Tip You can easily create the override signature of any of the Extensibility Method Definitions that are generated in your `DataContext` and entity classes simply by typing in the word *partial* and letting IntelliSense take over.

Validation is a critical aspect of creating any enterprise application. LTS has some native functionality built in that helps you validate the data being passed around in your model and database. By default, when using the LTS designer, the properties of your entities receive basic schema-validation attributes. This means that the data types in your object model will match the data types in the database, and these will be verified by the compiler during your build. This schema validation also includes the use of nulls in the database, which translate to nullable types in your object model.

Schema validation is a good start in building your application but doesn't cover all your bases and doesn't give me the opportunity to give you another code sample. Listing 4-41 takes advantage of the `OnPROPERTYNAMEChanging()` partial method that is created in all your entity classes. In this example, the property is `Name` on the `Department` entity, and you are overriding it to enforce some rules on the naming of the property. Because the schema validation stops at `string/nvarchar`, checking the possibility of someone entering something goofy in this property is a possibility (for example, 123blah***). In this example, you are using a regular expression to check whether the value of the `Name` property is `alpha`.

Listing 4-41. *Property Validation Extension*

```
partial void OnNameChanging(string name)
{

    if (!Regex.IsMatch(name,"[^a-zA-Z]") == false)
    {
        throw new Exception("Department Name has to be Alpha's!");
    }

}
```

Tip When overriding extension methods, it can be helpful to create a new partial class to store them in for improved organization.

Another important extension method is the `OnValidate()` method, which is called prior to the entities' values being saved to the database. You can use the `OnValidate()` method when you need to perform validation against multiple properties. For example, consider validating the `Name` and the `GroupName` properties on the `Department` table to ensure that they are not identical. Listing 4-42 shows the implementation of this example, by overriding the `OnValidate()` partial method.

Listing 4-42. *Overriding the OnValidate() Partial Method*

```
partial void OnValidate()
{
    if (this.Name == this.GroupName)
    {
        throw new Exception("Department and GroupName cannot be the same");
    }

}
```

You have now examined the concepts around extending entity classes in your model, but the focus has primarily been on query validation. From an insert, update, and delete validation standpoint, you have a few more things to learn before you can move on.

In Listing 4-38, you saw that you can override `InsertENTITYNAME`, `UpdateENTITYNAME`, and `DeleteENTITYNAME` to call a custom SQL statement. However, you can also add validation logic in these partial methods prior to SQL being submitted to your database. I'm not going to provide a code example for this, because I think with the other validation examples you get the point of what you can and can't do; however, I will tell you about the granddaddy of all extensibility points in LTS: `SubmitChanges()`.

As you can guess, this is the method that gives you access to everything in the change hierarchy. LTS provides the `ChangeSet` object, part of the `DataContext` class, that enables you to retrieve all the entities that have been added, modified, or deleted. Listing 4-43 shows an example of some code that overrides SubmitChanges, to validate that if an Employee entity is being added, an EmployeeDepartmentHistory entity is also being added. Granted, this example would be handled by using referential integrity in the database, but for the purpose of demonstrating the functionality of the ChangeSet object and the override of SubmitChanges, the example gets the point across.

Listing 4-43. *Override SubmitChanges() for Greater Control of Your Modified Entities*

```
public override void SubmitChanges(ConflictMode failureMode)
{
    ChangeSet cs = this.GetChangeSet();
    var x = cs.AddedEntities;

    bool emp = false;
    bool edh = false;

    foreach (var r in x)
    {
        if (r.GetType().Name == "Employee")
        {
            emp = true;
        }
        if (r.GetType().Name == "EmployeeDepartmentHistory")
        {
            edh = true;
        }

    }

     if (emp == true && edh == false)
     {
         throw new Exception("You have to submit an employee department history
                    when creating a new employee");
     }

     base.SubmitChanges(failureMode);
}
```

Transactions

The last topic I want to cover in this chapter is transactions in LTS. By default, every query that goes through the DataContext that calls SubmitChanges() is wrapped in a SQL server transaction. This means that data integrity should always be maintained when using LTS, because the entire transaction is either committed or rolled back. If a transaction is not in scope, a new one will automatically be created.

LTS also provides a way to explicitly create and use your own transactions through the TransactionScope class. The TransactionScope class is part of the System.Transaction namespace, and it does require a new reference to be added to your solution. After you have added the reference to the System.Transaction namespace, it is easy to enlist a new transaction, as you can see in Listing 4-44. Here you have an example that uses the TransactionScope class to control the commit action of the transaction.

In the default scenario without TransactionScope, SubmitChanges() is the trigger that ultimately fires COMMIT TRANSACTION in the database. Alternatively, in Listing 4-44, you have enrolled the DataContext class in a custom transaction; thus you control the time at which COMMIT TRANSACTION is executed in the database.

Listing 4-44. *Using the TransactionScope Class*

```
Department d = db.Departments.Single<Department>(r => r.Name == "Executive");
d.Name = "TransactionDepartment";

using (TransactionScope ts = new TransactionScope())
{
    db.SubmitChanges();
    ts.Complete();

}
```

The functionality seen in Listing 4-44 gives you the fine-grained control over your transactions that you will need in n-tier applications. This control is not limited to just the SubmitChanges() method: you can include any method in the DataContext—for example, ExecuteQuery() in a custom transaction—and control its COMMIT, ROLLBACK, or other functionality.

Along with the TransactionScope functionality that LTS provides, you can also use native database transactions to control the execution of your commands. In Listing 4-45, you can see an example of a try...catch...finally block that is using database transactions to control rollback and commit functions.

In this example, you are first checking to see whether db.Connection is closed. If it is, you are opening it, because you cannot enlist a new transaction without an open connection. Next you begin the transaction, calling SubmitChanges() and calling Commit() or Rollback(), depending on the results of the try...catch block.

Listing 4-45. *Explicitly Using Native Database Transactions with LTS*

```
Department d = db.Departments.Single<Department>
    (r => r.Name == "TransactionDepartment2");

d.Name = "TransactionDepartment3";

if(db.Connection.State == ConnectionState.Closed)
{
    db.Connection.Open();
}

db.Transaction = db.Connection.BeginTransaction();
```

```
try
{
    db.SubmitChanges();
    db.Transaction.Commit();
}
catch
{
    db.Transaction.Rollback();
    throw;
}
finally
{
    db.Transaction = null;

}
```

Another important aspect about transactions I want to touch on is the transaction isolation level. I'm not going to go into too much depth on this topic because Chapter 11 discusses concurrency, and this book isn't about database design; there are a few points, however, that you should understand about isolation and LTS.

Isolation level is, of course, what is used by the database to control locking and how/when one change is seen by other changes. LTS uses the standard `System.Data.IsolationLevel` enumeration for controlling the isolation level. The following are the enumeration values that can be set on your `DataContext.Transaction.IsolationLevel` property:

`Chaos`: The pending changes from more highly isolated transactions cannot be overwritten.

`ReadUncommitted`: A dirty read is possible, meaning that no shared locks are issued and no exclusive locks are honored.

`ReadCommitted` (LTS default): Shared locks are held while the data is being read to avoid dirty reads, but the data can be changed before the end of the transaction, resulting in nonrepeatable reads or phantom data.

`RepeatableRead`: Locks are placed on all data that is used in a query, preventing other users from updating the data. Prevents nonrepeatable reads, but phantom rows are still possible.

`Serializable`: A range lock is placed on `System.Data.DataSet`, preventing other users from updating or inserting rows into the `DataSet` until the transaction is complete.

`SnapShot`: Reduces blocking by storing a version of the data that one application can read while another is modifying the same data. Indicates that from one transaction, you cannot see changes made in other transactions even if you requery.

Along with the option of setting the isolation level in C# on the `DataContext` class, you can also use `SET TRANSACTION ISOLATION LEVEL` in T-SQL. Although you can do it with T-SQL, the only time that you would really ever use this technique is if you choose to use sprocs or native T-SQL transactions. Typically, you can get by with the default `ReadCommittted` LTS isolation level and .NET transactions, but there are circumstances where you might want to use SQL depending on the requirements and the volume of traffic in your application.

In general, I use .NET transactions over native database transactions when working with LTS because of the extra overhead (that is, code) that you have to write when working with database transactions. LTS has highly optimized connection handling and cleanup code, and it is error prone to have to explicitly call `Open()` or `Close()`. Additionally, because using database transactions require a more specialized skill set, from a pure convenience factor, .NET transactions are preferred because they can be controlled in your C# code.

Summary

In this chapter, you learned about some of the advanced topics in LTS by working with a two-tier application. When debugging LTS, it is critical that you look not only at the SQL in the debug visualizer but also at the amount of "chatter" that takes between the framework and the database server.

LTS provides a large number of extension points and the ability to customize most of the ORM functionality. Some examples of customization include calling external stored procedures, inline SQL, and custom validation code. Furthermore, by using the power of LINQ, you have the ability to create complex relationships and projections in the comfort of your own C# code.

In Chapter 9, you will learn everything that I didn't cover in the last two chapters. This includes inheritance, many-to-many relationships, and n-tier development using LTS. You will be mapping and building the FBP application that you started in Chapter 3 and will round out your LTS knowledge. Chapter 5, alternatively, is going to be the beginning of the examination of the ADO.NET Entity Framework.

PART 3

Entity Framework Examined

CHAPTER 5

Getting Started with the ADO.NET Entity Framework

In the preceding two chapters, you learned the ins and outs of LTS by examining real-world examples. In this chapter, you will be going back to the basics, but instead of looking more at LTS, you will be diving into the ADO.NET Entity Framework. In order to learn to run, you first need to walk, and therefore this chapter is the introduction to the ADO.NET Entity Framework (EF). EF is a much larger topic than LTS, so I devote three chapters (rather than two) to EF's inner workings. This chapter presents the following topics:

Entity Data Model (EDM) structure: The metadata for all EF development and the core of the architecture

EF designer and wizard: The user interface and wizard that comes with EF

EdmGen (`EdmGen.exe`): An Entity Data Model generation tool that ships with EF

Generated code from the EF toolset: The source code that is generated from the EF UI and the EdmGen tools

What Is EF?

It is difficult and probably incorrect to classify EF as an ORM because it is far more advanced than that. EF strives to accomplish something more sophisticated than your standard ORM tool by embracing the conceptual model as something concrete. EF accomplishes this by providing a framework for creating an abstract model on top of your relational model, hence overcoming the impedance mismatch.

The nucleus of EF is its layer of abstraction that is divided into conceptual, mapping, and logical layers making up the EDM. In addition, EF utilizes two APIs, object services and the entity client, for working with the EDM and also uses two data manipulation constructs, Entity SQL (ESQL) and LINQ to Entities.

After reading the list of technologies in EF, you probably already understand why it might be considered incorrect to call EF an ORM, but if you are still unclear, I promise after reading the next few chapters and after going through these technologies with concrete examples, EF will become clear.

Note EF does not ship with Visual Studio 2008. EF is a separate download slated to be available sometime in the first half of 2008 as an update to the VS 2008 release.

Exploring the Designer

I think the best place to start on your journey is with the EF designer, as you did with the LTS designer in Chapter 4. By taking a Bottom Up approach using the `AdventureWorks` database and a simple Windows Forms application, you can focus on the examples and the inner workings of EF instead of getting caught up with specific architecture or design constructs.

Start by opening Visual Studio 2008 and creating a new Window Forms application project—I just called mine `EF_Samples`. After the project has loaded, you are going to add a new ADO.NET Entity Data Model (EDM) to the project. As you can see in Figure 5-1, there is a new project template for EF, which allows you to create an `.edmx` file. Simply stated, the `.edmx` file is the physical XML file that contains the metadata for the conceptual, mapping, and logical layers of EF.

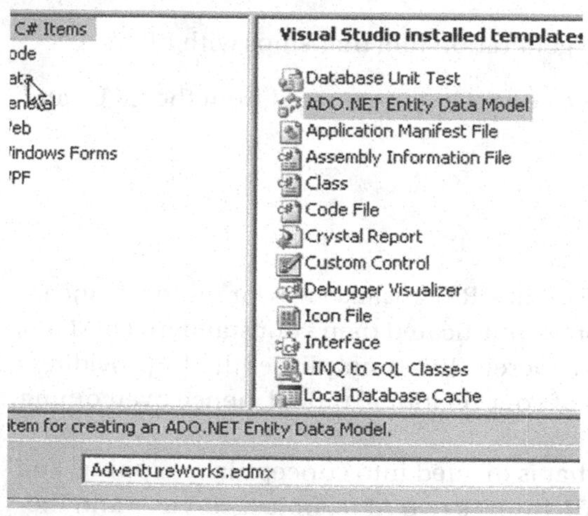

Figure 5-1. *EDM project template*

Caution To successfully generate an EDM file, all entities must have primary keys. If you generate files from a table without a primary key, the project will not compile.

Before you examine the .edmx file and the metadata involved in the EDM, let's continue with the EF project template and the wizard associated with it. After you click the Add button, the Entity Data Model Wizard pops up (see Figure 5-2). The first screen gives you the option to select Empty Model or Generate from Database. The Empty Model option enables you to hand-code the XML metadata for your model, and then the framework generates your classes at compile time. Alternatively, the Generate from Database option, which you will be using to work with `AdventureWorks`, is your standard Bottom Up approach, where you select a table, view, or stored procedure, and code generation occurs.

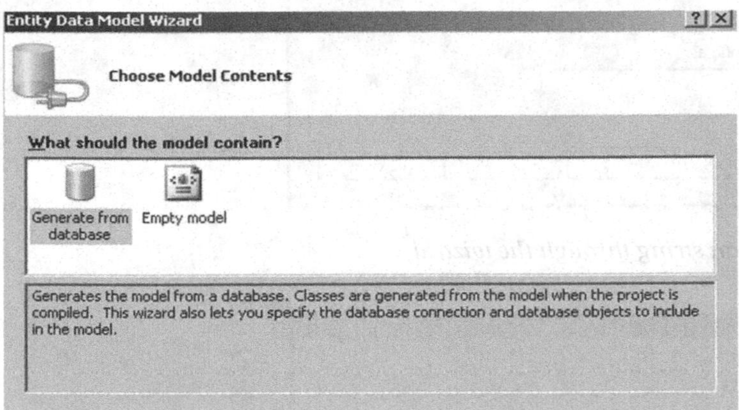

Figure 5-2. *The EDM Wizard provides two choices for your model.*

Prior to selecting the database objects that will be associated with the EDM, you need to provide your connection information. In Figure 5-3, you can see the next EDM Wizard screen that allows you to select an existing connection or a new connection. The New Connection option opens the standard Visual Studio Add Connection window (not shown), which allows you to specify Windows or SQL authentication. In addition, the EDM Wizard connection screen gives you the opportunity to exclude sensitive data from your connection string and change the key value in your `.config` file.

As you might expect, after selecting your connection settings, your next step is to select the database objects that you want to include in your model. In Figure 5-4, you can see the tree view for tables, views, and stored procedures. To start out, you are going to be selecting only a handful of tables from the `AdventureWorks` database. These tables are the same ones that you worked with in Chapters 3 and 4, so you should already be familiar with them. To refresh your memory, these tables include `Contact`, `Employee`, `EmployeeDepartmentHistory`, and `Department`.

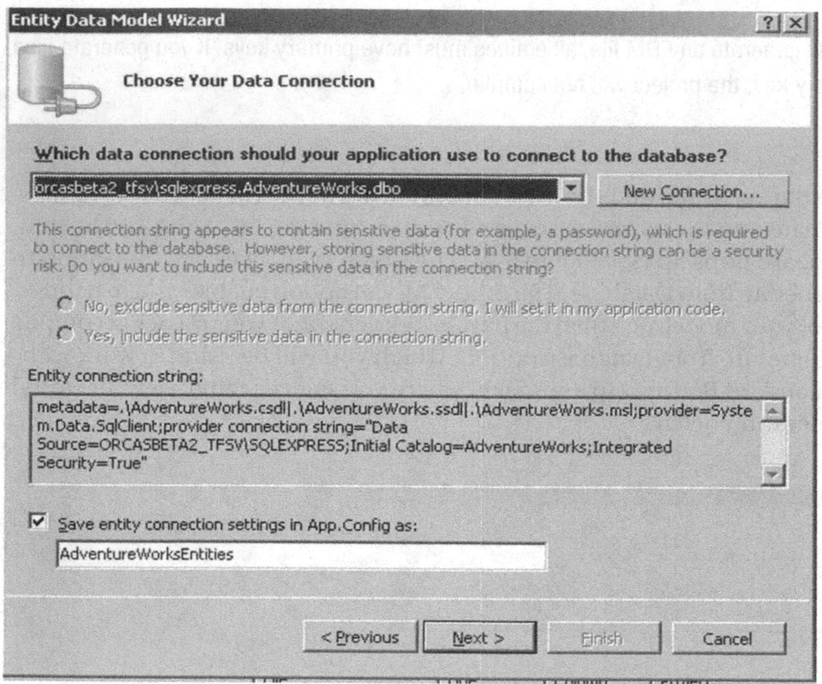

Figure 5-3. *Set the EDM connection string through the wizard.*

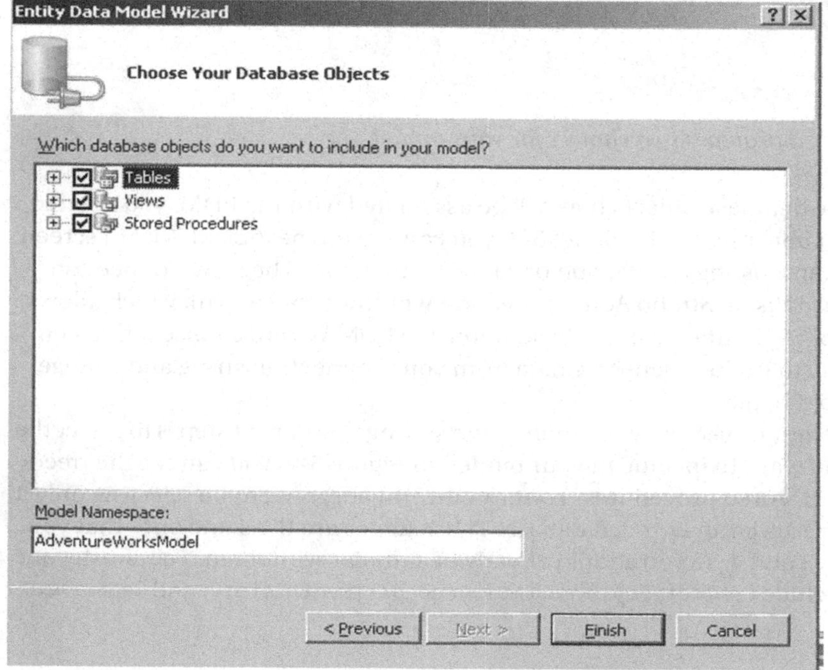

Figure 5-4. *Select the database object to be added to your model.*

After selecting the database objects that you initially want included in your model, you are presented with your design surface. Figure 5-5 shows the EF design surface, with the database objects you selected in the wizard already enumerated. As you can see, the design surface shows the relationships between the entities and displays all your fields from the database.

You may have noted that I just referred to these structures as *entities*; this is because these structures are no longer tables but representations of tables. The entities in this designer have scalar properties that map to your database fields and have navigational properties that represent the associations between the entities.

Along with the design surface holding the entities, you have another window that holds the mapping data between these entities. In Figure 5-6, you can see the Entity Mapping Details window, which provides UI functionality to manipulate the mapping between conceptual and logical models. This mapping functionality is not limited to table and entity relationships because you can also click on the relationship connectors between tables to manipulate association mapping information.

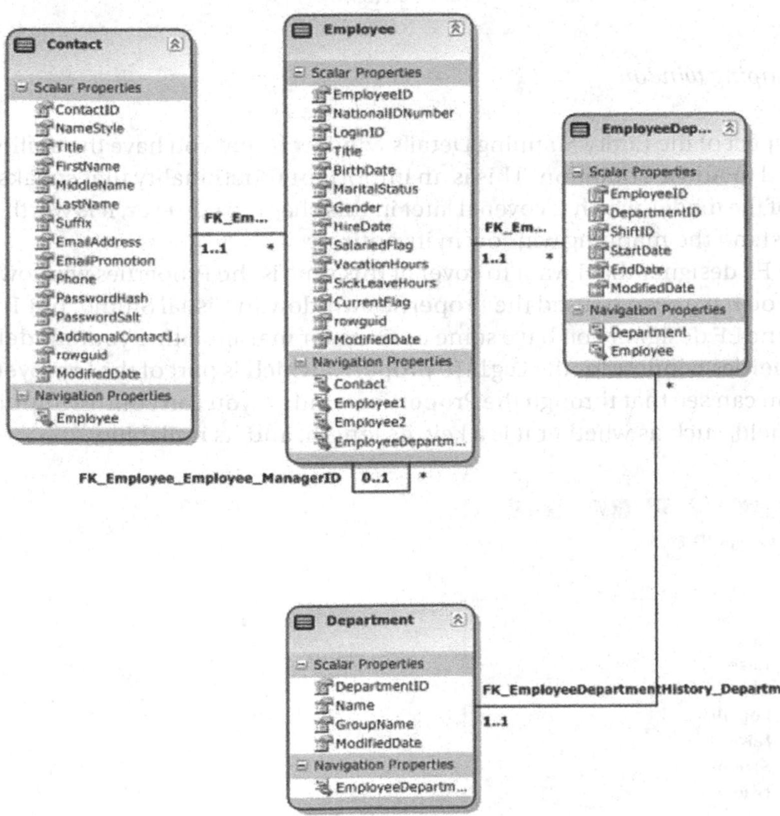

Figure 5-5. *EF design surface*

Entity Mapping Details - Contact

Column	Operator	Value / Property
⊟ Tables		
⊟ Maps to Contact		
<Add a Condition>		
⊟ Column Mappings		
ContactID (int)	<-->	ContactID (Int32)
NameStyle (bit)	<-->	NameStyle (Boolean)
Title (nvarchar)	<-->	Title (String)
FirstName (nvarchar)	<-->	FirstName (String)
MiddleName (nvarchar)	<-->	MiddleName (String)
LastName (nvarchar)	<-->	LastName (String)
Suffix (nvarchar)	<-->	Suffix (String)
EmailAddress (nvarchar)	<-->	EmailAddress (String)
EmailPromotion (int)	<-->	EmailPromotion (Int32)
Phone (nvarchar)	<-->	Phone (String)
PasswordHash (varchar)	<-->	PasswordHash (String)
PasswordSalt (varchar)	<-->	PasswordSalt (String)
AdditionalContactInfo (xml)	<-->	AdditionalContactInfo (String)
rowguid (uniqueidentifier)	<-->	rowguid (Guid)
ModifiedDate (datetime)	<-->	ModifiedDate (DateTime)
<Add a Table or View>		

Figure 5-6. *EF designer mapping window*

Another important aspect of the Entity Mapping Details window is that you have the ability to Add a Table or View and to Add a Condition. This is an important functionality that speaks to the conceptual nature of the model, which is covered later in this chapter; however, it is worth noting now so you understand the mapping window in its entirety.

Another aspect of the EF designer that I want to cover at this time is the Properties window. I'm quite sure that all of you have seen or used the Properties window in Visual Studio, but I want to show you that in the EF designer you have options for manipulating your model. Figure 5-7 shows the Properties window for the `LoginID` property, which is part of the `Employee` entity. In this example, you can see that through the Properties window you can control important metadata about the field, such as whether it is a key, its length, and its nullability.

Properties

AdventureWorksModel.Employee.LoginID Property

Default Value	
Entity Key	**false**
Fixed Length	**false**
Max Length	**256**
Name	**LoginID**
Nullable	**false**
Type	**String**
Unicode	**true**

Figure 5-7. *EF designer Properties window*

The final feature of the EF designer that I want to discuss in this section is the Entity Model Browser window. Figure 5-8 shows the Entity Model Browser, which is a new Explorer tab in VS 2008. In this window, you have a holistic view of the EDM. That is, you can view and manipulate (through the Properties window) the conceptual and logical model. Additionally, when hovering over an item in this window, the metadata (the XML) is displayed in a tool tip (not shown), which is helpful when you are learning the EDM.

It is important to understand that this section has not covered all the functionality in the EF designer. This section has presented the basics to get you moving and learning more about the framework. Throughout this and the next two chapters, you will be examining the designer and learning the intricacies that have not been covered in this section.

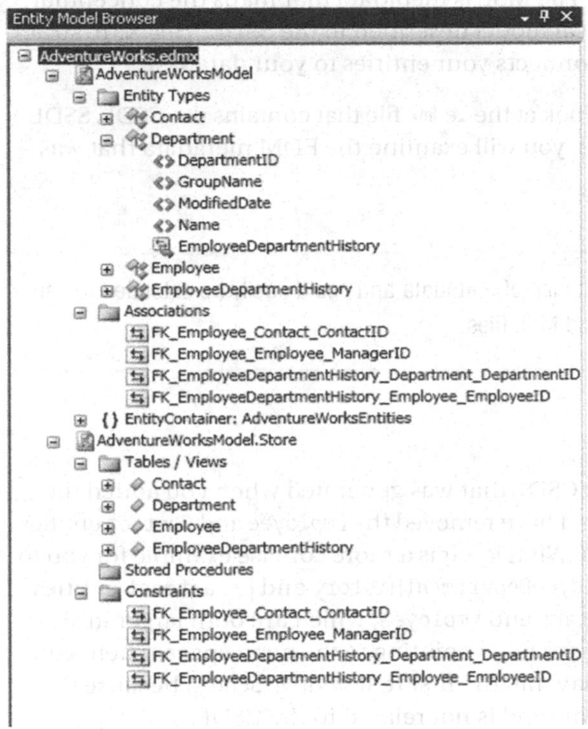

Figure 5-8. *Entity Model Browser window*

Understanding the EDM

You have now seen the basics of creating an EDM with the EF designer, but what exactly does this mean? According to MSDN, "The Entity Data Model (EDM) is a specification for defining the data used by applications built on the Entity Framework" (`http://msdn2.microsoft.com/en-us/library/bb387122(VS.90).aspx`). Although this definition is a little vague, it does effectively define the EDM.

As previously mentioned, the EDM is broken into three metadata structures that make up the conceptual, mapping, and logical layers used by EF. These structures are classified as the design schema (your `.edmx` file) and consist of the following aspects:

Conceptual Schema Definition Language (CSDL): The CSDL represents the conceptual model of your data. This XML structure includes your entities and their relationships and represents your object code.

Stored Schema Definition Language (SSDL): The SSDL represents the database structure and the data in your database. This XML structure is used to describe the logical layer of your solution.

Mapping Specification Language (MSL): The MSL is metadata that maps the conceptual model described in the CSDL to the logical model described in the SSDL. This XML structure is your mapping information that connects your entities to your database.

The easiest way to understand EDM is to look at the `.edmx` file that contains the CSDL, SSDL, and MSL structures. In the following sections, you will examine the EDM metadata that was generated from the designer.

■ **Note** EF has an open architecture for the persistence of metadata and could easily be extended to use other forms of data storage besides CSDL, SSDL, and MSL files.

CSDL

Listing 5-1 shows a condensed version of the CSDL that was generated when you added the tables through the EF designer. In this example, I have removed the `Employee` and `Contact` entities and their relationships with the other entities. What is left is a more concise example for you to start with. In this example, you have the `EmployeeDepartmentHistory` and `Department` entities and their associations (instead of having `Contact` and `Employee`, which are both larger in size).

The first real node in Listing 5-1 is the `Schema` node pointing to the namespace schema that contains the information about the CSDL. I say that the first real node is `Schema` because the `<edmx:ConceptualModels>` node is `.edmx` specific and is not related to the CSDL.

The next node is the `<EntityContainer>` node, which is used to specify the classes and associations in the object model. `<EntitySet>` and `<AssociationSet>` are child nodes of `<EntityContainer>`. As you can see in this example, you have two `<EntitySet>` nodes, which contain the `Department` and `EmployeeDepartmentHistory` data, and you have one `<AssociationSet>` node that contains the foreign-key relationship between these two entities.

Moving on, your next node is the `<EntityType>` node, which contains the data about the `Department` entity. Here you have the `<Key>` node, which defines the primary key in the entity, and then you have `<Property>` nodes, which define the properties on the class, including their name, type, and nullability. Additionally, another child node of `<EntityType>` is `<NavigationProperty>`. The `<NavigationProperty>` node, as seen in Listing 5-1, is used to describe the foreign-key relationship between entities. Think of this as the association property or your shortcut from one entity to another.

The final node in this example is the `<Association>` node, used to describe the details surrounding the association between entities. In this example, you can see that the `<Association>` node contains the foreign-key data, and then contains child nodes that describe the roles and multiplicities of the association. Here we have a one-to-many relationship that is specified by using the multiplicity attribute on each of the `<End>` child nodes.

Listing 5-1. *Example CSDL*

```
<edmx:ConceptualModels>
    <Schema Namespace="AdventureWorksModel" Alias="Self"
        xmlns="http://schemas.microsoft.com/ado/2006/04/edm">
        <EntityContainer Name="AdventureWorksEntities">
          <EntitySet Name="Department"
              EntityType="AdventureWorksModel.Department" />
          <EntitySet Name="EmployeeDepartmentHistory"
              EntityType="AdventureWorksModel.EmployeeDepartmentHistory" />
          <AssociationSet Name="
              FK_EmployeeDepartmentHistory_Department_DepartmentID"
              Association="AdventureWorksModel.
              FK_EmployeeDepartmentHistory_Department_DepartmentID">
              <End Role="Department" EntitySet="Department" />
              <End Role="EmployeeDepartmentHistory"
                  EntitySet="EmployeeDepartmentHistory" />
          </AssociationSet>
        </EntityContainer>
        <EntityType Name="Department">
          <Key>
            <PropertyRef Name="DepartmentID" />
          </Key>
          <Property Name="DepartmentID" Type="Int16" Nullable="false" />
          <Property Name="Name" Type="String" Nullable="false" MaxLength="50" />
          <Property Name="GroupName" Type="String" Nullable="false"
              MaxLength="50" />
          <Property Name="ModifiedDate" Type="DateTime" Nullable="false" />
          <NavigationProperty Name="EmployeeDepartmentHistory"
               Relationship="AdventureWorksModel.
               FK_EmployeeDepartmentHistory_Department_DepartmentID"
               FromRole="Department" ToRole="EmployeeDepartmentHistory" />
        </EntityType>
        <EntityType Name="EmployeeDepartmentHistory">
          <Key>
            <PropertyRef Name="EmployeeID" />
            <PropertyRef Name="DepartmentID" />
            <PropertyRef Name="ShiftID" />
            <PropertyRef Name="StartDate" />
          </Key>
```

```
      <Property Name="EmployeeID" Type="Int32" Nullable="false" />
      <Property Name="DepartmentID" Type="Int16" Nullable="false"/>
      <Property Name="ShiftID" Type="Byte" Nullable="false" />
      <Property Name="StartDate" Type="DateTime" Nullable="false" />
      <Property Name="EndDate" Type="DateTime" />
      <Property Name="ModifiedDate" Type="DateTime" Nullable="false" />
      <NavigationProperty Name="Department" Relationship="AdventureWorksModel.
          FK_EmployeeDepartmentHistory_Department_DepartmentID"
          FromRole="EmployeeDepartmentHistory" ToRole="Department" />
    </EntityType>
    <Association Name="FK_EmployeeDepartmentHistory_Department_DepartmentID">
      <End Role="Department" Type="AdventureWorksModel.Department"
          Multiplicity="1" />
      <End Role="EmployeeDepartmentHistory"
          Type="AdventureWorksModel.EmployeeDepartmentHistory"
          Multiplicity="*" />
      <ReferentialConstraint>
        <Principal Role="Department">
          <PropertyRef Name="DepartmentID" />
        </Principal>
        <Dependent Role="EmployeeDepartmentHistory">
          <PropertyRef Name="DepartmentID" />
        </Dependent>
      </ReferentialConstraint>
    </Association>
  </Schema>
</edmx:ConceptualModels>
```

SSDL

As mentioned earlier, the SSDL found in the .edmx file is used to formally describe the persistence store used with the EDM. The SSDL is similar to the CSDL, with the biggest difference being the data types used in the metadata. In the case of the SSDL, the data types being described are those from the database, whereas in the CSDL, the data types are those of the object model (that is, .NET types).

Listing 5-2 shows the matching SSDL for Listing 5-1, which is a condensed version of what you created earlier in this chapter. In Listing 5-2, you can see that the structure and the nodes used are identical to the CSDL in Listing 5-1. There are only a few differences between this example and the CSDL example. One difference is the value of the Type attribute that is part of the <Property> node. In this example, you can see that the types that are specified are database types, not .NET types (for example, nvarchar and smallint). Another difference is the existence of the StoreGeneratedPattern="identity" attribute and the maxlength attribute on the <Property> node.

Listing 5-2. *SSDL Example*

```
<edmx:StorageModels>
  <Schema Namespace="AdventureWorksModel.Store" Alias="Self"
    xmlns="http://schemas.microsoft.com/ado/2006/04/edm/ssdl">
    <EntityContainer Name="HumanResources">
      <EntitySet Name="Department"
          EntityType="AdventureWorksModel.Store.Department" />
      <EntitySet Name="EmployeeDepartmentHistory"
          EntityType="AdventureWorksModel.Store.EmployeeDepartmentHistory" />
      <AssociationSet
          Name="FK_EmployeeDepartmentHistory_Department_DepartmentID"
          Association="AdventureWorksModel.
          Store.FK_EmployeeDepartmentHistory_Department_DepartmentID">
        <End Role="Department" EntitySet="Department" />
        <End Role="EmployeeDepartmentHistory"
          EntitySet="EmployeeDepartmentHistory" />
      </AssociationSet>
    </EntityContainer>
    <EntityType Name="Department">
      <Key>
        <PropertyRef Name="DepartmentID" />
      </Key>
      <Property Name="DepartmentID" Type="smallint" Nullable="false"
         StoreGeneratedPattern="identity" />
      <Property Name="Name" Type="nvarchar" Nullable="false" MaxLength="50" />
      <Property Name="GroupName" Type="nvarchar"
          Nullable="false" MaxLength="50" />
      <Property Name="ModifiedDate" Type="datetime" Nullable="false" />
    </EntityType>
    <EntityType Name="EmployeeDepartmentHistory">
      <Key>
        <PropertyRef Name="EmployeeID" />
        <PropertyRef Name="StartDate" />
        <PropertyRef Name="DepartmentID" />
        <PropertyRef Name="ShiftID" />
      </Key>
      <Property Name="EmployeeID" Type="int" Nullable="false" />
      <Property Name="DepartmentID" Type="smallint" Nullable="false" />
      <Property Name="ShiftID" Type="tinyint" Nullable="false" />
      <Property Name="StartDate" Type="datetime" Nullable="false" />
      <Property Name="EndDate" Type="datetime" />
      <Property Name="ModifiedDate" Type="datetime" Nullable="false" />
    </EntityType>
```

```
      <Association Name="FK_EmployeeDepartmentHistory_Department_DepartmentID">
        <End Role="Department"
           Type="AdventureWorksModel.Store.Department" Multiplicity="1" />
        <End Role="EmployeeDepartmentHistory"
           Type="AdventureWorksModel.Store.EmployeeDepartmentHistory"
           Multiplicity="*" />
        <ReferentialConstraint>
          <Principal Role="Department">
            <PropertyRef Name="DepartmentID" />
          </Principal>
          <Dependent Role="EmployeeDepartmentHistory">
            <PropertyRef Name="DepartmentID" />
          </Dependent>
        </ReferentialConstraint>
      </Association>
    </Schema>
  </edmx:StorageModels>
```

MSL

MSL is the mapping glue that is used to tie the CSDL types and the SSDL types together. Whereas the CSDL and the SSDL are nearly identical, the MSL is slightly different. That being said, the MSL metadata is very intuitive and easy to understand and does have many similarities to the CSDL and SSDL languages. Listing 5-3 is the MSL example that maps together the CSDL in Listing 5-1 and the SSDL in Listing 5-2.

In Listing 5-3, you can see that like the SSDL and CSDL, the MSL references a namespace—but unlike the other two schemas, the MSL uses the <Mapping> node to house this information. The next node, <EntityContainerMapping>, does exactly as its name indicates: it maps entity containers. In this example, the two containers being mapped are HumanResources StorageEntityContainer and AdventureWorkEntities CdmEntityContainer. As you may have guessed, the StorageEntityContainer attribute is used for your SSDL mapping, and CdmEntityContainer is used for your CSDL mapping.

The next node is the <EntitySetMapping> node, which as its name suggests is used to map entity sets. The first <EntitySetMapping> node is for the Department entity set and contains an <EntityTypeMapping>, <MappingFragment>, and <ScalarProperty> child nodes. The <EntityTypeMapping> node contains a TypeName attribute, which is the type of the entity. The <MappingFragment> node contains the information to map back to the SSDL; in this example, it is the StoreEntitySet attribute with the Department EntityType. Finally, you have the <ScalarProperty> nodes, which contain their Name and the ColumnName that they map to.

Like Department, there is also the EmployeeDepartmentHistory <EntitySetMapping> node. The structure is about the same as Department, so there isn't really a need to go over each of the child nodes. The final node in the MSL is <AssociationSetMapping>, which contains the <EndProperty> and <Condition> child nodes. The <AssociationSetMapping> node contains the Name of the foreign key, the TypeName of the association, and the StoreEntitySet information that contains the mapping to the SSDL. The <EndProperty> nodes contain the <ScalarProperty> child nodes, which map to columns in the SSDL. Finally, the <Condition> node contains any referential constraints that may exist in the data store.

Listing 5-3. *MSL Example*

```
<edmx:Mappings>
   <Mapping Space="C-S"
      xmlns="urn:schemas-microsoft com:windows:storage:mapping:CS">
     <EntityContainerMapping StorageEntityContainer="HumanResources"
       CdmEntityContainer="AdventureWorksEntities">
       <EntitySetMapping Name="Department">
         <EntityTypeMapping TypeName="IsTypeOf(AdventureWorksModel.Department)">
           <MappingFragment StoreEntitySet="Department">
             <ScalarProperty Name="DepartmentID" ColumnName="DepartmentID" />
             <ScalarProperty Name="Name" ColumnName="Name" />
             <ScalarProperty Name="GroupName" ColumnName="GroupName" />
             <ScalarProperty Name="ModifiedDate" ColumnName="ModifiedDate" />
           </MappingFragment>
         </EntityTypeMapping>
       </EntitySetMapping>
       <EntitySetMapping Name="EmployeeDepartmentHistory">
         <EntityTypeMapping
             TypeName="IsTypeOf(AdventureWorksModel.EmployeeDepartmentHistory)">
           <MappingFragment StoreEntitySet="EmployeeDepartmentHistory">
             <ScalarProperty Name="EmployeeID" ColumnName="EmployeeID" />
             <ScalarProperty Name="DepartmentID" ColumnName="DepartmentID" />
             <ScalarProperty Name="ShiftID" ColumnName="ShiftID" />
             <ScalarProperty Name="StartDate" ColumnName="StartDate" />
             <ScalarProperty Name="EndDate" ColumnName="EndDate" />
             <ScalarProperty Name="ModifiedDate" ColumnName="ModifiedDate" />
           </MappingFragment>
         </EntityTypeMapping>
       </EntitySetMapping>
       <AssociationSetMapping
           Name="FK_EmployeeDepartmentHistory_Department_DepartmentID"
           TypeName="AdventureWorksModel.
           FK_EmployeeDepartmentHistory_Department_DepartmentID"
           StoreEntitySet="EmployeeDepartmentHistory">
         <EndProperty Name="Department">
           <ScalarProperty Name="DepartmentID" ColumnName="DepartmentID" />
         </EndProperty>
         <EndProperty Name="EmployeeDepartmentHistory">
           <ScalarProperty Name="EmployeeID" ColumnName="EmployeeID" />
           <ScalarProperty Name="StartDate" ColumnName="StartDate" />
           <ScalarProperty Name="DepartmentID" ColumnName="DepartmentID" />
           <ScalarProperty Name="ShiftID" ColumnName="ShiftID" />
         </EndProperty>
         <Condition ColumnName="DepartmentID" IsNull="false" />
       </AssociationSetMapping>
     </EntityContainerMapping>
   </Mapping>
 </edmx:Mappings>
```

Metadata Schemas

After reviewing Listings 5-1, 5-2, and 5-3, you should have a good idea of the structure of the metadata that makes up the EDM. However, these examples do not enumerate the entire schema for CSDL, SSDL, and MSL types, so let's take a closer look at the XSDs associated with this metadata.

All of the XSD for the EDM can be found in the Visual Studio `Schemas` directory. These files are as follows:

- `System.Data.Resources.CSDLSchema.xsd` (CSDL)
- `System.Data.Resources.SSDLSchema.xsd` (SSDL)
- `System.Data.Resources.CSMSL.xsd` (MSL)

Figure 5-9 shows the CSDL `Schema` node and its children. The `Schema` node can have a `Using` node (which is used for imports), an `Association` node (which is used to define relationships), a `ComplexType` node (which is used for extensibility and complex types), an `EntityType` node (which defines `EntityTypes`), and an `EntityContainer` (which contains `Entity` and `Association` sets).

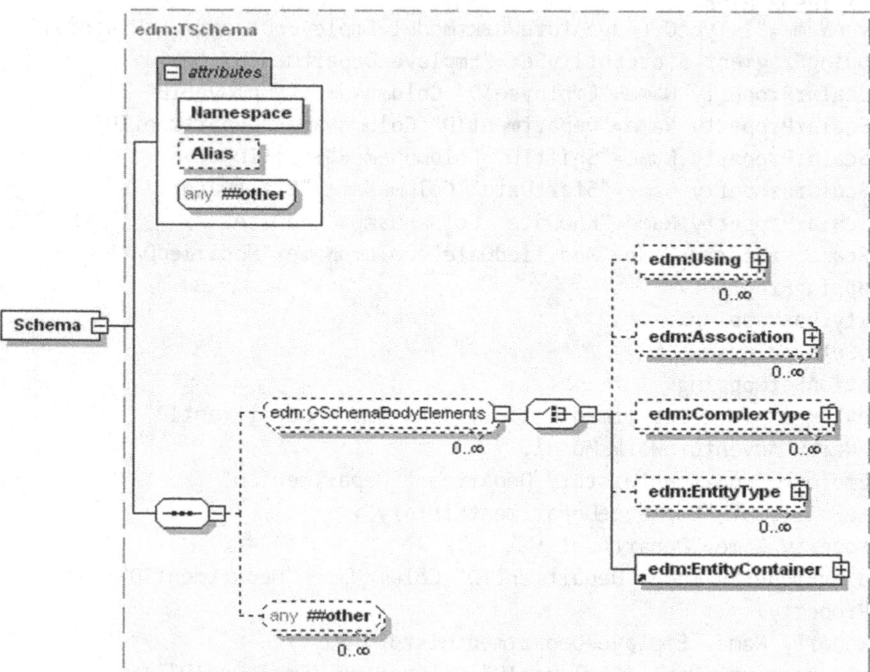

Figure 5-9. *CSDL Schema node*

■ **Note** The `Documentation` node is used when generating classes from your metadata in the XML comment section of your source code. Although this node is not expanded, in Figure 5-10 it contains a `Summary` and `Description` node for your use.

Expanding the tree, you can see the `Using` node and its attributes, as shown in Figure 5-10. The `Using` node is used to provide an alias to shorten the syntax needed to refer to types in another namespace.

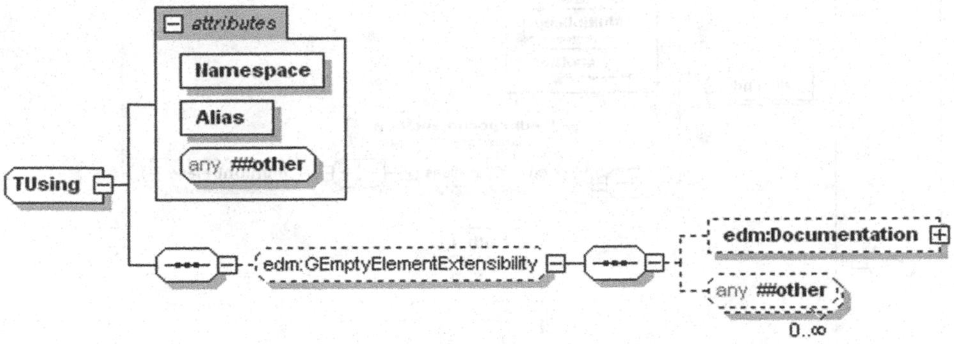

Figure 5-10. *CSDL Using node*

The next node in the hierarchy is `Association`, seen in Figure 5-11. The `Association` node contains the `End` node, which holds the data about the attributes of the association (for example, `Type`, `Role`, `Multiplicity`). Additionally, the `Association` node contains the `ReferentialConstraint` node, which provides the `Principal` and `Dependent` nodes for defining constraints in your model.

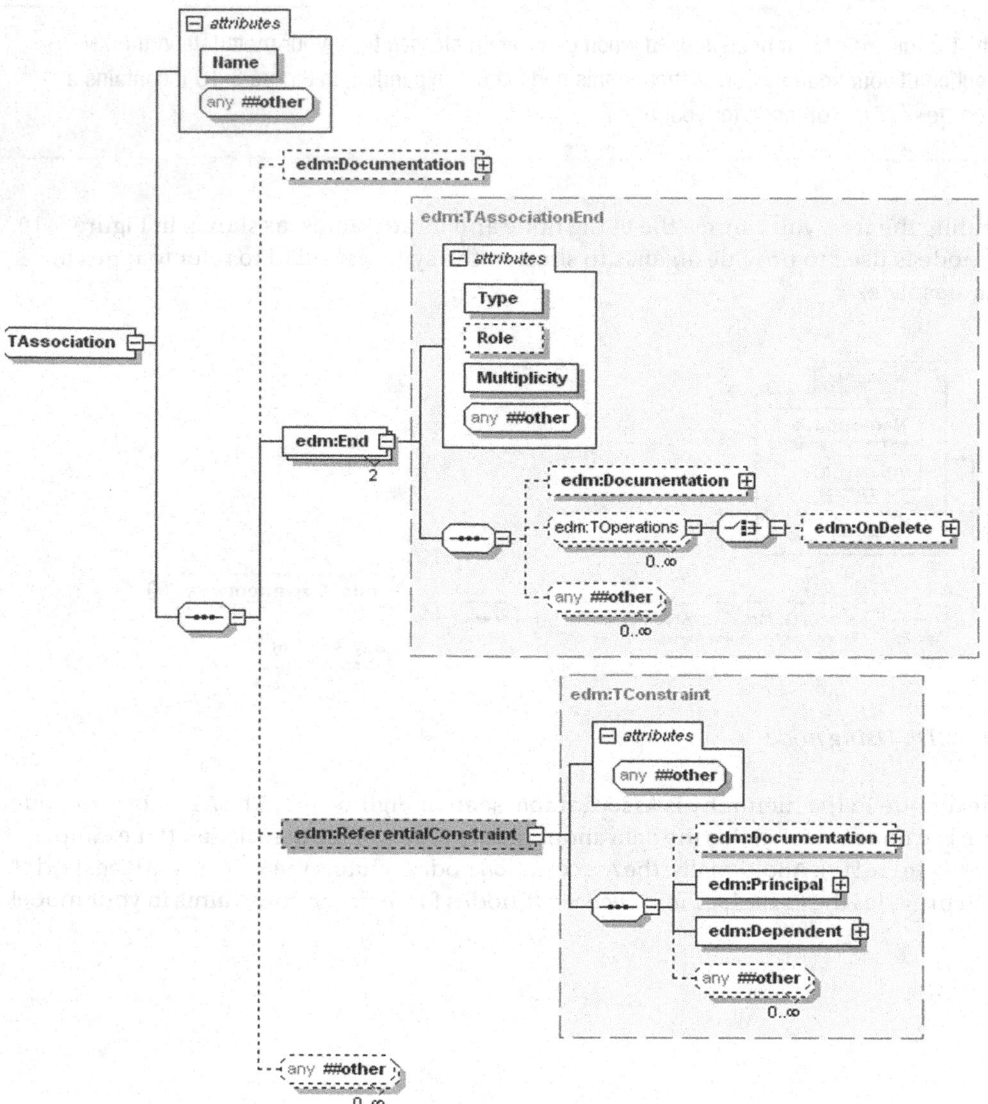

Figure 5-11. *CSDL Association node*

The `ComplexType` node seen in Figure 5-12 contains a `Property` child node for defining properties of `ComplexTypes`. As the name infers, this node is used for defining `Complex` custom types in your model.

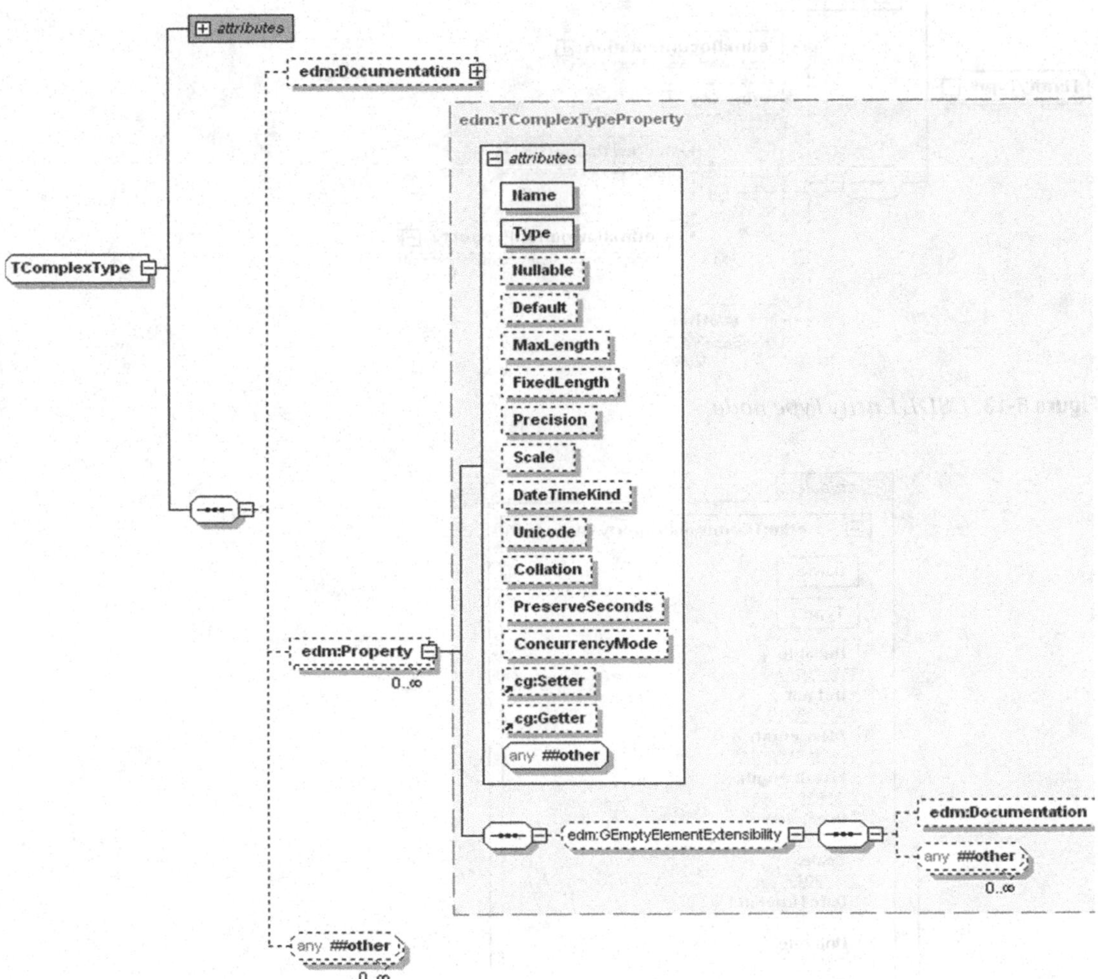

Figure 5-12. *CSDL ComplexType node*

Figure 5-13 shows the `EntityType` node. As you saw in Listing 5-1, the `EntityType` node is used to define entities in your model (for example, `Department`). This node contains three child nodes—`Key`, `Property`, and `NavigationProperty`—all of which are used to describe and define your entities.

Figure 5-14 shows the `Property` node from Figure 5-13 expanded. As you can see, there are a considerable number of attributes to choose from to describe your entities. As an example, we can include the two required attributes `Name` and `Type`, as well as `Nullable`, `Default`, and `MaxLength` as optional attributes.

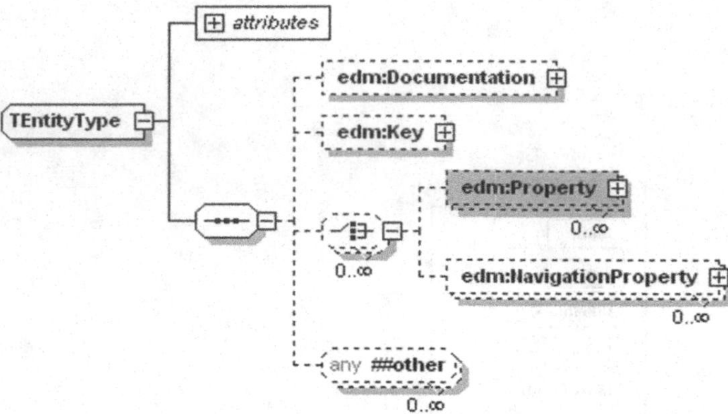

Figure 5-13. *CSDL EntityType node*

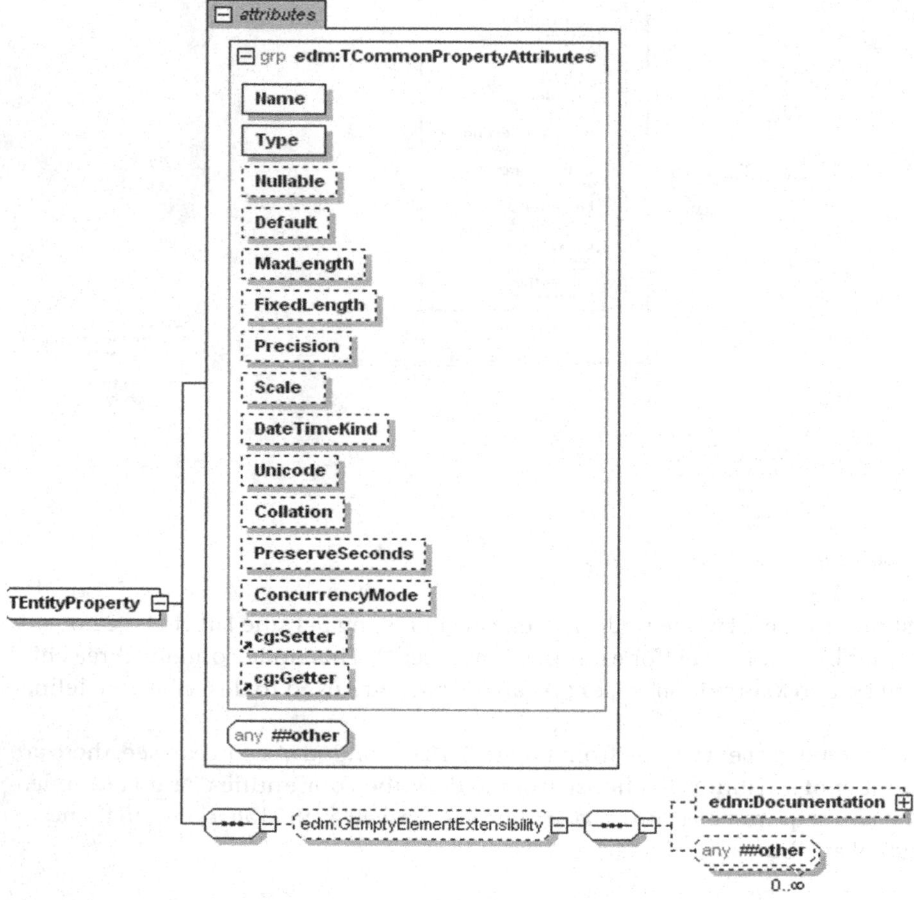

Figure 5-14. *CSDL Property node*

The last node in the hierarchy is the EntityContainer node, shown in Figure 5-15. As you can see, this node is used to hold EntitySet and AssociationSet nodes. As in Listing 5-1, an EntitySet and an AssociationSet are used to hold entities and associations, respectively.

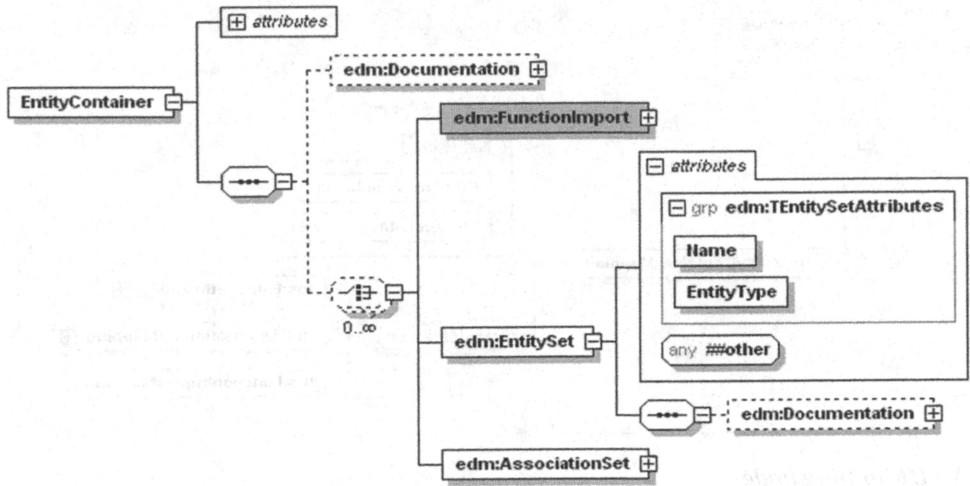

Figure 5-15. *CSDL EntityContainer node*

Although I could easily spend another 20 pages going through all the nodes and attributes in the CSDL schema, I think at this point you should understand your options. Additionally, because the SSDL specification is so similar to the CSDL specification, I am not going to enumerate the SSDL schema. Instead, I want to jump right into the System.Data.Resources.CSMSL.xsd to visually explore the MSL composition.

Figure 5-16 shows the MSL Mapping node. In this diagram, the EntityContainerMapping node is also expanded because the real guts of the MSL start there. The Mapping node does very little other than providing a Space attribute (also known as a namespace) and an Alias node. Alternatively, the EntityContainerMapping node provides the EntitySetMapping node, AssocationSetMapping node, and FunctionImportMapping node. Additionally, the EntityContainerMapping node contains two attributes (CdmEntitycontainer and StorageEntityContainer), which you saw in Listing 5-3, that define the conceptual and storage containers.

Rather than go through each of the child nodes of the EntityContainerMapping nodes, I instead focus on the EntitySetMapping node. The reason for this is that AssocationSetMapping, which is used for mapping association sets, and FunctionImportMapping, which is used for mapping stored procedures (covered in depth in Chapter 6), are similar structurally to EntitySetMapping. After all, the purpose of this exercise isn't to cover every detail of the MSL but, rather, to provide a solid foundation that you can build software applications on.

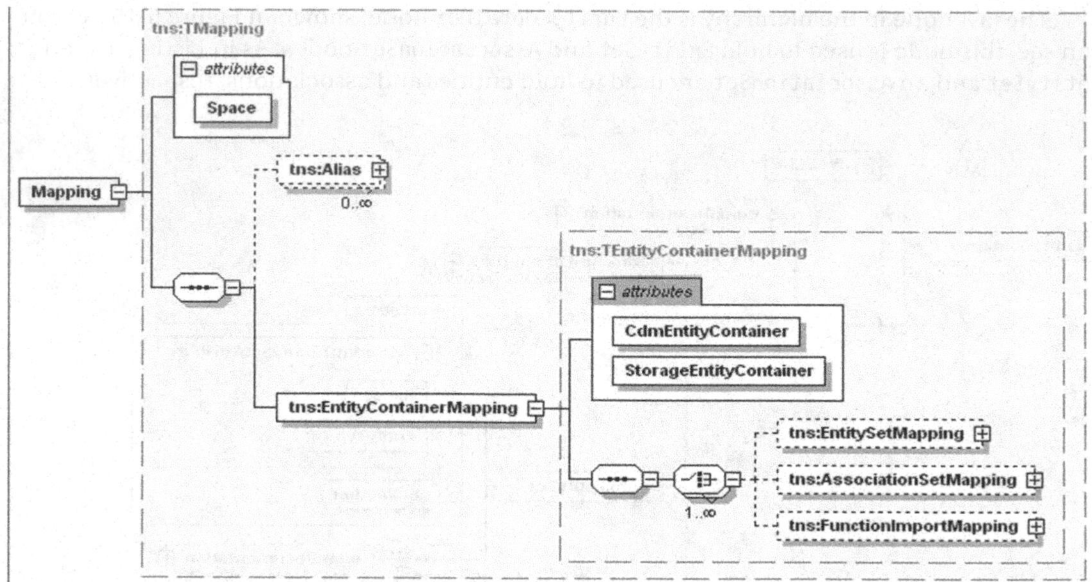

Figure 5-16. *MSL Mapping node*

Figure 5-17 shows the expanded `EntitySetMapping` node. In this example, we have the `Name` attribute, which is required, and the `TypeName` and `StoreEntitySet` optional attributes. Additionally, there are a number of child nodes. First is `QueryView`, which, as you look more at advanced topics in the coming chapters, will make more sense, but for now just know that it is a node that allows you to specify an ESQL view for defining complex logic. The next child is the `EntityTypeMapping` node, which is used just for that, entity type mapping. After that you have the `MappingFragment` node, which specifies the storage information and the conceptual mapping details.

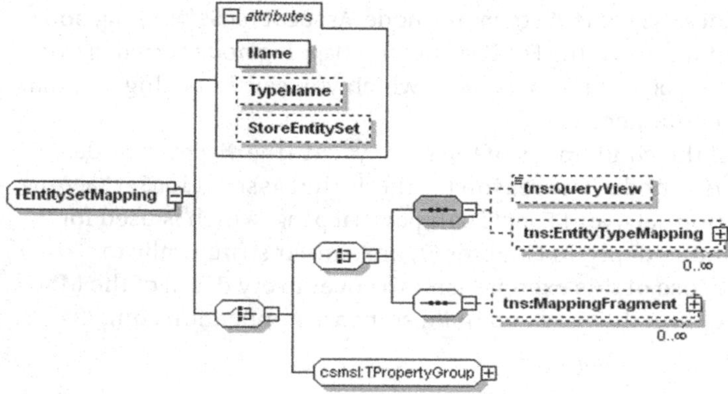

Figure 5-17. *MSL EntitySetMapping node*

In Figure 5-18, you can see that the `EntityTypeMapping` node is expanded to expose a `MappingFragment`. As you saw in Listing 5-3, an `EntityTypeMapping` node contains a `MappingFragment`, which in turn contains a group of properties describing the mapping between the conceptual and storage structures. Additionally, the `EntityTypeMapping` node also contains the `ModificationFunctionMapping` node with details on the functions for mapping your stored procedures.

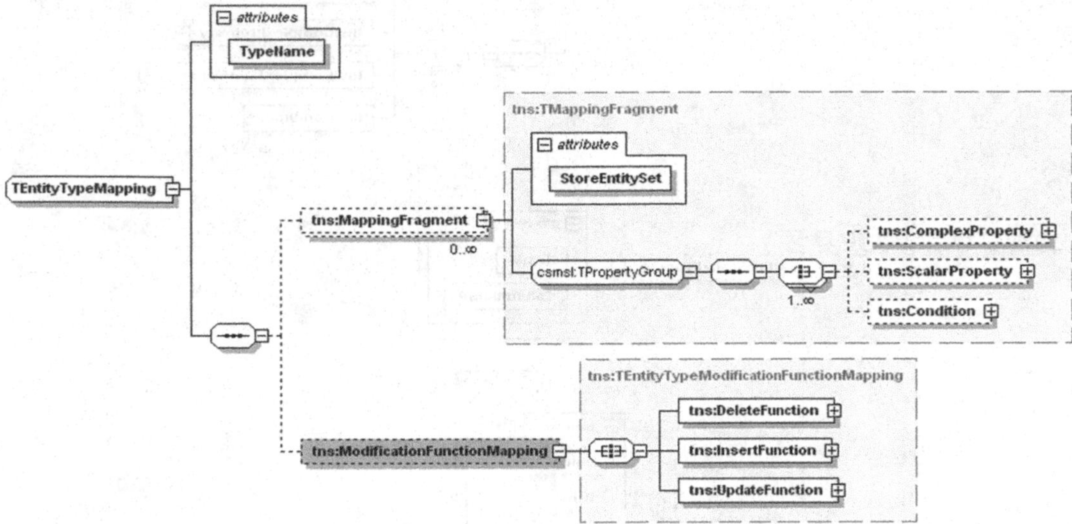

Figure 5-18. *MSL EntityTypeMapping*

The final topic of the MSL schema is the `PropertyGroup` containing the `ComplexProperty`, `ScalarProperty`, and `Condition` nodes. Figure 5-19 shows the expanded `PropertyGroup` used throughout the MSL schema. As you can see, `ComplexProperty` is just that—complex; it provides additional child nodes for defining mapping details, conditions, and types. Alternatively, `ScalarProperty` is very simple because it contains only two attributes (`Name` and `ColumnName`) to define the mapping details between CSDL and SSDL. Finally, the `Condition` node contains attributes for defining a condition in your mapping (for example, `Value`, `Name`, `ColumnName`, `IsNull`).

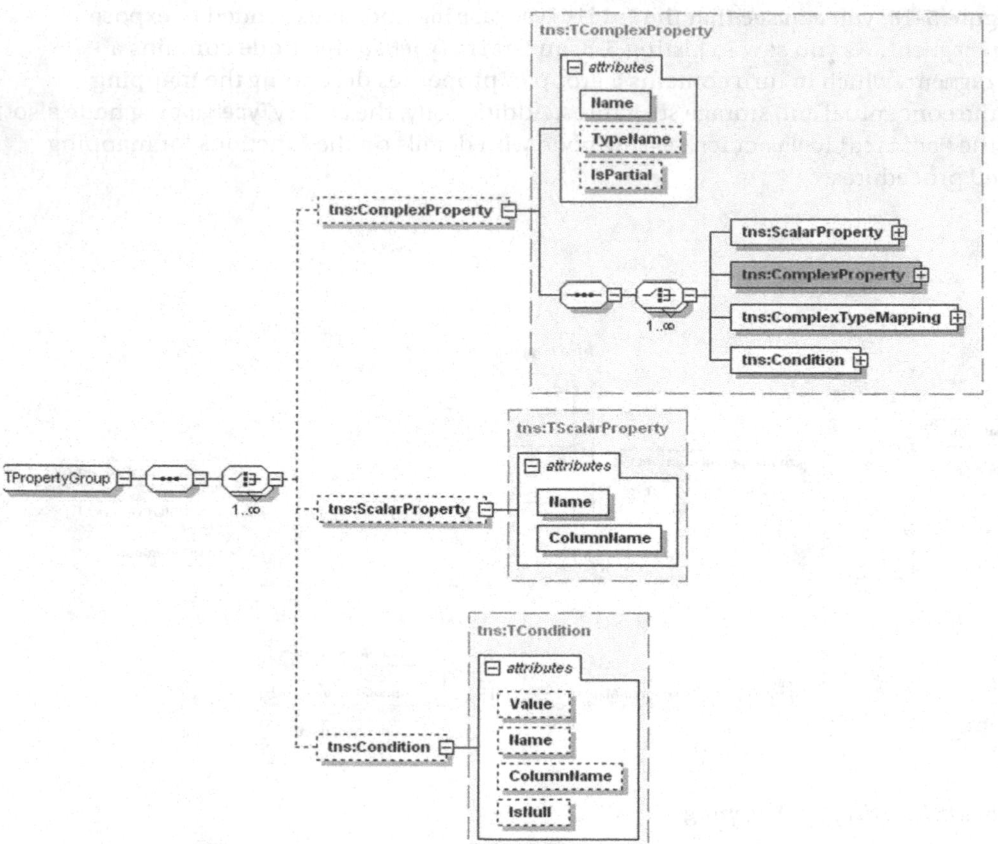

Figure 5-19. *MSL PropertyGroup*

Designer Metadata

You have now seen the basic metadata structure that makes up the EDM, specifically the `.edmx` file, but there is a lot more code generated from the EDM Wizard than this. Let's first take a look at what the designer is doing when you add database objects to the design surface.

Listing 5-4 shows a condensed version of the `AdventureWorks.edmx.designer` file that was created when you added your database objects through the EDM Wizard. I don't want to spend too much time on this because it doesn't have much impact on your application, but for the sake of thoroughness, it's worth taking a quick look.

The `edmx.designer` file generated by EF, like LTS, uses Microsoft's domain-specific language tools (DSL tools) to create the designer. The XML that is generated is pretty self-explanatory: it contains various nodes and attributes with positional and structural information needed by the DSL engine. One item to note about the `edmx.designer` syntax is that the nomenclature is similar to what is seen in the EDM. For example, in the CSDL and SSDL, you have `<EntityType>` nodes; in the MSL, you have `<EntityTypeMapping>` nodes; and in the `edmx.designer`, you have `<entityTypeShape>` nodes. This congruence between the various forms of the EF metadata is a useful troubleshooting tool.

Listing 5-4. *The Designer Metadata Needed for the UI*

```
<?xml version="1.0" encoding="utf-8"?>
<EntityDesignerDiagram dslVersion="1.0.0.0"
  absoluteBounds="0, 0, 11, 8.5" name="AdventureWorks">
  <entityDesignerViewModelMoniker namespace="/AdventureWorksModel" />
  <nestedChildShapes>
    <entityTypeShape Id="eb992da9-9104-494a-bc97-26be5fdaadda"
      absoluteBounds="3, 6.125, 1.5, 1.7566536458333335">
      <entityTypeMoniker name="/AdventureWorksModel/Department" />
      <nestedChildShapes>
        <elementListCompartment Id="23350cf6-0a62-4200-98e3-ec64d03737a7"
          absoluteBounds="3.015, 6.535, 1.4700000000000002,
          0.8648478190104163" name="Properties" titleTextColor="Black"
          itemTextColor="Black" />
        <elementListCompartment Id="b9b3b167-d005-4400-b37f-72a85281c454"
          absoluteBounds="3.015, 7.4098478190104169, 1.4700000000000002,
          0.37180582682291674" name="Navigation" titleTextColor="Black"
          itemTextColor="Black" />
      </nestedChildShapes>
    </entityTypeShape>
    <entityTypeShape Id="ae7646df-df35-477b-8270-637841d854e8"
       absoluteBounds="5.25, 1.875, 1.5, 2.2496956380208335">
       <entityTypeMoniker name="/AdventureWorksModel/EmployeeDepartmentHistory" />
       <nestedChildShapes>
         <elementListCompartment Id="14e7fda7-22a7-4d0e-906e-f04f45330f9d"
           absoluteBounds="5.265, 2.285, 1.4700000000000002, 1.19354248046875"
           name="Properties" titleTextColor="Black" itemTextColor="Black" />
         <elementListCompartment Id="cd519a57-b565-400c-9c70-a1abcf4d07a9"
           absoluteBounds="5.265, 3.48854248046875, 1.4700000000000002,
           0.53615315755208326" name="Navigation" titleTextColor="Black"
           itemTextColor="Black" />
       </nestedChildShapes>
    </entityTypeShape>
    <associationConnector edgePoints="[(4.5 : 7.00332682291667);
        (6 : 7.00332682291667); (6 : 4.12469563802083)]" fixedFrom="Algorithm"
        fixedTo="Algorithm">
        <associationMoniker
          name="/AdventureWorksModel/Department/
          FK_EmployeeDepartmentHistory_Department_DepartmentID" />
        <relativeChildShapes />
        <nodes>
          <entityTypeShapeMoniker Id="eb992da9-9104-494a-bc97-26be5fdaadda" />
          <entityTypeShapeMoniker Id="ae7646df-df35-477b-8270-637841d854e8" />
        </nodes>
    </associationConnector>
  </nestedChildShapes>
</EntityDesignerDiagram>
```

Generated Classes

The last set of code generated by the wizard is the largest set, the classes. Starting with the core of the model is the class that inherits from `System.Data.Objects.ObjectContext`. Listing 5-5 shows the `AdventureWorksEntities` partial class, the context class that you use to manipulate and work with the entities in your model. This example (unlike the previous examples in the chapter) is not condensed because I think it is important for you to see the entire contents of the file so you understand what is being generated.

To start, the `AdventureWorksEntities` class has three constructors. The default constructor obviously accepts zero arguments, but does pass `name=AdventureWorksEntities` and `AdventureWorksEntities` into the base class, `ObjectContext`. The first parameter in this case is the connection string name that exists in your `.config` file, and the second parameter is `defaultContainerName`. The second constructor accepts a single argument, a `connectionString`, and then passes that connection string to the base `ObjectContext` along with the `defaultContainerName` of `AdventureWorksEntities`. The third and final constructor provides a way to pass in an `EntityClient.EntityConnection` object (which is covered in more depth in coming chapters), and then passes that to the `ObjectContext` base along with `defaultContainerName`.

■ **Note** The C# code generated by the EDM Wizard uses the global namespace alias qualifier to ensure the least number of namespace conflicts.

After the constructors, the next functionality you see in the `AdventureWorksEntities` class is each of your entities (`Department`, `EmployeeDepartmentHistory`, `Employee`, and `Contact`) being exposed as a `Get` property that returns `System.Data.ObjectQuery<TEntity>`. You will look at and work with the `ObjectQuery` class later in this chapter, but, to give you an idea, this class is used to represent a query against a data store.

Finally, after the `Get` properties, you have `Adds` for each of your entities. For the `Add` functionality, there are four separate methods that accept your entity types (`Department`, `Employee`, and so forth). Each of these `Add` methods calls `base.AddObject` on the `ObjectContext` to add the entity to the `ObjectContext` by passing in the name of the `EntitySet` and the entity object.

Listing 5-5. *Generated ObjectContext for AdventureWorks*

```
/// <summary>
/// There are no comments for AdventureWorksEntities in the schema.
/// NOTE: Comments for all public generated code can be changed by modifying the
/// "Documentation" property in the EF designer
/// </summary>
public partial class AdventureWorksEntities :
global::System.Data.Objects.ObjectContext
{
        /// <summary>
        /// Initializes a new AdventureWorksEntities object using the connection
        /// string found in the 'AdventureWorksEntities' section of the application
        /// configuration file.
```

```
/// </summary>
public AdventureWorksEntities() :
        base("name=AdventureWorksEntities", "AdventureWorksEntities")
{}

/// <summary>
/// Initialize a new AdventureWorksEntities object.
/// </summary>
public AdventureWorksEntities(string connectionString) :
        base(connectionString, "AdventureWorksEntities")
{}

/// <summary>
/// Initialize a new AdventureWorksEntities object.
/// </summary>
public AdventureWorksEntities
    (global::System.Data.EntityClient.EntityConnection connection) :
        base(connection, "AdventureWorksEntities")
{}

[global::System.ComponentModel.BrowsableAttribute(false)]
public global::System.Data.Objects.ObjectQuery<Department> Department
{
    get
    {
        if ((this._Department == null))
        {
            this._Department = base.CreateQuery<Department>("[Department]");
        }
        return this._Department;
    }
}

private global::System.Data.Objects.ObjectQuery<Department>
    _Department = null;

[global::System.ComponentModel.BrowsableAttribute(false)]
public global::System.Data.Objects.ObjectQuery<Employee> Employee
{
    get
    {
        if ((this._Employee == null))
        {
            this._Employee = base.CreateQuery<Employee>("[Employee]");
        }
        return this._Employee;
    }
}
```

```
private global::System.Data.Objects.ObjectQuery<Employee> _Employee = null;

[global::System.ComponentModel.BrowsableAttribute(false)]
public global::System.Data.Objects.ObjectQuery
    <EmployeeDepartmentHistory> EmployeeDepartmentHistory
{
    get
    {
        if ((this._EmployeeDepartmentHistory == null))
        {
            this._EmployeeDepartmentHistory =
                base.CreateQuery<EmployeeDepartmentHistory>
                ("[EmployeeDepartmentHistory]");
        }
        return this._EmployeeDepartmentHistory;
    }
}

private global::System.Data.Objects.ObjectQuery
    <EmployeeDepartmentHistory> _EmployeeDepartmentHistory = null;

[global::System.ComponentModel.BrowsableAttribute(false)]
public global::System.Data.Objects.ObjectQuery<Contact> Contact
{
    get
    {
        if ((this._Contact == null))
        {
            this._Contact = base.CreateQuery<Contact>("[Contact]");
        }
        return this._Contact;
    }
}

private global::System.Data.Objects.ObjectQuery<Contact> _Contact = null;

public void AddToDepartment(Department department)
{
    base.AddObject("Department", department);
}

/// <summary>
/// There are no comments for Employee in the schema.
/// </summary>
public void AddToEmployee(Employee employee)
```

```
    {
        base.AddObject("Employee", employee);
    }

    public void AddToEmployeeDepartmentHistory
        (EmployeeDepartmentHistory employeeDepartmentHistory)
    {
        base.AddObject("EmployeeDepartmentHistory", employeeDepartmentHistory);
    }

    public void AddToContact(Contact contact)
    {
        base.AddObject("Contact", contact);
    }
}
```

Note `System.Data.ObjectQuery<TEntity>` can be formulated through an ESQL statement, a Query Builder method, or LINQ.

After `ObjectContext`, you have only entity code left to examine to complete the examination of the code that is generated by the EDM Wizard. There is no reason to look at all the entities that are generated because the structure is identical for each of them. Instead, let's just look at the `Department` class.

Listing 5-6 shows the `Department` partial class. As with all the generated entities, they are automatically set with attributes that specify to EF their namespace and entity set name. Additionally, all entities are marked as `serializable` and are defined with a data contract for serialization.

The entities in your model all contain a static `Create` method that returns a new type of entity. In Listing 5-6, you can see the `CreateDepartment` static method, which accepts the values of the `Department` properties and returns a new `Department` class.

Listing 5-6. *The Department Entity Class*

```
[global::System.Data.Objects.DataClasses.EdmEntityTypeAttribute
    (NamespaceName="AdventureWorksModel", Name="Department")]
[global::System.Runtime.Serialization.DataContractAttribute()]
[global::System.Serializable()]
public partial class Department :
global::System.Data.Objects.DataClasses.EntityObject
{
        /// <summary>
        /// Create a new Department object.
        /// </summary>
        /// <param name="departmentID">Initial value of DepartmentID.</param>
```

```
/// <param name="name">Initial value of Name.</param>
/// <param name="groupName">Initial value of GroupName.</param>
/// <param name="modifiedDate">Initial value of ModifiedDate.</param>
public static Department CreateDepartment
   (short departmentID, string name, string groupName,
   global::System.DateTime modifiedDate)
{
    Department department = new Department();
    department.DepartmentID = departmentID;
    department.Name = name;
    department.GroupName = groupName;
    department.ModifiedDate = modifiedDate;
    return department;
}

[global::System.Data.Objects.DataClasses.EdmScalarPropertyAttribute
    (EntityKeyProperty=true, IsNullable=false)]
[global::System.Runtime.Serialization.DataMemberAttribute()]
public short DepartmentID
{
    get
    {
        return this._DepartmentID;
    }
    set
    {
        this.ReportPropertyChanging("DepartmentID");
        this._DepartmentID = global::System.Data.Objects.DataClasses.
             StructuralObject.SetValidValue(value);
        this.ReportPropertyChanged("DepartmentID");
    }
}

private short _DepartmentID;

[global::System.Data.Objects.DataClasses.EdmScalarPropertyAttribute
     (IsNullable=false)]
[global::System.Runtime.Serialization.DataMemberAttribute()]
public string Name
{
    get
    {
        return this._Name;
    }
```

```
        set
        {
            this.ReportPropertyChanging("Name");
            this._Name = global::System.Data.Objects.DataClasses.
                StructuralObject.SetValidValue(value, false, 50);
            this.ReportPropertyChanged("Name");
        }
    }

    private string _Name;

    [global::System.Data.Objects.DataClasses.
        EdmScalarPropertyAttribute(IsNullable=false)]
    [global::System.Runtime.Serialization.DataMemberAttribute()]
    public global::System.DateTime ModifiedDate
    {
        get
        {
            return this._ModifiedDate;
        }
        set
        {
            this.ReportPropertyChanging("ModifiedDate");
            this._ModifiedDate = global::System.Data.Objects.DataClasses.
                StructuralObject.SetValidValue(value,
                global::System.DateTimeKind.Unspecified, true);
            this.ReportPropertyChanged("ModifiedDate");
        }
    }

    private global::System.DateTime _ModifiedDate;

    [global::System.Data.Objects.DataClasses.
        EdmRelationshipNavigationPropertyAttribute("AdventureWorksModel",
        "FK_EmployeeDepartmentHistory_Department_DepartmentID",
        "EmployeeDepartmentHistory")]
    [global::System.Xml.Serialization.XmlIgnoreAttribute()]
    [global::System.Xml.Serialization.SoapIgnoreAttribute()]
    [global::System.ComponentModel.BrowsableAttribute(false)]
    public global::System.Data.Objects.DataClasses.EntityCollection
        <EmployeeDepartmentHistory> EmployeeDepartmentHistory
    {
        get
        {
            return
```

```
                ((global::System.Data.Objects.DataClasses.IEntityWithRelationships)

                 (this)).RelationshipManager.GetRelatedCollection
                 <EmployeeDepartmentHistory>("AdventureWorksModel.
                 FK_EmployeeDepartmentHistory_Department_DepartmentID",
                 "EmployeeDepartmentHistory");
            }
        }
    }
```

Each of the properties in the class is a standard .NET get/set property, but all of them also contain attributes to specify details about the field (for example, `EntityKeyProperty` and `IsNullable`) and contain serialization attributes that mark them as `DataMemberAttributes`. Additionally, the set portion of the properties contains some tracking calls that the engine needs to monitor whether a field is "dirty." These calls use the abstract base class `EntityObject` to call `ReportPropertyChanging` and `ReportPropertyChanged`.

■ **Note** For the sake of brevity, not all the generated properties for the `Department` class are shown in Listing 5-6. However, all the properties follow the same get/set pattern where `StructuralObject.SetValidValue` is executed.

In addition to the properties that expose direct fields on the entity, you also have a get property that exposes an `EntityCollection<EmployeeDepartmentHistory>` `EmployeeDepartmentHistory`. This, as you've probably guessed, is the association between `Department` and `EmployeeDepartmentHistory`, stating that a `Department` can be associated with multiple `EmployeeDepartmentHistory` entities. With this property, you have three "ignore" attributes to tell the compiler that the property is not `serializable` or browsable. Additionally, this property is using the `RelationshipManager.GetRelatedCollection` method, part of the `System.Data.Object.DataClasses` namespace and also part of object services, which is discussed in more depth in Chapter 6.

Using EDMGen

Along with the robust designer tools that integrate directly into the Visual Studio IDE, you also have the option of using the command-line tool, EdmGen (`EdmGen.exe`) to create your EDM metadata. The EdmGen tool can be used for the following EF tasks:

- Generating CSDL, SSDL, and MSL files from a data source or from one another
- Generating source code files from metadata (that is, CSDL, SSDL, MSL) or from a data source
- Validating an existing EDM
- Generating mapping views from SSDL, CSDL, or MSL data

Table 5-1 enumerates all the command-line options that you have with EdmGen. To use this tool, you must always supply one of the "mode" options seen in Table 5-1 and then any of the other flags that are needed.

Table 5-1. *EdmGen.exe Command-Line Options*

Flag	Description
`/mode:EntityClassGeneration`	Generates objects from a CSDL file
`/mode:FromSsdlGeneration`	Generates MSL, CSDL, and objects from an SSDL file
`/mode:ValidateArtifacts`	Validates the SSDL, MSL, and CSDL files
`/mode:ViewGeneration`	Generates mapping views from SSDL, MSL, and CSDL files
`/mode:FullGeneration`	Generates SSDL, MSL, CSDL, and objects from the database
`/project:<string>`	The base name to be used for all the artifact files (short form: `/p`)
`/provider:<string>`	The name of the ADO.NET data provider to be used for SSDL generation (shortform: `/prov`)
`/connectionstring:<connection string>`	The connection string to the database that you would like to connect to (shortform: `/c`)
`/incsdl:<file>`	The file from which the conceptual model is read
`/refcsdl:<file>`	A CSDL file containing the types that the `/incsdl` file is dependent on
`/inmsl:<file>`	The file from which to read the mapping
`/inssdl:<file>`	The file from which to read the storage model
`/outcsdl:<file>`	The file to which the generated conceptual model is written
`/outmsl:<file>`	The file to which the generated mapping is written
`/outssdl:<file>`	The file to which the generated storage model is written
`/outobjectlayer:<file>`	The file to which the generated object layer is written
`/outviews:<file>`	The file to which the pregenerated view objects are written
`/language:CSharp`	Generates code using the C# language
`/language:VB`	Generates code using the VB language
`/namespace:<string>`	The namespace name to use for the conceptual model types
`/entitycontainer:<string>`	The name to use for the `EntityContainer` in the conceptual model

Table 5-1. *EdmGen.exe Command-Line Options (Continued)*

Flag	Description
`/help`	Displays the usage message (short form: `/?`)
`/nologo`	Suppresses the copyright message

Note EdmGen is installed with EF in your .NET Framework directory, which is typically installed in `C:\Windows\Microsoft.NET\Framework\v3.5`.

Although Table 5-1 is quite self-explanatory and the use of EdmGen is straightforward, let's take a look at a few examples that you could use to work with EdmGen. Listing 5-7 shows three examples using EdmGen. The first example shows the syntax for generating a complete EDM from the `AdventureWorks` database. In this example, EdmGen will create the CSDL, SSDL, MSL, object, and source code for all tables in the `AdventureWorks` database. The second example generates the entire EDM, but starts with an SSDL file instead of a database. The third and final example validates the EDM metadata.

Listing 5-7. *Example EdmGen.exe Syntax*

```
EdmGen.exe /mode:FullGeneration /project:AdventureWorks
    /provider:System.Data.SqlClient
    /connectionstring:"server=.\sqlexpress;integrated
    security=true;database=AdventureWorks"

EdmGen.exe /mode:FromSSDLGeneration /inssdl:AdventureWorks.ssdl
    /project:AdventureWorks

EdmGen.exe /mode:ValidateArtifacts /inssdl:AdventureWorks.ssdl
    /inmsl:AdventureWorks.msl
    /incsdl:AdventureWorks.csdl
```

Note The `/project:` flag used in Listing 5-7 tells EdmGen to assign that value/namespace to the generated code and filenames.

Summary

In this chapter, you were introduced to EF and learned about the native EF tools. The heart of EF is the EDM, which consists of the conceptual, logical, and mapping structures. Out of the box, each of these structures is separated into XML files that can be built by using the wizard, by using EdmGen, or by hand-coding them.

The toolset provided with EF is remarkably robust. You have the option of using the EF designer, which is integrated directly into the Visual Studio 2008 IDE to manipulate and work with the EDM and your object model. Additionally, you also have the option to use the command-line tool, EdmGen, to generate or validate the metadata and source code in your model.

In the next chapter, you will write some code. You will take the basic EDM model that you created in this chapter and use LINQ to Entities to work with the model. Additionally, you will explore the various CRUD options that you have in EF and will begin examining the EF API.

CHAPTER 6

Using the ADO.NET Entity Framework

Chapter 5 introduced you to the Entity Framework (EF) and the toolset that comes with it. In this chapter, you will broaden your knowledge of EF by writing some code to use EF as an ORM. To increase your knowledge of EF, you will be working on independent examples that relate back to the HR structure in the `AdventureWorks` database. Because the ultimate goal is to build a data-centric application, this chapter begins to introduce you to the CRUD functionality in EF as well as lay the foundation for the more advanced discussions in the coming chapters.

When working with the EDM, you have two APIs at your disposal: Object Services and the entity client. The entity client is a lower-level .NET data provider, which provides a mechanism for interacting directly with your conceptual model by using the new query language, Entity SQL (ESQL). The Object Services API is principally built on top of the entity client provider and provides the functionality to query in ESQL along with LINQ to Entities (that is, object queries). As the title of this book infers, the focus of this text is primarily on Object Services and LINQ to Entities; however, because ESQL is a critical part of EF, it is explored in Chapter 7.

Object Services: LINQ to Entities

Object Services is one of two APIs in EF. Object Services enables you to execute CRUD operations with strongly typed objects and entity types. Object Services supports two execution models against the EDM: LINQ (specifically LINQ to Entities) and Entity SQL. This section covers the application of LINQ to Entities in EF.

When looking at the usage of LINQ with EF, it is important that you first understand the `ObjectContext` class. In Chapter 5, you examined the `AdventureWorksEntities` class generated by EF. The `AdventureWorksEntities` class is an example of a class that extends the `ObjectContext` class. According to MSDN, the purpose of the `ObjectContext` class is for "interacting with data in the form of objects that are instances of entity types defined in an EDM" (`http://msdn2.microsoft.com/en-us/library/system.data.objects.objectcontext.aspx`). This quote just about sums it up—but to restate, the `ObjectContext` class is the conduit for interacting with the objects that are a representation of your database. This class also has the following functionality:

- A database connection that is an `EntityConnection` object
- Object model metadata that is stored in the `MetadataWorkspace` object
- State management and object tracking, controlled by `ObjectStateManager`

Querying

It is impossible to build a data-centric application if you can't retrieve data. In the preceding chapter, you built out a simple EDM with four tables and let EF generate the code associated with those structures. You also created a Windows Forms application to use as a test harness.

Let's start by writing a simple query with the EDM that you generated in Chapter 5. Listing 6-1 provides a simple example using LINQ to Entities to retrieve all the `EmployeeIDs` in the `EmployeeDepartmentHistory` table. As you can see, the C# code is easy to understand because it is formed like a standard LINQ query. In this example, you have a new `AdventureWorksEntities` class, a LINQ select against the `EmployeeDepartmentHistory` entity, and finally a loop that iterates through the results, pulling the `EmployeeIDs`.

■ Note The generated SQL seen in this chapter's examples was captured by using SQL Profiler.

Immediately following the C# example (in Listing 6-1), you can see the SQL generated by the query. Clearly, the SQL generated from EF is more complex than what you would typically write in this situation. The reason for this is that EF (and really, ADO.NET under the covers) is using an algorithm for creating canonical query trees (CQTs). I am not going to go into too much detail about CQTs because that is another book; however, it is important for you to understand that the CQTs generated by EF are highly optimized to run at peak efficiency. To create a provider-neutral mechanism for communicating with any data store, and to be able to ensure performance in both simple and complex situations, CQTs are the means to the end.

Listing 6-1. *Simple Query Using EF*

```
// C# Example

using(AdventureWorksEntities aw = new AdventureWorksEntities())
{

    var departmentHistories = from dep in aw.EmployeeDepartmentHistory
                              select dep;

    foreach (var edh in departmentHistories)
    {
        Debug.Print(edh.EmployeeID.ToString());

    }
}
```

```
-- SQL Generated from EF
SELECT
1 AS [C1],
[Extent1].[EmployeeID] AS [EmployeeID],
[Extent1].[DepartmentID] AS [DepartmentID],
[Extent1].[ShiftID] AS [ShiftID],
[Extent1].[StartDate] AS [StartDate],
[Extent1].[EndDate] AS [EndDate],
[Extent1].[ModifiedDate] AS [ModifiedDate]
FROM [HumanResources].[EmployeeDepartmentHistory] AS [Extent1]
```

■ **Tip** Use the `using` keyword when creating your `ObjectContext` (see Listing 6-1) to ensure that appropriate cleanup of connections occurs.

In Listing 6-1, you used `var` as the return value and for the iteration over the return value. What type is returned here? The type returned is actually your standard `System.Linq.IQueryable<T>` interface, and in this case `T` is your `EmployeeDepartmentHistory` entity.

Another important facet regarding the query in Listing 6-1 is the `ObjectQuery` class, the type that is returned from the `aw.EmployeeDepartmentHistory` call. The `ObjectQuery` class is a generic class that is part of `System.Data.Objects`. The purpose of the `ObjectQuery` class is to return collections of typed entities. Because `ObjectQuery` is associated with your `ObjectContext`, it has the metadata and connection information needed to translate your LINQ query into T-SQL.

Because the type returned from LINQ is an `IQueryable` interface, and the `ObjectQuery` type is used in the query, you can rewrite your query as seen in Listing 6-2. In this example, you are strongly typing the `ObjectQuery` and the LINQ query results. The reason to be explicit with the types is the same reason that you strongly type variables in the world of software development: to make it easier to understand and gain a negligible performance increase. I'm an advocate of Listing 6-2 over 6-1 because I believe that it is more intuitive and easier to understand; however, the SQL code in Listing 6-2 is identical to the SQL code in Listing 6-1. Thus, this type of formatting really becomes a philosophical debate more than a debate about patterns or anti-patterns because the performance increase with Listing 6-2, if any, is truly negligible.

Listing 6-2. *Another Way to Query Using EF*

```
// C# Example

using(AdventureWorksEntities aw = new AdventureWorksEntities())
{


    ObjectQuery<EmployeeDepartmentHistory> edh = aw.EmployeeDepartmentHistory;


    IQueryable<EmployeeDepartmentHistory> edhQuery = from d in edh
                                                     select d;
```

```
    IEnumerable<EmployeeDepartmentHistory> edhList = edhQuery.ToList();

    foreach (EmployeeDepartmentHistory f in edhList)
    {
        Debug.Print(f.EmployeeID.ToString());
    }
}

-- SQL Generated from EF

SELECT
1 AS [C1],
[Extent1].[EmployeeID] AS [EmployeeID],
[Extent1].[DepartmentID] AS [DepartmentID],
[Extent1].[ShiftID] AS [ShiftID],
[Extent1].[StartDate] AS [StartDate],
[Extent1].[EndDate] AS [EndDate],
[Extent1].[ModifiedDate] AS [ModifiedDate]
FROM [HumanResources].[EmployeeDepartmentHistory] AS [Extent1]
```

Listings 6-1 and 6-2 provide simple examples of querying against the EmployeeDepartmentHistory entity, but what if you want to access an association entity (that is, a navigation property)? Listing 6-3 shows the same query as Listing 6-1, but instead of retrieving the EmployeeID, it uses the dot operator to retrieve the EmailAddress property as part of the Contact class. Unfortunately, following this example results in a NullReferenceException—specifically, "Object reference not set to an instance of an object."

The reason for the error when running the code in Listing 6-3 is that only objects that are explicitly requested in your query are returned. This is true regardless of the relationship between the entities—for example, the relationship between EmployeeDepartmentHistory and Employee. Although this behavior may initially seem counterintuitive, it is actually a common pattern with ORMs. The reason for this behavior comes down to EFs needing to be aware of the scope of both the query and the data that is returned (that is, object tracking).

Listing 6-3. *Invalid Query with Association*

```
using(AdventureWorksEntities aw = new AdventureWorksEntities())
{

    var departmentHistories = from dep in aw.EmployeeDepartmentHistory
                              select dep;

    foreach (var edh in departmentHistories)
    {
        Debug.Print(edh.Employee.Contact.EmailAddress);

    }
}
```

You have two options to enable your query to load association objects. You can specify a query path or instead explicitly load related objects. In both cases, you need to weigh your options because there is a trade-off between a chatty interface and retrieving large amounts of data in a single query. The first option, to specify a query path, is used to predefine the object graph returned by your query. This provides a mechanism for retrieving all your objects in a single SQL query. The second option, using explicit loads, creates multiple SQL queries and round-trips to the database to populate your entities.

Listing 6-4 shows a query path that loads the `Employee` entity. As you can see, you use the `Include` keyword to extend your entity (`EmployeeDepartmentHistory.Include`). All you have to do is pass the name of the association entity, as a string, that you want included in the query. In addition to the C# code in Listing 6-4, you also have the SQL generated by EF. Here, EF generates a monster SQL query, but as previously mentioned, this pattern is to account for both simple and more complex scenarios.

Listing 6-4. *Query with Association Using Query Path*

```
//C# Example

using(AdventureWorksEntities aw = new AdventureWorksEntities())
{
    IQueryable<EmployeeDepartmentHistory> departmentHistories =
                from dep in aw.EmployeeDepartmentHistory.Include("Employee")
                select dep;

    foreach (EmployeeDepartmentHistory edh in departmentHistories)
    {
        Debug.Print(edh.Employee.BirthDate.ToString());

    }
}

-- SQL Generated from EF

SELECT
1 AS [C1],
[Extent1].[EmployeeID] AS [EmployeeID],
[Extent1].[DepartmentID] AS [DepartmentID],
[Extent1].[ShiftID] AS [ShiftID],
[Extent1].[StartDate] AS [StartDate],
[Extent1].[EndDate] AS [EndDate],
[Extent1].[ModifiedDate] AS [ModifiedDate],
1 AS [C2],
[Extent2].[EmployeeID] AS [EmployeeID1],
[Extent2].[NationalIDNumber] AS [NationalIDNumber],
[Extent2].[LoginID] AS [LoginID],
[Extent2].[Title] AS [Title],
```

```
[Extent2].[BirthDate] AS [BirthDate],
[Extent2].[MaritalStatus] AS [MaritalStatus],
[Extent2].[Gender] AS [Gender],
[Extent2].[HireDate] AS [HireDate],
[Extent2].[SalariedFlag] AS [SalariedFlag],
[Extent2].[VacationHours] AS [VacationHours],
[Extent2].[SickLeaveHours] AS [SickLeaveHours],
[Extent2].[CurrentFlag] AS [CurrentFlag],
[Extent2].[rowguid] AS [rowguid],
[Extent2].[ModifiedDate] AS [ModifiedDate1],
[Extent2].[ContactID] AS [ContactID],
[Extent2].[ManagerID] AS [ManagerID]
FROM  [HumanResources].[EmployeeDepartmentHistory] AS [Extent1]
LEFT OUTER JOIN [HumanResources].[Employee] AS [Extent2]
ON [Extent1].[EmployeeID] = [Extent2].[EmployeeID]
```

Listing 6-4 includes the Employee entity in the query, but the Employee entity is only the first level in the hierarchy. What if you want to include the Contact entity? Fortunately, it is equally easy. Listing 6-5 shows the syntax for including the Contact entity in the query. In this example, all you need to do is pass in the Employee.Contact string into the Include method. This tells EF to include both the Employee and Contact entities in the query that is generated. Along with the C# code, you also have the SQL code that is being executed to eager-load both of these entities. Again, the SQL code is complicated but is structurally what you would expect to see in most applied scenarios (that is, table joins).

Listing 6-5. *Query with Association Using Multilayer Query Path*

```
//C# Example

using(AdventureWorksEntities aw = new AdventureWorksEntities())
{

    IQueryable<EmployeeDepartmentHistory> departmentHistories =
                from dep in
                aw.EmployeeDepartmentHistory.Include("Employee.Contact")
                select dep;

    foreach (EmployeeDepartmentHistory edh in departmentHistories)
    {
        Debug.Print(edh.Employee.Contact.EmailAddress);

    }
}

-- SQL Generated from EF
```

```
SELECT
1 AS [C1],
[Extent1].[EmployeeID] AS [EmployeeID],
[Extent1].[DepartmentID] AS [DepartmentID],
[Extent1].[ShiftID] AS [ShiftID],
[Extent1].[StartDate] AS [StartDate],
[Extent1].[EndDate] AS [EndDate],
[Extent1].[ModifiedDate] AS [ModifiedDate],
1 AS [C2],
[Extent2].[EmployeeID] AS [EmployeeID1],
[Extent2].[NationalIDNumber] AS [NationalIDNumber],
[Extent2].[LoginID] AS [LoginID],
[Extent2].[Title] AS [Title],
[Extent2].[BirthDate] AS [BirthDate],
[Extent2].[MaritalStatus] AS [MaritalStatus],
[Extent2].[Gender] AS [Gender],
[Extent2].[HireDate] AS [HireDate],
[Extent2].[SalariedFlag] AS [SalariedFlag],
[Extent2].[VacationHours] AS [VacationHours],
[Extent2].[SickLeaveHours] AS [SickLeaveHours],
[Extent2].[CurrentFlag] AS [CurrentFlag],
[Extent2].[rowguid] AS [rowguid],
[Extent2].[ModifiedDate] AS [ModifiedDate1],
[Extent3].[ContactID] AS [ContactID],
[Extent3].[NameStyle] AS [NameStyle],
[Extent3].[Title] AS [Title1],
[Extent3].[FirstName] AS [FirstName],
[Extent3].[MiddleName] AS [MiddleName],
[Extent3].[LastName] AS [LastName],
[Extent3].[Suffix] AS [Suffix],
[Extent3].[EmailAddress] AS [EmailAddress],
[Extent3].[EmailPromotion] AS [EmailPromotion],
[Extent3].[Phone] AS [Phone],
[Extent3].[PasswordHash] AS [PasswordHash],
[Extent3].[PasswordSalt] AS [PasswordSalt],
[Extent3].[AdditionalContactInfo] AS [AdditionalContactInfo],
[Extent3].[rowguid] AS [rowguid1],
[Extent3].[ModifiedDate] AS [ModifiedDate2],
[Extent2].[ManagerID] AS [ManagerID]
FROM   [HumanResources].[EmployeeDepartmentHistory] AS [Extent1]
LEFT OUTER JOIN [HumanResources].[Employee] AS [Extent2]
 ON [Extent1].[EmployeeID] = [Extent2].[EmployeeID]
LEFT OUTER JOIN [Person].[Contact] AS [Extent3]
 ON [Extent2].[ContactID] = [Extent3].[ContactID]
```

As I mentioned earlier, there are two techniques for specifying the span of the entities that get loaded. You have seen the first technique, using a query path; now let's take a look at the second technique.

Listing 6-6 explicitly loads the `EmployeeDepartmentHistory` with the `Employee` entity. In this example, you first use the `ObjectQuery` class to load the `Employee` entity. Next you create a `foreach` loop to iterate over the employees, and explicitly call `Load()` during each iteration. Finally, you retrieve the `DepartmentID`, a property on the `EmployeeDepartmentHistory` entity. The `Load` method, which is part of the `EntityCollection` class, is explicitly loading the related object data into your `ObjectContext`.

Listing 6-6 also shows the SQL that is generated from the C# query. The first query in this listing is the `SELECT` to retrieve the `Employee` data. The second query is the `SELECT` to retrieve the `EmployeeDepartmentHistory` data. The query to retrieve the `EmployeeDepartmentHistory` data is executed during every iteration of the `foreach` loop. Obviously, Listing 6-6 shows only two of the queries, but the SQL is basically the same on each iteration, with only the `EntityKeyValue` parameter changing.

■ **Note** To use the `Load()` method in a `foreach` loop, you must specify `multipleactiveresultsets=true` in your connection string. The reason is that Object Services is trying to open a new data reader on each execution, thus requiring multiple active result sets at the database level. This functionality is applicable to only SQL Server 2005 or later, because previous versions did not support multiple active result sets.

Listing 6-6. *Explicitly Loading Entities*

```
//C# Example

using(AdventureWorksEntities aw = new AdventureWorksEntities())
{
    ObjectQuery<Employee> employees =
                                        aw.Employee;

    foreach (Employee emp in employees)
    {
        emp.EmployeeDepartmentHistory.Load();
        Debug.Print
            (emp.EmployeeDepartmentHistory.First().DepartmentID.ToString());
     }
}

-- SQL Generated from EF

SELECT
1 AS [C1],
[Extent1].[EmployeeID] AS [EmployeeID],
[Extent1].[NationalIDNumber] AS [NationalIDNumber],
```

```
[Extent1].[LoginID] AS [LoginID],
[Extent1].[Title] AS [Title],
[Extent1].[BirthDate] AS [BirthDate],
[Extent1].[MaritalStatus] AS [MaritalStatus],
[Extent1].[Gender] AS [Gender],
[Extent1].[HireDate] AS [HireDate],
[Extent1].[SalariedFlag] AS [SalariedFlag],
[Extent1].[VacationHours] AS [VacationHours],
[Extent1].[SickLeaveHours] AS [SickLeaveHours],
[Extent1].[CurrentFlag] AS [CurrentFlag],
[Extent1].[rowguid] AS [rowguid],
[Extent1].[ModifiedDate] AS [ModifiedDate],
[Extent1].[ContactID] AS [ContactID],
[Extent1].[ManagerID] AS [ManagerID]
FROM [HumanResources].[Employee] AS [Extent1]

-- SQL Generated from EF

exec sp_executesql N'SELECT
1 AS [C1],
[Extent1].[EmployeeID] AS [EmployeeID],
[Extent1].[DepartmentID] AS [DepartmentID],
[Extent1].[ShiftID] AS [ShiftID],
[Extent1].[StartDate] AS [StartDate],
[Extent1].[EndDate] AS [EndDate],
[Extent1].[ModifiedDate] AS [ModifiedDate]
FROM [HumanResources].[EmployeeDepartmentHistory] AS [Extent1]
WHERE [Extent1].[EmployeeID] = @EntityKeyValue1',
N'@EntityKeyValue1 int',@EntityKeyValue1=1

exec sp_executesql N'SELECT
1 AS [C1],
[Extent1].[EmployeeID] AS [EmployeeID],
[Extent1].[DepartmentID] AS [DepartmentID],
[Extent1].[ShiftID] AS [ShiftID],
[Extent1].[StartDate] AS [StartDate],
[Extent1].[EndDate] AS [EndDate],
[Extent1].[ModifiedDate] AS [ModifiedDate]
FROM [HumanResources].[EmployeeDepartmentHistory] AS [Extent1]
WHERE [Extent1].[EmployeeID] = @EntityKeyValue1',
N'@EntityKeyValue1 int',@EntityKeyValue1=285
```

So far, we have been considering only very simple SELECT* queries. These queries don't apply to most real-world problems. Let's take a look at some ways to make our queries more applicable to real-world scenarios.

One technique that can be used to retrieve an entity from a persisted store without creating and executing an object query is the GetObjectByKey method. The GetObjectByKey method is part of the ObjectContext class and returns an object representation of your entity based on the EntityKey that you supply. In Listing 6-7, you can see an example of the usage of GetObjectByKey. In this example, you have the code to retrieve an Employee entity by the EmployeeID key. The first thing that is happening here is that you are creating a new KeyValuePair class with EmployeeID set to the integer 21. Next, you create a new EntityKey, and then pass this EntityKey into the ObjectContext.

Now, in this case you've probably noticed that the ObjectContext is not in a using block as you have seen in other examples. This is going to be a point of discussion in the next few chapters, but here is what you need to know right now. By making your ObjectContext *shared*, you can increase performance because the object graph and data is cached in the ObjectContext. For example, the query in Listing 6-7 will be executed only a single time if you are using a shared ObjectContext, whereas it will be executed every time if you are disposing of the ObjectContext (the using block). This probably seems like a great idea; caching is great. However, the ObjectContext is not thread-safe, and as your working set grows and the database changes, issues can occur. Chapter 10 covers techniques for handling the ObjectContext in your application.

Listing 6-7. *Query the Persistent Store by Key*

```
//C# Example

AdventureWorksEntities aw = new AdventureWorksEntities();

IEnumerable<KeyValuePair<string, object>> entityKeyValues =
                new KeyValuePair<string, object>[] {
                          new KeyValuePair<string, object>("EmployeeID", 21) };

EntityKey ek =
    new EntityKey("AdventureWorksEntities.Employee", entityKeyValues);
Employee myEmp = (Employee)aw.GetObjectByKey(ek);

Debug.Print(myEmp.BirthDate.ToString());


-- SQL Generated from EF

SELECT
1 AS [C1],
[Project1].[EmployeeID] AS [EmployeeID],
[Project1].[NationalIDNumber] AS [NationalIDNumber],
[Project1].[LoginID] AS [LoginID],
[Project1].[Title] AS [Title],
[Project1].[BirthDate] AS [BirthDate],
[Project1].[MaritalStatus] AS [MaritalStatus],
[Project1].[Gender] AS [Gender],
[Project1].[HireDate] AS [HireDate],
[Project1].[SalariedFlag] AS [SalariedFlag],
```

```
[Project1].[VacationHours] AS [VacationHours],
[Project1].[SickLeaveHours] AS [SickLeaveHours],
[Project1].[CurrentFlag] AS [CurrentFlag],
[Project1].[rowguid] AS [rowguid],
[Project1].[ModifiedDate] AS [ModifiedDate],
[Project2].[ContactID] AS [ContactID],
[Project3].[ManagerID] AS [ManagerID]
FROM    ( SELECT cast(1 as bit) AS X ) AS [SingleRowTable1]
LEFT OUTER JOIN  (SELECT
       [Extent1].[EmployeeID] AS [EmployeeID],
       [Extent1].[NationalIDNumber] AS [NationalIDNumber],
       [Extent1].[LoginID] AS [LoginID],
       [Extent1].[Title] AS [Title],
       [Extent1].[BirthDate] AS [BirthDate],
       [Extent1].[MaritalStatus] AS [MaritalStatus],
       [Extent1].[Gender] AS [Gender],
       [Extent1].[HireDate] AS [HireDate],
       [Extent1].[SalariedFlag] AS [SalariedFlag],
       [Extent1].[VacationHours] AS [VacationHours],
       [Extent1].[SickLeaveHours] AS [SickLeaveHours],
       [Extent1].[CurrentFlag] AS [CurrentFlag],
       [Extent1].[rowguid] AS [rowguid],
       [Extent1].[ModifiedDate] AS [ModifiedDate]
       FROM [HumanResources].[Employee] AS [Extent1]
       WHERE 21 = [Extent1].[EmployeeID] ) AS [Project1] ON 1 = 1
LEFT OUTER JOIN  (SELECT
       [Extent2].[EmployeeID] AS [EmployeeID],
       [Extent2].[ContactID] AS [ContactID]
       FROM [HumanResources].[Employee] AS [Extent2]
       WHERE 21 = [Extent2].[EmployeeID] ) AS [Project2] ON 1 = 1
LEFT OUTER JOIN  (SELECT
       [Extent3].[EmployeeID] AS [EmployeeID],
       [Extent3].[ManagerID] AS [ManagerID]
       FROM [HumanResources].[Employee] AS [Extent3]
       WHERE 21 = [Extent3].[EmployeeID] ) AS [Project3] ON 1 = 1
```

Another useful method that is part of the `ObjectContext` is the `TryGetObjectByKey` method. Similar to the `GetObjectByKey` method, this can be used to retrieve an object from the persistence layer by an `EntityKey`. The difference with this method is that it accepts a reference object as a parameter, and returns a Boolean indicating whether it was successful or failed in the retrieval.

As you can see in Listing 6-8, this built-in functionality is useful because it reduces the amount of code that you have to write. For example, if you were using only the `GetObjectByKey` method, you would need to have a null check, along with a `try…catch` block around the call in case an `ObjectNotFoundException` occurred.

Listing 6-8. *Using This TryGetObjectByKey to Retrieve an Entity*

```
//C# Example

IEnumerable<KeyValuePair<string, object>> entityKeyValues =
                new KeyValuePair<string, object>[] {
                      new KeyValuePair<string, object>("EmployeeID", 999999) };


EntityKey ek =
    new EntityKey("AdventureWorksEntities.Employee", entityKeyValues);

object entity;

bool isGood = aw.TryGetObjectByKey(ek,out entity);

if (isGood)
{
    Employee emp = (Employee)entity;
    Debug.Print(emp.BirthDate.ToString());
}
```

Using Query Operators

So far, we've covered some of the basic functionality to retrieve data by using LINQ with EF. However, I have yet to provide a breakdown of LINQ to Entities and the execution and syntactical options that you have. It is important to note that entire books have been written on the syntax and architecture of LINQ, and the purpose of this text is ORM, so I provide only an overview of the LINQ constructs. When working with LINQ, you have two options when querying any store: query expression types and method-based expression types. For the most part, you have seen only the query expression types in this chapter, so let's explore this concept first.

A query is stored in a variable when working with LINQ. If the query returns a sequence of data, the variable must be a queryable type. Because this variable is nothing more than a query, the execution against your data store is deferred until it is iterated over in a `foreach` loop or forced to execute against your data store.

As an alternative to queries that are deferred, you also have queries that return a singleton result and are executed immediately. Some examples include the aggregate methods (`Average`, `Count`, `Max`, `Min`, `Sum`) along with the element methods (`First`, `Last`, `LastOrDefault`, `Single`, `Skip`, `Take`, `TakeWhile`). In addition, you also have the option of using the `ToList` and `ToArray` methods to force immediate execution of a sequence-based query.

Listing 6-9 shows two queries to retrieve the `Employee` entity. The first query is similar to the other examples in this chapter; it is a query expression. The second query uses method-based syntax to achieve the same results. Notice in both cases I have added the `ToList` method to force eager execution of the query. Additionally, note in Listing 6-9 that in both cases the exact same SQL is generated by EF.

You may be wondering at this point, "If both syntactical structures generate the same SQL code, which one is better?" The fact is that it comes down to personal preference. In my opinion, the query-based expression syntax is more readable and easier to understand because it is similar to SQL; however, there is fundamentally no difference between the two when it comes to the conversion from C# to SQL.

Listing 6-9. *Query and Method-Based LINQ Expressions*

```
//C# Example

List<Employee> emp = (from r in aw.Employee
                      where r.SickLeaveHours > 40
                      select r).ToList();

List<Employee> emp2 = aw.Employee.Where(s => s.SickLeaveHours > 40).ToList();

-- SQL Generated from EF

SELECT
1 AS [C1],
[Extent1].[EmployeeID] AS [EmployeeID],
[Extent1].[NationalIDNumber] AS [NationalIDNumber],
[Extent1].[LoginID] AS [LoginID],
[Extent1].[Title] AS [Title],
[Extent1].[BirthDate] AS [BirthDate],
[Extent1].[MaritalStatus] AS [MaritalStatus],
[Extent1].[Gender] AS [Gender],
[Extent1].[HireDate] AS [HireDate],
[Extent1].[SalariedFlag] AS [SalariedFlag],
[Extent1].[VacationHours] AS [VacationHours],
[Extent1].[SickLeaveHours] AS [SickLeaveHours],
[Extent1].[CurrentFlag] AS [CurrentFlag],
[Extent1].[rowguid] AS [rowguid],
[Extent1].[ModifiedDate] AS [ModifiedDate],
[Extent1].[ContactID] AS [ContactID],
[Extent1].[ManagerID] AS [ManagerID]
FROM [HumanResources].[Employee] AS [Extent1]
WHERE ( CAST( [Extent1].[SickLeaveHours] AS int)) > 40
```

Note For the most part, the architecture and execution of LINQ queries is the same among all LINQ applications (LINQ to SQL, LINQ to Entities, and so forth). I would recommend reviewing the "Getting Started with LINQ" documentation on MSDN (`http://msdn2.microsoft.com/en-us/library/bb397916(VS.90).aspx`) before writing any LINQ-based application.

In Listing 6-9, you saw the use of the `where` clause in your LINQ query. LINQ and LINQ to Entities provide you with a robust set of standard query operators for a plethora of operations. Although I am not going to go through all of them, it is worth exploring a few other query operators before moving on to the next topic.

Examples of the standard query operators that come with LINQ include functionality for filtering, projection, sorting, aggregation, paging, and grouping. Starting from the top of this list, you have already seen examples of projection with the use of the `select` keyword in this chapter. As projection is functionally the transformation of a result set into a different form, the `select` and `select many` operators are the methods for accomplishing this. Similarly, filtering (like projection) is the function of limiting the result set that is returned. Filtering is done with the `where` clause, using standard .NET comparison operators as seen in Listing 6-9.

Note LINQ provides two patterns for querying. First, you can use LINQ C# keywords such as `select`, `where`, and `orderby` inside your LINQ query. Second, you can use method-based queries (extension methods), in which you use the dot operator followed by `Select`, `Where`, `OrderBy`, and so forth. In both cases, you can take advantage of strongly typed queries, IntelliSense, and the fact that the CLR is doing the heavy lifting for you by translating your queries into method calls.

In addition to manipulating the result set, you also have the ability to order the results by using LINQ query expressions such as `OrderBy`, `OrderByDescending`, `Reverse`, `ThenBy`, and `ThenByDescending` methods. Furthermore, along with query expressions for ordering (`OrderBy`, `OrderByDescending`, and so forth), you can also use the LINQ C# keywords `orderby`, `descending`, and `ascending` within your query. Similar to the ordering functionality is the grouping functionality that LINQ provides. Grouping, which is the function of grouping data based on some criteria, can be accomplished by using the `GroupBy` method.

Listing 6-10 shows an example of the `OrderBy` and `GroupBy` methods in LINQ to Entities. The first example uses a query expression to retrieve the `Employee` entity, and the `orderby` keyword to order by the `Employee.HireDate`. The SQL for the first example, also seen in Listing 6-10, is what you would expect: a SQL `SELECT` statement with an `ORDERBY` at the end of the expression.

The second example uses the `GroupBy` method as a method call at the end of the query expression. This could alternatively be expressed as `group r by r.HireDate`, but I wanted to show off the capability to mix and match method and query expressions in LINQ. In this example, you can see that you have a lambda expression indicating to group by `Employee.HireDate`. Another interesting fact about this example is that it is returning a generic `List` of `IGrouping` interfaces. The `IGrouping` interface is a LINQ interface that allows you to group a collection of objects that have a common key. The SQL that is generated for the `GroupBy` example is also seen in Listing 6-10 and is probably different than you would expect. The SQL that is generated does not use the `GROUPBY` keyword in T-SQL. Instead, it is using a `SELECT DISTINCT` and an `ORDERBY` (with a couple `JOIN`s) to achieve the same results.

Listing 6-10. *OrderBy and GroupBy in LINQ to Entities*

```
//C# Example OrderBy

List<Employee> emp = (from r in aw.Employee
                      orderby r.HireDate
                      select r).ToList();
```

```
//C# Example GroupBy

List<IGrouping<DateTime,Employee>> emp2 = (from r in aw.Employee
                                           select r).GroupBy(s=>s.HireDate).ToList();


-- SQL Generated from EF -> OrderBy example

SELECT
[Project1].[C1] AS [C1],
[Project1].[EmployeeID] AS [EmployeeID],
[Project1].[NationalIDNumber] AS [NationalIDNumber],
[Project1].[LoginID] AS [LoginID],
[Project1].[Title] AS [Title],
[Project1].[BirthDate] AS [BirthDate],
[Project1].[MaritalStatus] AS [MaritalStatus],
[Project1].[Gender] AS [Gender],
[Project1].[HireDate] AS [HireDate],
[Project1].[SalariedFlag] AS [SalariedFlag],
[Project1].[VacationHours] AS [VacationHours],
[Project1].[SickLeaveHours] AS [SickLeaveHours],
[Project1].[CurrentFlag] AS [CurrentFlag],
[Project1].[rowguid] AS [rowguid],
[Project1].[ModifiedDate] AS [ModifiedDate],
[Project1].[ContactID] AS [ContactID],
[Project1].[ManagerID] AS [ManagerID]
FROM ( SELECT
       [Extent1].[EmployeeID] AS [EmployeeID],
       [Extent1].[NationalIDNumber] AS [NationalIDNumber],
       [Extent1].[ContactID] AS [ContactID],
       [Extent1].[LoginID] AS [LoginID],
       [Extent1].[ManagerID] AS [ManagerID],
       [Extent1].[Title] AS [Title],
       [Extent1].[BirthDate] AS [BirthDate],
       [Extent1].[MaritalStatus] AS [MaritalStatus],
       [Extent1].[Gender] AS [Gender],
       [Extent1].[HireDate] AS [HireDate],
       [Extent1].[SalariedFlag] AS [SalariedFlag],
       [Extent1].[VacationHours] AS [VacationHours],
       [Extent1].[SickLeaveHours] AS [SickLeaveHours],
       [Extent1].[CurrentFlag] AS [CurrentFlag],
       [Extent1].[rowguid] AS [rowguid],
       [Extent1].[ModifiedDate] AS [ModifiedDate],
       1 AS [C1]
       FROM [HumanResources].[Employee] AS [Extent1]
)  AS [Project1]
ORDER BY [Project1].[HireDate] ASC
```

```
-- SQL Generated from EF -> Example GroupBy

SELECT
[Project2].[HireDate] AS [HireDate],
[Project2].[C1] AS [C1],
[Project2].[C2] AS [C2],
[Project2].[EmployeeID] AS [EmployeeID],
[Project2].[NationalIDNumber] AS [NationalIDNumber],
[Project2].[LoginID] AS [LoginID],
[Project2].[Title] AS [Title],
[Project2].[BirthDate] AS [BirthDate],
[Project2].[MaritalStatus] AS [MaritalStatus],
[Project2].[Gender] AS [Gender],
[Project2].[HireDate1] AS [HireDate1],
[Project2].[SalariedFlag] AS [SalariedFlag],
[Project2].[VacationHours] AS [VacationHours],
[Project2].[SickLeaveHours] AS [SickLeaveHours],
[Project2].[CurrentFlag] AS [CurrentFlag],
[Project2].[rowguid] AS [rowguid],
[Project2].[ModifiedDate] AS [ModifiedDate],
[Project2].[ContactID] AS [ContactID],
[Project2].[ManagerID] AS [ManagerID]
FROM ( SELECT
       [Distinct1].[HireDate] AS [HireDate],
       1 AS [C1],
       [Extent2].[EmployeeID] AS [EmployeeID],
       [Extent2].[NationalIDNumber] AS [NationalIDNumber],
       [Extent2].[ContactID] AS [ContactID],
       [Extent2].[LoginID] AS [LoginID],
       [Extent2].[ManagerID] AS [ManagerID],
       [Extent2].[Title] AS [Title],
       [Extent2].[BirthDate] AS [BirthDate],
       [Extent2].[MaritalStatus] AS [MaritalStatus],
       [Extent2].[Gender] AS [Gender],
       [Extent2].[HireDate] AS [HireDate1],
       [Extent2].[SalariedFlag] AS [SalariedFlag],
       [Extent2].[VacationHours] AS [VacationHours],
       [Extent2].[SickLeaveHours] AS [SickLeaveHours],
       [Extent2].[CurrentFlag] AS [CurrentFlag],
       [Extent2].[rowguid] AS [rowguid],
       [Extent2].[ModifiedDate] AS [ModifiedDate],
       CASE WHEN ([Extent2].[EmployeeID] IS NULL) THEN
           CAST(NULL AS int) ELSE 1 END AS [C2]
       FROM   (SELECT DISTINCT
              [Extent1].[HireDate] AS [HireDate]
              FROM [HumanResources].[Employee] AS [Extent1] ) AS [Distinct1]
```

```
        LEFT OUTER JOIN [HumanResources].[Employee] AS [Extent2] ON
        ([Extent2].[HireDate] = [Distinct1].[HireDate]) OR
        (([Extent2].[HireDate] IS NULL) AND ([Distinct1].[HireDate] IS NULL))
)  AS [Project2]
ORDER BY [Project2].[HireDate] ASC, [Project2].[C2] ASC
```

The next query operators that you have at your disposal in LINQ to Entities are the set methods. These often overlooked methods can provide you with much finer-grained control of your queries. The purpose of the set methods is to refine the result set based on the existence (or nonexistence) of elements in the same or another set. Examples of these methods include `All`, `Any`, `Concat`, `Contains`, `DefaultIfEmpty`, `Distinct`, `EqualAll`, `Except`, `Intersect`, and `Union`.

Obviously, I'm not going to give you examples for all of these. Instead, I want to show you the one that I like best because it is different from the other functions. The `Intersect` method is used to combine two queries into one intersection. Listing 6-11 shows the `Intersect` functionality in LINQ. This example has one query with the criteria of `EmailAddress` starting with *a*, and a second query with the criteria of the title starting with *M*. By using the `Intersect` method, you can combine these two queries into one. Additionally, in this example, you can see that I am using an anonymous type that returns the `FirstName`, `MiddleName`, and `LastName`. Finally, the SQL code is also shown in Listing 6-11 and, as you can see, is what you would hope to see from the combination of these two expressions.

Listing 6-11. *Intersect Function*

```
//C# Example

var firstQuery = from s in aw.Contact
                 where s.EmailAddress.StartsWith("a")
                 select new
                 {
                     s.FirstName,
                     s.MiddleName,
                     s.LastName
                 };

var secondQuery = from t in aw.Contact
                  where t.Title.StartsWith("M")
                  select new
                  {
                      t.FirstName,
                      t.MiddleName,
                      t.LastName
                  };


firstQuery = firstQuery.Intersect(secondQuery);
```

```
foreach (var u in firstQuery)
{
    Debug.Print(u.LastName);
}

-- SQL Generated from EF

SELECT
[Intersect1].[C1] AS [C1],
[Intersect1].[FirstName] AS [C2],
[Intersect1].[MiddleName] AS [C3],
[Intersect1].[LastName] AS [C4]
FROM  (SELECT
       1 AS [C1],
       [Extent1].[FirstName] AS [FirstName],
       [Extent1].[MiddleName] AS [MiddleName],
       [Extent1].[LastName] AS [LastName]
       FROM [Person].[Contact] AS [Extent1]
       WHERE (CAST(CHARINDEX(N'a', [Extent1].[EmailAddress]) AS int)) = 1
INTERSECT
       SELECT
       1 AS [C1],
       [Extent2].[FirstName] AS [FirstName],
       [Extent2].[MiddleName] AS [MiddleName],
       [Extent2].[LastName] AS [LastName]
       FROM [Person].[Contact] AS [Extent2]
       WHERE (CAST(CHARINDEX(N'M', [Extent2].[Title]) AS int)) = 1) AS [Intersect1]
```

Another important operation that you can use with LINQ to Entities is a join method. There are two operators that can be used for joining: the `Join` and `GroupJoin` methods. As you might expect, the purpose of the `Join` and `GroupJoin` methods is to create an association between two objects in an ad hoc manner. Join methods are used when you don't have a defined foreign-key relationship or a navigation property, but need an association query.

Listing 6-12 shows a simple example of using a join in LINQ. In this example, you are joining the `Employee` and `Contact` entities on the `Title` attribute. Granted, this is not a scenario that you would ever likely face in real life because the `Title` attribute is not unique enough for this association to be functional, but for the purpose of demonstrating the syntax, it gets the point across.

As you can see in Listing 6-12, to use the `Join` keyword, just follow the standard SQL pattern of joining the two entities to each other by using some attribute as the tie. In this example, you also have an anonymous type that is returned, containing the joined entities. Listing 6-12 also shows the SQL that is generated from EF for this join query. There isn't too much to say about the SQL because it is structurally typical to what you would write when joining two tables.

Listing 6-12. *LINQ Join Query*

```
//C# Example

var q =
        (from c in aw.Contact
        join emp in aw.Employee
        on c.Title equals emp.Title into totEmpCont
        select new { c, totEmpCont }).ToList();

-- SQL Generated from EF

SELECT
[Project1].[ContactID] AS [ContactID],
[Project1].[NameStyle] AS [NameStyle],
[Project1].[Title] AS [Title],
[Project1].[FirstName] AS [FirstName],
[Project1].[MiddleName] AS [MiddleName],
[Project1].[LastName] AS [LastName],
[Project1].[Suffix] AS [Suffix],
[Project1].[EmailAddress] AS [EmailAddress],
[Project1].[EmailPromotion] AS [EmailPromotion],
[Project1].[Phone] AS [Phone],
[Project1].[PasswordHash] AS [PasswordHash],
[Project1].[PasswordSalt] AS [PasswordSalt],
[Project1].[AdditionalContactInfo] AS [AdditionalContactInfo],
[Project1].[rowguid] AS [rowguid],
[Project1].[ModifiedDate] AS [ModifiedDate],
[Project1].[C1] AS [C1],
[Project1].[C2] AS [C2],
[Project1].[EmployeeID] AS [EmployeeID],
[Project1].[NationalIDNumber] AS [NationalIDNumber],
[Project1].[LoginID] AS [LoginID],
[Project1].[Title1] AS [Title1],
[Project1].[BirthDate] AS [BirthDate],
[Project1].[MaritalStatus] AS [MaritalStatus],
[Project1].[Gender] AS [Gender],
[Project1].[HireDate] AS [HireDate],
[Project1].[SalariedFlag] AS [SalariedFlag],
[Project1].[VacationHours] AS [VacationHours],
[Project1].[SickLeaveHours] AS [SickLeaveHours],
[Project1].[CurrentFlag] AS [CurrentFlag],
[Project1].[rowguid1] AS [rowguid1],
```

```
    [Project1].[ModifiedDate1] AS [ModifiedDate1],
    [Project1].[ContactID1] AS [ContactID1],
    [Project1].[ManagerID] AS [ManagerID]
    FROM ( SELECT
           [Extent1].[ContactID] AS [ContactID],
           [Extent1].[NameStyle] AS [NameStyle],
           [Extent1].[Title] AS [Title],
           [Extent1].[FirstName] AS [FirstName],
           [Extent1].[MiddleName] AS [MiddleName],
           [Extent1].[LastName] AS [LastName],
           [Extent1].[Suffix] AS [Suffix],
           [Extent1].[EmailAddress] AS [EmailAddress],
           [Extent1].[EmailPromotion] AS [EmailPromotion],
           [Extent1].[Phone] AS [Phone],
           [Extent1].[PasswordHash] AS [PasswordHash],
           [Extent1].[PasswordSalt] AS [PasswordSalt],
           [Extent1].[AdditionalContactInfo] AS [AdditionalContactInfo],
           [Extent1].[rowguid] AS [rowguid],
           [Extent1].[ModifiedDate] AS [ModifiedDate],
           1 AS [C1],
           [Extent2].[EmployeeID] AS [EmployeeID],
           [Extent2].[NationalIDNumber] AS [NationalIDNumber],
           [Extent2].[ContactID] AS [ContactID1],
           [Extent2].[LoginID] AS [LoginID],
           [Extent2].[ManagerID] AS [ManagerID],
           [Extent2].[Title] AS [Title1],
           [Extent2].[BirthDate] AS [BirthDate],
           [Extent2].[MaritalStatus] AS [MaritalStatus],
           [Extent2].[Gender] AS [Gender],
           [Extent2].[HireDate] AS [HireDate],
           [Extent2].[SalariedFlag] AS [SalariedFlag],
           [Extent2].[VacationHours] AS [VacationHours],
           [Extent2].[SickLeaveHours] AS [SickLeaveHours],
           [Extent2].[CurrentFlag] AS [CurrentFlag],
           [Extent2].[rowguid] AS [rowguid1],
           [Extent2].[ModifiedDate] AS [ModifiedDate1],
           CASE WHEN ([Extent2].[EmployeeID] IS NULL)
THEN CAST(NULL AS int) ELSE 1 END AS [C2]
           FROM  [Person].[Contact] AS [Extent1]
           LEFT OUTER JOIN [HumanResources].[Employee] AS [Extent2] ON
([Extent1].[Title] = [Extent2].[Title]) OR (([Extent1].[Title] IS NULL) AND
([Extent2].[Title] IS NULL))
)  AS [Project1]
ORDER BY [Project1].[ContactID] ASC, [Project1].[C2] ASC
```

The last topic to cover about querying with LINQ to Entities is those singleton methods that I mentioned earlier in the chapter. These methods are broken into two categories: aggregate methods and element methods. The first group, the aggregate methods, are used to compute a single value from a result set. These methods are the Min, Max, Average (and so forth) methods that can be used with LINQ expressions.

Listing 6-13 shows how you can use the Max method to return the maximum BirthDate from the Employee table. In this example, the Max method is used to return the youngest employee in the data store. The SQL for this example can also be seen in Listing 6-13. As you can see, the SQL that is generated uses the T-SQL MAX function to return the results from your query.

Listing 6-13. *Aggregate Method Max*

```
//C# Example

DateTime q = (from g in aw.Employee
              select g.BirthDate).Max();

Debug.Print(q.ToString());

-- SQL Generated from EF

SELECT
[GroupBy1].[A1] AS [C1]
FROM   ( SELECT cast(1 as bit) AS X ) AS [SingleRowTable1]
LEFT OUTER JOIN  (SELECT
       MAX([Extent1].[BirthDate]) AS [A1]
       FROM [HumanResources].[Employee] AS [Extent1] ) AS [GroupBy1] ON 1 = 1
```

The second type of singleton methods are the element methods in LINQ. This is the last LINQ to Entities query example in this chapter. Here, the element operations are used to retrieve a specific element from a result set sequence. These methods are the First, Last, Single, Skip, Take (and so forth) methods, which are natively part of LINQ.

Listing 6-14 shows the First method. This example has a simple query that is retrieving the first married employee. As you might expect, this translates into a query that is doing a SELECT TOP(1), which can be seen in Listing 6-14.

Listing 6-14. *Using the First Method to Retrieve the First Employee in the Query*

```
//C# Example

Employee x = (from emp in aw.Employee
              where emp.MaritalStatus == "M"
              select emp).First();

--SQL Generated from EF

SELECT
[Limit1].[C1] AS [C1],
[Limit1].[EmployeeID] AS [EmployeeID],
[Limit1].[NationalIDNumber] AS [NationalIDNumber],
[Limit1].[LoginID] AS [LoginID],
```

```
[Limit1].[Title] AS [Title],
[Limit1].[BirthDate] AS [BirthDate],
[Limit1].[MaritalStatus] AS [MaritalStatus],
[Limit1].[Gender] AS [Gender],
[Limit1].[HireDate] AS [HireDate],
[Limit1].[SalariedFlag] AS [SalariedFlag],
[Limit1].[VacationHours] AS [VacationHours],
[Limit1].[SickLeaveHours] AS [SickLeaveHours],
[Limit1].[CurrentFlag] AS [CurrentFlag],
[Limit1].[rowguid] AS [rowguid],
[Limit1].[ModifiedDate] AS [ModifiedDate],
[Limit1].[ContactID] AS [ContactID],
[Limit1].[ManagerID] AS [ManagerID]
FROM ( SELECT TOP (1)
       [Extent1].[EmployeeID] AS [EmployeeID],
       [Extent1].[NationalIDNumber] AS [NationalIDNumber],
       [Extent1].[ContactID] AS [ContactID],
       [Extent1].[LoginID] AS [LoginID],
       [Extent1].[ManagerID] AS [ManagerID],
       [Extent1].[Title] AS [Title],
       [Extent1].[BirthDate] AS [BirthDate],
       [Extent1].[MaritalStatus] AS [MaritalStatus],
       [Extent1].[Gender] AS [Gender],
       [Extent1].[HireDate] AS [HireDate],
       [Extent1].[SalariedFlag] AS [SalariedFlag],
       [Extent1].[VacationHours] AS [VacationHours],
       [Extent1].[SickLeaveHours] AS [SickLeaveHours],
       [Extent1].[CurrentFlag] AS [CurrentFlag],
       [Extent1].[rowguid] AS [rowguid],
       [Extent1].[ModifiedDate] AS [ModifiedDate],
       1 AS [C1]
       FROM [HumanResources].[Employee] AS [Extent1]
       WHERE N'M' = [Extent1].[MaritalStatus]
) AS [Limit1]
```

Updating, Inserting, and Deleting

Until now, this entire chapter has focused on the query functionality of LINQ to Entities and EF. The fact is, however, that updating, inserting, and deleting with LINQ to Entities are equally important and equally simple.

Listing 6-15 shows an update transaction. In this example, you query for the Employee with the EmployeeID that is equal to 1. After retrieving the Employee entity, you are modifying the MaritalStatus and calling SaveChanges on the ObjectContext.

Beneath the C# code is the SQL code that is generated from the SaveChanges call. In this example, I have not included the first SELECT to retrieve the Employee; instead I have included only the UPDATE to change the MaritalStatus. The UPDATE statement generated by EF is a fairly standard parameterized SQL statement that sets the MaritalStatus based on the EmployeeID.

Listing 6-15. *Update an Object in EF*

```
//C# Example

Employee x = (from emp in aw.Employee
              where emp.EmployeeID == 1
              select emp).First();

x.MaritalStatus = "S";
aw.SaveChanges();

--SQL Generated from EF

exec sp_executesql N'update [HumanResources].[Employee]
set [MaritalStatus] = @0
where ([EmployeeID] = @1)
',N'@0 nvarchar(1),@1 int',@0=N'S',@1=1
```

After examining the simple technique in Listing 6-15 for updating an entity using EF, you may be asking yourself, "How does EF know what to update?" In the preceding chapter, you saw that each setter method in the generated entity properties has more than just a set value statement; it also has some additional code for tracking.

In Listing 6-16, you can see the `MaritalStatus` getter and setter of the `Employee` class. The set functionality is calling `this.ReportPropertyChanging` and `this.ReportPropertyChanged`. The `this` is referencing your entities' (`Employee`) abstract base class `System.Data.Objects.DataClasses.EntityObject`, and the method calls tell the EF change tracker that the property is changing or has changed. Along with the change-tracking notifications, you also have a call to `System.Data.Objects.DataClasses.StructuralObject.SetValidValue` to set the value of the property. The `StructuralObject` class is the abstract base class of the `EntityObject` class and is used as a helper class for code generation. The `SetValidValue` internal static method is one of the many helper methods in `StructuralObject` and is used to check whether a value is valid and then to set that value.

Listing 6-16. *Change Tracking in EF*

```
get
{
    return this._MaritalStatus;
}
set
{
    this.ReportPropertyChanging("MaritalStatus");
    this._MaritalStatus = global::System.Data.Objects.DataClasses.
         StructuralObject.SetValidValue(value, false, 1);
     this.ReportPropertyChanged("MaritalStatus");
}
```

Listing 6-16 includes a simple example of updating an entity with EF, but let's take a look at an example that is more congruent with what you might see in the real world. Listing 6-17 first queries to find all single female employees over the age of 18. In this example, I have provided two alternate techniques for retrieving the same query. The first technique is to use the IQueryable interface with the Include("Contact") span in a query expression pattern. The second example, which is commented out, uses a method-based expression and returns an ObjectQuery because it has to do so in order to use the Include span on your ObjectContext. Although, as mentioned earlier, both examples generate the same SQL code, it is worth noting here that using the IQueryable interface with the query expression requires one less cast and is a more generic interface than ObjectQuery.

Regardless of the technique you use to create your query, after the query is created in this example, you are looping through the collection (IQueryable or ObjectQuery) and setting the Employee.Contact.EmailPromotion and the Employee.CurrentFlag properties. Upon completion of the loop, SaveChanges is called and the entire object graph is updated.

From a SQL standpoint, what occurs here is that first a join query is executed to retrieve the Employee and Contact tables. This query (not shown) also has the criterion that says, "find all single female employees over 18 years of age." After the first query, no SQL is executed until the ObjectContext.SaveChanges method is called, at which time individual update transactions are called for each of the values that have changes. After the C# in Listing 6-17, you have two examples of the SQL update statements that are executed. The first is to update the Employee table, and the second is to update the Contact table.

Listing 6-17. *Update Across Multiple Entities*

```
//C# Example
IQueryable<Employee> emp =
                from s in aw.Employee.Include("Contact")
                where s.BirthDate <= new DateTime(1989, 11, 23)
                && s.Gender == "F" && s.MaritalStatus == "S"
                select s;

//ObjectQuery<Employee> emp = (ObjectQuery<Employee>)aw.Employee.Include("Contact")
//                 .Where(s=>s.BirthDate <= new DateTime(1989, 11, 23)
//                 && s.Gender == "F" && s.MaritalStatus == "S");


foreach (Employee x in emp)
{
                x.Contact.EmailPromotion = 1;
                x.CurrentFlag = true;

}

aw.SaveChanges();

--SQL Generated from EF
```

```
exec sp_executesql N'update [HumanResources].[Employee]
set [MaritalStatus] = @0
where ([EmployeeID] = @1)
',N'@0 nvarchar(1),@1 int',@0=N'S',@1=1

exec sp_executesql N'update [Person].[Contact]
set [EmailPromotion] = @0
where ([ContactID] = @1)
',N'@0 int,@1 int',@0=1,@1=1001
```

Now that you know how to query and create basic update statements in EF, it is time to look at inserting entities. Listing 6-18 shows how you go about inserting a new entity into your data store. In this example, you are creating a new `Department`, calling the `AddDepartment` method, which is part of your derived `ObjectContext` class, and then calling `SaveChanges` to commit the item to the data store. Also included in the example is the SQL that is generated by EF, which is, as you would expect, a standard SQL insert into the `Department` table.

There are a few items that I should mention regarding the topic of inserting new entities through EF. First, all non-nullable properties and relationship properties have to be set; otherwise, you will receive an error when you execute `SaveChanges`. There are a few ways to handle properties such as `ModifiedDate` that could easily be generated for you, which you will look at in the next chapter. Nonetheless, the data store is still going to require some value in non-nullable fields regardless of how it is created.

Second, when working with identity fields (for example the `DepartmentID` field), EF first generates a temporary key for the field prior to `SaveChanges` and then replaces this key with the value generated from the insert. Finally, along the same lines, primary-key constraints (any constraints, really) still apply, so if a key is not a database identity, you must use a unique value for that field.

Listing 6-18. *Insert a New Department by Using EF*

```
//C# Example

Department dept = new Department();
dept.GroupName = "MyGroup1";
dept.Name = "MyName";
dept.ModifiedDate = DateTime.Now;
aw.AddToDepartment(dept);
int changes = aw.SaveChanges();

--SQL Generated from EF

exec sp_executesql N'insert [HumanResources].[Department]
([Name], [GroupName], [ModifiedDate])
values (@0, @1, @2)
```

```
select [DepartmentID]
from [HumanResources].[Department]
where @@ROWCOUNT > 0 and [DepartmentID] = scope_identity()',
N'@0 nvarchar(6),@1 nvarchar(8),@2
datetime',@0=N'MyName',@1=N'MyGroup1',@2=''2007-12-17 18:32:56:500''
```

Note Listing 6-18 shows the `ObjectContext.SaveChanges` call returning an integer, `changes`. This integer is populated with the number of changes (updates, deletes, and inserts) that have been committed, and can be useful when building out an instrumented framework.

The `AddToDepartment` method that you saw in Listing 6-18 is a generated method, and part of your `ObjectContext`. Before we move on to deletes, let's take a look at what the `AddToDepartment` method is doing. Listing 6-19 shows the `AddToDepartment` method, which is calling `base.AddObject` and passing in the `entitySetName` and the new entity.

Because the base in this case is the `System.Data.Objects.ObjectContext` class, you also have the option of calling `AddObject` directly from your code. I point this out because the `AddObject` call is a loosely typed call, whereas the `AddToDepartment` call is strongly typed. Therefore, the `AddObject` call can easily be used as a general-purpose (foreshadowing) call that can accept any type of entity.

Listing 6-19. *AddToDepartment Method*

```
public void AddToDepartment(Department department)
{
    base.AddObject("Department", department);
}
```

You have now seen the basics of queries, inserts, and updates; so there is only one topic left to discuss in this chapter: deletes. Like its sibling CRUD operations, deletes in EF revolve around the `ObjectContext` class. Listing 6-20 shows a query against the `Department` table, where the `GroupName` field is equal to `MyGroup1`. Because the query is called with the `First` method, the value is returned immediately and is then passed to the `ObjectContext.DeleteObject` method. After the entity is passed to the `DeleteObject` method on the `ObjectContext`, EF and the object-tracking services mark this entity as dirty, so when `SaveChanges` is called, the delete SQL is generated and executed.

Listing 6-20. *Delete an Entity with EF*

```
//C# Example

Department dept = aw.Department.Where(s => s.GroupName == "MyGroup1").First();
aw.DeleteObject(dept);
int changes = aw.SaveChanges();
```

```
--SQL Generated from EF

SELECT TOP (1)
[Extent1].[DepartmentID] AS [DepartmentID],
[Extent1].[Name] AS [Name],
[Extent1].[GroupName] AS [GroupName],
[Extent1].[ModifiedDate] AS [ModifiedDate]
FROM [HumanResources].[Department] AS [Extent1]
WHERE N'MyGroup1' = [Extent1].[GroupName]

exec sp_executesql N'delete [HumanResources].[Department]
where ([DepartmentID] = @0)',N'@0 smallint',@0=17
```

Compiled Queries

Before finishing up this chapter, I want to briefly touch on compiled query functionality in LINQ to Entities, because it can greatly improve performance in your application. LINQ to Entities gives you a class, aptly named `CompiledQuery`, which provides the functionality to reuse queries. The queries, which are primed for use with the `CompiledQuery` class, are those queries that need to be executed many times and are structurally similar.

As you can see in Listing 6-21, the compiled query is a regular LINQ to Entities query with explicit parameters. The first parameter is an `ObjectContext`, which in this example is the `AdventureWorksEntities` `ObjectContext`. The reason for the `ObjectContext` parameter is so that the query can be compiled prior to the creation of an instance of the `ObjectContext`. This allows for reuse of the compiled query across multiple instances of an `ObjectContext`, as long as they represent the same model (for example, `AdventureWorks`).

In Listing 6-21, the compiled query is creating a structure to search against the `Contact` entity by using the `StartsWith` function. Here you are creating a delegate in the form of a `var` that returns an `IQueryable` interface, which can be used to return the contacts whose `FirstName` starts with a specific string. Next, the delegate is being consumed in a loop, where an instance of your `ObjectContext` is being passed in along with the letter *A*. The results of this query are all of the contacts whose `FirstName` begins with *A*.

Listing 6-21. *A Compiled Query Using LINQ to Entities*

```
var contacts =
CompiledQuery.Compile((AdventureWorksEntities1 adventureworks, string startsWith) =>
                                    from contact in adventureworks.Contact
                                    where contact.FirstName.StartsWith(startsWith)
                                    orderby contact.FirstName
                                    select contact);



using (AdventureWorksEntities1 aw = new AdventureWorksEntities1())
{
```

```
        foreach (var contact in contacts(aw, "A"))
        {

            Debug.Print(contact.FirstName.ToString());

        }

    }
```

■ **Note** Listing 6-21 demonstrates a technique for using the `CompiledQuery` class. However, it is recommended that you structure your compiled queries by using the `Func` anonymous delegate in a `static` class, as seen in Listing 6-5.

Listing 6-22 shows the SQL generated from the LINQ to Entities query in Listing 6-21. Here you have a parameterized query that is using the letter *A* as a condition in the `WHERE` clause. The advantage of using the `CompiledQuery` class is that the query is cached for the `appdomain`, so the next time you execute this query with a different `startsWith` parameter, you will see a performance gain.

Listing 6-22. *SQL Generated from the Compiled Query*

```
exec sp_executesql N'SELECT
[Project1].[ContactID] AS [ContactID],
[Project1].[NameStyle] AS [NameStyle],
[Project1].[Title] AS [Title],
[Project1].[FirstName] AS [FirstName],
[Project1].[MiddleName] AS [MiddleName],
[Project1].[LastName] AS [LastName],
[Project1].[Suffix] AS [Suffix],
[Project1].[EmailAddress] AS [EmailAddress],
[Project1].[EmailPromotion] AS [EmailPromotion],
[Project1].[Phone] AS [Phone],
[Project1].[PasswordHash] AS [PasswordHash],
[Project1].[PasswordSalt] AS [PasswordSalt],
[Project1].[AdditionalContactInfo] AS [AdditionalContactInfo],
[Project1].[rowguid] AS [rowguid],
[Project1].[ModifiedDate] AS [ModifiedDate]
FROM ( SELECT
       [Extent1].[ContactID] AS [ContactID],
       [Extent1].[NameStyle] AS [NameStyle],
       [Extent1].[Title] AS [Title],
       [Extent1].[FirstName] AS [FirstName],
       [Extent1].[MiddleName] AS [MiddleName],
       [Extent1].[LastName] AS [LastName],
```

```
        [Extent1].[Suffix] AS [Suffix],
        [Extent1].[EmailAddress] AS [EmailAddress],
        [Extent1].[EmailPromotion] AS [EmailPromotion],
        [Extent1].[Phone] AS [Phone],
        [Extent1].[PasswordHash] AS [PasswordHash],
        [Extent1].[PasswordSalt] AS [PasswordSalt],
        [Extent1].[AdditionalContactInfo] AS [AdditionalContactInfo],
        [Extent1].[rowguid] AS [rowguid],
        [Extent1].[ModifiedDate] AS [ModifiedDate]
        FROM [Person].[Contact] AS [Extent1]
        WHERE (CAST(CHARINDEX(
        @prm_5563352d5b4b4e9b85ad64e021b7fb49,
        [Extent1].[FirstName]) AS int)) = 1
)  AS [Project1]
ORDER BY [Project1].[FirstName] ASC',
N'@prm_5563352d5b4b4e9b85ad64e021b7fb49
 nvarchar(1)',@prm_5563352d5b4b4e9b85ad64e021b7fb49=N'A'
```

Summary

In this chapter, you learned about using LINQ to Entities and Object Services for querying data in EF. Object queries are an efficient and easy-to-use technique for retrieving data in EF. Along with the functionality that Object Services provides, you also have the robust native LINQ query functionality provided by LINQ to Entities.

LINQ offers you two techniques for retrieving data: method-based queries and query expressions. In general, query expressions are easier to read—but under the cover, the same SQL code is generated. Furthermore, in both cases you have the option of using a plethora of built-in functions for aggregation and set-based logic.

Another topic introduced in this chapter is using LINQ to Entities and Object Services for updates, inserts, and deletes. Although we have only scratched the surface of this topic, you did learn that the `ObjectContext.SaveChanges` method is powerful and can span across entire object graphs and associations.

In the next chapter, you will examine advanced topics of EF, including inheritance, ESQL, and the entity client. Additionally, you will learn more techniques for handling CRUD operations as well as begin to examine the foundation for architecture that is used in Chapter 10.

CHAPTER 7

Advanced ADO.NET Entity Framework

Chapter 6 introduced you to the basics of EF by exploring CRUD operations through LINQ to Entities and Object Services. In this chapter, you will continue your investigation of EF by looking at more-advanced scenarios in isolated examples. To start with, you will examine the three types of inheritance supported by EF. Next you will take a look at the entity client and learn the basics behind ESQL. Finally, you will learn how to use stored procedures in your model.

Inheritance

The subject of inheritance in the EDM and in ORM tools is a critical one. Although the fundamental purpose of inheritance is to allow a derived type to extend features of a parent type, there is much more to it. Inheritance is the most important part of object-oriented development, and, when used correctly in an ORM, inheritance enables you to create a domain model that is hierarchal and polymorphic, thus overcoming much of the impedance mismatch.

EF supports the three types of inheritance, as discussed in Chapter 2. These types are not technology specific, but rather are recognized as the sum of inheritance patterns for ORM tools. To refresh your memory, ORM inheritance can be accomplished through the following:

- A single Table per Class hierarchy
- A Table per Concrete Class
- A table class to its own table

It is important at this point that you understand that inheritance in the EDM (and LINQ to SQL) does not support method inheritance as the CLR does. This is, of course, because the EDM does not actually implement any methods that are involved in the ORM paradigm. Additionally, it is important to note that inheritance in EF follows the CLR in that only single-type inheritance is allowed.

Note In this section on inheritance, you will be taking a break from using the `AdventureWorks` database and will use a custom database called `EFSamples` to avoid unnecessary complexities.

Single-Table Mapping

Single-table mapping is the simplest form of inheritance and thus a good place to begin. *Single-table mapping*, as its name suggests, is when an entire inheritance hierarchy is stored in a single database table. Although this is one of the most basic designs for inheritance in ORM tools, it is also one of the best performing because the table contains the flattened structure and unioned relationships.

In single-table mapping, a discriminator column is used. A *discriminator column* is a column in your database table that provides a code representing the type to be created. To start with an example, you need to first create a new table called `Account` in the new database called `EFSamples`. In this table, you need to add the `AccountNumber`, `AccountType`, `Balance`, `Term`, `Principal`, and `Tax` columns. Listing 7-1 shows the T-SQL to create this table.

Listing 7-1. *T-SQL to Create the Account Table*

```
CREATE TABLE [dbo].[Account](
      [AccountNumber] [int] NOT NULL,
      [AccountType] [char](10) NOT NULL CONSTRAINT [DF_Account_AccountType]
      DEFAULT ((0)),
      [Balance] [int] NULL,
      [Term] [int] NULL,
      [Principal] [int] NULL,
      [Tax] [int] NULL,

 CONSTRAINT [PK_Account] PRIMARY KEY CLUSTERED
(
      [AccountNumber] ASC

)WITH (IGNORE_DUP_KEY = OFF) ON [PRIMARY]
) ON [PRIMARY]
```

After you have created the new `Account` table, the next step is to create a new `.edmx` file in your Visual Studio solution. For this example, I named the new file `EFSamples`, connected to the database, and imported the `Account` table that was created in Listing 7-1. Figure 7-1 shows the result of the import. As you can see, you have a single entity in the model called `Account`. This is not exactly an inheritance example, but a starting point.

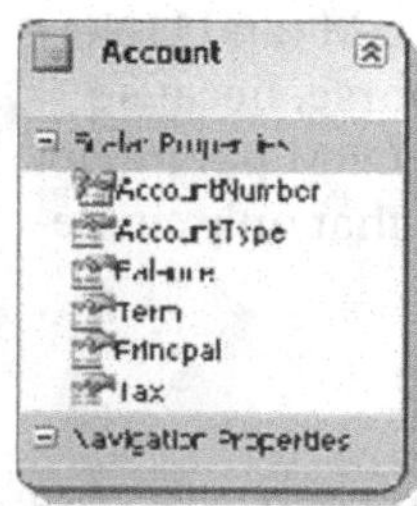

Figure 7-1. *The Account entity*

Continuing with our single-table mapping example, the next task is to modify the `Account` entity to create two additional subclasses. I'm not going to discuss all the details about using the EF designer for creating entities, because this is discussed in the next chapter, but I do want to take a moment to describe how you go about splitting up the `Account` class.

First, the easiest way to create a new subclass entity is to right-click on the design surface and choose Add ➤ Entity from the menu. Next, a new dialog box pops up that provides you with a text box for typing the Entity Name and selecting the Base Type. Figure 7-2 shows the dialog box in which I typed Loan for the entity name and Account for the base type.

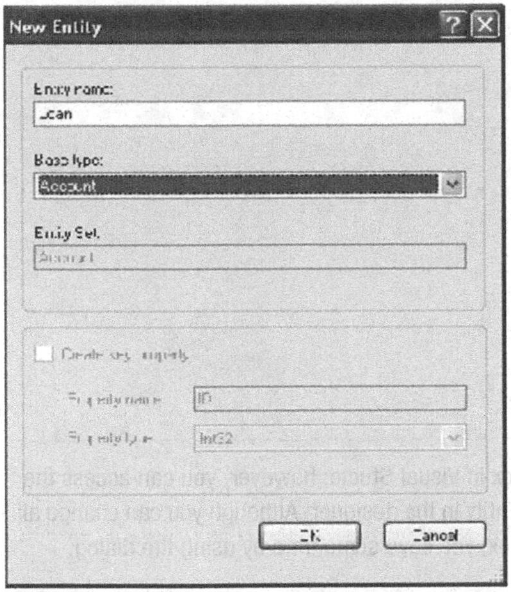

Figure 7-2. *New Entity dialog box*

After you click OK, you have created a new entity on the design surface called `Loan`, with an arrowhead-line connector to the `Account` base class. To move the scalar properties from the `Account` class to the `Loan` (and `Mortgage`) classes, all you have to do is cut and paste from one to the other. Figure 7-3 shows the refactored entity model containing an example of an `Account` class that has a subclass of `Loan`, which has a subclass of `Mortgage`. You may have noticed that the `AccountType` column is not shown in Figure 7-3; don't worry, this is not a mistake and is explained in the next few paragraphs.

So far in this example, we have created a new `Account` table and a class hierarchy to go with it, but you still have to change the mapping details to support this new hierarchy. Although the EF designer is intuitive and does many things for you, it doesn't automatically map your properties or set the discriminator columns when you add a new entity that is not an import from the database (for example, `Loan`).

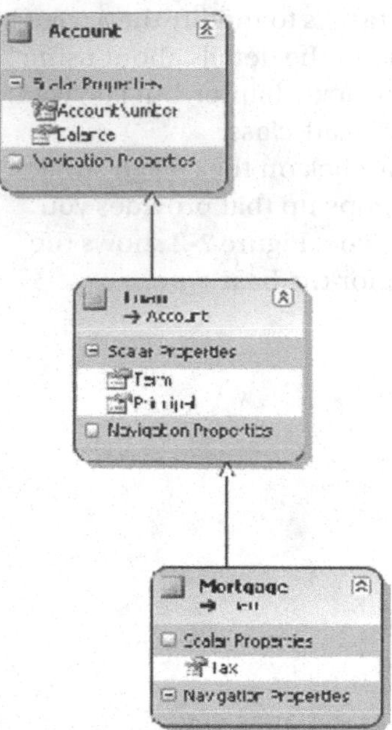

Figure 7-3. *Inheritance hierarchy*

■ **Tip** You can optionally drag a new entity from the toolbox in Visual Studio; however, you can access the dialog box seen in Figure 7-2 only when right-clicking Add Entity in the designer. Although you can change all the settings shown in Figure 7-2 without using the dialog box, you save some time by using the dialog.

Figure 7-4 shows the mapping window for the `Loan` class. As you can see, the `Account` table columns `Term` and `Principal` are mapped to the `Term` and `Principal` properties in the `Loan` entity. I have also created a new condition that says `When AccountType = 1`. It is important to note that because we are using the `AccountType` as a conditional variable in the model, we do not need to have an explicit column mapping in the designer, as seen in Figure 7-4. Setting the `AccountType` condition tells EF and the mapping configuration that when the discriminator value is `1`, the type is `Loan`. Additionally, in the `Account` and `Mortgage` mapping detail windows (not shown), I have mapped the appropriate columns to properties and have created conditions where `AccountType 0` is an `Account` type and `AccountType 2` is a `Mortgage` type.

Now that you have mapped the entities and set the discriminator value, you can recompile. After you have recompiled successfully, the MSL mapping file is generated in your bin directory. Listing 7-2 provides the MSL mapping file from this example. The file has `MappingFragments` for each of the entities in the model, and each of the fragments has a `Condition` node that maps the `AccountType` column to a value.

Column	Operator	Value / Property
Tables		
Maps to Account		
When AccountType	=	1
<Add a Condition>		
Column Mappings		
AccountType (int)	↔	
Term (int)	↔	Term (Int32)
Principal (int)	↔	Principal (Int32)
Tax (decimal)	↔	
<Add a Table or View>		

Figure 7-4. *Mapping Details window*

Listing 7-2. *MSL Generated from the Account Inheritance Example*

```
<EntityContainerMapping StorageEntityContainer="dbo"
CdmEntityContainer="EFSamplesEntities">
    <EntitySetMapping Name="Account">
      <EntityTypeMapping TypeName="EFSamplesModel.Account">
        <MappingFragment StoreEntitySet="Account">
          <ScalarProperty Name="AccountNumber" ColumnName="AccountNumber" />
          <ScalarProperty Name="Balance" ColumnName="Balance" />
          <Condition ColumnName="AccountType" Value="0" />
        </MappingFragment>
      </EntityTypeMapping>
      <EntityTypeMapping TypeName="IsTypeOf(EFSamplesModel.Mortgage)">
        <MappingFragment StoreEntitySet="Account">
          <ScalarProperty Name="Balance" ColumnName="Balance" />
          <ScalarProperty Name="Term" ColumnName="Term" />
          <ScalarProperty Name="Principal" ColumnName="Principal" />
          <ScalarProperty Name="AccountNumber" ColumnName="AccountNumber" />
          <ScalarProperty Name="Tax" ColumnName="Tax" />
          <Condition ColumnName="AccountType" Value="2" />
        </MappingFragment>
      </EntityTypeMapping>
      <EntityTypeMapping TypeName="EFSamplesModel.Loan">
        <MappingFragment StoreEntitySet="Account">
          <ScalarProperty Name="AccountNumber" ColumnName="AccountNumber" />
          <ScalarProperty Name="Balance" ColumnName="Balance" />
          <ScalarProperty Name="Term" ColumnName="Term" />
          <ScalarProperty Name="Principal" ColumnName="Principal" />
          <Condition ColumnName="AccountType" Value="1" />
        </MappingFragment>
      </EntityTypeMapping>
    </EntitySetMapping>
  </EntityContainerMapping>
```

The only thing left to do with our single-table mapping example is to write some C# to test it out. First, however, you need to insert some data into the Account table by executing this statement: INSERT INTO Account(AccountNumber, AccountType, Balance, Term, Principal, Tax) VALUES (123,'2',5000,24,1000,100). With this code, I have inserted a new row with the Account type of 2 to test the Mortgage discriminator. Listing 7-3 contains a simple example that gets the Account entity, loops through the result set, and prints the Type of the entity. In this example, the output is EFSamplesModel.Mortgage, thus proving that the discriminator column works.

Listing 7-3. *C# Code to Test the Discriminator*

```
EFSamplesEntities ef = new EFSamplesEntities();

ObjectQuery<Account> acc = ef.Account;

foreach (var c in acc)
{
    Debug.Print(c.GetType().ToString());

}
```

Listing 7-4 shows the SQL that is generated from the C# in Listing 7-3. As you can see, the SELECT statement that gets generated is a standard SELECT statement with nothing unusual except the WHERE clause, which limits the query to only the conditions that you specified in your mapping file. This means that your discriminator values must be explicitly expressed in your EDM; otherwise, an error will occur.

Listing 7-4. *Select Statement Created from Discriminator Inheritance*

```
SELECT
[Extent1].[AccountType] AS [AccountType],
[Extent1].[AccountNumber] AS [AccountNumber],
[Extent1].[Balance] AS [Balance],
[Extent1].[Term] AS [Term],
[Extent1].[Principal] AS [Principal],
[Extent1].[Tax] AS [Tax]
FROM [dbo].[Account] AS [Extent1]
WHERE ([Extent1].[AccountType] = '0') OR ([Extent1].[AccountType] = '2')
OR ([Extent1].[AccountType] = '1')
```

Table per Type

In Table per Type inheritance, each type in your hierarchy is mapped to its own table in the database. Using the same example of the Account, Loan, and Mortgage entities, the first task is to create three tables in your database, all with a common key, AccountNumber. Listing 7-5 provides the T-SQL scripts for creating the three tables for this example. As you can see, all three tables have the AccountNumber as their primary key column.

Listing 7-5. *T-SQL to Create the Account, Loan, and Mortgage Tables*

```
CREATE TABLE [dbo].[Account](
	[AccountNumber] [int] NOT NULL,
	[Balance] [int] NULL,
 CONSTRAINT [PK_Account_1] PRIMARY KEY CLUSTERED
(
	[AccountNumber] ASC
)WITH (IGNORE_DUP_KEY = OFF) ON [PRIMARY]
) ON [PRIMARY]


CREATE TABLE [dbo].[Loan](
	[AccountNumber] [int] NOT NULL,
	[Term] [int] NULL,
	[Principal] [int] NULL,
 CONSTRAINT [PK_Loan] PRIMARY KEY CLUSTERED
(
	[AccountNumber] ASC
)WITH (IGNORE_DUP_KEY = OFF) ON [PRIMARY]
) ON [PRIMARY]

CREATE TABLE [dbo].[Mortgage](
	[AccountNumber] [int] NOT NULL,
	[Tax] [int] NULL,
 CONSTRAINT [PK_Mortgage] PRIMARY KEY CLUSTERED
(
	[AccountNumber] ASC
)WITH (IGNORE_DUP_KEY = OFF) ON [PRIMARY]
) ON [PRIMARY]
```

Note In the Table per Type example, I have not included any database referential integrity between the Account, Loan, and Mortgage tables because you will be looking at this mapping later in the chapter. However, note that in a real-world solution there would be constraints on these tables in the database.

Because the steps to create the model in the designer are identical to the one from Figure 7-3, I am not going to go through the creation of the entities in the designer. However, I do want to show you a few interesting details about the entity code being generated that were not covered in the preceding section.

Listing 7-6 provides the Account property, which is part of your object context. The reason that I want to point this out is that this is the only entity that gets exposed from your object context; the entity that contains the identity plus Account is the *entity set* in this example. This is worth noting because in previous examples in earlier chapters, each entity was exposed through the object context class.

Listing 7-6. *Account Entity Set Exposed Through Object Context*

```
 [global::System.ComponentModel.BrowsableAttribute(false)]
public global::System.Data.Objects.ObjectQuery<Account> Account
{
    get
    {
        if ((this._Account == null))
        {
            this._Account = base.CreateQuery<Account>("[Account]");
        }
        return this._Account;
    }

}
```

Another interesting aspect of the code that is generated for the inheritance model is the static Create method generated for all the classes in the hierarchy. In Listing 7-7, you can see the static method from the Loan entity. In this example, the method is creating a new Loan class and setting the AccountNumber. What is most interesting about this example is that the entity key, AccountNumber, is being used even for the creation of the Loan entity.

Listing 7-7. *Static CreateLoan Method Exposed in the Loan Entity*

```
public static Loan CreateLoan(int accountNumber)
{
    Loan loan = new Loan();
    loan.AccountNumber = accountNumber;
    return loan;
}
```

The next step in the process is to map the entity hierarchy to the tables that you created in Listing 7-5. Figure 7-5 shows the mapping details window for the Loan class. Here you can see that unlike the single-table example, where you had to specify a discriminator as a condition, in this example you simply need to map the AccountNumber column in the Loan table to the AccountNumber property of the Account class.

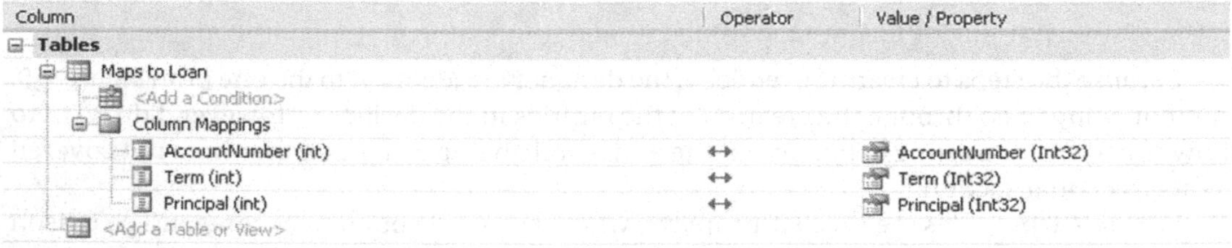

Column	Operator	Value / Property
Tables		
Maps to Loan		
<Add a Condition>		
Column Mappings		
AccountNumber (int)	↔	AccountNumber (Int32)
Term (int)	↔	Term (Int32)
Principal (int)	↔	Principal (Int32)
<Add a Table or View>		

Figure 7-5. *Mapping the Loan class*

The mapping of the Table per Type approach is very easy. In Listing 7-8, you can see the MSL mapping file from the bin directory. In this metadata mapping file are three MappingFragment nodes—Account, Loan, and Mortgage, respectively—and each MappingFragment contains a ScalarProperty that maps to the column AccountNumber.

Listing 7-8. *MSL File for Table per Type Mapping*

```
<EntityContainerMapping StorageEntityContainer="dbo" CdmEntityContainer="Entities">
  <EntitySetMapping Name="AccountSet">

    <EntityTypeMapping TypeName="IsTypeOf(TablePerType.Account)">
      <MappingFragment StoreEntitySet="Account">
        <ScalarProperty Name="Balance" ColumnName="Balance" />
        <ScalarProperty Name="AccountNumber" ColumnName="AccountNumber" />
      </MappingFragment>
    </EntityTypeMapping>

    <EntityTypeMapping TypeName="IsTypeOf(TablePerType.Loan)">
      <MappingFragment StoreEntitySet="Loan">
        <ScalarProperty Name="AccountNumber" ColumnName="AccountNumber" />
        <ScalarProperty Name="Principal" ColumnName="Principal" />
        <ScalarProperty Name="Term" ColumnName="Term" />
      </MappingFragment>
    </EntityTypeMapping>

    <EntityTypeMapping TypeName="IsTypeOf(TablePerType.Mortgage)">
      <MappingFragment StoreEntitySet="Mortgage">
        <ScalarProperty Name="AccountNumber" ColumnName="AccountNumber" />
        <ScalarProperty Name="Tax" ColumnName="Tax" />
      </MappingFragment>
    </EntityTypeMapping>

  </EntitySetMapping>
</EntityContainerMapping>
```

The C# code seen in Listing 7-9 is nearly identical to the code in Listing 7-3, with the exception that a few names have changed. Before I discuss the code, however, you need to insert some data into the three tables (Account, Loan, and Mortgage) by executing the following SQL statements that make the AccountNumber key identical in all three:

```
INSERT INTO Mortgage(AccountNumber, Tax) VALUES (123,200)

INSERT INTO Loan(AccountNumber, Term, Principal) VALUES (123,12,20)

INSERT INTO Account(AccountNumber, Balance) VALUES (123,1000)
```

Listing 7-9 shows a simple example of retrieving the Account EntitySet from the object context as an ObjectQuery. Next, the example loops through the result set and prints out the type of class.

In this example, you have inserted data into all three tables, and so the bottom class in the hierarchy (that is, TablePerType.Mortgage) is what is printed out. Interestingly enough in this example, if you remove the data from the Mortgage table, then the Type that gets printed is TablePerType.Loan instead of Mortgage.

Listing 7-9. *C# to Retrieve the Account Entity Set*

```
Entities en = new Entities();

ObjectQuery<TablePerType.Account> acc = en.AccountSet;

foreach (var c in acc)
{
    Debug.Print(c.GetType().ToString());

}
```

As you might expect in this example, because there are three tables involved instead of one, the T-SQL being generated from EF is quite a bit more complex. Listing 7-10 shows the SQL that is generated when executing the C# in Listing 7-9. Fundamentally, the SQL in this example is a SELECT statement with two left outer joins on the Loan and Mortgage table using the AccountNumber column.

Listing 7-10. *SQL Generated from the Table per Type Mapping*

```
SELECT CASE WHEN ( NOT (([Project2].[C1] = 1) AND ([Project2].[C1] IS NOT NULL)))
THEN '0X' WHEN (([Project2].[C1] = 1) AND ([Project2].[C1] IS NOT
NULL) AND ( NOT (([Project1].[C1] = 1) AND ([Project1].[C1] IS NOT NULL))))
THEN '0X0X' ELSE '0X0X0X' END AS [C1],
[Extent1].[AccountNumber] AS [AccountNumber],
[Extent1].[Balance] AS [Balance],
CASE WHEN ( NOT (([Project2].[C1] = 1) AND ([Project2].[C1] IS NOT NULL)))
THEN CAST(NULL AS int) WHEN (([Project2].[C1] = 1) AND
([Project2].[C1] IS NOT NULL) AND ( NOT (([Project1].[C1] = 1)
AND ([Project1].[C1] IS NOT NULL)))) THEN [Project2].[Term] ELSE
[Project2].[Term] END AS [C2],
CASE WHEN ( NOT (([Project2].[C1] = 1) AND ([Project2].[C1] IS NOT NULL)))
THEN CAST(NULL AS int) WHEN (([Project2].[C1] = 1) AND
([Project2].[C1] IS NOT NULL) AND ( NOT (([Project1].[C1] = 1)
AND ([Project1].[C1] IS NOT NULL)))) THEN [Project2].[Principal] ELSE
[Project2].[Principal] END AS [C3],
CASE WHEN ( NOT (([Project2].[C1] = 1) AND ([Project2].[C1] IS NOT NULL)))
THEN CAST(NULL AS int) WHEN (([Project2].[C1] = 1) AND
([Project2].[C1] IS NOT NULL) AND ( NOT (([Project1].[C1] = 1)
AND ([Project1].[C1] IS NOT NULL)))) THEN CAST(NULL AS int) ELSE [Project1].[Tax]
END AS [C4]
FROM   [dbo].[Account] AS [Extent1]
```

```
LEFT OUTER JOIN  (SELECT
       [Extent2].[AccountNumber] AS [AccountNumber],
       [Extent2].[Tax] AS [Tax],
       cast(1 as bit) AS [C1]
       FROM (SELECT
      [Mortgage].[AccountNumber] AS [AccountNumber],
      [Mortgage].[Tax] AS [Tax]
      FROM [dbo].[Mortgage] AS [Mortgage]) AS [Extent2] )
AS [Project1] ON [Extent1].[AccountNumber] = [Project1].[AccountNumber]
LEFT OUTER JOIN  (SELECT
       [Extent3].[AccountNumber] AS [AccountNumber],
       [Extent3].[Term] AS [Term],
       [Extent3].[Principal] AS [Principal],
       cast(1 as bit) AS [C1]
       FROM [dbo].[Loan] AS [Extent3] ) AS [Project2]
ON [Extent1].[AccountNumber] = [Project2].[AccountNumber]
```

Table per Concrete Class

The Table per Concrete Class mapping technique is similar to both the Table per Type and the single-table mapping. Unlike the Table per Type example, where only the needed fields are stored in a table, the Table per Concrete Class technique puts all the fields of your concrete class into a single table. For this example, all the entities and tables get the number 2 appended to the end of their names. In addition, Account2 becomes an abstract class, and a single table called Loan2 gets created. Because this technique of inheritance mapping is typically used with a single layer of inheritance, in this example the Mortgage entity has been removed.

■ Note The number 2 is being appended on the end of the names in these examples only so that it is possible to run these examples in the same database and solution files.

Listing 7-11 shows the T-SQL used to create the Loan2 table. As you can see from this code, the Loan2 table now contains the AccountNumber and the Balance fields from the abstract Account2 class.

Listing 7-11. *SQL Used to Generate the Loan Table*

```
CREATE TABLE [dbo].[Loan2](
       [AccountNumber] [int] NOT NULL,
       [Balance] [int] NULL,
       [Term] [int] NULL,
       [Principal] [int] NULL,
 CONSTRAINT [PK_Loan2] PRIMARY KEY CLUSTERED
(
       [AccountNumber] ASC
)WITH (IGNORE_DUP_KEY = OFF) ON [PRIMARY]
) ON [PRIMARY]
```

The entity model looks nearly identical to the one seen in Figure 7-3, with the exception that the number 2 is appended to the entity names and the `Mortgage` entity no longer exists. One thing that is not different is that the `Account2` entity is an abstract class. To add the `Account2` entity, you can drag a new entity from the toolbox or you can follow the same steps that you saw in Figure 7-2. To make an entity abstract, such as the `Account2` entity, you need to change the Inheritance Modifier property, as seen in Figure 7-6.

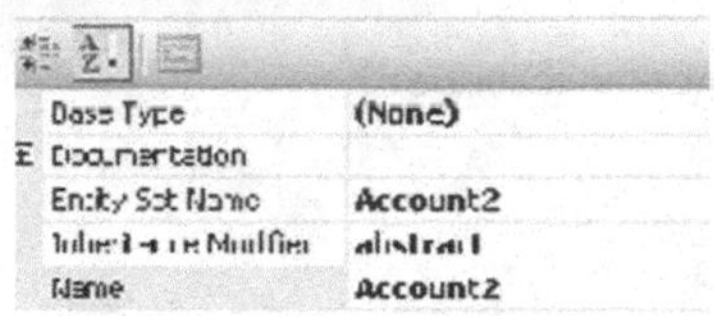

Figure 7-6. *Setting the Inheritance Modifier to abstract*

Another significant difference with this technique for mapping inheritance is the actual mapping details. Because the `Account2` class is abstract and does not have a physical table called `Account2`, it has to map to the `Loan2` table. In Figure 7-7, you can see the UI mapping details for the abstract `Account2` entity.

Column	Operator	Value / Property
Tables		
Maps to Loan2		
<Add a Condition>		
Column Mappings		
AccountNumber (int)	↔	AccountNumber (Int32)
Balance (int)	↔	Balance (Int32)
Term (int)	↔	
Principal (int)	↔	
<Add a Table or View>		

Figure 7-7. *Mapping the Account2 class to the Loan2 table*

Before looking at the MSL mapping file, I want to show you the CSDL conceptual file because with the abstract `Account2` class there is a new attribute now in the metadata. Listing 7-12 shows the CSDL data for the `Account2` entity and the `Loan2` entity. In this example, notice the use of the `Abstract` attribute that is set to `true` for the `Account2` entity and also the `BaseType` attribute that is set to `EFSamplesModel1.Account2` for the `Loan2` entity.

Listing 7-12. *Abstract Inheritance in CSDL*

```
<EntityContainer Name="Entities">
    <EntitySet Name="Account2" EntityType="EFSamplesModel1.Account2" />
</EntityContainer>
```

```
<EntityType Name="Account2" Abstract="true">
    <Key>
      <PropertyRef Name="AccountNumber" />
    </Key>
    <Property Name="AccountNumber" Type="Int32" Nullable="false" />
    <Property Name="Balance" Type="Int32" Nullable="true" />
</EntityType>

<EntityType Name="Loan2" BaseType="EFSamplesModel1.Account2">
    <Property Name="Principal" Type="Int32" Nullable="true" />
    <Property Name="Term" Type="Int32" Nullable="true" />
</EntityType>
```

The MSL mapping data can be seen in Listing 7-13. Here you have two `MappingFragments`, similar to the other examples, but instead of the `Account2` entity mapping to an `Account` table, it maps directly to the `Loan` table.

Listing 7-13. *Mapping Metadata for the Table per Concrete Class Technique*

```
<EntityContainerMapping StorageEntityContainer="dbo" CdmEntityContainer="Entities">
    <EntitySetMapping Name="Account2">

      <EntityTypeMapping TypeName="IsTypeOf(EFSamplesModel1.Account2)">
        <MappingFragment StoreEntitySet="Loan2">
          <ScalarProperty Name="AccountNumber" ColumnName="AccountNumber" />
          <ScalarProperty Name="Balance" ColumnName="Balance" />
        </MappingFragment>
      </EntityTypeMapping>

      <EntityTypeMapping TypeName="EFSamplesModel1.Loan2">
        <MappingFragment StoreEntitySet="Loan2">
          <ScalarProperty Name="AccountNumber" ColumnName="AccountNumber" />
          <ScalarProperty Name="Principal" ColumnName="Principal" />
          <ScalarProperty Name="Term" ColumnName="Term" />
        </MappingFragment>
      </EntityTypeMapping>

    </EntitySetMapping>
</EntityContainerMapping>
```

The next step to complete in this example is to write some C# code to use the inheritance structure. As with the other examples thus far in this chapter, Listing 7-14 shows a small example of querying against the `Account2` entity set. In this example, the `Type` that is printed is `EFSamplesModel1.Loan2` (as you may have expected).

Listing 7-14. *Use the Account2 Entity Set*

```
EFSamplesModel1.Entities en = new EFSamplesModel1.Entities();

ObjectQuery<Account2> acc = en.Account2;

foreach (var c in acc)
{

    Debug.Print(c.GetType().ToString());

}
```

The SQL generated by this query is a standard T-SQL select from the Loan2 table. Listing 7-15 shows the SQL that is created for this type of inheritance.

Listing 7-15. *SQL Generated from Table per Concrete Class Inheritance*

```
SELECT
'0X0X' AS [C1],
[Extent1].[AccountNumber] AS [AccountNumber],
[Extent1].[Balance] AS [Balance],
[Extent1].[Principal] AS [Principal],
[Extent1].[Term] AS [Term]
FROM [dbo].[Loan2] AS [Extent1]
```

In this section, you have seen the three types of inheritance that EF supports. One thing to keep in mind is that there is not one inheritance strategy that is going to solve all problems. In reality, you will likely end up with a combination of these techniques in your application, depending on the issue(s) you are trying to solve.

Entity Client Provider

Until now, this discussion of EF has revolved around Object Services and LINQ to Entities; EF, however, offers another API to work with your data, the Entity Client Provider. The EntityClient is a standard ADO.NET data provider. With the EntityClient, you have a gateway to query against your EDM and your conceptual model. As an ADO.NET provider, the EntityClient (that is, System.Data.EntityClient) uses the well-known provider pattern enabling developers to work with common classes such as Connection, Command, DataReader, and so forth.

The EntityClient is a powerful API because it is not data store–specific. The EntityClient works in conjunction with SQLClient, and Microsoft has launched a partner program to enable additional vendors to develop data access clients to work with the EntityClient (http://blogs.msdn.com/adonet/archive/2007/02/14/entity-client.aspx). What this means in simple terms is that in the near term, you will be able to have an EDM model that is database independent.

You are probably wondering how this is possible. Well, as mentioned earlier, the EntityClient doesn't support LINQ—it supports only entity-level queries written in ESQL. With this restriction, the design can be data provider–independent because there is a common dialect being used to query against the EDM; thus, this dialect can be translated to the data provider class into T-SQL, psql, and so forth. Now, without LINQ, you lose the strongly typed queries that you have seen so far, but ESQL is a very feature rich language for queries.

Note In ESQL version 1.0, INSERT, UPDATE, and DELETE operations are not supported. ESQL can be used only for querying at this time.

ESQL

It is impossible to discuss the EntityClient without discussing ESQL, so let's take a closer look at this new query language. ESQL is a query language that is similar to T-SQL. However, despite all the similarities, ESQL is very different.

Rather than provide a list of all the differences between ESQL and T-SQL, let's take a look at some examples and then discuss the semantics. Listing 7-16 shows a simple query against the AdventureWorks.edmx model to retrieve the Employee entity. As you can see, in this example you use an EntityConnection, an EntityCommand, and a DataReader to retrieve the LoginID from the Employee table. If you have worked with ADO.NET, this pattern should be very familiar to you. Additionally, your ESQL in this example is nothing more than the name of the Employee entity.

Listing 7-16. *Retrieving the Employee Entity by Using ESQL*

```
using (EntityConnection conn = new EntityConnection("name=AdventureWorksEntities1"))
{

    conn.Open();
    string myQuery = "AdventureWorksEntities1.Employee";

    using (EntityCommand cmd = new EntityCommand(myQuery, conn))
    {

        using (DbDataReader rdr =
                cmd.ExecuteReader(CommandBehavior.SequentialAccess))
        {

            while (rdr.Read())
            {

                Debug.Print(rdr["LoginID"].ToString());

            }

        }

    }

}
```

The SQL that is generated from the C# in Listing 7-16 can be seen in Listing 7-17. Here you have a SQL SELECT statement that explicitly names each of the fields and is executed against the Employee table.

Listing 7-17. *SQL Generated from the ESQL*

```
SELECT
[Extent1].[EmployeeID] AS [EmployeeID],
[Extent1].[NationalIDNumber] AS [NationalIDNumber],
[Extent1].[LoginID] AS [LoginID],
[Extent1].[Title] AS [Title],
[Extent1].[BirthDate] AS [BirthDate],
[Extent1].[MaritalStatus] AS [MaritalStatus],
[Extent1].[Gender] AS [Gender],
[Extent1].[HireDate] AS [HireDate],
[Extent1].[SalariedFlag] AS [SalariedFlag],
[Extent1].[VacationHours] AS [VacationHours],
[Extent1].[SickLeaveHours] AS [SickLeaveHours],
[Extent1].[CurrentFlag] AS [CurrentFlag],
[Extent1].[rowguid] AS [rowguid],
[Extent1].[ModifiedDate] AS [ModifiedDate]
FROM [HumanResources].[Employee] AS [Extent1]
```

In Listing 7-16, you saw an EntityConnection being used to query against the EDM. The connection string in this example is the one that is generated by the designer and stored in your app.config file. To refresh your memory, this connection string can be seen in Listing 7-18. In the connection string, you have a configuration that specifies the metadata files (for example, CSDL, SSDL, MSL) as well as the data provider (for example, SqlClient) and the actual connection information. The reason that I am revisiting this is that I want you to recognize that the EDM files are specified in this setting, so when creating a new EntityConnection, you are connecting to these files along with the database.

Listing 7-18. *EF Connection String*

```
<add name="AdventureWorksEntities1"
connectionString="metadata=.\AdventureWorks.csdl|.\AdventureWorks.ssdl|.
\AdventureWorks.msl;provider=System.Data.SqlClient;provider connection
string=&quot;Data Source=YourComputer;Initial Catalog=AdventureWorks;Integrated
Security=True;MultipleActiveResultSets=True&quot;"
providerName="System.Data.EntityClient" />
```

In this last example, in which you queried for the Employee entity, you were using the EntityClient. However, it is important to recognize that ESQL can also be used with the ObjectServices API with strong types. Listing 7-19 shows an example of using the same ESQL query with an ObjectContext (for example, AdventureWorksEntities1) and an ObjectQuery. In this example, the SQL that is generated (not shown) is nearly identical to what is seen in Listing 7-17.

Listing 7-19. *Using ObjectQuery and Object Services with ESQL*

```
using (AdventureWorksEntities1 aw = new AdventureWorksEntities1())
{

    string myQuery = "AdventureWorksEntities1.Employee";
```

```
    foreach (Employee emp in new ObjectQuery<Employee>(myQuery, aw))
    {

        Debug.Print(emp.LoginID.ToString());

    }

}
```

Let's take a look at another example, but this time let's add a condition to the query. Listing 7-20 shows a simple `select` statement to retrieve the `Employee` entity with the `EmployeeID` equal to `1`. As you can see in this example, the syntax for querying is very similar to what you would write in T-SQL. Additionally, in this example, what is being returned is a collection of rows in the form of a `DbDataRecord`, hence the reason for the cast from `DataReader`.

Listing 7-20. *Using an ESQL Select with a Condition*

```
using (EntityConnection conn = new EntityConnection("name=AdventureWorksEntities1"))
{

    conn.Open();

     string myQuery =
       "select p from AdventureWorksEntities1.Employee as p where p.EmployeeID = 1";

     using (EntityCommand cmd = new EntityCommand(myQuery, conn))
     {

         using (DbDataReader rdr =
              cmd.ExecuteReader(CommandBehavior.SequentialAccess))
         {

              while (rdr.Read())
              {
                  DbDataRecord ddr = (DbDataRecord)rdr["p"];
                  Debug.Print(ddr["EmployeeID"].ToString());


              }

         }

     }

}
```

The SQL that is generated from our ESQL can be seen in Listing 7-21. Here you have a standard `SELECT` statement against the `Employee` table, with a `WHERE` clause to specify `EmployeeID = 1`.

Listing 7-21. *SQL Generated from ESQL Select*

```
SELECT
1 AS [C1],
[Extent1].[EmployeeID] AS [EmployeeID],
[Extent1].[NationalIDNumber] AS [NationalIDNumber],
[Extent1].[LoginID] AS [LoginID],
[Extent1].[Title] AS [Title],
[Extent1].[BirthDate] AS [BirthDate],
[Extent1].[MaritalStatus] AS [MaritalStatus],
[Extent1].[Gender] AS [Gender],
[Extent1].[HireDate] AS [HireDate],
[Extent1].[SalariedFlag] AS [SalariedFlag],
[Extent1].[VacationHours] AS [VacationHours],
[Extent1].[SickLeaveHours] AS [SickLeaveHours],
[Extent1].[CurrentFlag] AS [CurrentFlag],
[Extent1].[rowguid] AS [rowguid],
[Extent1].[ModifiedDate] AS [ModifiedDate]
FROM [HumanResources].[Employee] AS [Extent1]
WHERE [Extent1].[EmployeeID] = 1
```

In the example in Listing 7-20, a collection of rows was returned, requiring you to work with column names and a DbDataRecord object. Alternatively, in ESQL you have another option to work directly with the values being returned as you did in Listing 7-16. Listing 7-22 is a similar example to what you saw in Listing 7-20 with two key differences. First, rather than using a SELECT, which always returns a collection of rows, you are using a SELECT VALUE that returns the values of the table in string form. The second difference is, of course, that you no longer need to use the DbDataRecord because you can directly access the values returned from the query.

Listing 7-22. *Using the SELECT VALUE to Return String Values*

```
using (EntityConnection conn = new EntityConnection("name=AdventureWorksEntities1"))
{

    conn.Open();

    string myQuery =
        "select value p from AdventureWorksEntities1.Employee
                 as p where p.EmployeeID = 1";

     using (EntityCommand cmd = new EntityCommand(myQuery, conn))
     {

         using (DbDataReader rdr =
             cmd.ExecuteReader(CommandBehavior.SequentialAccess))
         {
```

```
            while (rdr.Read())
            {
                Debug.Print(rdr["EmployeeID"].ToString());

            }
        }
    }
}
```

The SQL that is generated when using the SELECT VALUE is nearly identical to the SQL generated when using the SELECT. The one difference (see Listing 7-23) is that the [C1] cast seen in Listing 7-21 is no longer part of the query because the EF doesn't need this field.

Listing 7-23. *SQL Generated from the ESQL SELECT VALUE*

```
SELECT
[Extent1].[EmployeeID] AS [EmployeeID],
[Extent1].[NationalIDNumber] AS [NationalIDNumber],
[Extent1].[LoginID] AS [LoginID],
[Extent1].[Title] AS [Title],
[Extent1].[BirthDate] AS [BirthDate],
[Extent1].[MaritalStatus] AS [MaritalStatus],
[Extent1].[Gender] AS [Gender],
[Extent1].[HireDate] AS [HireDate],
[Extent1].[SalariedFlag] AS [SalariedFlag],
[Extent1].[VacationHours] AS [VacationHours],
[Extent1].[SickLeaveHours] AS [SickLeaveHours],
[Extent1].[CurrentFlag] AS [CurrentFlag],
[Extent1].[rowguid] AS [rowguid],
[Extent1].[ModifiedDate] AS [ModifiedDate]
FROM [HumanResources].[Employee] AS [Extent1]
WHERE [Extent1].[EmployeeID] = 1
```

So far, you have seen that ESQL supports both collection-based queries and item-based queries. ESQL also supports composite expressions, providing you with a mechanism for retrieving association entities. Listing 7-24 provides an example of a query with multiple expressions. In this example, you use a navigation property to retrieve the Contact entity data associated with the Employee entity. Because the EDM doesn't care about normalization, in most situations you can build multilevel ESQL expressions across entities, without using a JOIN.

Another important aspect of the example in Listing 7-23 is the aliasing that I'm doing in the query. Just like the as keyword in T-SQL, the as keyword in ESQL can be used to alias the results returned from your query. In this case, the Contact entity is being aliased as c, so to retrieve this data you have to cast the collection of rows associated to a DbDataRecord.

Listing 7-24. *Query Across Associations by Using ESQL*

```
using (EntityConnection conn = new EntityConnection("name=AdventureWorksEntities1"))
{

    conn.Open();

    string myQuery =
    "select p, p.Contact as c from AdventureWorksEntities1.Employee as p";

    using (EntityCommand cmd = new EntityCommand(myQuery, conn))
    {

        using (DbDataReader rdr =
            cmd.ExecuteReader(CommandBehavior.SequentialAccess))
        {

            while (rdr.Read())
            {
                DbDataRecord ddr = (DbDataRecord)rdr["c"];
                Debug.Print(ddr["FirstName"].ToString());


            }

        }

     }

}
```

■ **Note** Listing 7-24 shows two expressions in the query, so two sets of row collections are being returned, one for the Contact (c) entity and one for the Employee (p) entity.

In Listing 7-25, you can see the SQL that is generated from EF and the ESQL that you wrote in Listing 7-24. Here you have the relationship between the Employee and Contact entities represented with a LEFT OUTER JOIN using the ContactID.

Listing 7-25. *SQL Generated from Composite ESQL*

```
SELECT
1 AS [C1],
[Extent1].[EmployeeID] AS [EmployeeID],
[Extent1].[NationalIDNumber] AS [NationalIDNumber],
[Extent1].[LoginID] AS [LoginID],
[Extent1].[Title] AS [Title],
[Extent1].[BirthDate] AS [BirthDate],
[Extent1].[MaritalStatus] AS [MaritalStatus],
[Extent1].[Gender] AS [Gender],
[Extent1].[HireDate] AS [HireDate],
[Extent1].[SalariedFlag] AS [SalariedFlag],
[Extent1].[VacationHours] AS [VacationHours],
[Extent1].[SickLeaveHours] AS [SickLeaveHours],
[Extent1].[CurrentFlag] AS [CurrentFlag],
[Extent1].[rowguid] AS [rowguid],
[Extent1].[ModifiedDate] AS [ModifiedDate],
[Extent2].[ContactID] AS [ContactID],
[Extent2].[NameStyle] AS [NameStyle],
[Extent2].[Title] AS [Title1],
[Extent2].[FirstName] AS [FirstName],
[Extent2].[MiddleName] AS [MiddleName],
[Extent2].[LastName] AS [LastName],
[Extent2].[Suffix] AS [Suffix],
[Extent2].[EmailAddress] AS [EmailAddress],
[Extent2].[EmailPromotion] AS [EmailPromotion],
[Extent2].[Phone] AS [Phone],
[Extent2].[PasswordHash] AS [PasswordHash],
[Extent2].[PasswordSalt] AS [PasswordSalt],
[Extent2].[AdditionalContactInfo] AS [AdditionalContactInfo],
[Extent2].[rowguid] AS [rowguid1],
[Extent2].[ModifiedDate] AS [ModifiedDate1]
FROM  [HumanResources].[Employee] AS [Extent1]
LEFT OUTER JOIN [Person].[Contact] AS [Extent2] ON [Extent1].[ContactID] =
[Extent2].[ContactID]
```

Another interesting aspect regarding entity navigation and associations using ESQL is the one-to-many relationships. Listing 7-26 shows the code that you would use to go from `Contact` to `Employee`. In this example, I am asking for the `Employee` entity from the `Contact` entity.

It is important to realize that in the `AdventureWorks` model, not all `Contact` entities are necessarily going to be an `Employee` entity. This, of course, results in null values being returned because the query does not have a condition to limit the results to non-null values. Additionally, because of the nature of the relationship between the `Contact` and `Employee` entities, instead of a `DbDataRecord` being returned, a second `DbDataReader` is returned, thus the need for the second `while` loop in Listing 7-26.

Listing 7-26. *Query to Retrieve Employee Entities from Contact Entities*

```
using (EntityConnection conn = new EntityConnection("name=AdventureWorksEntities1"))
{

    conn.Open();

    string myQuery =
    "select c, c.Employee as p from AdventureWorksEntities1.Contact as c";

    using (EntityCommand cmd = new EntityCommand(myQuery, conn))
    {

        using (DbDataReader rdr =
           cmd.ExecuteReader(CommandBehavior.SequentialAccess))
        {

            while (rdr.Read())
            {
                DbDataReader edr = (DbDataReader)rdr["p"];
                while (edr.Read())
                {
                    Debug.Print(edr["EmployeeID"].ToString());
                }


            }

        }

    }

}
```

As you can imagine, the SQL that is generated from the C# code in Listing 7-26 is more complex than the SQL you saw in Listing 7-25. Listing 7-27 shows the SQL generated from the code in Listing 7-26. Here you can see that you have one `SELECT` statement with a subquery in the `FROM`, and finally a `JOIN` between the `Contact` and `Employee` tables.

Listing 7-27. *SQL Generated from ESQL Association Between Contact and Employee*

```
SELECT
[Project1].[ContactID] AS [ContactID],
[Project1].[NameStyle] AS [NameStyle],
[Project1].[Title] AS [Title],
[Project1].[FirstName] AS [FirstName],
[Project1].[MiddleName] AS [MiddleName],
[Project1].[LastName] AS [LastName],
```

```
[Project1].[Suffix] AS [Suffix],
[Project1].[EmailAddress] AS [EmailAddress],
[Project1].[EmailPromotion] AS [EmailPromotion],
[Project1].[Phone] AS [Phone],
[Project1].[PasswordHash] AS [PasswordHash],
[Project1].[PasswordSalt] AS [PasswordSalt],
[Project1].[AdditionalContactInfo] AS [AdditionalContactInfo],
[Project1].[rowguid] AS [rowguid],
[Project1].[ModifiedDate] AS [ModifiedDate],
[Project1].[C1] AS [C1],
[Project1].[C2] AS [C2],
[Project1].[EmployeeID] AS [EmployeeID],
[Project1].[NationalIDNumber] AS [NationalIDNumber],
[Project1].[LoginID] AS [LoginID],
[Project1].[Title1] AS [Title1],
[Project1].[BirthDate] AS [BirthDate],
[Project1].[MaritalStatus] AS [MaritalStatus],
[Project1].[Gender] AS [Gender],
[Project1].[HireDate] AS [HireDate],
[Project1].[SalariedFlag] AS [SalariedFlag],
[Project1].[VacationHours] AS [VacationHours],
[Project1].[SickLeaveHours] AS [SickLeaveHours],
[Project1].[CurrentFlag] AS [CurrentFlag],
[Project1].[rowguid1] AS [rowguid1],
[Project1].[ModifiedDate1] AS [ModifiedDate1]
FROM ( SELECT
       [Extent1].[ContactID] AS [ContactID],
       [Extent1].[NameStyle] AS [NameStyle],
       [Extent1].[Title] AS [Title],
       [Extent1].[FirstName] AS [FirstName],
       [Extent1].[MiddleName] AS [MiddleName],
       [Extent1].[LastName] AS [LastName],
       [Extent1].[Suffix] AS [Suffix],
       [Extent1].[EmailAddress] AS [EmailAddress],
       [Extent1].[EmailPromotion] AS [EmailPromotion],
       [Extent1].[Phone] AS [Phone],
       [Extent1].[PasswordHash] AS [PasswordHash],
       [Extent1].[PasswordSalt] AS [PasswordSalt],
       [Extent1].[AdditionalContactInfo] AS [AdditionalContactInfo],
       [Extent1].[rowguid] AS [rowguid],
       [Extent1].[ModifiedDate] AS [ModifiedDate],
       1 AS [C1],
       [Extent2].[EmployeeID] AS [EmployeeID],
       [Extent2].[NationalIDNumber] AS [NationalIDNumber],
       [Extent2].[LoginID] AS [LoginID],
       [Extent2].[Title] AS [Title1],
       [Extent2].[BirthDate] AS [BirthDate],
```

```
        [Extent2].[MaritalStatus] AS [MaritalStatus],
        [Extent2].[Gender] AS [Gender],
        [Extent2].[HireDate] AS [HireDate],
        [Extent2].[SalariedFlag] AS [SalariedFlag],
        [Extent2].[VacationHours] AS [VacationHours],
        [Extent2].[SickLeaveHours] AS [SickLeaveHours],
        [Extent2].[CurrentFlag] AS [CurrentFlag],
        [Extent2].[rowguid] AS [rowguid1],
        [Extent2].[ModifiedDate] AS [ModifiedDate1],
        CASE WHEN ([Extent2].[EmployeeID] IS NULL) THEN CAST(NULL AS int)
ELSE 1 END AS [C2]
        FROM  [Person].[Contact] AS [Extent1]
        LEFT OUTER JOIN [HumanResources].[Employee] AS [Extent2] ON
[Extent1].[ContactID] = [Extent2].[ContactID]
)  AS [Project1]
ORDER BY [Project1].[ContactID] ASC, [Project1].[C2] ASC
```

Along with the ability to navigate across relationships, ESQL also supports traditional `SELECT-FROM-WHERE-GROUPBY-HAVING-ORDERBY` query expressions (`http://blogs.msdn.com/adonet/archive/2007/05/30/entitysql.aspx`). However, unlike T-SQL, ESQL does not permit the use of the * wildcard.

Listing 7-28 shows example code using the `ORDER BY` expression. In this example, you are selecting the `VacationHours` and `EmployeeID` from the `Employee` entity and sorting the results in descending order.

Listing 7-28. *ESQL ORDER BY*

```
using (EntityConnection conn = new EntityConnection("name=AdventureWorksEntities1"))
{

    conn.Open();
    string myQuery =
       "select p.VacationHours, p.EmployeeID from AdventureWorksEntities1.Employee
                as p order by p.VacationHours desc";

    using (EntityCommand cmd = new EntityCommand(myQuery, conn))
    {

       using (DbDataReader rdr =
             cmd.ExecuteReader(CommandBehavior.SequentialAccess))
       {
           while (rdr.Read())
           {
               Debug.Print(rdr["VacationHours"].ToString());
```

```
            }
        }

    }

}
```

The SQL generated when using the standard T-SQL expressions is what you would expect. The expression is simply being added to the T-SQL dialect. Listing 7-29 shows the SQL that is emitted from Listing 7-28. As you can see, the ORDER BY is added to the end of the SELECT expression.

Listing 7-29. *SQL Generated with an ORDER BY*

```
SELECT
[Project1].[C1] AS [C1],
[Project1].[VacationHours] AS [VacationHours],
[Project1].[EmployeeID] AS [EmployeeID]
FROM ( SELECT
       [Extent1].[EmployeeID] AS [EmployeeID],
       [Extent1].[VacationHours] AS [VacationHours],
       1 AS [C1]
       FROM [HumanResources].[Employee] AS [Extent1]
)  AS [Project1]
ORDER BY [Project1].[VacationHours] DESC
```

■ **Caution** SELECT VALUE can have only one expression in the projection list. This means that the VALUE keyword can be used only on a single entity that doesn't span across multiple tables.

Another useful ESQL feature is that you can use functions such as AVG, MIN, MAX, and so forth in your expression as you can with T-SQL. Listing 7-30 shows an example of a query to retrieve the average vacation hours from the Employee entity. The SQL generated (not shown), like the SQL generated in Listing 7-29, basically just passes the ESQL expression through to the T-SQL query.

Listing 7-30. *ESQL Query with Function*

```
using (EntityConnection conn = new EntityConnection("name=AdventureWorksEntities1"))
{

    conn.Open();
    string myQuery =
              "select avg(p.VacationHours) as vac from
                  AdventureWorksEntities1.Employee as p";
```

```
    using (EntityCommand cmd = new EntityCommand(myQuery, conn))
    {

        using (DbDataReader rdr =
            cmd.ExecuteReader(CommandBehavior.SequentialAccess))
        {
            while (rdr.Read())
            {

                Debug.Print(rdr["vac"].ToString());


            }
        }

    }

}
```

Another powerful feature of ESQL is the support for inheritance and polymorphic queries. You have already seen some of the polymorphic functionality in the navigation queries seen earlier, but Listing 7-31 contains an actual query that demonstrates inheritance. In this example, we have gone back to the `EFSamplesEntities` EDM that you created earlier in the chapter. Here you have an ESQL query against the `Account` entity that uses the `IS OF` keywords to tell the engine that you want only entities of the `Mortgage` type.

As you may realize, the ability to use `IS OF` and `TYPEOF` (not shown) ESQL keywords is extremely useful. Although this example is simple, picture an enterprise system that has a model with multiple levels of inheritance. Having the ability to use polymorphism and inheritance in a query language is a new paradigm, and one that will make our lives easier.

Listing 7-31. *ESQL Polymorphic Query*

```
using (EntityConnection conn = new EntityConnection("name=EFSamplesEntities"))
{

    conn.Open();
    string myQuery =
                    "SELECT VALUE e FROM EFSamplesEntities.Account
                        as e WHERE e IS OF (EFSamplesModel.Mortgage)";


    using (EntityCommand cmd = new EntityCommand(myQuery, conn))
    {

        using (DbDataReader rdr =
             cmd.ExecuteReader(CommandBehavior.SequentialAccess))
        {
```

```
            while (rdr.Read())
            {
                Debug.Print(rdr["Balance"].ToString());
            }
        }
    }
}
```

Listing 7-32 shows the SQL that is generated from the polymorphic ESQL query in Listing 7-31. Here you can see that the `AccountType` discriminator is being set to `2` in the query, thus returning only data of type `Mortgage`.

Listing 7-32. *SQL Generated by the Polymorphic ESQL Query*

```
SELECT
'0X0X0X' AS [C1],
[Extent1].[AccountNumber] AS [AccountNumber],
 CAST( [Extent1].[Balance] AS int) AS [C2],
[Extent1].[Term] AS [Term],
[Extent1].[Principal] AS [Principal],
 CAST( [Extent1].[Tax] AS int) AS [C3]
FROM [dbo].[Account] AS [Extent1]
WHERE [Extent1].[AccountType] = ( CAST( '2' AS int))
```

In this section, you learned about the `EntityClient` and ESQL. As stated previously, the purpose of this book is not to be a comprehensive guide to ESQL, and so this section covered only a fraction of ESQL. If you plan on using ESQL in your application, it is advisable that you do more research on the topic. However, to close this section on ESQL, let's take a quick look at what T-SQL functionality is *not* available through ESQL according to MSDN (`http://msdn2.microsoft.com/en-us/library/bb738573(VS.90).aspx`):

DML: ESQL does not support DML statements (`INSERT`, `UPDATE`, `DELETE`).

DDL: ESQL does not support DDL statements (`CREATE`, `ALTER`, `DROP`, and so forth).

Grouping Functions: ESQL does not support grouping functions (`CUBE`, `ROLLUP`, and so forth).

Analytic Functions: ESQL does not support analytic functions.

Hints: ESQL does not support query hints.

Built-in functions and operators: ESQL supports only a subset of T-SQL functions and operators.

Stored Procedures

If you have read any of the earlier chapters in this book, you know that I am against using stored procedures (sprocs) with ORM. However, it would be irresponsible of me to neglect to discuss the functionality because it is natively supported in EF. Additionally, although I think using sprocs for CRUD is incorrect when working with ORM tools, there are times (such as when using Reporting or Security functions) when a sproc is recommended.

Sprocs can be used in EF without making any modifications to the conceptual model or the client code. The only changes that need to be made are in the SSDL, CSDL, and the MSL files. For the sake of brevity, I am not going to go walk you through using sprocs through the UI, because all you really need to know is what changes are happening under the covers. Additionally, after you see the MSL and SSDL changes, the wizard in the EF designer and the model browser will make perfect sense.

Let's start by looking at a simple sproc to retrieve the data in the `Department` table. Listing 7-33 shows a stored procedure for retrieving departments by `DepartmentID`.

Listing 7-33. *GetDepartment Sproc*

```
CREATE PROCEDURE [dbo].[GetDepartment]
   @DepartmentID int
AS
    SELECT DepartmentID,[Name],GroupName,ModifiedDate
   FROM HumanResources.Department
WHERE DepartmentID = @DepartmentID;
```

The sproc is considered a *function* in the context of EF and so is defined that way in the metadata files. Listing 7-34 provides the SSDL, CSDL, and MSL details for using the sproc. As you can see in Listing 7-34, all the metadata that EF needs to connect and use the `GetDepartment` sproc is stored in the XML.

Listing 7-34. *Metadata to Use a Sproc*

```
<--SSDL-->
<Function Name="GetDepartment" Aggregate="false" BuiltIn="false"
    NiladicFunction="false" IsComposable="false"
    ParameterTypeSemantics="AllowImplicitConversion" Schema="dbo">
    <Parameter Name="DepartmentID" Type="int" Mode="In" />
</Function>

<--CSDL-->
<FunctionImport Name="GetDepartment">
    <Parameter Name="DepartmentID" Mode="In" Type="Int32" />
</FunctionImport>

<--MSL-->
<FunctionImportMapping FunctionImportName="GetDepartment"
    FunctionName="AdventureWorksModel.Store.GetDepartment" />
```

After the metadata is defined in the mapping files, a new method called GetDepartment is created in your ObjectContext. The new method really does only one thing, which is call base.ExecuteFunction<Department> and pass the sproc name and parameter to the call and return a System.Data.Objects.ObjectResult. Because the sproc is exposed through your ObjectContext, you can call it as seen in Listing 7-35.

Listing 7-35. *Calling a Sproc*

```
AdventureWorksEntities2 aw2 = new AdventureWorksEntities2();

foreach(AdventureWorksModel.Department dep in aw2.GetDepartment(100))
{
    Debug.Print(dep.GroupName.ToString());

}
```

Along with using a sproc directly through the ExecuteQuery functionality in the ObjectContext class, you can also use sprocs for actual object-to-database mapping. The MSL mapping schema gives you a way to specify InsertFunction, UpdateFunction, and DeleteFunction in XML. By specifying this information, you are effectively overriding the generation of dynamic SQL and forcing EF to use sprocs for these functions.

Listing 7-36 shows the metadata mapping that you can use to override the dynamic SQL generation of INSERT, UPDATE, and DELETE queries. As you can see in this example, each of the functions is mapped to a sproc, and each of the sproc's parameters is specified. Because this functionality overrides the default dynamic SQL generation, there is no explicit C# code that has to be written to use the sprocs; the binding happens automatically. In addition, the MSL file entries in the CSDL and SSDL files (not shown) are made to point to the appropriate sprocs (similar to Listing 7-34).

Listing 7-36. *Mapping to Sprocs*

```
<EntityTypeMapping TypeName="IsTypeOf(AdventureWorksModel.Department)">
<ModificationFunctionMapping>

<InsertFunction FunctionName="AdventureWorks.CreateDepartment">
< ResultBinding Name="DepartmentID" ParameterName="DepartmentID"/>
<ScalarProperty Name="Name" ParameterName="Name"/>
  <ScalarProperty Name="GroupName" ParameterName="GroupName"/>
</InsertFunction>

<UpdateFunction FunctionName=" AdventureWorks.UpdateDepartment">
  < ResultBinding Name="DepartmentID" ParameterName="DepartmentID"
  Version="current"/>
<ScalarProperty Name="Name" ParameterName="Name" Version="current"/>
  <ScalarProperty Name="GroupName" ParameterName="GroupName" Version="current"/>
</UpdateFunction>
```

```
<DeleteFunction FunctionName="AdventureWorks.DeleteDepartment">
  < ResultBinding Name="DepartmentID" ParameterName="DepartmentID"/>
</DeleteFunction>

</ModificationFunctionMapping>
</EntityTypeMapping>
```

Summary

In this chapter, you learned about inheritance, ESQL, and the EntityClient and the basics around sprocs. The three types of inheritance, single-table, Table per Type, and Table per Concrete Class are all supported in EF. There is no skeleton key when it comes to mapping inheritance, so it is best to choose the design that meets the requirements of your application.

When building your application, it is important to consider the pros and cons of using ESQL. ESQL is a very powerful language that is provider-neutral, so if you need greater control and prefer the standard ADO.NET pattern, ESQL might be the right tool for you. Keep in mind that this chapter only scratched the surface of ESQL, so it is important that you do more research on the subject before choosing that direction.

Along with ESQL, EF also offers native support for sprocs. The native support in EF provides you with a mechanism for using sprocs in purely declarative manner by manipulating the metadata instead of the code.

In Chapter 8, I will walk you through the development of the Bank of Pluto domain model, which will be used as a real-world case study throughout the rest of the book. Chapter 8 changes direction by moving away from EF and LTS to focus specifically on the business case of the Bank of Pluto.

PART 4

The Bank of Pluto Case Study

CHAPTER 8

A Domain Model for the First Bank of Pluto

After exploring the fundamentals of ORM, LTS, EF, and the patterns and practices needed to work with these tools, you are now at the point where you can start developing a domain model. In this chapter, you will develop a common domain model for the First Bank of Pluto (FBP). This domain model will utilize many of the patterns and design practices covered in the first part of this book. Additionally, this domain model will be used throughout the rest of the book as the foundation for development using LINQ to SQL and EF. Thus, the domain model will be developed using persistent ignorance and will be modified as necessary in the chapters relating specifically to LINQ to SQL and EF.

As you are probably aware, it is bad practice to develop software without detailed requirements. I don't know about you, but I like to understand what I'm trying to accomplish before I start writing code. In an effort to keep the focus of the text on the design and development of the domain model rather than process methodology (for example, waterfall or extreme programming), I will be narrating the requirements in use case form for simplicity and understanding. However, to bring all readers up to speed on this format, I will also provide a brief description and overview of the use case, and then continue with the concrete examples that elaborate the First Bank of Pluto.

Requirements and Use Cases

The FBP is a new Internet-based lending institution. The core focus of the FBP is retail loans, including auto loans and mortgages. The bank has not yet opened, and management is looking for you to design and develop a solution for their core business. Although the bank's core business is now lending, they are looking to expand into a savings and checking retail bank at some point in the future. However, the Plutonian Deposit Insurance Corporation (PDIC) will allow the FBP to go into only the lending business at this time, because the FBP does not have the capital to back up a full-service banking organization.

The bank has provided you with a set of use cases that are to be used as requirements. Unlike a typical client/consultant relationship, in this situation you're stuck with the use cases and cannot get any direct feedback because the owners of FBP speak only Plutonian. It is your responsibility to build the system from the information provided, and the owners do not want any extra functionality that goes beyond their core business.

I know many software developers who associate use cases with a particular development methodology such as the Rational Unified Process (RUP). Although this association is accurate, the fact is that use cases are excellent requirements-gathering artifacts regardless of the methodology used for your development.

The fundamental concept of a use case revolves around the ability to capture the functional requirements of a software system. *Use cases* are mechanisms to describe the interactions that take place in a software system. The use case starts with the actor. An *actor* is someone or something that is outside the system. This can be a user interaction or a system interaction. The goal of the use case is to describe in simple steps the interactions of the system. This is accomplished from the perspective of the actor and is an end-to-end set of events.

The events described in a use case are most often written in the language of a business analyst, which is to say the language is not technical. In fact, it is my experience that the best use cases are the ones narrated as a "black box" versus ones that try to mix in technical jargon.

Note The UML 2.0 standard has a diagram specifically designed for the use case (coincidently called the use case diagram). However, this diagram is not being used in this text because, as mentioned in Chapter 2, it is overkill in most real-world scenarios. The narrative use case is a far better tool to clarify system requirements because they are written in the domain expert's language, which means there is no need for a specialized skill set.

The following are the use cases that the FBP has supplied you with.

1A: User Registration

Primary actor: User.

Context of use: The user wants to apply for a loan at the First Bank of Pluto; however, the user must first register in the system.

Scope: FBP's Customer Management System.

Status: Draft.

Stakeholders and interests:

- User: Wants to initiate the loan application process but needs a registered user ID and password.
- FBP: Wants to gather preliminary information from the applicant.

Precondition: None.

Minimal guarantees: The user will receive a confirmation that the user ID and password were created and will be redirected to the loan application page.

Trigger: The user supplies the necessary registration information to the FBP and clicks the Save button.

Success guarantees: The user receives confirmation and is redirected to the application page.

Main success scenario:

1. The user fills in the User Name, Password, and Email address fields on the registration form and clicks the Submit button.
2. The FBP validates the registration form.
3. The registration is accepted, and the user information is stored.
4. The user is notified that registration is complete and is redirected to the application (Use Case 1B).

Extensions:

1. Information is missing on the registration form.

    1a. The FBP informs the user of the missing information and requests that it be fixed.

2. The user provides a duplicate user ID or e-mail address.

    2a. The FBP validates against the database and informs the user of the problem and that the fields need to be fixed.

Related information: Store all of the registration information in the FBP Customer Management System.

1B: Loan Application

Primary actors: User, applicant, and Loan System.

Context of use: The user wants to apply for a loan at the FBP but must first complete a loan application.

Scope: FBP's Loan System.

Status: Draft.

Stakeholders and interests:

- User: Before a person can be an applicant, that person must register as a user in the system (see Use Case 1A).
- Applicant: Wants to complete the application process.
- FBP: Wants to gather all necessary information for the loan application.
- FBP: Wants to minimize costs and time to complete the loan application process.

Precondition: The applicant has completed the registration phase (Use Case 1A).

Minimal guarantees: The applicant will receive either a rejection or a loan agreement.

Trigger: The applicant completes the loan application on the FBP web site.

Success guarantees: The applicant is informed of the decision.

Main success scenario:

1. The applicant fills in First Name, Last Name, Date of Birth, Tax ID (SSN), Gender, Requested Amount, and Loan Type (mortgage or auto) and submits the application.
2. The FBP researches the applicant's credit history from the Plutonian Credit Reporting Agency (PCRA).
3. The credit history is added to the application.
4. The application is evaluated (see Use Case 1C) in real time.
5. The applicant is notified that the loan was approved.
6. The money is posted to the applicant's (borrower's) account.

Extensions:

1. The application is missing information.
   - **1a.** Inform the applicant that there is missing information and halt submission until the issues are resolved.

Related information: The FBP Customer Management System and Loan System will be used to access information concerning the applicant, retrieve a credit score, and determine the loan decision.

1C: Loan Application Evaluation

Primary actors: Applicant and Loan System.

Context of use: The loan application has all the required information and needs to be evaluated to determine whether it is credit worthy.

Scope: FBP's Loan System.

Stakeholders and interests:

- FBP: Wants to approve applications that are good risks and provide a reasonable interest rate.
- FBP: Wants to reject higher-risk applications.

Precondition: The application has all required information for evaluation (see Use Case 1B).

Minimal guarantees: The application will be either rejected or approved with an accompanying interest rate.

Trigger: The application has been submitted on the FBP web site.

Success guarantees: A decision is determined, and the applicant is informed of the decision.

Main success scenario:

1. Retrieve the credit score and evaluate against the following criteria:
   - Score 0–400 = rejected
   - Score 401–500 = approved (8 percent interest rate)
   - Score 501–600 = approved (7 percent interest rate)
   - Score 701+– = approved (6 percent interest rate)
2. Approve or reject the loan application and supply the interest rate on approved applications.

Extensions: None.

Related information: The FBP Loan System will be used to access the information required to send to the PCRA and will determine the credit worthiness of the applicant.

1D: Account/Loan Summary

Primary actors: Borrower, user, and Loan System.

Context of use: After the loan application has been approved and the money disbursed, the borrowers need to be able to log in and view a summary of their accounts.

Scope: FBP's Loan System and Customer Management System.

Stakeholders and interests:

- FBP: Wants to provide its customers with a way to see basic information about their accounts.

Precondition: The loan is approved and money is disbursed to the borrower's account.

Minimal guarantees: The balance, interest rate, account number, and loan period will be displayed to the borrower.

Trigger: The application has been approved and the loan has been disbursed.

Success guarantees: A summary screen is displayed to the customer.

Main success scenario:

- Retrieve the balance, interest rate, account number, and loan and display it to the user.

Extensions: None.

Related information: The FBP Loan System and Customer Management System will be used to access the information needed to show the loan summary to the customer.

The Model

Like a typical client, the requirements found in the FBP use cases are sparse. Instead of walking you through every detail of modeling the use cases, I will give you the condensed version so you can dive directly into the code. Modeling a domain can be a daunting task, so be aware that doing it with any efficiency takes practice.

In Figure 8-1, I started with the stakeholders in the system and worked my way through the use cases described earlier in the chapter. I define a *stakeholder* in the domain model as someone or something that has their neck on the line. A stakeholder can be a person, company, or organization. However, it is important to understand that a stakeholder is the lowest level in the hierarchy. For example, a stakeholder may be a person, but a stakeholder is not a user. A person is a user, which is to say a person has the role of a user, but a user is not a stakeholder, the person is. This is a bit confusing, but I assure you that it is one of the easiest ways to keep the model in order and will make more sense as we move through the examples in the text.

■ **Note** The code that you are writing in this chapter is a starting point for a POCO (that is, persistent ignorant) domain model. As with most software projects, we will be refactoring and extending this code throughout the book to accommodate for changing requirements and infrastructure (for example, EF, LINQ to SQL) shortcomings.

When building an object model, you need to go back to the basics, which I call the *is a, has a, does a* relationships. This is a fundamental concept that you learn when going through object-oriented development training, but it is often lost in overengineering and overanalysis of a project. I approach each use case by asking myself, "What are the *is a, has a,* and *does a* relationships?" Figure 8-1 shows the top-level relationship structure of the FBP domain.

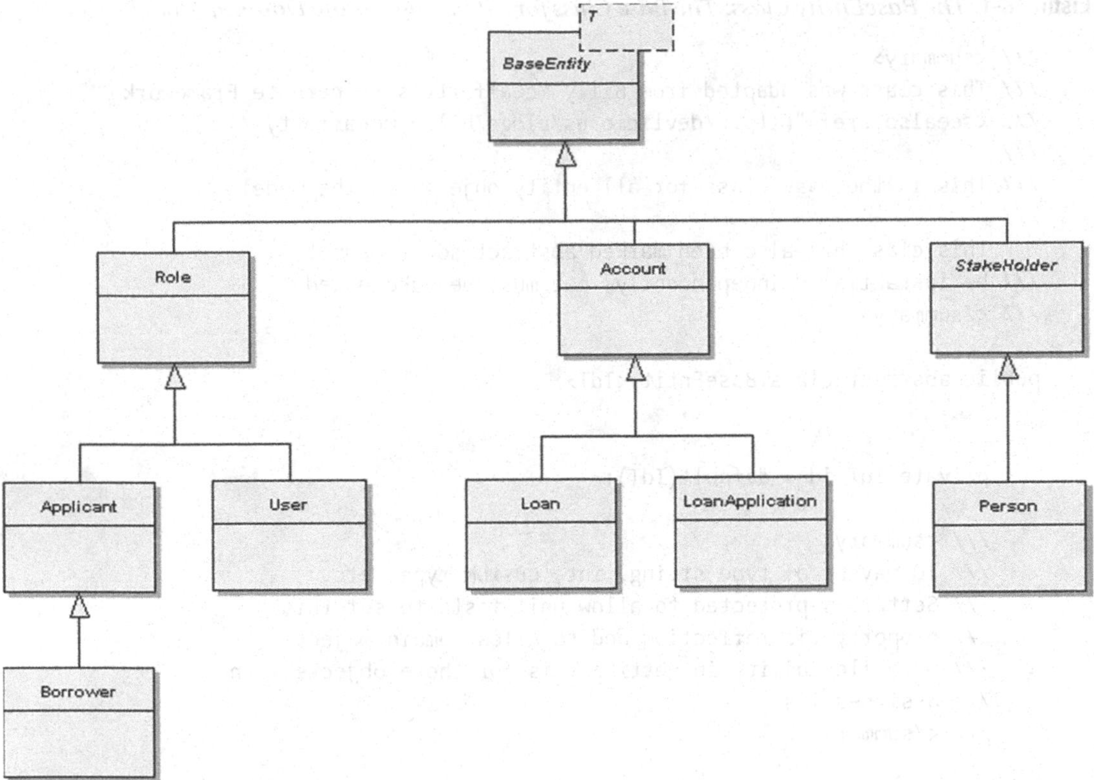

Figure 8-1. *Class diagram of the domain model*

Base Classes

Now that you have a rough idea of the relationships between the classes in the system, let's start writing some code to build out the domain model. The first thing I like to do after building my class diagram is to create my base class structure. I have created a new class library project in Visual Studio 2008 called `BoP.Core`. *BoP* stands for *Bank of Pluto,* of course, and the word *Core* denotes that this is the central point of the domain model. This is where most of the foundational POCO objects will be created to enumerate the bank's domain.

The first object I have created can be seen in Listing 8-1 and is the `BaseEntity` class. This is the class from which all entities in the domain model derive, because it contains functionality to handle *identity* and *equality*. In Listing 8-1, which was adapted from Billy McCafferty's NHibernate DAO framework (`www.devlicio.us/blogs/billy_mccafferty`), you have a generic abstract class that can accept an ID of any .NET type, thereby giving you flexibility when working with identity attributes in your model and database. In addition, as is common practice, I have overridden `Equals`, `ToString`, and `GetHashCode` to account for the equality predicaments that one can run into when building a domain model foundation.

Listing 8-1. *The BaseEntity Class: The Base Class for All Entities in the Domain Model*

```
/// <summary>
/// This class was adapted from Billy McCafferty's NHibernate Framework
/// <seealso cref="http://devlicio.us/blogs/billy_mccafferty"/>
///
/// This is the base class for all entity objects in the model.
///
/// This class has also been marked abstract so it cannot
/// be instantiated independently, but must be subclassed.
/// </summary>

public abstract class BaseEntity<IdT>
{

    private IdT id = default(IdT);

    /// <summary>
    /// ID may be of type string, int, custom type, etc.
    /// Setter is protected to allow unit tests to set this
    /// property via reflection and to allow domain objects
    /// more flexibility in setting this for those objects with
    /// assigned IDs.
    /// </summary>

    public IdT ID {
        get { return id; }
        protected set { id = value; }
    }

    public override sealed bool Equals(object obj) {
        BaseEntity<IdT> compareTo = obj as BaseEntity<IdT>;

        return (compareTo != null) &&
               (HasSameNonDefaultIdAs(compareTo) ||

                // Since the IDs aren't the same, either of them must be
                // transient to compare business value signatures

                (((IsTransient()) || compareTo.IsTransient()) &&
                 HasSameBusinessSignatureAs(compareTo)));
    }

    /// <summary>
    /// Transient objects are not associated with an item already in storage.
    /// For instance, a <see cref="Applicant" /> is transient if its ID is 0.
    /// </summary>
```

```
public bool IsTransient() {
    return ID == null || ID.Equals(default(IdT));
}

/// <summary>
/// Must be provided to properly compare two objects
/// </summary>
public override int GetHashCode()
{
    return this.ToString().GetHashCode();
}

private bool HasSameBusinessSignatureAs(BaseEntity<IdT> compareTo) {

    return GetHashCode().Equals(compareTo.GetHashCode());
}

/// <summary>
/// Returns true if self and the provided persistent
/// object have the same ID values and the IDs are
/// not of the default ID value
/// </summary>

private bool HasSameNonDefaultIdAs(BaseEntity<IdT> compareTo) {

    return (ID != null && ! ID.Equals(default(IdT))) &&
           (compareTo.ID != null && ! compareTo.ID.Equals(default(IdT))) &&
           ID.Equals(compareTo.ID);
}

/// <summary>
/// Overriden to return the class type
/// of this object.
/// </summary>
///
/// <returns>
/// the class name for this object
/// </returns>
///

public override string ToString()
{
    StringBuilder str = new StringBuilder();
    str.Append(" Class: ").Append(GetType().FullName);
    return str.ToString();
}

}
```

Now that you have a base class for your entities, you need to create a base class for your stakeholders. With the exception of the entities in your model, the stakeholders are probably your most important structure. As I mentioned earlier, a stakeholder is a conceptually primitive type—a `Person`, `Company`, or `Organization`, not a `User` or `Applicant`, which are considered `Roles` in our model (see Listing 8-3).

In Listing 8-2, you have another abstract class called `StakeHolder`. This class, as the name implies, is used as the superclass for all stakeholders in the model. You will notice that the `StakeHolder` inherits from our `BaseEntity` class and passes the type `int` as the identity of the class. Because we can inherit from only one class in C#, and because we know that a stakeholder in the system is an *entity* (see Chapter 2 for a more detailed definition), we have to build our inheritance chain this way to ensure that our stakeholders have the appropriate identity management.

You may be thinking that this is slightly limiting because you are forced to have all stakeholders use type `int` as their identity type—and it is limiting—but for the purpose of these examples, it is the best solution. If you really think that you will need different identity types for each of your stakeholders, you can create a separate interface to assign the type; however, I will not be covering that in this text.

Along with deriving from `BaseEntity` and `StakeHolder`, the fundamental purpose behind the class is to store and manage the `Roles` of the stakeholder. As you can see in Listing 8-2, this is implemented by using a `Ilist<Role>` container, with the standard collection methods implemented in the class.

Listing 8-2. *The StakeHolder Class: The Base Class from Which All Stakeholders in the System Are Derived*

```
/// <summary>
/// The base class that all other stakeholders
/// extend from.  A stakeholder is a person,
/// company, or organization that has an interest
/// in the domain, and has also been validated or confirmed
/// to exist.
/// </summary>

public abstract class StakeHolder:BaseEntity<int>
{

        List<Role> roles;

        /// <summary>
        /// Default constructor initializes the Role collection
        /// </summary>
        public StakeHolder()
        {
            roles = new List<Role>();
        }
```

```
/// <summary>
/// Property exposing Roles as List<>
/// used to get List of Roles and Set the internal
/// collection
/// </summary>
public List<Role> Roles
{
   get{
           return roles;
     }
   set
     {
          foreach (Role r in value)
             roles.Add(r);
     }
 }


 /// <summary>
 /// Check if there are any roles associated with this
 /// stakeholder.
 /// </summary>
 ///
 /// <returns>
 /// is the roles list empty.
 /// </returns>

 public virtual bool IsRolesEmpty()
 {
      return (Roles.Count == 0);
 }

 /// <summary>
 /// Every subclass of this class must provide a name.  Depending
 /// on the subclass, the way the name is constructed may be
 /// different.  Example:  A name of a person vs. a company name
 /// </summary>
 ///
 /// <returns>
 /// the name of this stakeholder.
 /// </returns>

 public abstract String GetName();
```

```
/// <summary>
/// Adds a role to this stakeholder.  Also makes sure
/// to assign the stakeholder to the role as well.
///
/// </summary>
/// <param name="r">
/// the role to add
/// </param>

public virtual void AddRole(Role r)
{
     r.StakeHolder = this;
     r.StakeHolderId = this.StakeHolderId;
     Roles.Add(r);
}

/// <summary>
/// Removes the Role.
/// The stakeholder reference is also set to null.
///
/// </summary>
/// <param name="r">
/// the role to remove
/// </param>
/// <returns>
/// was the role removed
/// </returns>

public virtual bool RemoveRole(Role r)
{
       Roles.Remove(r);

       bool success = (Roles.IndexOf(r) < 0);
       if (success)
            r.StakeHolder = null;

       return success;
}


/// <summary>
/// Get the number of roles on this stakeholder
/// </summary>
///
/// <returns>
/// the number of roles for the stakeholder
/// </returns>
///
```

```
public virtual int NumberOfRoles()
{
     return Roles.Count;
}


/// <summary>
/// Check if the role is contained in this stakeholder.
///
/// </summary>
/// <param name="a">
/// the role to check for
/// </param>
/// <returns>
/// was the role found
/// </returns>

public virtual bool ContainsRole(Role a)
{
      return Roles.Contains(a);
}


/// <summary>
/// Every role has a name, see if a role exists
/// on this stakeholder by the designated name.
/// </summary>
///
/// <param name="roleName">
/// the role name to search for
/// </param>
///
/// <returns>
/// does the role exist by the given role name
/// </returns>

public virtual bool ContainsRoleOfName(String roleName)
{
      Role role = GetRoleOfName(roleName);
      return (role != null);                 }


/// <summary>
/// Every role has a name, return the role based on the role name
/// passed in.  If the role does not exist by the given name,
/// null is returned.
/// </summary>
///
```

```
        /// <param name="roleName">
        /// the role name to search for
        /// </param>
        ///
        /// <returns>
        /// the role by the given name
        /// </returns>

        public virtual Role GetRoleOfName(string roleNamc)
        {
            if ((roleName != null) && (roleName.Length > 0))
            {

                for (int i = 0; i < Roles.Count; i++)
                {
                    if (roleName.Equals(Roles[i].Name))
                        return Roles[i];
                }
            }

            return null;
        }

}
```

You have probably already guessed the next class that you need to create in order to build out the structural code of the model. Yes, the Role class is the next piece that needs to be developed, and you can find it in Listing 8-3. I have already talked about the conceptual value of the Role class in the model; however, I still want to touch on a few design topics surrounding this class. First, it is critical to understand that a role is not an entity in the system; it is a value object, because a role must be associated with a stakeholder and does not have an identity of its own. This design principle is evident in the implementation code of the class (for example, the StakeHolder get/set property). Next, the Role class is an abstract class, and thus should be used as the superclass for all roles in the system. Finally, the Role class contains a convenience method for returning the associated Person (that is, stakeholder) to allow for easier coding against the model. This is not to say that you should add a significant number of convenience or helper methods to this (or any) abstract class; however, in this scenario a cross-cutting method is helpful.

Listing 8-3. *The Role Class: The Base Class for All Roles Defined in the System*

```
/// <summary>
/// For every stakeholder, there should be only
/// one instance of that particular stakeholder in the domain.
/// A stakeholder can take on many different
/// roles to represent himself based on the
/// domain that stakeholder is involved in.
///
```

```
/// For example, Bill (who is a person and hence a stakeholder)
/// could be seen as a policeman for his profession, but is also
/// seen as a coach for his high school football team,
/// and is seen as a borrower if he has an auto loan.
/// All of the above would be represented as Roles on Bill.
/// Every role defined for a stakeholder should extend off of
/// this class.
///
/// </summary>
///
public class Role
{
    /// <summary>
    /// Default Constructor needed for reflection
    /// </summary>
    public Role()
    { }

    /// <summary>
    /// Constructor to set the name of this role.
    /// Every role has a "nice" name or "display name"
    /// indicating the type of role it is.
    /// Every class that extends off the role is responsible for
    /// providing a nice name for its role.
    /// </summary>
    ///
    /// <param name="name">
    /// display name for this role.
    /// </param>

    public Role(string name)
    {
        if (Name != null)
            this.Name = name;
    }

    /// <summary>
    /// Returns the "nice" name or "display" name for this role.
    /// Every class that subclasses this
    /// role class is responsible for supplying a display name.
    /// </summary>
    ///
    /// <returns>
    /// the name for this role.
    /// </returns>
    public string Name { get; set; }
```

```
/// <summary>
/// Gets/Sets the stakeholder for this role.
/// EVERY role should be associated with a stakeholder
/// </summary>
///
/// <returns>
/// the stakeholder for this implementing this role.
/// </returns>
public virtual StakeHolder StakeHolder{ get; set; }

/// <summary>
/// Convenience method.  Get the stakeholder's name, which may be a person's
/// name or company's name.
/// </summary>
///
/// <returns>
/// the name
/// </returns>
public virtual String GetName()
{
    if (StakeHolder == null)
        return "Undefined";
    else
        return StakeHolder.GetName();
}


/// <summary>
/// Convenience method.  Get the stakeholder as a person.
/// Returns null if the stakeholder can't be narrowed to a Person.
/// </summary>
///
/// <returns>
/// the stakeholder as a person
/// </returns>
public virtual Person Person
{
    get
    {
        if (StakeHolder is Person)
            return ((Person)StakeHolder);
        else
            return (null);
    }
```

```
            set
            {
                StakeHolder = value;
            }
        }

        /// <summary>
        /// Returns a string representation of the object.
        ///
        /// </summary>
        /// <returns>
        /// a string representation of the object.
        /// </returns>
        public override String ToString()
        {
            StringBuilder buf = new StringBuilder();
            lock (this)
            {
                buf.Append(base.ToString());
                buf.Append("Role Model");
            }
            buf.Append("\r\n");
            return buf.ToString();
        }
    }
```

Note I have added a method to return a `Person` in the `Role` class because the business requirements tell me that the main stakeholder in this model is an individual. If the requirements changed to require a commercial or organizational stakeholder, it would be perfectly acceptable to include these convenience methods in the `Role` abstract class.

Entities

Continuing on with the model, the next step is to start the development of the actual business domain objects. These are the objects that ultimately get mapped to the database and are the main reason for this book. These classes are the easy part of the solution, and therefore I will not be showing examples of each class in the domain model. Trust me, after you have seen a couple of property classes, you'll understand the concept. These classes are represented in Figure 8-1, and for the most part are simple classes that contain properties/attributes of the domain.

In Listing 8-4, you can see that I have created the `Account` class, which is an entity in the system and thus inherits from `BaseEntity`. Additionally, the `Account` class uses one of the new VS 2008 features, automatic properties that you will see throughout the text. Also notice the `Loan` class, which is a subclass of `Account` and thus inherits from `Account` for its identity.

Listing 8-4. *The Account and Loan Classes: Entities in the System*

```
/// <summary>
/// The account class is a general use object in the system.
/// This class is instantiated when a person's loan is approved,
/// and is also subclassed for more-granular control (e.g., Loan).
/// </summary>

public class Account:BaseEntity<int>
{
    public Account() { }

    public int AccountNumber{ get; set; }
    public int Balance { get; set; }

}


/// <summary>
/// The Loan class is a subclass of Account.
/// This class contains loan-specific information
/// and is created after an application is approved.
/// </summary>

public class Loan:Account
{
    public float InterestRate { get; set; }
    public int Period { get; set; }
    public float Amount
    {
        get { return base.Balance; }
        set { base.Balance = value; }
    }

}
```

The next area of focus in the model is the stakeholders, which (as you have seen in Listings 8-2 and 8-3) have a different inheritance structure than the standard entity object (for example, Account) in your domain model. These classes inherit directly from the StakeHolder base, which handles the plumbing code for Role management and implements the BaseEntity functionality.

Listing 8-5 shows an example of the Person stakeholder, the main focus of the FBP application. The Person class implements all the attributes that you would expect a person to have: First Name, Last Name, Tax ID, Gender, and so forth. Additionally, the Person class overrides the GetName method from the StakeHolder class and returns a concatenated first and last name. I know you are probably thinking to yourself that this class is lacking a lot of information, but I want to point out again that the purpose of this exercise is to create a basic foundation so we can elaborate the patterns and structure of the framework.

Listing 8-5. *The Person Class: The Key Stakeholder in the FBP Application*

```
/// <summary>
/// The Person class represents an individual and contains
/// logical attributes about that individual that make him or her unique.
/// These attributes consist of (but are not limited to) Gender,
/// DOB, First Name, Last Name, Tax ID, etc.
///
/// Within the domain, there should be only one existence of a
/// particular person, but a single person can have many roles.
/// See the <see cref="Role"/> class for details.
/// </summary>

public class Person: StakeHolder
{
    public string FirstName { get; set; }
    public string LastName { get; set; }
    public string Gender { get; set; }
    public DateTime DOB{ get; set; }
    public string TaxId { get; set; }
    public string Email { get; set; }

    public override string GetName()
    {
        return FirstName + " " + LastName;
    }
}
```

■ **Tip** Remember when modeling your domain to think about interactions and attribution of your object in the primitive form. This will lead you to a cleaner model and will help improve the usability of your framework.

Roles

Now that you have examples of a nonstakeholder entity (for example, `Account`) and an entity stakeholder (for example, `Person`), you need to look at creating roles in the system. This concept of a role is one I have mentioned throughout this chapter because it can be difficult to grasp. As you can see in Listing 8-6, we have the `User` class as an example of a role in the system. The `User` role is used when a consumer of the web site registers with the system. The `User` class contains the necessary security information to authenticate to the FBP system. Along with the `User` class, in Listing 8-6 the `Applicant` class is also enumerated.

Listing 8-6. *The User and Applicant Classes: Examples of Roles in the FBP Application*

```
/// <summary>
/// The User class, as the name implies, is the "User"
/// role in the system. This role is placed on any stakeholder
/// in the domain to provide the required information
/// for logging on and off of the system.  This Role is
/// created after a user of the web site registers.
/// </summary>

public class User:Role
{
    private const string ROLE_NAME = "User";

    public User() : base(ROLE_NAME) { }

    public string UserId { get; set; }
    public string Password { get; set; }
    public bool Active { get; set; }

}

/// <summary>
/// The Applicant class is a Role in the system and is a
/// transient object. A Person in the system is only
/// temporarily an Applicant because they become a Borrower
/// after their application is approved.
/// </summary>

public class Applicant:Role
{
    private const string ROLE_NAME = "Applicant";

    public Applicant() : base(ROLE_NAME) { }

    public LoanApplication LoanApp { get; set; }
}
```

The Applicant class is another role in the system and is used during the application process. Notice that both the Applicant and User classes are passing a ROLE_NAME constant to the Base class constructor. The purpose of this identifier is for tracking changes in the collection of the Role class in relationship to the stakeholder. The use of the constant in this scenario is purely a preference of mine, and can easily be changed to be populated through reflection or some other means. In addition, the Applicant role is fundamentally a transient object, which means that it is used only on a temporary basis during the application process. This is because when the application is approved, the consumer of the system is no longer an Applicant but a Borrower, and if the application is rejected, the Applicant role is removed from the system. Don't worry too much about persistent or transient classes right now, because as we dive into LINQ to SQL and the EF, I will be addressing and elaborating on these situations in depth.

Managers

Up to this point, you have been working mostly with common foundational structures—for example, entities and stakeholders. What about the domain-specific logic that makes the application go? The logic that actually does some work is all handled in the Manager and Factory layers (DAO Factory, if you want to get specific). The DAO implementation is covered in the next section, but I want you to look at the best way to implement the manager functionality in the FBP application.

Before you start looking at Listing 8-7 (which presents some manager interfaces and implementation code), let's discuss the manager concept. What is a manager? Most of us have a manager at work, but that is a really bad analogy because I've met many worthless managers who do very little. That is not what we want for the managers in our system; we want managers who are hard workers. I like to think of a manager as someone who directs others, works hard, and handles coordination of work. You should think about these attributes every time you create a manager in your system.

For example, in Listing 8-7, you can see that we have created an `IUserManager` interface. What does a manager of users do in a banking application? Obviously, the manager of users would handle user-specific functions, such as authentication and password management. This pattern can be applied throughout the model, by creating separate managers for the entities in the system that need to do work. These managers are in turn used by your presentation layer, for event-driven UI interactions.

If there is one thing to remember here, it is that the manager does not handle the CRUD or creational patterns and operations—that is reserved for your DAO layer. The manager accomplishes the other functions that are needed for the system to run. Don't worry if you are confused at this point; as you continue through the text and as the FBP application comes to life, these patterns will become clearer.

Listing 8-7 shows two examples of interfaces in the `BoP.Core` solution that provide you with the contract for creating a concrete `UserManager` or `LoanApplicationManager`. In both examples, you can see in the XML comments that we are also defining specific exception types to be raised from the implementation of the interface. These exceptions are also being created in the `BoP.Core` solution, and examples can be seen in Listing 8-8.

Listing 8-7. *The UserManager and LoanApplicationManager: Examples of "Workers" in the FBP Application*

```
/// <summary>
/// Provides the operations for working with the domain model
/// by implementing business logic to work with the DAO layer.
/// </summary>
public interface IUserManager
{

    /// <summary>
    /// A method that will authenticate a user based on their
    /// userName and password.  If the userName and password are correct,
    /// the user will be returned with their person/profile information.
    /// </summary>
    ///
```

```
/// <param name="userName">
/// user name to log in
/// </param>
///
/// <param name="password">
/// password of the user
/// </param>
///
/// <returns>
/// the authenticated user
/// </returns>
///
/// <exception cref="BoP.Core.InvalidUserNameException">
/// the user could not be found based on that username
/// </exception>
///
/// <exception cref="BoP.Core.InvalidPasswordException">
/// password provided is incorrect
/// </exception>
///
/// <exception cref="BoP.Core.UserDisabledException">
/// the user is disabled
/// </exception>
///
/// <exception cref="BoP.Core.AuthenticateException">
/// an unexpected exception occurs
/// </exception>
///
User Authenticate(String userName, String password);

/// <summary>
/// A Method for Creating a new user
/// This is a helper method to encapsulate DAO functionality
/// </summary>
/// <param name="u"></param>
User CreateUser(User u);

/// <summary>
/// Method for retrieving a forgotten password.
/// An email is sent with the user's password.
/// </summary>
/// <param name="email"></param>
/// <returns>Password</returns>
string ForgotPassword(string email);
```

```
    /// <summary>
    /// Method for retrieving a forgotten username.
    /// An email is sent with the user's UserName.
    /// </summary>
    /// <param name="email"></param>
    /// <returns>Emails UserName</returns>
    string ForgotUserName(string email);

        /// <summary>
        /// a method that will log out a given user
        /// </summary>
        /// <param name="user"></param>
        void Logout(User user);

    }

/// <summary>
/// The ILoanApplicationManager Interface is used to define
/// the contract for creating a new LoanApplicationManager
/// concrete class.  This class provides the necessary "worker"
/// functions for manipulating a LoanApplication
/// </summary>
public interface ILoanApplicationManager
{

        /// <summary>
        /// A method that saves the
        /// loan application before or after
        /// decisioning and credit history
        /// </summary>
        ///
        /// <param name="la">
        /// Loan Application
        /// </param>
        ///
        /// <returns>
        /// Loan Application
        /// </returns>
        ///
        /// <exception cref="BoP.Core.SaveLoanException">
        /// an unexpected exception occurs
        /// </exception>
        LoanApplication SaveLoanApplication(LoanApplication la);
```

```
    /// <summary>
    /// A method that reviews the
    /// loan application and determines
    /// if the applicant is worthy of the loan
    /// </summary>
    ///
    /// <param name="la">
    /// Loan Application
    /// </param>
    ///
    /// <returns>
    /// Loan Application
    /// </returns>
    ///
    /// <exception cref="BoP.Core.DecisionLoanException">
    /// an unexpected exception occurs
    /// </exception>
    LoanApplication DecisionLoanApplication(LoanApplication la);

    /// <summary>
    /// A method that populates the credit
    /// history on a loan application
    /// credit score.
    /// </summary>
    ///
    /// <param name="la">
    /// Loan Application
    /// </param>
    ///
    /// <returns>
    /// Loan Application
    /// </returns>
    ///
    /// <exception cref="BoP.Core.CreditHistoryException">
    /// an unexpected exception occurs
    /// </exception>
    ///
    LoanApplication GetCreditHistory(LoanApplication la);

}
```

■ **Tip** It is best practice to create custom exceptions that inherit from `System.ApplicationException` in your domain model to allow for optimized error handling and self-description.

Listing 8-8. *An Example of a Domain Model Custom Exception*

```
/// <summary>
/// Used as a base exception class for exceptions
/// thrown from the user manager, especially when dealing
/// with authentication
/// </summary>

public class AuthenticateException:ApplicationException
{
    /// <summary>
    /// Creates new AuthenticateException without detail message.
    /// </summary>

    public AuthenticateException()
    {}

    /// <summary>
    /// Constructs a new AuthenticateException with
    /// the specified detail message.
    /// </summary>
    ///
    /// <param name="msg">
    /// the detail message.
    /// </param>

    public AuthenticateException(String msg):base(msg)
    {}

    /// <summary>
    /// Constructs AuthenticateException with detail
    /// message and inner exception
    /// </summary>
    ///
    /// <param name="msg">
    /// Detail message
    /// </param>
    /// <param name="inner">
    /// Exception to wrap
    /// </param>

    public AuthenticateException(string msg, Exception inner)
                        : base(msg, inner)
    {
    }

}
```

DAO Implementation

In Chapter 2, I discussed the DAO pattern and the concept of abstracting the layer between your domain model and your data access layer. In this chapter, I'm going to start building the structure for the DAO implementation in the FBP model. I want to stress the word *start* because the concrete DAO implementation is specific to the ORM solution that you will be using in your application. Therefore, we will be building the interfaces that are part of the `BoP.Core` project but will not build the concrete implementation until we move into the development of LINQ to SQL and EF in the coming chapters.

The first thing you need to know is that the DAO solution built in this text is an adaptation of Billy McCafferty's generic DAO implementation for NHibernate, which he adapted from the Java Hibernate generic DAO solution. What does this mean to you? Well, instead of implementing a concrete DAO factory and a concrete DAO object for each of your domain objects, you can now implement a generic solution that encapsulates this functionality. Basically, I just saved you hours of tedious coding.

To start with, you will be creating PI C# interfaces in the `BoP.Core` solution that contain the contracts for our CRUD operations. These interfaces, which are seen in Listing 8-9, are consumed by the `BoP.Data` solution (which will be created in the coming chapters). The `BoP.Data` solution will contain the DAO factories for our ORM solutions (for example, LINQ to SQL, EF) and will consume the contracts stored in our `BoP.Core` solution. To keep things organized, the new data interfaces will be stored in a subnamespace of `BoP.Core` called `BoP.Core.DAOInterfaces`.

Listing 8-9 shows the `IDao` interface and the `IDaoFactory` examples. These two interfaces do not contain any ORM-specific implementation logic and can be used for general functionality in your model. The `IDao` interface contains the method signatures for your CRUD operations, which will be used to manipulate your persistent objects and communicate with your ORM. Although the `IDaoFactory` contains interfaces specific to the domain model you have just created, you will notice that it now contains multiple interfaces that relate back to the entities in your domain model. You may be thinking that you were taught to store your interfaces in separate physical files for readability and maintenance. However, because these are broad-purpose interfaces, I don't see any issue with keeping them in a single file; however, feel free to extract them into separate files if you feel the need. Overall, the `IDaoFactory` is a good way to keep the data access separate from your domain model implementation.

Listing 8-9. *The DAO Interfaces in the BoP.Core Solution*

```
/// <summary>
/// This interface was adapted from Billy McCafferty's NHibernate Framework
/// <see cref="http://devlicio.us/blogs/billy_mccafferty"/>
///
/// The purpose of this interface is to provide a
/// general-purpose contract for CRUD operations
/// executed in the ORM layer
/// </summary>
/// <typeparam name="T"></typeparam>
/// <typeparam name="IdT"></typeparam>
```

```
public interface IDao<T, IdT>
{
    T GetById(IdT id, bool shouldLock);
    List<T> GetAll();
    T Save(T entity);
    void Delete(T entity);
    void CommitChanges();
}

/// <summary>
/// This interface was adapted from Billy McCafferty's NHibernate Framework
/// <see cref="http://devlicio.us/blogs/billy_mccafferty"/>
///
/// The purpose of this interface is to provide
/// the contracts for retrieving DAO objects
/// in a decoupled manner
/// </summary>

public interface IDaoFactory
{
    IAccountDao GetAccountDao();
    ICreditHistoryDao GetCreditHistoryDao();
    ILoanDao GetLoanDao();
    ILoanApplicationDao GetLoanApplicationDao();
    IUserDao GetUserDao();
    IPersonDao GetPersonDao();
    IApplicantDao GetApplicantDao();
}

#region Inline interface declarations

public interface IAccountDao : IDao<Account, int> { }
public interface ILoanDao : IDao<Loan, int> { }
public interface ILoanApplicationDao : IDao<LoanApplication, int> { }
public interface ICreditHistoryDao : IDao<CreditHistory, int> { }
public interface IUserDao : IDao<User, int> { }
public interface IPersonDao : IDao<Person, int> { }
public interface IApplicantDao : IDao<Applicant, int> { }

#endregion
```

Class Service Infrastructure

Another important function to put into your domain model is the ability to disconnect the instantiation of objects. I'm not going to get into a discussion on inversion of control or a debate on the use of reflection, but I will say that it is generally good practice to have the ability to late-bind to your model to limit coupling between layers.

Listing 8-10 shows the ClassServiceFactory, whose name is a bit misleading. The ClassServiceFactory is a *factory* class that uses the Service and ServiceTable classes (not shown) to handle the late-binding infrastructure. Think of Service as an encapsulation of the metadata needed to create a class through reflection, a ServiceTable as a Hashtable to store this metadata, and the ClassServiceFactory as the interface used to create the object. In addition to handling class/object instantiation, the Class Service infrastructure uses a caching mechanism to maintain and track the lifetime of objects to improve performance. Finally, as you can see in Listing 8-10, by default the infrastructure uses the web.config file as the mechanism for storing the class creation settings, but can be extended to use a different provider.

The functionality of the Class Service infrastructure, partially seen in Listing 8-10, can be summarized as follows:

Disconnected architecture: Creates objects in a service-oriented model.

Late binding: Declarative instantiation simplifies the creation of objects.

Caching: Improves performance by tracking the object life span.

Extensibility: Implements an interface model, allowing for custom enhancements and extensions.

Listing 8-10. *The ClassServiceFactory Class Creating Objects in a Disconnected Manner*

```
/// <summary>
/// This code was adapted from the ClassServiceFactory found in
/// org.eclipse.jdt.apt.core.  For more information please see:
/// http://www.eclipse.org/
/// An implementation of the service factory interface. It's built to
/// instantiate class references based on the assembly name and the class name.
/// A "service name" is provided and then the corresponding service name entry
/// is searched for in web.config. The assembly and class name are retrieved
/// based on that service name, and an object reference is instantiated.
/// </summary>
public class ClassServiceFactory:IServiceFactory
{

        private const String ASSEMBLY_NAME = "assemblyName";
        private const String CLASS_NAME = "className";
        private const String LIFE_SPAN = "lifeSpan";

        [NonSerialized()]
        private ServiceTable serviceTable;

        private const String SECONDARY_SERVICE_PROVIDER = "SecondaryServiceFactory";
```

```
public ClassServiceFactory():base(){}

/// <summary>
/// Finds and returns a "service" based on the
/// service name provided.  The config file is searched
/// for a service name given.  If found, then an attempt
/// is made to instantiate the object based on the defined assembly name
/// and the class name.
/// If the service name cannot be found in the configuration and a secondary
/// service factory is defined, the secondary is called in an attempt to
/// find the object.
/// </summary>
public Object FindByServiceName(String serviceName)
{
       lock(this)
       {
               Object retObj = null;
               Service service = GetService(serviceName);

             // check to see if a secondary service provider
             // exists and attempt to call it by the service name
              if (service == null)
              {
                   IServiceFactory secondaryServiceProvider =
                        GetSecondaryServiceProvider();
                   if (secondaryServiceProvider != null)
                     retObj = secondaryServiceProvider.
                          FindByServiceName(serviceName);
              }

              // Otherwise, the service is not null and should be ready
              // If it is not ready, then throw an exception
              else if (service.IsReady())
              {
                   retObj = service.GetObject();
              }

              // Throw an exception.  This should not happen
              else
              {
                   throw new FinderException("Service:  " + serviceName +
                      " is not in a ready state but should be");
              }
```

```
            // if the retObj is null, then we throw an
            // ObjectNotFoundException
            if (retObj == null)
                throw new ObjectNotFoundException();

            return(retObj);

            }
    }

    /// <summary>
    /// Returns the service table. If for some reason the
    /// service table is empty/null, a new one is automatically
    /// created.
    /// </summary>
    private ServiceTable GetServiceTable()
    {
            if (serviceTable == null)
                  serviceTable = new ServiceTable();

            return(serviceTable);
      }

    /// <summary>
    /// Attempts to return the service definition based
    /// on the service name. If the service is not
    /// found in the service table, the configuration file
    /// is searched. If it is not found through the
    /// configuration file, null will be returned.
    /// </summary>
    private Service GetService(String serviceName)
    {
            Service theService = GetServiceTable().GetService(serviceName);

            if (theService == null)
                 theService = LoadFromConfigFile(serviceName);

            return(theService);
    }

    /// <summary>
    /// Attempts to create the service from the configuration
    /// file provided it exists based on the service name.
    /// The service will also be loaded into the service table
    /// for future reference.
```

```
/// If the service cannot be created, null will be returned.
/// If the configuration provided is invalid for some reason,
/// a FinderException will be thrown.
/// </summary>
private Service LoadFromConfigFile(String serviceName)
{
        Service newService = null;

        //If we find any '/' in the service name, replace them with "."
        String convertedServiceName = serviceName;
        int index = convertedServiceName.IndexOf("/");
        while (index >= 0)
        {
                convertedServiceName =
                convertedServiceName.Substring(0,index) + "." +
                convertedServiceName.Substring(index+1,
                (convertedServiceName.Length - (index+1)));
                index = convertedServiceName.IndexOf("/");
        }

         //Now attempt to find the configuration
         //entry for this service name

         String assemblyName = null;
         String className =  null;
         int lifeSpan = Service.LIFESPAN_INDEFINITE;

         Hashtable serviceEntries =
          (Hashtable)ConfigurationSettings.GetConfig
          ("BoP.Util.ClassServiceFactory/" +
                convertedServiceName);

         //If this service definition exists.

         if (serviceEntries != null)
         {
                //Check for an assembly name.  If it
                // exists, then a class name must also exist,
                // otherwise it's an invalid state

                if (serviceEntries.ContainsKey(ASSEMBLY_NAME))
                {
                        assemblyName =
                        (String)serviceEntries[ASSEMBLY_NAME];
```

```
        if (!serviceEntries.ContainsKey(CLASS_NAME))
            throw new FinderException("Class name not
               defined for service: " + serviceName);

        className = (String)serviceEntries[CLASS_NAME];
    }

    //Check for a life span definition

    if (serviceEntries.ContainsKey(LIFE_SPAN) &&
       (!serviceName.Equals(SECONDARY_SERVICE_PROVIDER)))
    {
        String span = (String)serviceEntries[LIFE_SPAN];
        try
        {
            lifeSpan = Int32.Parse(span);
            if (lifeSpan < 0)
               lifeSpan = Service.LIFESPAN_IMMEDIATE;
        }
        catch(Exception exc)
        {
             throw new FinderException("Life span
             value not recognized for service:  " +
                 serviceName);
        }
    }

    //Now if an assembly name is defined, then create the
    //service with the assembly name and class name.
    //Otherwise, just create a shell for the service that
    //will be used by the remote service.

    if (assemblyName != null)
    {
         newService = new Service(serviceName,
              assemblyName, className);
    }
    else
    {
        IServiceFactory secondaryServiceFactory =
             GetSecondaryServiceProvider();
        if (secondaryServiceFactory != null)
             newService = new
             Service(serviceName,
              secondaryServiceFactory);
```

```
                    else
                        throw new FinderException("Service: " +
                            serviceName + " is defined as remote
                              but a secondary service provider was
                                     not found");
                }

                //Set the life span to what was defined)
                //and add it to the table

                newService.SetLifeSpan(lifeSpan);
                GetServiceTable().Add(serviceName,newService);
            }

            return(newService);
        }

        /// <summary>
        /// Attempts to find the secondary service factory that would
        /// be registered with this implementation.  This is used
        /// as a way to possibly link in a ServiceFactory that
        /// could reference remote objects.
        /// </summary>
        private IServiceFactory GetSecondaryServiceProvider()
        {
            IServiceFactory factory2 = null;
            Service service = GetService(SECONDARY_SERVICE_PROVIDER);
            if (service != null)
                factory2 = (IServiceFactory)service.GetObject();

            return(factory2);
        }
    }
```

Summary

In this chapter, you have learned how to apply many of the patterns that you learned in Chapter 2 and have created the foundation of the PI domain model that is used throughout the text. Building a robust domain model can be a complicated task, but having a solid set of requirements is the first step.

Use cases are an excellent tool for gathering requirements. In this chapter, you were given a set of four use cases that were provided to you by the FBP. With these use cases, you were able to build the relationships and associations in the domain model. Starting off with a class diagram, it is easy to build the base classes, entities, and roles into the domain model.

The base classes in your domain model are critical because they provide the core of your structure. This structure is used to handle equality and identity, which is essential when using ORM in your application. In addition to the base classes for handling entities, you were introduced to the stakeholder role concept in this chapter.

The stakeholder is a primitive type in your domain model (that is, a validated person, company, or organization). In terms of the FBP application, the only stakeholder is `Person`. However, your domain model is built to allow for extensions. Along with the introduction of stakeholder, the concept of a role was explained. A role in the domain model is an extension of a stakeholder, in that a stakeholder can be part of any number of roles. This can include the `User` role, the `Applicant` role, or any other nonstakeholder role you can think of.

Modeling entities is one aspect of the solution; however, you shouldn't neglect the managers and the DAO layer. The managers, simply stated, are the workers of your domain. They do all the stuff that is not considered CRUD. Alternatively, the DAO layer performs CRUD operations in your model. It's important to remember that a generic DAO pattern saves you a lot of tedious coding and increases reusability.

Overall, this chapter has introduced the basics of building a foundation layer in your domain model. In the next chapter, you will be using this domain model with LTS as the ORM. Chapter 9 utilizes all your knowledge to develop and build an enterprise class application for the First Bank of Pluto.

CHAPTER 9

Mapping the FBP

The time has come. In this chapter, you will be putting together the framework for the FBP application. To accomplish this, you will need to draw on everything you have learned in the previous chapters, as well as learn a couple of new concepts that you will be exploring as you move through this chapter.

In Chapters 4 and 5, the approach was from the bottom up and in a two-tier environment; in this chapter, the approach is from the top down, in a DDD pattern, preparing the solution for n-tier deployment.

To accomplish an enterprise approach with LTS, you will need to make some changes and extensions to the FBP POCO model that you built in Chapter 8. In the following sections, you will learn more about inheritance, external mappings, and performance optimizations. This chapter concludes with a functioning model of the FBP.

Creating Classes with the Object Relational Designer

In earlier chapters, I mentioned that the LTS GUI has minimal Top Down development support, making it difficult to approach a problem from a DDD perspective. As you may recall from Chapter 1, Top Down development occurs when you model your domain on business or conceptual needs rather than the database. Although it is true that LTS has minimal support for Top Down development, in order to be thorough, I want to illustrate the functionality that it provides you.

In Chapters 4 and 5, you saw that LTS has very strong drag-and-drop support from the bottom up because it utilizes the Server Explorer and the DBML designer surface. Another aspect of the designer is the class toolbox functionality, which provides a mechanism for visually creating entities.

In Figure 9-1, you can see the Object Relational Designer toolbox. This toolbox gives you the option of visually creating your classes inside the DBML design surface, which in turn generates the classes in the `designer.cs` file with your `DataContext` object.

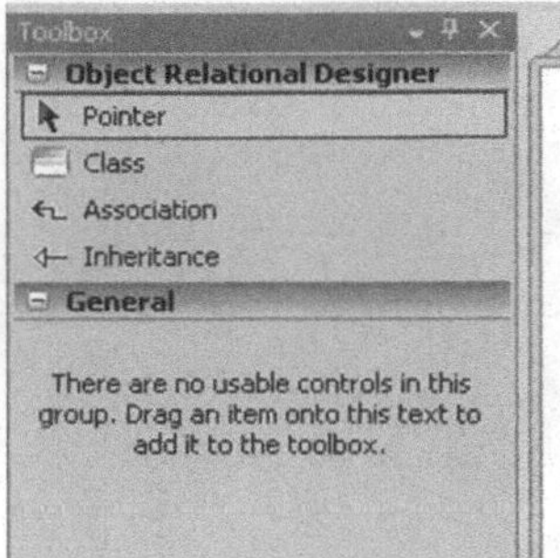

Figure 9-1. *The Object Relational Designer toolbox*

Figure 9-2 shows a new class on the design surface. With the UI, you have the ability to add properties, associations, and inheritance to your class. Additionally, as you can see in Figure 9-3, you can control the mapping attributes from the Visual Studio Properties window. The Properties window can control the attributes at the class and member level of your class (Figure 9-3 shows only the class level).

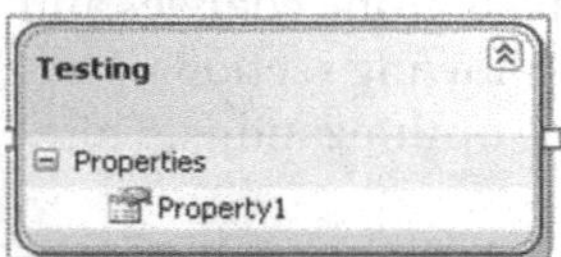

Figure 9-2. *A new class created from the toolbox*

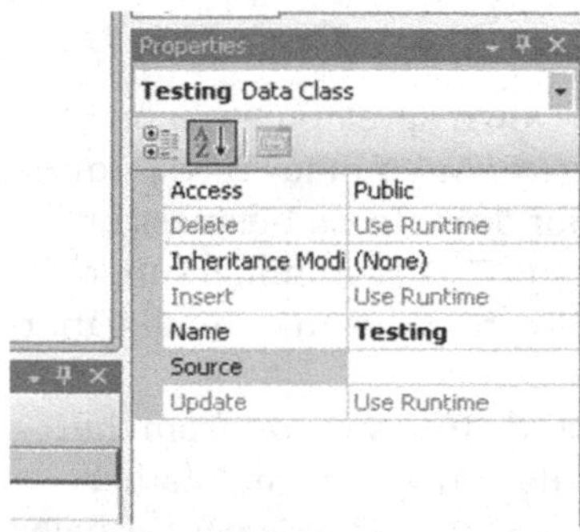

Figure 9-3. *The Properties window can control the mapping attributes of the class.*

Although the Object Relational Designer can be useful for quick throw-away apps, it is inadequate for anything remotely complex. It lacks the functionality of most commercial ORM tools, many of which allow greater control over the classes, and does not compare with its competition, EF. Nonetheless, some of you may find it useful while you are learning the basics of LTS; thus I thought it necessary to give a brief synopsis.

Using Inheritance

Unlike the Object Relational Designer, the role of inheritance in your application is a critical one. I have mentioned it in previous chapters, but I have yet to give a concrete example and explanation about how LTS handles inheritance.

LTS supports the simplest form of inheritance: single-table mapping. *Single-table mapping,* as its name suggests, occurs when an entire inheritance hierarchy is stored in a single database table. Although this is one of the most basic designs for inheritance in ORM tools, it is one of the best performing, because the table contains the flattened structure and union relationships.

LTS implements single-table mapping by using a *discriminator column.* This is a column in your database table that provides a code representing the type to be created. Figure 9-4 shows an example of the abstract Account class that has a subclass of Loan. In most real-world applications, you would further subclass Loan into types such as Mortgage, Personal, and Student, but for the FBP application we are going to leave this at a single level.

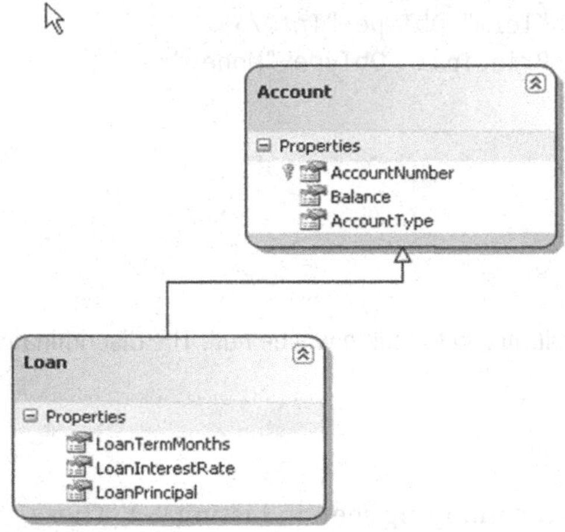

Figure 9-4. *The Account hierarchy*

Listing 9-1 shows the XML mapping for the Account and Loan hierarchy. In the XML mapping file (BoP.map), you can see that you have a single table, Accounts, with two different types, BoP.Core.Account and BoP.Core.Loan (see Listing 9-2 for the C# code). The AccountType column is marked with the IsDiscriminator="true" attribute, which is required. Additionally, the nested Type node of the BoP.Core.Loan class has two other attributes, InheritanceCode="1" and IsInheritanceDefault="True".

The inheritance code tells the LTS framework how to map the discriminator column to the entities. This means that if there is a 1 in the AccountType column, the mapping is to the Loan class. If you had another type, such as Checking, you would have a discriminator of 2, and the mapping file would reflect this. The IsInheritanceDefault attribute is required when using inheritance in LTS because the framework needs to know what the default cast is going to be.

Listing 9-1. *Mapping Inheritance in LTS*

```
<Database Name="BoP" Provider="System.Data.Linq.SqlClient.Sql2005Provider"
    xmlns="http://schemas.microsoft.com/linqtosql/mapping/2007">

  <Table Name="Accounts">
    <Type Name="BoP.Core.Account" >
      <Column Name="Balance" Member="Balance" DbType="Money"/>
      <Column Name="AccountNumber" Member="AccountNumber"
         DbType="Int NOT NULL IDENTITY" IsPrimaryKey="true"
         IsDbGenerated="true" AutoSync="OnInsert" />
      <Column Name="AccountType" Member="AccountType"
         DbType="Int" IsDiscriminator="true" />
        <Type Name="BoP.Core.Loan" InheritanceCode="1" IsInheritanceDefault="True">
          <Column Name="LoanInterestRate" Member="InterestRate"
             DbType="Decimal(18,0)" />
          <Column Name="LoanTermMonths" Member="Term" DbType="Int"/>
          <Column Name="LoanPrincipal" Member="Principal" DbType="Money"/>
        </Type>
    </Type>
  </Table>
</Database>
```

Note Single-table inheritance means that many of the columns in the table will be null. The discriminator will determine which columns are populated.

Listing 9-2 shows the C# entities that represent the mapping seen in Listing 9-1. These entities are PI, which is to say they do not have any ties back to LTS. Additionally, the subclass `Loan` is using nullable types because these properties can be null in the database.

Listing 9-2. *C# Entities Being Mapped in Listing 9-1*

```
public abstract class Account
{
    public Account() { }

    public int AccountNumber { get; set; }
    public decimal Balance { get; set; }
    public int AccountType{ get; set; }

}
```

```
public class Loan:Account
{

    public decimal? InterestRate { get; set; }
    public int? Term{ get; set; }
    public decimal? Principal { get; set; }
}
```

Just so you are clear on the mapping aspect of inheritance in LTS, Figure 9-5 shows the table structure of the Accounts table. As you can see, the Accounts table contains the fields for both the Account class and the Loan class.

Table - dbo.Accounts | Summary

Column Name	Data Type	Allow Nulls
AccountNumber	int	☐
Balance	money	☐
AccountType	int	☑
LoanInterestRate	decimal(18, 0)	☑
LoanTermMonths	int	☑
LoanPrincipal	money	☑
		☐

Figure 9-5. *Accounts table, which represents the Account and Loan classes*

Now that you understand how single-table inheritance works in LTS, you need to write some code to take advantage of it. Listing 9-3 demonstrates one way to use inheritance in your application. In this example, you are querying for accounts and then looping through the Loan items in the Accounts collection. You could also use the is keyword if you wanted to test the type before casting, but because this example has only one subclass, that is not necessary.

Listing 9-3. *Using the Inheritance Structure in Your Code*

```
IQueryable<Account> accounts =
    db.Accounts.Where(r => r.AccountNumber == 10000);

foreach (Loan a in accounts)
{
    Console.WriteLine("Interest Rate = " + a.LoanInterestRate);
}
```

Another useful feature of LTS and its inheritance functionality is that you have the ability to use enums for your discriminator with very little effort. For example, if you created a new enum called AccountType and changed the AccountType property in Listing 9-2 from int to AccountType (see Listing 9-4), LTS would handle the rest for you.

Listing 9-4. *Using an Enum for the Discriminator*

```
public enum AccountType: int
    {
        Account = 0,
        Loan = 1

    }

public AccountType AccountType{ get; set; }
```

Using Compiled Queries

At this point, you are probably wondering when I am going to start discussing FBP. It is coming shortly, but first you need to look at one other function in LINQ that can improve performance when building LTS applications: compiled queries.

LTS gives you a class, aptly named `CompiledQuery`, which provides you with the functionality to reuse queries. The queries, which are primed for use with the `CompiledQuery` class, are those queries that need to be executed many times and are structurally similar.

Using the `CompiledQuery` class is a bit tricky because it returns a delegate. To further complicate things, the best way to use the `CompiledQuery` class is with a shared static function that returns the `Func` anonymous delegate. In Listing 9-5, you can see that I have created a new static `Func` called `EmployeesByManagerId`; in a static class, this returns employees by their `ManagerId`. The query uses a lambda expression, accepts a `DataContext` and an `int`, and then returns an `IQueryable<Employee>` interface.

Listing 9-5. *An Example of a Compiled Query in LTS*

```
static class CompiledQueries
{

    public static Func<AdventureWorksDataContext, int, IQueryable<Employee>>
        EmployeesByManagerId =
          CompiledQuery.Compile(
             (AdventureWorksDataContext db, int managerId) =>
                from c in db.Employees where
                   c.ManagerID == managerId select c);
}
```

Using the compiled query is easy because it returns an `IQueryable` interface. In Listing 9-6, you can see an example in which I am passing in the database `DataContext` and the integer `someManagerId`, and then looping through the results. The benefit of using the `CompiledQuery` class in the static function is that it is compiled once per `appdomain` and then is cached for the entire life cycle of the application domain.

Listing 9-6. *Consuming the Compiled Query Is the Same As Using Any IQueryable Interface*

```
int someManagerId = 0;

foreach (Employee x in
    CompiledQueries.EmployessByManagerId(db, someManagerId))
{
        //Do Something
        Debug.Print(x.LoginID);

}
```

■ **Note** Listing 9-6 is an example of how to consume a compiled query. In most applications, you would wrap the call in another method and pass in the `int` parameter for greatest reuse.

Building a Foundation

It's time to start working on the foundation of FBP. In Listing 9-1, when you were examining some inheritance basics in LTS, I provided you with an external XML mapping file. As I have mentioned throughout this book, this is the preferred method for mapping your model to your database because it helps keep your domain model separate from third-party hooks (that is, PI).

To use the external mapping file and begin building out your foundation, you need to create a new `DataContext` class. By this point, you should have a solid understanding of the `DataContext` class, so it shouldn't be difficult for you to create one. Before you do that, I want to lay out the structure of the Visual Studio solution so you have an idea of how the application is going to materialize. The following is the structure of the `BoP` (also known as the First Bank of Pluto, or FBP) foundation:

- `BoP` solution: Visual Studio 2008 solution
- `BoP.Core`: VS project that contains your domain model and your data/DAO interfaces
- `BoP.Data`: VS project that contains LTS-specific classes, factories, concrete DAOs, and mapping metadata
- `BoP.Util`: VS project that contains utility classes to work with your model
- `BoP.Workers`: VS project that contains the managers that manipulate the model
- `BoP.Tests`: Unit tests for the `BoP` application

The four projects compile into assemblies, named the same as their project names; these make up the foundation of the FBP application. Inside the projects, there may be subnamespaces (for example, `BoP.Core.DataInterfaces`, `BoP.Core.Domain`), which will become apparent as you move forward with development. Additionally, this foundation does not contain any user-interface information because the purpose of the foundation is to be UI independent.

In later chapters, you will implement some user-interface patterns on top of the foundation, but for now the testing and example aspect of the foundation will be done through NUnit 2.4.3.

■ **Note** NUnit is an open source unit-testing framework that has largely become the de facto standard for automated unit-testing .NET projects. Those not familiar with NUnit can learn about it and download it from `www.nunit.org`.

Back to the `DataContext`: to start your journey, you are going to create a new class called `BoPDataContext` in the `BoP.Data` project. This class, which can be seen in Listing 9-7, is your LTS `DataContext` for the FBP application. As you can see, this class inherits from `System.Data.Linq.DataContext`. It implements the static functionality of reading in your `BoP.map` file and pulls your connection string from your `.config` file. `BoP.map` is your XML mapping file, while the `BoP` connection string connects to your database. Additionally, this class is sealed; you don't want developers subclassing it because there is a specific interface for using it (which you will see in the next example).

Listing 9-7. *FBP Custom DataContext Class*

```
namespace BoP.Data.LTS
{
    public sealed class BoPDataContext : System.Data.Linq.DataContext
    {
        static XmlMappingSource map =
                                XmlMappingSource.FromXml
                                (System.IO.File.ReadAllText("BoP.map"));

        static string connectionString =
             ConfigurationManager.ConnectionStrings["BoP"].ToString();

        public BoPDataContext() :
              base(connectionString, map) { }

        public BoPDataContext(string connection)
            : base(connection, map) { }

    }
}
```

■ **Note** Listing 9-7 is in the `BoP.Data.LTS` namespace because this implementation is LTS specific. Also, note that table functions have yet to be added because your entity model is incomplete.

If you read the preceding paragraph, you are probably saying, "Wait a second; how can I have a connection string without a database?" You are correct; I have yet to create a database, and I don't plan to create one until I finish developing the domain model. This again is the purpose of Top Down development: to focus on the domain instead of the database. When the time comes, you will use the `DataContext`'s `CreateDatabase` method to generate the database from our domain model and metadata, but first you need to continue building out the foundation. For the time being, just forget about the database and leave your `connectionStrings` node in your `.config` file empty.

After you have built out the basic `BoPDataContext` class, the next step is to create a singleton around your `DataContext`. In Listing 9-8, you have a new class called `BoPDataContextManager`, which controls the creation of the `BoPDataContext`. Although putting your `DataContext` in a singleton is not strictly necessary, it can be beneficial when working with n-tiered applications. It is important to note that the class in Listing 9-8 will need to be modified when using it in a web or n-tier environment because it does not support the HTTP request scope or transactions other than the LTS default. As you continue to build out the foundation, you will add additional code to this class and your `BoPDataContext` to support more advanced scenarios.

Listing 9-8. *The Singleton for Wrapping Your BoPDataContext*

```
namespace BoP.Data.LTS
{
    /// <summary>
    /// Simple class to implement DataContext singleton.
    /// </summary>
    public sealed class BoPDataContextManager
    {
        private BoPDataContext db;

        #region Thread-safe, lazy Singleton

        /// <summary>
        /// This is a thread-safe, lazy singleton.
        /// See http://www.yoda.arachsys.com/csharp/singleton.html
        /// for more details about its implementation.
        /// </summary>
        public static BoPDataContextManager Instance {
            get {
                return Nested.BoPDataContextManager;
            }
        }

        /// <summary>
        /// Initializes BoPDataContext.
        /// </summary>
        private BoPDataContextManager() {
            InitDB();
        }
```

```
    /// <summary>
    /// Assists with ensuring thread-safe, lazy singleton
    /// </summary>
    private class Nested
    {
        static Nested() { }
        internal static readonly BoPDataContextManager BoPDataContextManager =
            new BoPDataContextManager();
    }

    #endregion

    private void InitDB() {
        db = new BoPDataContext();
    }

    public BoPDataContext GetContext()
    {
        return db;

    }}}
```

Although you are not finished in the `BoP.Data` project, after building the `BoPDataContextManager`, the next step is to move back to the `BoP.Core` project. In the beginning of this chapter, you looked at a simple inheritance structure with the `Account` class and the `Loan` class, which is in fact part of the FBP model. However, as you may recall from Chapter 8, there is a `BaseEntity<T>` class. This is the abstract base class for your domain model, which was not used in Listing 9-2 but needs to be. Unfortunately, there is no clean way of mapping a generic class such as `BaseEntity<T>` in an external XML file. Therefore, we have to work around this issue by creating an override of `ID` on our derived class so that the field maps appropriately. In Listing 9-9, you can see an example of this implementation in the `Account` class.

Listing 9-9. *LTS XML Mapping Limitations*

```
public abstract class Account:BaseEntity<int>
{
    public Account()
    {}

   public override int ID
   {
       get
       {
           return base.ID;
       }
```

```
        set
        {
            base.ID = value;
        }
    }

    //Other properties not shown
}
```

Continuing on, the changes in `BoP.map` from Listing 9-1, with the inclusion of the implementation of `BaseEntity<T>`, are minimal. Instead of using `Member = AccountNumber`, you should use `Member = ID`, and the `AccountNumber` property will be removed. This direction of using the `ID` property as the mapping for all primary keys simplifies the model and makes it easier to work with in complex situations. Additionally, as you will see when we implement the concrete DAO functionality, the generic class `BaseEntity<T>` is useful in creating dynamic structures for handling your data access.

In the `Account/Loan` example, we have a single table mapping to the `Accounts` table. Moving on with the FBP application, you next need to start building out the XML mapping file. You may be wondering how to create the mapping file. This is where the limitations of LTS come into play. Because there isn't a way to "import" your domain assemblies into the ORM, you are left with two choices. One, you can write the file by hand, which is what I am doing. This technique does give you the most control over the metadata and is fundamentally what the contract-first camp says you should do. Two, you can build out your database tables and run SqlMetal to generate your mapping file. This approach is okay, but because LTS is limited to single-table inheritance, you will still have to modify the mapping file to include inheritance in your solutions. Three (yes, I know I said there were two solutions—I lied), you can write a small application that uses reflection to import your domain assemblies and then spits out XML mapping data. I have yet to write one of these, but from a technical standpoint, this should not be a difficult application to write. The way you approach the mapping is up to you. For the purposes of this book, I am writing the mapping file by hand because I believe that it is the truest form of DDD.

Listing 9-10 shows the basic mapping file for the solution. I say *basic* because it does not include all types in the FBP solution, but does provide the core mapping needed in the application. As you can see, the structure is broken into three (nonexistent) database tables: `Accounts`, `Roles`, and `StakeHolders`. This structure is identical to what was presented in Chapter 8.

Listing 9-10. *XML Mapping the FBP Solution*

```
<?xml version="1.0" encoding="utf-8"?>
<Database Name="BoP" Provider="System.Data.Linq.SqlClient.Sql2005Provider"
xmlns="http://schemas.microsoft.com/linqtosql/mapping/2007">

<Table Name="Accounts">
    <Type Name="BoP.Core.Account" InheritanceCode="0">
        <Column Name="AccountNumber" Member="ID" DbType="Int NOT NULL IDENTITY"
            IsPrimaryKey="true" IsDbGenerated="true" AutoSync="OnInsert" />
        <Column Name="Balance" Member="Balance" DbType="Money"/>
```

```
      <Column Name="AccountType" Member="AccountType" DbType="Int"
          IsDiscriminator="true" />
      <Type Name="BoP.Core.Loan" InheritanceCode="1" IsInheritanceDefault="True">
          <Column Name="LoanInterestRate" Member="InterestRate"
              DbType="Decimal(18,0)" />
          <Column Name="LoanTermMonths" Member="Term" DbType="Int"/>
          <Column Name="LoanPrincipal" Member="Principal" DbType="Money"/>
       </Type>
   </Type>
</Table>

<Table Name="Roles" Member="Roles">
   <Type Name="BoP.Core.Domain.Role">
       <Column Name="RoleType" Member="RoleType" DbType="Int NOT NULL"
           IsDiscriminator="true" />
       <Column Name="StakeHolderId" Member="StakeHolderId" DbType="Int NOT NULL"
           IsPrimaryKey="true" />
       <Association Name="FK_Roles_StakeHolders" Member="StakeHolders"
           ThisKey="StakeHolderId" OtherKey="StakeHolderId"  DeleteOnNull="true"
           IsForeignKey="true" />
       <Type Name="BoP.Core.Domain.User" InheritanceCode="0"
           IsInheritanceDefault="True">
           <Column Name="UserId" Member="UserId" DbType="NVarChar(50) NOT NULL"
               CanBeNull="false" />
           <Column Name="Password" Member="Password" DbType="NVarChar(50) NOT NULL"
               CanBeNull="false" />
           <Column Name="Active" Member="Active" DbType="Char(1) NOT NULL"
               CanBeNull="false" />
       </Type>
  </Type>
</Table>

<Table Name="StakeHolders" Member="StakeHolders">
    <Type Name="BoP.Core.Domain.StakeHolder">
        <Column Name="StakeHolderType" Member="StakeHolderType"
             DbType="Int NOT NULL" IsDiscriminator="true" />
        <Column Name="StakeHolderId" Member="StakeHolderId"
             DbType="Int NOT NULL IDENTITY" IsPrimaryKey="true" IsDbGenerated="true"
             AutoSync="OnInsert" />
        <Association Name="FK_Roles_StakeHolders" Member="Roles"
             ThisKey="StakeHolderId" OtherKey="StakeHolderId" DeleteRule="CASCADE"
             IsUnique="true" />
        <Type Name="BoP.Core.Domain.Person" InheritanceCode="0"
             IsInheritanceDefault="True">
            <Column Name="FirstName" Member="FirstName" DbType="NVarChar(50)"
                 CanBeNull="True" />
```

```
            <Column Name="LastName" Member="LastName" DbType="NVarChar(50)"
                CanBeNull="True" />
            <Column Name="Gender" Member="Gender" DbType="Char(1)"
                CanBeNull="True" />
            <Column Name="DOB" Member="DOB" DbType="DateTime" />
            <Column Name="Email" Member="Email" DbType="NVarChar(100) NOT NULL"
                CanBeNull="True" />
            <Column Name="TaxId" Member="TaxId" DbType="NVarChar(50)"
                CanBeNull="True"/>
        </Type>
    </Type>
</Table>

</Database>
```

Caution In this chapter, you are building a PI model by using LTS. Be aware that by not using the `INotifyPropertyChanged` interface in your entities, you are making LTS work hard and you are negatively impacting performance. When building a model for use with LTS, you need to weigh the pros and cons of using a PI.

In addition to the basic mapping in Listing 9-10, you can also see that you have some associations between the `StakeHolder/Person` and the `Role/User` structures. These associations were originally identified in Chapter 8, but let's take another look so you understand what is going on here. In Listing 9-11, you can see the `User` class and the `StakeHolder` class. They have been slightly modified since Chapter 8 to improve usability and provide greater control over the relationship between the two entities, and, in this example, the code comments have been removed.

Reviewing this code in Listing 9-11, you may notice that along with exposing a collection of roles as a `List<Role>` property, I have also mimicked the functionality by creating `Add`, `Remove`, and other methods. The reason for this goes back to the PI domain model concept, essentially the potential that extra logic around the association between `StakeHolder` and `Role` is needed. For example, in the `AddRole` method, some extra logic exists to conversely add the `StakeHolder` to the `Role` and update the `StakeHolderId`. This type of abstraction keeps your domain model portable and more likely to work with all ORM tools.

Listing 9-11. *Updated StakeHolder and Role Classes*

```
/// <summary>
/// The User class, as the name implies is the "User"
/// role in the system. This role is placed on any stakeholder
/// in the FBP to provide the required information
/// for logging on and off of the system. This Role is
/// created after a user of the web site registers.
/// </summary>
```

```
public class User:Role
{
    private const string ROLE_NAME = "User";
    public User() : base(ROLE_NAME) { }
    public string UserId { get; set; }
    public string Password { get; set; }
    public char Active { get; set; }
}

namespace BoP.Core.Domain
{
/// <summary>
/// The base class of stakeholder.  A stakeholder is a person,
/// company, or organization that has an interest
/// in the domain.
/// </summary>
public abstract class StakeHolder:BaseEntity<int>
{
    List<Role> roles;

   public StakeHolder ()
   {
       roles = new List<Role>();
   }

   public int StakeHolderType { get; set; }

   public int StakeHolderId
   {
       get { return base.ID; }
       set { base.ID = value; }
   }

   public List<Role> Roles
   {
       get { return roles; }
       set
       {
           foreach (Role r in value)
               roles.Add(r);
       }
   }

   public virtual bool IsRolesEmpty()
   {
       return (Roles.Count == 0);
   }
```

```
public virtual String GetName()
{
   return string.empty;
}

public virtual void AddRole(Role r)
{
     r.StakeHolder = this;
     r.StakeHolderId = this.StakeHolderId;
     Roles.Add(r);
}

public virtual bool RemoveRole(Role r)
{
     Roles.Remove(r);

     bool success = (Roles.IndexOf(r) < 0);

     if (success)
         r.StakeHolder = null;

     return success;
}

public virtual int NumberOfRoles()
{
     return Roles.Count;
}

public virtual bool ContainsRole(Role a)
{
     return Roles.Contains(a);
}

public virtual bool ContainsRoleOfName(String roleName)
{
     Role role = GetRoleOfName(roleName);
     return (role != null);
}

public virtual Role GetRoleOfName(string roleName)
{
     if ((roleName != null) && (roleName.Length > 0))
     {
```

```
            for (int i = 0; i < Roles.Count; i++)
            {
                if (roleName.Equals(Roles[i].Name))
                    return Roles[i];
            }
        }

            return null;
    }

  }
}
```

■ **Note** From a pure database design perspective, the BoP solution presented in Listing 9-10 is acceptable; however, with high volumes it is probably not ideal. Unfortunately, with the rudimentary inheritance model in LTS, you trade normalization for good ORM. As the FBP grows, you will ultimately need to refactor the structure to change inheritance to associations, to account for the deficient single-table inheritance pattern.

The next aspect of building out the FBP model is to work on the DAO structures. In Chapter 8, you saw the fundamentals of the data interfaces that needed to be created. These data interfaces exist in the BoP.Core project and define the contract for the concrete DAOs in the solution. To refresh your memory, the basic structure of the data interfaces can be seen in Listing 9-12. Here you have the IDao interface and the IDaoFactory interface, which are both part of the BoP.Core.DataInterface namespace.

Listing 9-12. *IDao and IDaoFactory Data Interface Contracts*

```
namespace BoP.Core.DataInterfaces
{
    /// <summary>
    /// This interface was adapted from Billy McCafferty's NHibernate Framework
    /// <see cref="http://devlicio.us/blogs/billy_mccafferty"/>
    ///
    /// The purpose of this interface is to provide a
    /// general purpose contract for CRUD operations
    /// executed in the ORM layer
    /// </summary>
    /// <typeparam name="T"></typeparam>
    /// <typeparam name="IdT"></typeparam>
    public interface IDao<T, IdT>
    {
        T GetById(IdT id);
        List<T> GetAll();
        T Save(T entity);
```

```
        void Delete(T entity);
        void CommitChanges();
    }
}

namespace BoP.Core.DataInterfaces
{
    /// <summary>
    /// This interface was adapted from Billy McCafferty's NHibernate Framework
    /// <see cref="http://devlicio.us/blogs/billy_mccafferty"/>
    ///
    /// The purpose of this interface is to provide
    /// the contracts for retrieving DAO objects
    /// in a decoupled manner
    /// </summary>

    public interface IDaoFactory
    {
        IAccountDao GetAccountDao();
        ICreditHistoryDao GetCreditHistoryDao();
        ILoanDao GetLoanDao();
        ILoanApplicationDao GetLoanApplicationDao();
        IUserDao GetUserDao();
        IPersonDao GetPersonDao();
        IApplicantDao GetApplicantDao();
    }

    #region Inline interface declarations

    public interface IAccountDao : IDao<Account, int> { }
    public interface ILoanDao : IDao<Loan, int> { }
    public interface ILoanApplicationDao : IDao<LoanApplication, int> { }
    public interface ICreditHistoryDao : IDao<CreditHistory, int> { }
    public interface IUserDao : IDao<User, int> { }
    public interface IPersonDao : IDao<Person, string> { }
    public interface IApplicantDao : IDao<Applicant, int> { }

    #endregion
}
```

The first concrete implementation of the interfaces, as seen in Listing 9-12, can also be observed in Listing 9-13. Here you have the `LTSDaoFactory`, which exposes the LTS DAO classes. This implementation is pretty straightforward: it exposes `GetENTITYDAO` methods, where `ENTITY` is the name of the entities that return new concrete DAOs as an interface. As you can see, the file is named `LTS` because this implementation is LTS specific.

Listing 9-13. *Concrete Implementation of DAOFactory*

```
namespace BoP.Data.LTS
{
    /// <summary>
    /// Exposes access to LTS DAO classes.  This framework
    /// was adapted from Billy McCafferty's NHibernate Framework.
    ///
    /// This is the concrete implementation of IDaoFactory, which
    /// is exposed from the BoP.Core.DataInterfaces domain model
    /// </summary>
    public class LTSDaoFactory : IDaoFactory
    {

        #region Inline DAO implementations

        public class AccountDao : AbstractLTSDao<Account, int>, IAccountDao{ }

        #endregion

        #region IDaoFactory Members

        public IAccountDao GetAccountDao()
        {
            return new AccountDao();
        }

        public IPersonDao GetPersonDao()
        {
            return new PersonDao();
        }


        public ICreditHistoryDao GetCreditHistoryDao()
        {
            throw new System.NotImplementedException();
        }

        public ILoanDao GetLoanDao()
        {
            throw new System.NotImplementedException();
        }

        public ILoanApplicationDao GetLoanApplicationDao()
        {
            return new LoanApplicationDao();
        }
```

```
        public IUserDao GetUserDao()
        {
            return new UserDao();
        }

        public IApplicantDao GetApplicantDao()
        {
            throw new System.NotImplementedException();
        }

        #endregion

    }
}
```

You may have noticed that in Listing 9-13 there is an inline implementation of the `AccountLTSDao` class, which inherits from the `AbstractLTSDao` and passes in the types needed for generic CRUD operations. The inline implementation is included because the `AbstractLTSDao` contains all the functionality that is needed for now, and so it is not contained in its own file with extensions. As your model grows, this may need to be moved into its own file, such as the `PersonLTSDao`, which you will be looking at shortly.

Listing 9-14 shows the `AbstractLTSDao` class containing the base implementation for your CRUD operations. This class takes advantage of the powerful functionality of generic types to create a multipurpose type-independent wrapper around the `DataContext`.

Starting at the top of the class, you can see that it inherits from the `IDao` interface, part of the `BoP.Core.DataInterface` namespace that enforces the generic type `T` and the generic identifier `IdT`. In addition, because of constraints within LTS, the `AbstractLTSDao` has to specify an additional constraint on the `T` so it is enforced as a class (for example, where `T:class`). The class also contains generic implementation code for `GetAll`, `Save`, `Delete`, and `SubmitChanges`, plus a signature for `GetById`. Notice that `GetTable` calls in all the methods that are using the `BaseType` instead of the type that is passed in. This is because you have used the pattern of mapping the base type as the table; thus you would receive an error if you tried to retrieve a derived type as `Table`.

Listing 9-14. *The Abstract DAO*

```
namespace BoP.Data.LTS
{
    public abstract class AbstractLTSDao<T, IdT> : IDao<T, IdT> where T:class
    {

        #region IDao<T,IdT> Members

        BoPDataContext db = BoPDataContextManager.Instance.GetContext();

        public virtual T GetById(IdT id)
        {
```

```
            return default(T);

        }

        public virtual List<T> GetAll()
        {
            Table<T> someTable = db.GetTable(typeof(T)) as Table<T>;
            return someTable.ToList<T>();
        }

        public virtual T Save(T entity)
        {
            ITable tab = db.GetTable(entity.GetType().BaseType);
            tab.Add(entity);
            db.SubmitChanges();
            return entity;
        }

        public virtual T SaveOrUpdate(T entity)
        {
            throw new NotImplementedException();
        }

        public virtual void Delete(T entity)
        {
            ITable tab = db.GetTable(entity.GetType().BaseType);
            tab.Remove(entity);
            db.SubmitChanges();

        }

        public virtual void CommitChanges()
        {
            db.SubmitChanges();
        }

        #endregion
    }}
```

One significant problem with using a PI model with LTS is that you lose support for deferred loading. This is because you are not using the LTS association `EntitySets` and `EntityRefs` in your model; thus LTS doesn't know the span to load. In this case, you have to explicitly specify the span with the `DataLoadOptions` class. For the FBP application, I'm doing this in the `LTSDataContextManager`. However, depending on your design, this is something you may want to do in your DAO implementation. In Listing 9-15, you can see an updated `InitDB` method that specifies that `Roles` should be loaded with `StakeHolders`.

Listing 9-15. *Specify the DataLoadOptions When Using a PI Model*

```
private void InitDB()
{
    db = new BoPDataContext();
    DataLoadOptions dlo = new DataLoadOptions();
    loadOptions.LoadWith<StakeHolder>(r => r.Roles);
    db.LoadOptions = dlo;

}
```

Caution By default, when using a PI model with LTS, you lose the ability to defer loading of associations, so you must specify the `LoadOptions` ahead of time if you want to use the "dot" functionality to work with associated entities.

At this point, you should know that `StakeHolder` is nothing more than a base class, so it doesn't make any sense to have a `StakeHolderLTSDao`. Instead, because the derived type `Person` is what you care about, this is the DAO that you would create. Before creating this DAO, you need to first think about the `IPersonDao` interface and what functionality needs to be exposed. Listing 9-16 shows the new `IPersonDao` interface, which adds two method signatures to the implementation. The first method returns a `Person` with a `taxid` parameter. The second signature is an all-purpose `GetByExample` method that accepts a `Person` type with some data associated with it.

Listing 9-16. *Updated IPersonDao Interface*

```
namespace BoP.Core.DataInterfaces
{
    public interface IPersonDao: IDao<Person, string>
    {
        Person GetByTaxId(string taxid);
        List<Person> GetByExample(Person p);
    }
}
```

Note Now that the `IPersonDao` interface is customized, it is extracted out of the `IDaoFactory` file into its own file in the `BoP.Core` project.

Because you have a new IPersonDao interface, let's take a look at the implementation code for the PersonDao. Listing 9-17 shows the PersonDao class. As you can see, the PersonDao class inherits from the AbstractLTSDao class and is strongly typed as Person. The class has implementation code for GetById, GetByTaxId, and GetByExample. Each of these methods uses standard LINQ queries to retrieve data from the database as well as uses the OfType<Person> return to cast/filter the results into the Person type.

Listing 9-17. *Implementation of the PersonDao Class*

```
namespace BoP.Data.LTS
{
    public class PersonDao: AbstractLTSDao<Person,string>,IPersonDao
{

    BoPDataContext db = BoPDataContextManager.Instance.GetContext();

    public override Person GetById(string id)
    {

        Person sh = (from p in db.GetTable<StakeHolder>().OfType<Person>()
                        where p.StakeHolderId == id
                        select p).First();

        return sh;


    }

    public Person GetByTaxId(string taxid)
    {

        Person sh = (from p in db.GetTable<StakeHolder>().OfType<Person>()
                         where p.TaxId == taxid
                         select p).First();


        return sh;

    }

    public List<Person> GetByExample(Person p)
    {
            List<Person> lp = (from s in
                                      db.GetTable<StakeHolder>().OfType<Person>()
                               where s.TaxId == p.TaxId ||
                               s.StakeHolderId == p.StakeHolderId ||
                               s.LastName == p.LastName ||
                               s.Gender == p.Gender ||
```

```
                            s.Email == p.Email ||
                            s.DOB == p.DOB ||
                            s.FirstName == p.FirstName
                            select s).ToList();
            return lp;

        }

}
}
```

■ **Tip** When working with inheritance in LTS, use the `OfType<T>` construct (see Listing 9-17) to focus the results of your query and reduce unnecessary database calls.

You may have already figured out that I am developing the first use case from Chapter 8, where the goal was to allow a user to register in the system with a username, password, and e-mail address. You have the mapping already, which you saw in Listing 9-10, and you saw the C# code in Listing 9-11, but we still need a manager (that is, a worker) to complete the "do" aspect of this process.

Listing 9-18 shows a portion of a concrete implementation of a `UserManager` class. In this example, you have the `CreateUser()` method, which accepts a `User` class and then saves the new `User` (and `Person`) by using the `DaoFactory` (which you created earlier in this chapter). Obviously, this `UserManager` is missing a significant amount of functionality, including `UpdateProfile`, `ForgotPassword`, and so forth. However, the purpose of this example is simply to demonstrate the concept behind creating a layer of abstraction and separating out the workers.

In addition to the `CreateUser()` method, you have a very rudimentary authenticate method and a `Logout()` signature. In a real-world application, the authentication process for an application like this would be much more robust and secure; however, for demonstration purposes, this example gets the point across about worker abstraction in your application.

The `CreateUser()` method has a number of "firsts" for you. For example, it is the first method to have any error handling in our model. As you may know, a well-designed application will throw custom errors that inherit from `ApplicationException`. The `CreaterUser()` method throws two of these custom exceptions based on the outcome of your query. Although this is the first example of this type of custom error handling, in a real-world solution, you would be following this pattern throughout your domain model to create a reliable application.

Listing 9-18. *A UserManager Class*

```
namespace BoP.Workers
{
    public class UserManager: IUserManager
    {
```

```
#region IUserManager Members

public void CreateUser(User user)
{
    IServiceFactory serviceFactory = new ClassServiceFactory();
    IDaoFactory df =
       (IDaoFactory)serviceFactory.FindByServiceName
           ("BoP/Core/DataInterfaces/IDaoFactory");

    IPersonDao ipd = df.GetPersonDao();

    Person testPerson = user.Person;

    ipd.Save(testPerson);

    testPerson.AddRole(user);

    ipd.CommitChanges();

}

public User Authenticate(string userName, string password)
{
    try
    {
        IServiceFactory serviceFactory = new ClassServiceFactory();
        IDaoFactory df =
            (IDaoFactory)serviceFactory.FindByServiceName
                ("BoP/Core/DataInterfaces/IDaoFactory");

        IUserDao iud = df.GetUserDao();

        User x = iud.GetByUserIdAndPassword(userName, password);

        if (x.Active == 'F')
            throw new UserDisabledException("Your Account Has Been Disabled.
                          Please Contact Customer Service.");


        return x;

    }
    catch (InvalidOperationException ioe)
    {
```

```
                throw new InvalidUserNameOrPassword
                    ("You have entered an incorrect username or password.
                        Please contact Customer Service.",ioe);

            }
            catch (Exception ex)
            {
                throw ex;
            }
        }

        public void Logout(User user)
        {
            throw new NotImplementedException();
        }
}
```

Caution The authentication method in the FBP application (see Listing 9-18) is not secure and should not be used in a production environment. As with all of the sample code, it is for ORM demonstration purposes only. When building a production application, consult the Microsoft Developer Network (MSDN) for application security best practices.

Another first in the `CreateUser()` method is the use of the `IUserDao/UserDao`. The `UserDao` is similar to the `PersonDao` you saw in Listing 9-17 in that it inherits from the `AbstractDao` base class. The difference is that you have only one additional method, `GetByUserIdAndPassword`, rather than `GetByExample`, `GetByBlah`, and so forth in the `PersonDao` (see Listing 9-19). The reason for this is to keep things as simple as possible. After all, a `User` is a role, without many needs except retrieval by `UserId` and `Password` (that is, authentication). Looking at Listing 9-18, you may be confused as to why I am using a `PersonDao` in one example and a `UserDao` in another example. To clarify, the purpose of these examples is to show that you have the option to use either DAO for these exercises.

Listing 9-19. *A New Method in the UserDao*

```
BoPDataContext db = BoPDataContextManager.Instance.GetContext();

public  User GetByUserIdAndPassword(string uid, string pwd)
{

    User u = (from p in db.GetTable<Role>().OfType<User>()
              where p.UserId == uid &&
              p.Password == pwd
              select p).First();
```

```
    return u;

}
```

Another sort-of first in Listing 9-18 is the introduction of the `ClassServiceFactory` class and its interface. I only briefly touched on this class in Chapter 8, so I think it prudent to discuss it now. The pattern for the `ClassServiceFactory` is one you may have seen before, because it is used in many .NET and Java frameworks. The sole purpose of the `ClassServiceFactory` class is to create and store services that are your factory or manager classes. This does *not* include the creation of entity classes or classes in the `BoP.Core` solution (interfaces don't count), but it does include everything else.

■ Tip Use C# interfaces to eliminate tight coupling in your domain model. A good domain model has an interface for most, if not all, critical classes to enforce contract of the implementation.

Listing 9-20 shows the `.config` file settings used by the `ClassServiceFactory` infrastructure for creating the `UserManager` and the `DaoFactory`. As you have seen in previous chapters, I like to start by showing you the metadata before looking at any code. I think that most programmers, looking at the XML in Listing 9-20 and reading the narratives in this text, can mentally derive the code that is needed to work with this XML. For example, Listing 9-20 could include several `sectionGroups` with `sectionNames`, each representing classes in your application. Below that, the sections are enumerated with attributes for `assemblyName`, `className`, and `lifeSpan`. From this, you should realize that the code in the `ClassServiceFactory` is using some form of reflection to create your classes generically and then store them in cache for some period of time.

Listing 9-20. *App.Config for Reflective Creation of Classes*

```
<configuration>
   <configSections>
      <sectionGroup name="BoP.Util.ClassServiceFactory">
         <section name="BoP.Core.Domain.IUserManager"
            type="System.Configuration.DictionarySectionHandler, System,
            Version=1.0.5000.0, Culture=neutral,
            PublicKeyToken=b77a5c561934e089" />
         <section name="BoP.Core.DataInterfaces.IDaoFactory"
            type="System.Configuration.DictionarySectionHandler, System,
            Version=1.0.5000.0, Culture=neutral,
            PublicKeyToken=b77a5c561934e089" />
      </sectionGroup>
   </configSections>
```

```
  <BoP.Util.ClassServiceFactory>
      <BoP.Core.Domain.IUserManager>
          <add key="assemblyName" value="BoP.Workers" />
          <add key="className" value="BoP.Workers.UserManager" />
          <add key="lifeSpan" value="0" />
      </BoP.Core.Domain.IUserManager>
      <BoP.Core.DataInterfaces.IDaoFactory>
          <add key="assemblyName" value="BoP.Data" />
          <add key="className" value="BoP.Data.LTS.LTSDaoFactory" />
          <add key="lifeSpan" value="0" />
      </BoP.Core.DataInterfaces.IDaoFactory>
  </BoP.Util.ClassServiceFactory>
</configuration>
```

■Tip Take a look at Microsoft's Enterprise Library to provide everyday functionality to your domain model. The Enterprise Library provides a framework for exception handling, logging, caching, security, and more, which can be combined with the ORM patterns learned in this book to create a powerful foundation for development.

In Chapter 8, you saw a portion of the ClassServiceFactory, but let's take another quick look at some of the key methods in the infrastructure before we go on to create the database.

Listing 9-21 shows two methods. The first method, GetService() from the ClassServiceFactory class, calls the second method in the listing, GetService() in the ServiceTable class. As you can see, if the service is not found in the ServiceTable, which is using the HttpRuntime.Cache for storing the object, a new one is loaded or created from the data in the .config file.

This is but one way to build this mousetrap, but there are literally hundreds of patterns for creating a mechanism for class creation. This text is not meant to be an exploration into all of these options but, rather, an explanation that no framework or domain model is complete without this type of creational functionality. Whether you use inversion of control, design by contract, or something else, that is totally up to you. At the end of this chapter, I discuss some next steps and point you to resources for learning more about techniques and solutions that can handle the creational aspect of your framework.

Listing 9-21. *The Basics Behind the ClassServiceFactory Infrastructure*

```
//From ClassServiceFactory class
private Service GetService(string serviceName)
{
    Service theService = GetServiceTable().GetService(serviceName);

    if (theService == null)
        theService = LoadFromConfigFile(serviceName);
```

```
    return(theService);
}

//From ServiceTable class
public virtual Service GetService(string serviceName)
{

    return ((Service)HttpRuntime.Cache[serviceName]);
}
```

Creating a Database

At this point, you have developed most of the core pieces of the framework code that you will need for the FBP application. Granted, I am still going to show you more in the coming paragraphs, and you don't have all the DAOs and factories in place, but you should now understand the patterns and techniques to complete the basic model and become a Jedi.

What this also means is that your `BoP.map` file has gotten to the point where it makes sense to generate your database. As I mentioned earlier, LTS gives you a convenient method for creating a database from your data context. Listing 9-22 shows an example of the code needed to create your database. In this example, you are using the overload constructor of `BoPDataContext`, which takes a connection and automatically loads the `BoP.map` file (see Listing 9-7).

In addition, in this example you are using the `DatabaseExists()` method to check whether the `.mdf` file already exists. Obviously, from this example I am executing this function in a one-off manner; however, along with the two database methods seen in Listing 9-21, the `DataContext` class also contains a `DeleteDatabase()` method. This functionality can be useful in distributed applications and applications that need small database structures. The one caveat is that the database that is created will not have objects such as stored procedures, triggers, user-defined functions, and check constraints. The database will contain only a representation of what is in your LTS mapping file.

Listing 9-22. *Creating a Database from Your Metadata with the DataContext*

```
BoP.Data.LTS.BoPDataContext bp = new BoPDataContext("C:\\BoPDB\\BoP.mdf");

if (!bp.DatabaseExists())
    bp.CreateDatabase();
```

In most enterprise applications, you will generate the `.mdf` file once, import it, and update it through DBA scripts or SQL Server Management Studio, and so that is what is being demonstrated here. Figure 9-6 shows the `.mdf` file in Management Studio with the `StakeHolder` table/columns expanded. As you can see, three tables were created from your `BoP.map` file: `Accounts`, `Roles`, and `StakeHolders`.

Now that you have a database, you need to update your `.config` file with a `connectionStrings` section that points to your database so your `DataContext` class can load the correct database information.

- C:\BoPDB\BoP.mdf
  - Database Diagrams
  - Tables
    - System Tables
    - dbo.Accounts
    - dbo.Roles
    - dbo.StakeHolders
      - Columns
        - StakeHolderType (int, not null)
        - StakeHolderId (PK, int, not null)
        - FirstName (nvarchar(50), null)
        - LastName (nvarchar(50), null)
        - Gender (char(1), null)
        - DOB (datetime, null)
        - TaxId (nvarchar(50), null)
        - Email (nvarchar(100), not null)
      - Keys
      - Constraints
      - Triggers
      - Indexes
      - Statistics
  - Views
  - Synonyms

Figure 9-6. *BoP database created from metadata*

Now that the basic structure of your foundation is in place, you need to write some tests to complete the use cases from Chapter 8. In Listing 9-23, you can see the first few tests, which involve the `UserManager` methods you have seen previously. In these tests, you are creating a new `UserManager`, creating a new `User`, associating a new `Person` with that `User` (using an object initializer), and then, in the second test, authenticating that `User`.

Listing 9-23. *UserManager Tests*

```
[TestFixture]
public class UseCaseTests
{
    IServiceFactory serviceFactory;
    private const string USERMAN = "BoP/Core/Domain/IUserManager";

    [Test]
    public void UserRegistration()
    {
        serviceFactory = new ClassServiceFactory();
        IUserManager um = (IUserManager)serviceFactory.FindByServiceName(USERMAN);

        User testUser = new User();
        testUser.Person = new Person { Email = "testPerson@bop.com" };
        testUser.Active = 'T';
        testUser.UserId = "testUser";
        testUser.Password = "testPassword";
        um.CreateUser(testUser);
```

```
            Assert.Greater(testUser.Person.StakeHolderId,0);

        }


        [Test]
        public void UserAuthentication()
        {
            serviceFactory = new ClassServiceFactory();
            IUserManager um = (IUserManager)serviceFactory.FindByServiceName(USERMAN);

            User testUser = um.Authenticate("testUser", "testPassword");
            Assert.IsNotNull(testUser);

        }
    }
```

■ **Note** The NUnit tests in some of the examples are larger in scope than you would typically want to use in a production application. When you write NUnit tests for your application, try to apply the ACID (Atomic, Consistent, Isolated, and Durable) rule of transactions to your tests.

These first tests and the code in this chapter should provide you with enough information to complete all the use cases from Chapter 8. Therefore, I don't plan to go through each test with each manager and factory (of course, you can download the complete project for review from the Source Code/Download area of the Apress web site, `www.apress.com`). However, before we move on, there are a few other test cases that I want to cover to complete this topic.

Listing 9-24 shows something a little different from what you saw in the previous examples. In this example, you have the `SaveLoanApplication` test, which is exactly what you would expect to see, and then you have the `GetLoanAppsByTaxId` example. In the `GetLoanAppsByTaxId` example, you are using the `PersonManager` to execute the `GetPersonByTaxId`, which uses the `TaxId` to return a `Person`.

Although Listing 9-24 doesn't show the manager code, what is happening behind the scenes is an association between the `Account` and the `StakeHolder` tables and entities. This association is an addition to the object model, but you can see at the bottom of Listing 9-24 the updated `BoP.map` file, which demonstrates this relationship.

Another important point about the test case `GetLoanAppsByTaxId` is that the test case itself is using LINQ (not LTS) to query the returned `Person`, which holds a collection of `Accounts`. The point of this example is to demonstrate that you still have the ability to use LINQ to work with your data structures, but instead of working directly with the database (that is, tightly coupling yourself to the ORM), you work with the abstract layer. One thing to note in this example is that I have added a `LoadWithOptions` to the `DataContext` to eager load the `Accounts` table with the `StakeHolder` table, similar to `Roles` and `StakeHolders`.

Listing 9-24. *Use LINQ to Query Against Your Data Structures*

```
[Test]
public void CreateLoanApplication()
{
    serviceFactory = new ClassServiceFactory();
    ILoanApplicationManager um =
        (ILoanApplicationManager)serviceFactory.FindByServiceName
            ("BoP/Core/Domain/ILoanApplicationManager");
    LoanApplication la = new LoanApplication();
    la.LoanPurpose = "Building a bridge to no where";
    la.RequestedAmount = 1000000;

    //Hardcode to a Person for testing -> you can always change
       // this to retrieve a "testPerson" if you like
    la.StakeHolderId = 1;
    um.SaveLoanApplication(la);
    Assert.IsNotEmpty(la.ID.ToString());

}

[Test]
public void GetLoanAppsByTaxId()
{
    serviceFactory = new ClassServiceFactory();
    IPersonManager um =
       (IPersonManager)serviceFactory.FindByServiceName
           ("BoP/Core/Domain/IPersonManager");
    Person p = um.GetPersonByTaxId("123-12-1234");

    var x = from s in p.Accounts
            select s;

    foreach (LoanApplication r in x)
    {
        Assert.IsNotEmpty(r.RequestedAmount);

    }

}

<Table Name="Accounts" Member="Accounts">
    <Type Name="BoP.Core.Domain.Account" InheritanceCode="0">
        <Column Name="AccountNumber" Member="ID" DbType="Int NOT NULL IDENTITY"
            IsPrimaryKey="true" IsDbGenerated="true" AutoSync="OnInsert" />
```

```
        <Column Name="Balance" Member="Balance" DbType="Money"/>
        <Column Name="StakeHolderId" Member="StakeHolderId" DbType="Int" />
        <Association Name="FK_Accounts_StakeHolders" Member="StakeHolders"
            ThisKey="StakeHolderId" OtherKey="StakeHolderId" IsForeignKey="true" />
        <Column Name="AccountType" Member="AccountType" DbType="Int"
            IsDiscriminator="true" />
        <Type Name="BoP.Core.Domain.LoanApplication" InheritanceCode="1"
            IsInheritanceDefault="True">
            <Column Name="RequestedAmount" Member="RequestedAmount"
                DbType="NVarChar(50) NOT NULL" />
            <Column Name="LoanPurpose" Member="LoanPurpose" DbType="NVarChar(MAX)"/>
            <Column Name="Approved" Member="Approved" DbType="Char(1) NOT NULL"/>
            <Column Name="CreditScore" Member="CreditScore" DbType="Int"/>
            <Type Name="BoP.Core.Domain.Loan" InheritanceCode="2">
                <Column Name="LoanInterestRate" Member="InterestRate"
                    DbType="Decimal(18,0)" />
                <Column Name="LoanTermMonths" Member="Term" DbType="Int"/>
               <Column Name="LoanPrincipal" Member="Principal" DbType="Money"/>
            </Type>
       </Type>
    </Type>
</Table>
```

Working with Many-to-Many Relationships

I'm not going to write a lot about many-to-many relationships in LTS because they are not natively supported by the LTS engine. There are several ways to overcome this deficiency in LTS, but I am going to discuss only one, the one that I like best.

The technique that I have used and have found easiest to digest is to create a join table that acts as a go-between for the entities that have the many-to-many relationship. For example, picture a `Product` table and an `Order` table, where each product can have multiple orders and vice versa. This relationship cannot be mapped natively by using LTS, so you need to have a join table to break up the relationship.

To solve this problem, you create a `ProductOrder` table that contains an association with `Product` and `Order` as well as its own primary key. Figure 9-7 shows a basic example of this relationship. After you have the join table in place, the query logic and modeling logic becomes easy because you are no longer modeling a many-to-many relationship. Instead, you are modeling two one-to-many relationships.

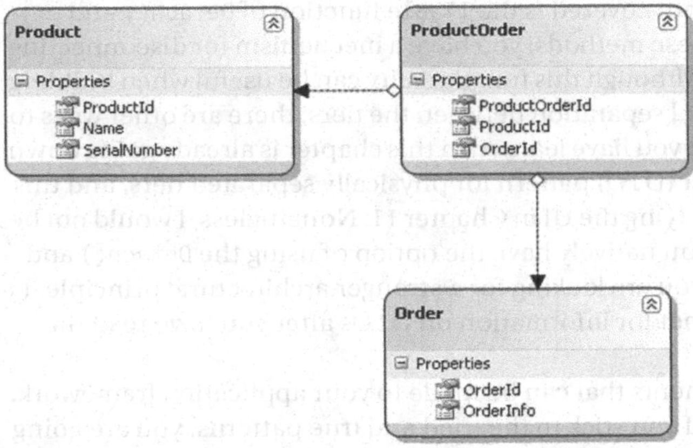

Figure 9-7. *The relationship between Product, ProductOrder, and Order*

Where to Go from Here

Although you have covered a lot of ground in the last few chapters on LTS, there are still plenty of places to go from here. As I mentioned earlier, you have several options for improving the solution design from an architecture perspective. Two specific projects come to mind as possibilities for improving the FBP code that you have seen in this text.

First, the Enterprise Library (`http://msdn2.microsoft.com/en-us/library/aa480453.aspx`) is an open source project from the Microsoft Patterns and Practices team. The Enterprise Library offers application blocks that could improve the everyday functions of the FBP solution. For example, the configuration block and the policy injection block both use dependency injection to "invert control," thus making it a good possibility for improving the creational (that is, `ClassServiceFactory`) code in this chapter. Additionally, the Enterprise Library offers excellent foundation blocks for caching, logging, validation, and exception handling.

Second, the Castle project (`www.castleproject.org/index.html`) is another open source framework for .NET that has components for various cross-cutting tasks needed in every application framework. The Castle project is partially considered a competitor of the Enterprise Library; however, its synergies and its implementation are much more lightweight than the Enterprise Library. One example is Castle's lightweight polymorphic container, which provides easy-to-use inversion of control. This container is much simpler to use than the Enterprise Library version but lacks some of the robust features that the Enterprise Library offers.

Another important topic that was not covered is the ITable function of Detach() and Attach() in the LTS framework. With these methods, you have a mechanism for disconnecting and reconnecting your entities to LTS. Although this functionality can be useful when building out a multi-tier application with physical separation between the tiers, there are other ways to overcome this problem. The design that you have learned in this chapter is already going down the path of using a Data Transfer Object (DTO) pattern for physically separated tiers, and this will be touched on when you look at applying the UI in Chapter 11. Nonetheless, I would not be doing my job if I didn't point out that you natively have the option of using the Detach() and Attach() methods in LTS. However, if you are looking for a stronger architectural principle, I would recommend searching the Internet for information on DTOs after you have read the introduction to them in Chapter 11.

Overall, there are always improvements that can be made to your application framework. What you need to keep in mind is that if you stick to the tried and true patterns, you are going to end up with a solid foundation for development.

Summary

To sum up, in this chapter you have learned everything that you need to know to design a robust framework by using LTS (or any ORM). Although LTS has deficiencies—including its limited inheritance model, lack of support for many-to-many relationships, and the performance impact of using PI—it is still a good ORM for building small- to medium-sized applications.

By using industry design patterns and building abstract layers around your domain model, you can help ensure portability and reusability of your framework. This chapter introduced you to the implementation of these principles, which you can carry on to any other DAO/ORM as needed.

In the next chapter, you will map the domain model for the FBP application by using EF as you have with LTS. The chapter explores the IPOCO functionality of EF and creates an enterprise data access framework for use by the First Bank of Pluto.

CHAPTER 10

Mapping the Bank of Pluto with the ADO.NET Entity Framework

Now that you have an understanding of how EF can be used, let's go back to the Bank of Pluto project and see how EF can be applied to your domain model. In this chapter, you will learn how to use EF as the ORM for the First Bank of Pluto. Additionally, you will be examining the aspects of reusability that the code developed in Chapter 3 and Chapter 6 provides when working with a non-PI ORM such as EF. Finally, you will be exploring some of the top-down designer functionality and the real-world mapping metadata that is required for `BoP`.

Persistence Ignorance/Custom Objects

The domain model that you created in Chapter 3 and mapped to LTS in Chapter 6 is a PI domain model that theoretically should be usable with all PI ORM tools. Unfortunately, EF is not a PI ORM tool; there is no way with this first release of EF to use a domain model sans hooks back to EF. Microsoft has acknowledged the need for PI and has indicated that this is something that they are potentially working on for the next version of EF (`http://blogs.msdn.com/dsimmons/archive/2007/06/02/persistence-ignorance-ok-i-think-i-get-it-now.aspx`). For now, however, we must defile our `BoP` model with technology-specific code to use EF.

Fortunately, EF is not completely an anti-PI pattern. The ADO.NET team has incorporated the Interface Plain Old CLR Object (IPOCO) pattern into the mix for working with custom objects in your model. What the IPOCO pattern means (and no, IPOCO is not an actual interface—it is a pattern) is that instead of requiring direct inheritance from a base class to use an ORM tool, you only have to implement one or more interfaces. In the case of EF, three interfaces are needed: `IEntityWithChangeTracker`, `IEntityWithKey`, and `IEntityWithRelationships`.

Unfortunately, using EF requires going beyond the IPOCO interface because you also have to decorate your classes (including properties) with EF-specific attributes. If you have learned anything thus far, you should know that adding technology-specific attributes to your domain models is ill-advised. Implementing an interface is one thing, because with good design and coding this can become a nonissue; however, EF also requires you to add redundant metadata attributes to your model. If you are thinking, like me, that this is a big problem and potentially a deterrent to using EF, all I can say here is that Microsoft is aware of the issue (see the previous link reference), and, in my opinion, the EF benefits (for example, conceptual model mapping, robust UI, efficient generated SQL, provider independence) outweigh the PI concerns and the attribute design flaw in version 1.

IPOCO Interfaces

As mentioned earlier, there are three interfaces, IEntityWithChangeTracker, IEntityWithKey, and IEntityWithRelationships, that you must implement in order to use a custom object with EF.

The IEntityWithChangeTracker interface, as its name suggests, enables your object to participate in EF change-tracking processes. The only method that needs to be implemented in your class is the SetChangeTracker method, which can be seen in Listing 10-1. The SetChangeTracker method is called by the Object Services framework in order to define a local instance of IEntityChangeTracker, which is used by your properties to notify the framework of changes.

Listing 10-1. *The SetChangeTracker Method*

```
IEntityChangeTracker _changeTracker = null;

void IEntityWithChangeTracker.SetChangeTracker
    (IEntityChangeTracker changeTracker)
{
    _changeTracker = changeTracker;

}
```

The next interface, IEntityWithKey, is technically an optional interface in the EF IPOCO construct; however, the performance impact of not implementing this interface is significant and so it is highly recommended that you think of this as a requirement in version 1 of EF. The purpose of the IEntityWithKey interface is to expose the EntityKey to Object Services. The EntityKey is used to determine identity and thus is used by EF to track and control objects in the ObjectContext of your application. Listing 10-2 shows a concrete implementation of EntityKey. Here you can see that the EntityKey is a .NET property that returns a System.Data.EntityKey, and in its set accessor functionality calls the EntityMemberChanging and EntityMemberChanged methods, which are part of the _changeTracker that you defined in Listing 10-1.

Listing 10-2. *IEntityWithKey Implementation*

```
EntityKey _entityKey = null;

System.Data.EntityKey IEntityWithKey.EntityKey
{
    get
    {
        return _entityKey;

    }
    set
    {
```

```
            // Set the EntityKey property, if it is not set.
            // Report the change if the change tracker exists.
            if (_changeTracker != null)
            {
                _changeTracker.EntityMemberChanging("-EntityKey-");
                _entityKey = value;
                _changeTracker.EntityMemberChanged("-EntityKey-");
            }
            else
            {
                _entityKey = value;
            }

        }
    }
```

The final interface that you need to implement in order to use a custom class with EF is the `IEntityWithRelationships` interface. This interface is needed by the framework when you have associations (relationships) between entities in your model. These relationships, as discussed in earlier chapters, are the navigation properties (also known as *foreign keys*) in your model. Listing 10-3 shows the implementation of the `IEntityWithRelationships` interface, which is the `RelationshipManager` read-only property.

Listing 10-3. *IEntityWithRelationships Implementation*

```
RelationshipManager _relationships = null;

RelationshipManager IEntityWithRelationships.RelationshipManager
{
    get
    {
        if (null == _relationships)
            _relationships = RelationshipManager.Create(this);
        return _relationships;
    }
}
```

Note Be aware when building your domain model that when you use EF as your ORM solution, you lose the ability to use the new automatic property feature in .NET 3.5 due to the change-tracking functionality that has to be in each property.

The next aspect of using a custom class in EF is to decorate the appropriate fields with attributes that provide metadata to the framework. At this point, you may be trying to understand the necessity of having these attributes. These attributes should be in your custom classes because they help to identify which classes should be persistable and which properties should be persisted. The framework uses this metadata to create the linkage(s) between the conceptual model and the object model.

Listing 10-4 shows the `Balance` property, which is part of the `Account` class. In this example, you have a standard .NET read/write property that is decorated with the `EDMScalarPropertyAttribute()`. Obviously, in this example, the property is a scalar type or a primitive, thus requiring the `EDMScalarPropertyAttribute()`; however, there are other options (such as `EDMComplexProperty()` and `EDMRelationshipNavigationProperty()`) that you will see later in this chapter. Along with the attribute decoration in this example, you additionally have calls to `PropertyChanging` and `PropertyChanged` in order to notify the framework change tracker that the property has been updated.

Listing 10-4. *EDMScalarPropertyAttribute in Use*

```
 [global::System.Data.Objects.DataClasses.EdmScalarPropertyAttribute()]
public int Balance
{
    get { return _balance;}
    set
    {
       _changeTracker.PropertyChanging("Balance");
       _balance = value;
       _changeTracker.PropertyChanged("Balance");

    }

}
```

■ **Tip** When using EF attributes in your domain model, it is easier to fully qualify the attribute by using the global namespace as seen in Listings 10-4 and 10-5 because then you don't need a `using` reference.

The next attribute that is required by the framework is a class-level attribute that identifies the class as a persistable entity. Listing 10-5 shows an example of the `EdmEntityTypeAttribute`. In this example, you are providing the `NamespaceName` parameter and the `Name` parameter to the `EdmEntityTypeAttribute`. As you can see, this particular example is for the `Account` class in the `BoP` domain model.

Listing 10-5. *The EdmEntityTypeAttribute*

```
 [global::System.Data.Objects.DataClasses.EdmEntityTypeAttribute
(NamespaceName = "BoP.Core.Domain", Name = "Account")]
```

The final attribute that you need to be aware of is one that is at the assembly level. The `EdmSchemaAttribute` in Listing 10-6 is required to denote an assembly that is going to participate in the EF persistence chain. This attribute should be added to your `AssemblyInfo.cs` file.

Listing 10-6. *The EdmSchemaAttribute*

```
[assembly: global::System.Data.Objects.DataClasses.EdmSchemaAttribute()]
```

Top-Down Designer

Although the EF designer doesn't support a true DDD approach, where you can derive your metadata from an existing domain model, it does have reasonable support for top-down development. The top-down designer is useful for developing entities and CSDL from scratch. This can be a helpful resource as you are learning the syntactical minutiae of the EDM and starting off development in EF.

Figure 10-1 shows the toolbox that contains the top-down EF development widgets. There are not a lot of items that you can use in the toolbox, just an Entity, Association, and Inheritance, but these, coupled with the properties you can set in the designer, enable you to visually create a conceptual model.

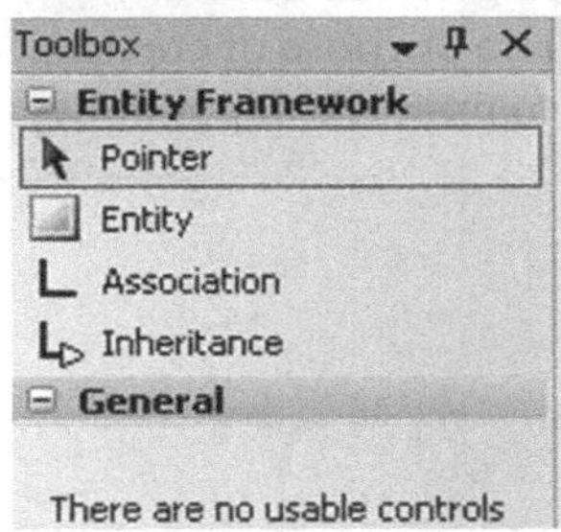

Figure 10-1. *Top-down toolbox*

As you can see in Figure 10-2, the top-down visual representation looks identical to what we have covered previously. In this example, you have a `BaseEntity` and an `Account` class that have no mapping behind them. Another way to think about this is that these classes exist only in the CSDL and nowhere else in the EDM (yet).

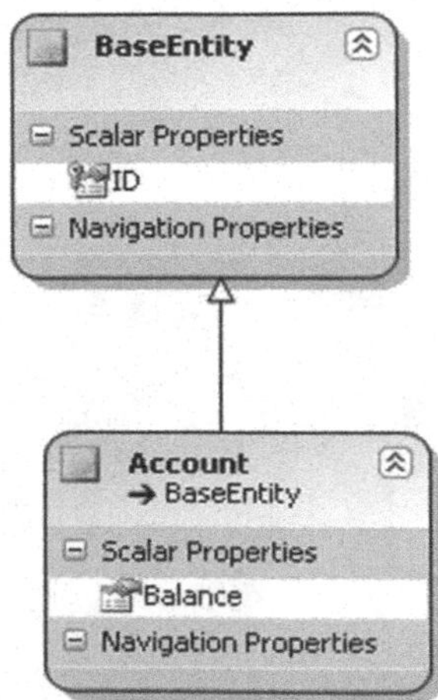

Figure 10-2. *Entities with no mapping*

Applying IPOCO to BoP

Now that you understand what generically needs to take place to enable the use of a custom business object, let's take a look at the application against the BoP model. To promote reuse and increase the abstraction, we are going to first modify our BaseEntity class to work with EF. As you may remember from earlier chapters, BaseEntity is the abstract class that all domain objects inherit from.

Note Although most ORM tools require a default constructor, EF doesn't; however, for greatest reusability of your model, I recommend keeping the default constructor in your domain classes.

Listing 10-7 shows the code from the BaseEntity abstract class. As you can see, BaseEntity is implementing the three IPOCO interfaces discussed earlier in this chapter. Additionally, notice the wrapper methods PropertyChanged and PropertyChanging. The purpose of creating this abstract layer that implements the IPOCO interfaces is to attempt to limit the dependency on EF-specific technology (that is, layered architecture).

Listing 10-7. *The New BaseEntity of Your Domain Model*

```
public abstract class BaseEntity<T> : IEntityWithRelationships,
IEntityWithChangeTracker, IEntityWithKey
{

    public BaseEntity()
    { }

    private T id = default(T);

    /// <summary>
    /// ID may be of type string, int, custom type, etc.
    /// Setter is protected to allow unit tests to set this
    /// property via reflection and to allow domain objects
    /// more flexibility in setting this for those objects with
    /// assigned IDs.
    /// </summary>
    ///

   public virtual T ID
   {
       get { return id; }
            set { id = value; }
   }
```

```
public override sealed bool Equals(object obj)
{
    BaseEntity<T> compareTo = obj as BaseEntity<T>;

    return (compareTo != null) &&
           (HasSameNonDefaultIdAs(compareTo) ||

            // Since the IDs aren't the same,
            //  either of them must be transient to
            // compare business value signatures
            (((IsTransient()) || compareTo.IsTransient()) &&
             HasSameBusinessSignatureAs(compareTo)));
     }

     /// <summary>
     /// Must be provided to properly compare two objects
     /// </summary>
     public override int GetHashCode()
     {
         return this.ToString().GetHashCode();
     }

     private bool HasSameBusinessSignatureAs(BaseEntity<T> compareTo) {

         return GetHashCode().Equals(compareTo.GetHashCode());
     }

     /// <summary>
     /// Returns true if self and the provided persistent
     /// object have the same ID values and the IDs are
     /// not of the default ID value
     /// </summary>
     private bool HasSameNonDefaultIdAs(BaseEntity<T> compareTo) {

         return (ID != null && ! ID.Equals(default(T))) &&
                (compareTo.ID != null && ! compareTo.ID.Equals(default(T))) &&
                ID.Equals(compareTo.ID);
     }

     /// <summary>
     /// Overriden to return the class type
     /// of this object.
     /// </summary>
     ///
     /// <returns>
     /// the class name for this object
     /// </returns>
```

```
///
public override string ToString()
{
    StringBuilder str = new StringBuilder();
    str.Append(" Class: ").Append(GetType().FullName);
    return str.ToString();
}


RelationshipManager _relationships = null;

RelationshipManager IEntityWithRelationships.RelationshipManager
{
    get
    {
        if (null == _relationships)
            _relationships = RelationshipManager.Create(this);
        return _relationships;
    }

}

IEntityChangeTracker _changeTracker = null;

void IEntityWithChangeTracker.SetChangeTracker
    (IEntityChangeTracker changeTracker)
{
    _changeTracker = changeTracker;


}

public void PropertyChanging(string propName)
{
    if (_changeTracker != null)
    {
        _changeTracker.EntityMemberChanging(propName);

    }


}
```

```
        public void PropertyChanged(string propName)
        {
            if (_changeTracker != null)
            {
                _changeTracker.EntityMemberChanged(propName);
            }


        }

        EntityKey _entityKey = null;

        System.Data.EntityKey IEntityWithKey.EntityKey
        {
            get
            {
                return _entityKey;

            }
            set
            {
                // Set the EntityKey property, if it is not set.
                // Report the change if the change tracker exists.
                if (_changeTracker != null)
                {
                    _changeTracker.EntityMemberChanging("-EntityKey-");
                    _entityKey = value;
                    _changeTracker.EntityMemberChanged("-EntityKey-");
                }
                else
                {
                    _entityKey = value;
                }

            }
        }

}
```

After you have created the BaseEntity class, the next step is to move on and begin updating the BoP domain classes with the appropriate attributes and changes to the getters and setters. I don't think that it is necessary to go through all the classes because the changes are basically the same across all the domain objects. However, let's take a look at a few examples so you have a better understanding of what needs to change.

Listing 10-8 shows the ubiquitous Account class (which you have seen many times previously). Here, however, there is an Account class that has been modified for use with EF.

In addition to the attributes and the calls to the BaseEntity for PropertyChanging and PropertyChanged, you also have an override of ID. You override ID instead of using the generic implementation of ID in the base class because EF does not easily allow for the mapping of generic types, thus the need for a concrete implementation of ID in your domain class. Finally, you also have a new attribute that was alluded to earlier, EdmRelationshipNavigationProperty. This attribute decorates the StakeHolder property, and as the name implies, is used for informing the framework of an association between two entities.

Listing 10-8. *The Account Class*

```
/// <summary>
/// The account class is a general-use object in the system.
/// This class is instantiated when a person's loan is accepted,
/// and is also subclassed for more granular control (e.g., Loan).
/// </summary>

[global::System.Data.Objects.DataClasses.EdmEntityTypeAttribute
    (NamespaceName = "BoP.Core.Domain", Name = "Account")]
public class Account:BaseEntity<int>
{
    private int _balance;
    private int _stakeHolderId;
    private StakeHolder _stakeHolder;
    private Person _person;

    public Account() {}

    [global::System.Data.Objects.DataClasses.EdmScalarPropertyAttribute
         (EntityKeyProperty = true, IsNullable = false)]
    public override int ID
    {
        get
        {
            return base.ID;
        }
        set
        {
            this.PropertyChanging("ID");
            base.ID = value;
            this.PropertyChanging("ID");
        }
    }

    [global::System.Data.Objects.DataClasses.EdmScalarPropertyAttribute()]
    public int StakeHolderId
    {
        get
```

```
        {
            return _stakeHolder;
        }
        set
        {
            this.PropertyChanging("StakeHolderId");
            _stakeHolderId = value;
            this.PropertyChanging("StakeHolderId");

        }

    }

    [global::System.Data.Objects.DataClasses.EdmScalarPropertyAttribute()]
    public StakeHolder StakeHolder
    {

        get { return _stakeHolder;}
        set
        {
            this.PropertyChanging("StakeHolder");
            _stakeHolder = value;
            this.PropertyChanging("StakeHolder");


         }


     }


     public virtual Person Person
     {
         get
         {
             if (StakeHolder is Person)
                   return ((Person)StakeHolder);
             else
                   return (null);
         }

         set
         {
             StakeHolder = value;
         }
     }
```

```
        [global::System.Data.Objects.DataClasses.EdmScalarPropertyAttribute()]
        public int Balance
        {
            get { return _balance;}
            set
            {
                this.PropertyChanging("Balance");
                _balance = value;
                this.PropertyChanged("Balance");

            }

        }

    }

}
```

The concept of associations in EF is important, so let's take a look at the StakeHolder and Person classes in the model. In Listing 10-9, you can see a condensed version of the StakeHolder and Person classes. The Person class inherits from the StakeHolder class, and the StakeHolder class has an association with the Account class. Also worth noting is that the StakeHolder class is an abstract class, so it cannot be instantiated directly.

Listing 10-9. *StakeHolder and Person Entities*

```
// The Abstract StakeHolder class

[Serializable]
[global::System.Data.Objects.DataClasses.
EdmEntityTypeAttribute(NamespaceName = "BoP.Core.Domain",
 Name = "StakeHolder")]
public abstract class StakeHolder : BaseEntity<int>
{
    [global::System.Data.Objects.DataClasses.
    EdmScalarPropertyAttribute(EntityKeyProperty = true,
    IsNullable = false)]
    public int StakeHolderId
    {
        get{    return base.ID;    }
        set{    base.ID = value;    }
    }

    [global::System.Data.Objects.DataClasses.
    EdmRelationshipNavigationPropertyAttribute("BoP.Core.Domain",
    "StakeHolderAccount", "Account")]
```

```
    public global::System.Data.Objects.DataClasses.EntityCollection<Account> Account
    {
        get{
            return
            ((global::System.Data.Objects.DataClasses.IEntityWithRelationships)
            (this)).RelationshipManager.GetRelatedCollection<Account>
            ("BoP.Core.Domain.StakeHolderAccount", "Account");
        }
    }

// The Person class

[Serializable]
[global::System.Data.Objects.DataClasses.EdmEntityTypeAttribute
(NamespaceName = "BoP.Core.Domain", Name = "Person")]
public class Person: StakeHolder
{
    private string _firstName;
    private string _lastName;
    private string _gender;
    private DateTime? _dob;
    private string _taxId;
    private string _email;

    [global::System.Data.Objects.DataClasses.EdmScalarPropertyAttribute()]
    public string FirstName
    {
        get{    return _firstName;    }
        set
        {
                this.PropertyChanging(System.Reflection.MethodInfo.
                GetCurrentMethod().Name);
                _firstName = value;
                this.PropertyChanging(System.Reflection.MethodInfo.
                GetCurrentMethod().Name);
        }
    }

    [global::System.Data.Objects.DataClasses.EdmScalarPropertyAttribute()]
    public string LastName
    {
        get{    return _lastName;    }
```

```
        set{

                this.PropertyChanging(System.Reflection.MethodInfo.
                GetCurrentMethod().Name);
              _ lastName = value;
                this.PropertyChanging(System.Reflection.MethodInfo.
                GetCurrentMethod().Name);
            }
    }

    [global::System.Data.Objects.DataClasses.EdmScalarPropertyAttribute()]
    public DateTime? DOB
    {
        get{    return _dob;    }
        set{
                this.PropertyChanging(System.Reflection.MethodInfo.
                GetCurrentMethod().Name);
                _dob = value;
                this.PropertyChanging(System.Reflection.MethodInfo.
                GetCurrentMethod().Name);
            }
    }
}
// Other properties removed for readability.  You get the point!
}
```

At this point, it is worth mentioning that the structure of the BoP application with EF as the ORM is identical to the structure of the domain model that you created in Chapter 6. In case you have forgotten what the structure looks like, here it is:

BoP solution: Visual Studio 2008 solution

BoP.Core: VS project that contains your domain model and your data/DAO interfaces

BoP.Data: VS project that contains EF-specific classes, factories, concrete DAOs, and mapping metadata

BoP.Util: VS project that contains utility classes to work with your model

BoP.Workers: VS project that contains the managers that manipulate the model

BoP.Tests: Unit tests for the BoP application

Although many things in the domain model foundation need to change to accommodate EF, the structure of the foundation remains constant across ORMs. Standardizing the structure has many advantages, including reusability, consistency, and a foundation for achieving the ubiquitous language that is vital in DDD.

■ **Note** The BaseEntity, Account, StakeHolder, Person, and LoanApplication classes seen in this section are all part of the BoP.Core solution.

Moving on to the next entity in the domain model, you have the LoanApplication entity, which inherits directly from the Account class. Listing 10-10 shows a portion of the source code for the LoanApplication class. There isn't anything extraordinary about the LoanApplication entity; it just uses your standard EdmScalarPropertyAttribute metadata, but it is worth looking at because it is inheriting from the Account class.

Listing 10-10. *LoanApplication Class*

```
 [Serializable]
[global::System.Data.Objects.DataClasses.
EdmEntityTypeAttribute(NamespaceName = "BoP.Core.Domain",
 Name = "LoanApplication")]
public class LoanApplication : Account
{
    private int _requestedAmount;
    private string _loanPurpose;
    private bool _approval;
    private int _creditScore;

    [global::System.Data.Objects.DataClasses.
    EdmScalarPropertyAttribute()]
    public int RequestedAmount
    {
        get {    return _requestedAmount;    }
        set {
                this.PropertyChanging(System.Reflection.MethodInfo.
                GetCurrentMethod().Name);
            _ requestedAmount = value;
                this.PropertyChanging(System.Reflection.MethodInfo.
                GetCurrentMethod().Name);
            }
    }

//Other properties removed for readability

}
```

To wrap up the domain class changes required to make EF function correctly, Figure 10-3 shows the conceptual diagram for the BoP entities. Here you can see a holistic view of the classes in the model and their interactions. Along with the classes covered in this section, you can also include a User class that is a Role in the solution and has an association with the Person entity. Additionally, you have the Loan entity, which is a descendant of the Account type.

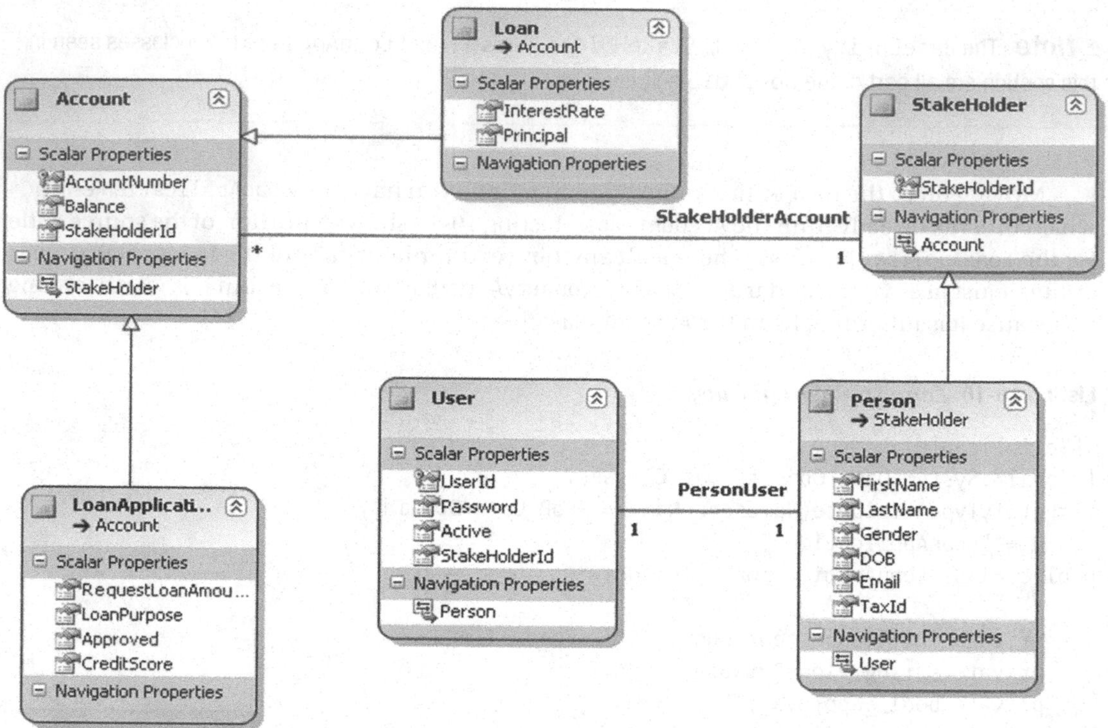

Figure 10-3. *Domain classes*

Mappings/Database

Creating the metadata mappings of the EDM is the next step to building the BoP application to run with EF. There are many ways to create these mappings, so I'm not going to say that one way is right over another. It is really up to you to choose what you feel most comfortable with.

The DDD camp and the contract-first camp would probably say that if you cannot import your model to generate the metadata, you should create the mapping by hand. In many cases, I do think coding your SSDL file by hand and then running EdmGen is probably the most consistent and repeatable approach; however, the EF UI does a pretty good job, so creating the model (as seen in Figure 10-3) and compiling and pulling the metadata that way is also a good choice. Yes, of course you can always create the database and generate the model that way too; however, as stated many times before, this doesn't build out a nice inheritance structure and requires you to change all sorts of links and associations to fit your domain model.

To further illustrate this scenario, I have hand-coded the SSDL and run EdmGen against the SSDL to generate my EDM files. As you will see shortly, after hand-coding, it is simple to create the tables for the application. Listing 10-11 shows the SSDL for the BoP application; here you have the database definitions for each of the tables in the model.

Listing 10-11. *BoP SSDL*

```
<Schema Namespace="BoP.Core.Domain.Store" Alias="Self"
    Provider="System.Data.SqlClient" ProviderManifestToken="2005"
    xmlns="http://schemas.microsoft.com/ado/2006/04/edm/ssdl">
  <EntityContainer Name="dbo">
    <EntitySet Name="Account" EntityType="BoP.Core.Domain.Store.Account" />
    <EntitySet Name="Loan" EntityType="BoP.Core.Domain.Store.Loan" />
    <EntitySet Name="LoanApplication"
        EntityType="BoP.Core.Domain.Store.LoanApplication" />
    <EntitySet Name="Person" EntityType="BoP.Core.Domain.Store.Person" />
    <EntitySet Name="User" EntityType="BoP.Core.Domain.Store.User" />
  </EntityContainer>
  <EntityType Name="Account">
    <Key>
      <PropertyRef Name="AccountNumber" />
    </Key>
    <Property Name="AccountNumber" Type="int" Nullable="false"
      StoreGeneratedPattern="Identity" />
    <Property Name="Balance" Type="decimal" />
    <Property Name="StakeHolderId" Type="int" />
  </EntityType>
  <EntityType Name="Loan">
    <Key>
      <PropertyRef Name="AccountNumber" />
    </Key>
    <Property Name="AccountNumber" Type="int" Nullable="false" />
    <Property Name="InterestRate" Type="decimal" />
    <Property Name="Principal" Type="money" />
  </EntityType>
  <EntityType Name="LoanApplication">
    <Key>
      <PropertyRef Name="AccountNumber" />
    </Key>
    <Property Name="AccountNumber" Type="int" Nullable="false" />
    <Property Name="RequestLoanAmount" Type="money" />
    <Property Name="LoanPurpose" Type="nvarchar(max)" />
    <Property Name="Approved" Type="char" Nullable="false" MaxLength="1" />
    <Property Name="CreditScore" Type="int" />
  </EntityType>
  <EntityType Name="Person">
    <Key>
      <PropertyRef Name="StakeHolderId" />
    </Key>
    <Property Name="FirstName" Type="nvarchar" MaxLength="50" />
```

```
    <Property Name="LastName" Type="nvarchar" MaxLength="50" />
    <Property Name="Gender" Type="char" MaxLength="1" />
    <Property Name="DOB" Type="datetime" />
    <Property Name="Email" Type="nvarchar" MaxLength="50" />
    <Property Name="TaxId" Type="nvarchar" MaxLength="50" />
    <Property Name="StakeHolderId" Type="int" Nullable="false" />
  </EntityType>
  <EntityType Name="User">
    <Key>
      <PropertyRef Name="UserId" />
    </Key>
    <Property Name="UserId" Type="nvarchar" Nullable="false" MaxLength="50" />
    <Property Name="Password" Type="nvarchar" MaxLength="50" />
    <Property Name="Active" Type="nchar" MaxLength="10" />
    <Property Name="StakeHolderId" Type="int" Nullable="false" />
  </EntityType>
</Schema>
```

The next mapping file is the CSDL conceptual mapping, which can be seen in Listing 10-12. This mapping file was generated by using the EdmGen tool from the hand-coded SSDL file in Listing 10-11. Although the file doesn't contain anything unusual, it is worth noting the AssociationSet and Association nodes that show the navigational properties in the domain model.

Listing 10-12. *CSDL BoP Mappings*

```
<?xml version="1.0" encoding="utf-8"?>
<Schema Namespace="BoP.Core.Domain" Alias="Self"
    xmlns="http://schemas.microsoft.com/ado/2006/04/edm">
  <EntityContainer Name="BoPObjectContext">
    <EntitySet Name="Account" EntityType="BoP.Core.Domain.Account" />
    <EntitySet Name="User" EntityType="BoP.Core.Domain.User" />
    <EntitySet Name="StakeHolder" EntityType="BoP.Core.Domain.StakeHolder" />
    <AssociationSet Name="StakeHolderAccount"
        Association="BoP.Core.Domain.StakeHolderAccount">
      <End Role="StakeHolder" EntitySet="StakeHolder" />
      <End Role="Account" EntitySet="Account" />
    </AssociationSet>
    <AssociationSet Name="PersonUser" Association="BoP.Core.Domain.PersonUser">
      <End Role="Person" EntitySet="StakeHolder" />
      <End Role="User" EntitySet="User" />
    </AssociationSet>
  </EntityContainer>
  <EntityType Name="Account">
    <Key>
      <PropertyRef Name="AccountNumber" />
    </Key>
    <Property Name="AccountNumber" Type="Int32" Nullable="false" />
```

```
  <Property Name="Balance" Type="Decimal" Precision="18" Scale="0" />
  <Property Name="StakeHolderId" Type="Int32" Nullable="true" />
  <NavigationProperty Name="StakeHolder"
      Relationship="BoP.Core.Domain.StakeHolderAccount" FromRole="Account"
      ToRole="StakeHolder" />
</EntityType>
<EntityType Name="Loan" BaseType="BoP.Core.Domain.Account">
  <Property Name="InterestRate" Type="Decimal" Precision="18" Scale="0" />
  <Property Name="Principal" Type="Decimal" Precision="19" Scale="4" />
</EntityType>
<EntityType Name="LoanApplication" BaseType="BoP.Core.Domain.Account">
  <Property Name="RequestLoanAmount" Type="Decimal" Precision="19" Scale="4" />
  <Property Name="LoanPurpose" Type="String" MaxLength="1073741823" />
  <Property Name="Approved" Type="String" Nullable="false" MaxLength="1"
      Unicode="false" FixedLength="true" />
  <Property Name="CreditScore" Type="Int32" />
</EntityType>
<EntityType Name="Person" BaseType="BoP.Core.Domain.StakeHolder">
  <Property Name="FirstName" Type="String" MaxLength="50" />
  <Property Name="LastName" Type="String" MaxLength="50" />
  <Property Name="Gender" Type="String" MaxLength="1" Unicode="false"
      FixedLength="true" />
  <Property Name="DOB" Type="DateTime" />
  <Property Name="Email" Type="String" MaxLength="50" />
  <Property Name="TaxId" Type="String" MaxLength="50" />
  <NavigationProperty Name="User" Relationship="BoP.Core.Domain.PersonUser"
      FromRole="Person" ToRole="User" />
</EntityType>
<EntityType Name="User">
  <Key>
    <PropertyRef Name="UserId" />
  </Key>
  <Property Name="UserId" Type="String" MaxLength="50" Nullable="false" />
  <Property Name="Password" Type="String" MaxLength="50" />
  <Property Name="Active" Type="String" MaxLength="10" FixedLength="true" />
  <Property Name="StakeHolderId" Type="Int32" Nullable="false" />
  <NavigationProperty Name="Person" Relationship="BoP.Core.Domain.PersonUser"
      FromRole="User" ToRole="Person" />
</EntityType>
<EntityType Name="StakeHolder" Abstract="true">
  <Key>
    <PropertyRef Name="StakeHolderId" />
  </Key>
  <Property Name="StakeHolderId" Type="Int32" Nullable="false" />
  <NavigationProperty Name="Account"
      Relationship="BoP.Core.Domain.StakeHolderAccount" FromRole="StakeHolder"
      ToRole="Account" />
```

```
  </EntityType>
  <Association Name="StakeHolderAccount">
    <End Type="BoP.Core.Domain.StakeHolder" Role="StakeHolder" Multiplicity="1" />
    <End Type="BoP.Core.Domain.Account" Role="Account" Multiplicity="*" />
  </Association>
  <Association Name="PersonUser">
    <End Type="BoP.Core.Domain.Person" Role="Person" Multiplicity="1" />
    <End Type="BoP.Core.Domain.User" Role="User" Multiplicity="1" />
  </Association>
</Schema>
```

The final mapping file is of course the MSL file. The MSL file is the mapping glue that connects the SSDL and the CSDL. Listing 10-13 shows the generated MSL file. Here you have the metadata that defines the EntityContainerMapping along with the properties and attributes needed by EF to connect the conceptual model to the storage model.

Listing 10-13. *MSL for the BoP Application*

```
<?xml version="1.0" encoding="utf-8"?>
<Mapping Space="C-S" xmlns="urn:schemas-microsoft-com:windows:storage:mapping:CS">
  <EntityContainerMapping StorageEntityContainer="dbo"
      CdmEntityContainer="BoPObjectContext">
    <EntitySetMapping Name="Account">
      <EntityTypeMapping TypeName="IsTypeOf(BoP.Core.Domain.Account)">
        <MappingFragment StoreEntitySet="Account">
          <ScalarProperty Name="StakeHolderId" ColumnName="StakeHolderId" />
          <ScalarProperty Name="AccountNumber" ColumnName="AccountNumber" />
          <ScalarProperty Name="Balance" ColumnName="Balance" />
        </MappingFragment>
      </EntityTypeMapping>
      <EntityTypeMapping TypeName="IsTypeOf(BoP.Core.Domain.Loan)">
        <MappingFragment StoreEntitySet="Loan">
          <ScalarProperty Name="AccountNumber" ColumnName="AccountNumber" />
          <ScalarProperty Name="Principal" ColumnName="Principal" />
          <ScalarProperty Name="InterestRate" ColumnName="InterestRate" />
        </MappingFragment>
      </EntityTypeMapping>
      <EntityTypeMapping TypeName="IsTypeOf(BoP.Core.Domain.LoanApplication)">
        <MappingFragment StoreEntitySet="LoanApplication">
          <ScalarProperty Name="AccountNumber" ColumnName="AccountNumber" />
          <ScalarProperty Name="CreditScore" ColumnName="CreditScore" />
          <ScalarProperty Name="Approved" ColumnName="Approved" />
          <ScalarProperty Name="LoanPurpose" ColumnName="LoanPurpose" />
          <ScalarProperty Name="RequestLoanAmount" ColumnName="RequestLoanAmount" />
        </MappingFragment>
      </EntityTypeMapping>
    </EntitySetMapping>
    <EntitySetMapping Name="User">
```

```
        <EntityTypeMapping TypeName="IsTypeOf(BoP.Core.Domain.User)">
          <MappingFragment StoreEntitySet="User">
            <ScalarProperty Name="StakeHolderId" ColumnName="StakeHolderId" />
            <ScalarProperty Name="UserId" ColumnName="UserId" />
            <ScalarProperty Name="Password" ColumnName="Password" />
            <ScalarProperty Name="Active" ColumnName="Active" />
          </MappingFragment>
        </EntityTypeMapping>
      </EntitySetMapping>
      <EntitySetMapping Name="StakeHolder">
        <EntityTypeMapping TypeName="IsTypeOf(BoP.Core.Domain.StakeHolder)">
          <MappingFragment StoreEntitySet="Person">
            <ScalarProperty Name="StakeHolderId" ColumnName="StakeHolderId" />
          </MappingFragment>
        </EntityTypeMapping>
        <EntityTypeMapping TypeName="BoP.Core.Domain.Person">
          <MappingFragment StoreEntitySet="Person">
            <ScalarProperty Name="StakeHolderId" ColumnName="StakeHolderId" />
            <ScalarProperty Name="TaxId" ColumnName="TaxId" />
            <ScalarProperty Name="Email" ColumnName="Email" />
            <ScalarProperty Name="DOB" ColumnName="DOB" />
            <ScalarProperty Name="Gender" ColumnName="Gender" />
            <ScalarProperty Name="LastName" ColumnName="LastName" />
            <ScalarProperty Name="FirstName" ColumnName="FirstName" />
          </MappingFragment>
        </EntityTypeMapping>
      </EntitySetMapping>
      <AssociationSetMapping Name="StakeHolderAccount"
            TypeName="BoP.Core.Domain.StakeHolderAccount" StoreEntitySet="Account">
        <EndProperty Name="Account">
          <ScalarProperty Name="AccountNumber" ColumnName="AccountNumber" />
        </EndProperty>
        <EndProperty Name="StakeHolder">
          <ScalarProperty Name="StakeHolderId" ColumnName="StakeHolderId" />
        </EndProperty>
      </AssociationSetMapping>
      <AssociationSetMapping Name="PersonUser" TypeName="BoP.Core.Domain.PersonUser"
          StoreEntitySet="User">
        <EndProperty Name="User">
          <ScalarProperty Name="UserId" ColumnName="UserId" />
        </EndProperty>
        <EndProperty Name="Person">
          <ScalarProperty Name="StakeHolderId" ColumnName="StakeHolderId" />
        </EndProperty>
      </AssociationSetMapping>
    </EntityContainerMapping>
  </Mapping>
```

Now that you have created the mapping files, the next step is to create your database so you have something to actually connect your domain model to. Reviewing the SSDL, you should notice that five tables are needed to make the BoP application function. Listing 10-14 shows the T-SQL that you can use to create the tables. Here you have the Account, Loan, LoanApplication, User, and Person tables.

Listing 10-14. *SQL Table Scripts for BoP Database*

```
CREATE TABLE [dbo].[Account](
       [AccountNumber] [int] IDENTITY(10000,1) NOT NULL,
       [Balance] [decimal](18, 0) NULL,
       [StakeHolderId] [int] NULL,
 CONSTRAINT [PK_Account] PRIMARY KEY CLUSTERED
(
       [AccountNumber] ASC
)WITH (IGNORE_DUP_KEY = OFF) ON [PRIMARY]
) ON [PRIMARY]

CREATE TABLE [dbo].[Loan](
       [AccountNumber] [int] NOT NULL,
       [InterestRate] [decimal](18, 0) NULL,
       [Principal] [money] NULL,
 CONSTRAINT [PK_Loan] PRIMARY KEY CLUSTERED
(
       [AccountNumber] ASC
)WITH (IGNORE_DUP_KEY = OFF) ON [PRIMARY]
) ON [PRIMARY]

CREATE TABLE [dbo].[LoanApplication](
       [AccountNumber] [int] NOT NULL,
       [RequestLoanAmount] [money] NULL,
       [LoanPurpose] [nvarchar](max) COLLATE SQL_Latin1_General_CP1_CI_AS NULL,
       [Approved] [char](1) COLLATE SQL_Latin1_General_CP1_CI_AS NOT NULL,
       [CreditScore] [int] NULL,
 CONSTRAINT [PK_LoanApplication] PRIMARY KEY CLUSTERED
(
       [AccountNumber] ASC
)WITH (IGNORE_DUP_KEY = OFF) ON [PRIMARY]
) ON [PRIMARY]

CREATE TABLE [dbo].[Person](
       [FirstName] [nvarchar](50) COLLATE SQL_Latin1_General_CP1_CI_AS NULL,
       [LastName] [nvarchar](50) COLLATE SQL_Latin1_General_CP1_CI_AS NULL,
       [Gender] [char](1) COLLATE SQL_Latin1_General_CP1_CI_AS NULL,
       [DOB] [datetime] NULL,
```

```
	[Email] [nvarchar](50) COLLATE SQL_Latin1_General_CP1_CI_AS NULL,
	[TaxId] [nvarchar](50) COLLATE SQL_Latin1_General_CP1_CI_AS NULL,
	[StakeHolderId] [int] NOT NULL,
 CONSTRAINT [PK_Person] PRIMARY KEY CLUSTERED
(
	[StakeHolderId] ASC
)WITH (IGNORE_DUP_KEY = OFF) ON [PRIMARY]
) ON [PRIMARY]

CREATE TABLE [dbo].[User](
	[UserId] [nvarchar](50) COLLATE SQL_Latin1_General_CP1_CI_AS NOT NULL,
	[Password] [nvarchar](50) COLLATE SQL_Latin1_General_CP1_CI_AS NULL,
	[Active] [nchar](10) COLLATE SQL_Latin1_General_CP1_CI_AS NULL,
	[StakeHolderId] [int] NOT NULL,
 CONSTRAINT [PK_User] PRIMARY KEY CLUSTERED
(
	[UserId] ASC
)WITH (IGNORE_DUP_KEY = OFF) ON [PRIMARY]
) ON [PRIMARY]
```

■ Note The database structure that I choose to use for the BoP EF application is basically a Table per Concrete Class inheritance structure. Although this design doesn't meet the requirements of all applications, it is generally a good model because it is inherently normalized, as compared to a Table per Hierarchy pattern (which is not).

Although a good majority of Chapter 12 is devoted to comparing and contrasting the differences in implementation between LTS and EF, it is worth noting here that unlike LTS, which requires a non-normalized database structure because of its simple form of inheritance, with EF we can structure our data model in a more normalized, logical manner.

Middle Tier/Context Manager

The next piece of functionality that needs to be added to your domain model is an object context. As you learned in earlier chapters, the purpose of the `ObjectContext` class is to encapsulate the CRUD functionality in your model. There are many ways to build out your object context and middle tier. However, we are going to follow a pattern similar to what we developed in Chapter 6 for the sake of consistency.

Listing 10-15 shows the `BoPObjectContext` class, which is part of the `BoP.Data` solution. In this class, three constructors are used for initialization of the connection and for providing the default entity container to the `ObjectContext` base class. Additionally, three methods return `ObjectQuerys` in the form of `Account`, `User`, and `StakeHolder` (the parent classes in the model).

Listing 10-15. *EF ObjectContext*

```
public class BoPObjectContext : global::System.Data.Objects.ObjectContext
{

        public BoPObjectContext() :
            base("name=BoPObjectContext", "BoPObjectContext")
        {
        }

        public BoPObjectContext(string connectionString) :
            base(connectionString, "BoPObjectContext")
        {
        }

        public BoPObjectContext
            (global::System.Data.EntityClient.EntityConnection connection) :
            base(connection, "BoPObjectContext")
        {
        }

        public global::System.Data.Objects.ObjectQuery<Account> Account
        {
            get
            {
                if ((this._Account == null))
                {
                    this._Account = base.CreateQuery<Account>("[Account]");
                }
                return this._Account;
            }
        }

        private global::System.Data.Objects.ObjectQuery<Account> _Account;

        public global::System.Data.Objects.ObjectQuery<User> User
        {
            get
            {
                if ((this._User == null))
                {
                    this._User = base.CreateQuery<User>("[User]");
                }
                return this._User;
            }
        }

        private global::System.Data.Objects.ObjectQuery<User> _User;
```

```
    public global::System.Data.Objects.ObjectQuery<StakeHolder> StakeHolder
    {
        get
        {
            if ((this._StakeHolder == null))
            {
                this._StakeHolder =
                    base.CreateQuery<StakeHolder>("[StakeHolder]");
            }
            return this._StakeHolder;
        }
    }

    private global::System.Data.Objects.ObjectQuery<StakeHolder> _StakeHolder;

}
```

Note The following examples are very similar to the code that you developed in Chapter 6, because the architecture is the same regardless of the ORM (LTS or EF), thus allowing for the greatest reusability.

The next piece of code for you to look at is a wrapper/manager around the `BoPObjectContext`, called the `BoPObjectContextManager` (see Listing 10-16). This is an example of a thread-safe, lazy singleton, but there is a catch with this pattern. The EF `ObjectContext` is not thread safe, and thus using this exact pattern is not the best approach for web applications. In Chapter 11, we will consider an n-tier disconnected model for EF (and LTS), where we modify the `BoPObjectManager` to use the `Attach()` and `Detach()` methods, but for this chapter let's stick to this pattern with the understanding that this is fine for Windows Forms applications and more information follows in Chapter 11.

Listing 10-16. *BoPObjectContextManager*

```
/// <summary>
/// Simple class to implement DataContext singleton.
/// </summary>
public sealed class BoPObjectContextManager
{
    private BoPObjectContext db;

    #region Thread-safe, lazy Singleton

    /// <summary>
    /// This is a thread-safe, lazy singleton.
    /// See http://www.yoda.arachsys.com/csharp/singleton.html
    /// for more details about its implementation.
    /// </summary>
```

```
        public static BoPObjectContextManager Instance
        {
            get
            {
                return Nested.BoPObjectContextManager;
            }
        }

        /// <summary>
        /// Initializes BoPDataContext.
        /// </summary>
        private BoPObjectContextManager()
        {
            InitDB();
        }

        /// <summary>
        /// Assists with ensuring thread-safe, lazy singleton
        /// </summary>
        private class Nested
        {
            static Nested() { }
            internal static readonly BoPObjectContextManager
               BoPObjectContextManager =  new BoPObjectContextManager();
        }
        #endregion

        private void InitDB()
        {

            db = new BoPObjectContext();
        }

        public BoPObjectContext GetContext()
        {
            return db;

        }
}
```

One aspect I have skipped over thus far is the DAO layer in the EF BoP application. It really hasn't changed much since Chapter 6, and so I didn't think it necessary to repeat the same points again. However, because the concrete implementation of the DAOs is changing because of syntactical differences between LTS and EF, we should review the structure again so it is fresh in your mind.

In Listing 10-17, you can see the data interfaces that exist in the BoP.Core project and define the contract for the concrete DAOs in the solution. The basic structure of the data interfaces is included in Listing 10-17. Here you have the IDao interface and the IDaoFactory interface, which are both part of the BoP.Core.DataInterface namespace.

Listing 10-17. *IDao and IDaoFactory Data Interface Contracts*

```
namespace BoP.Core.DataInterfaces
{
    /// <summary>
    /// This interface was adapted from Billy McCafferty's NHibernate Framework
    /// <see cref="http://devlicio.us/blogs/billy_mccafferty"/>
    ///
    /// The purpose of this interface is to provide a
    /// general-purpose contract for CRUD operations
    /// executed in the ORM layer
    /// </summary>
    /// <typeparam name="T"></typeparam>
    /// <typeparam name="IdT"></typeparam>
    public interface IDao<T, IdT>
    {
        T GetById(IdT id);
        List<T> GetAll();
        T Save(T entity);
        void Delete(T entity);
        void CommitChanges();
    }
}

namespace BoP.Core.DataInterfaces
{
    /// <summary>
    /// This interface was adapted from Billy McCafferty's NHibernate Framework
    /// <see cref="http://devlicio.us/blogs/billy_mccafferty"/>
    ///
    /// The purpose of this interface is to provide
    /// the contracts for retrieving DAO objects
    /// in a decoupled manner
    /// </summary>

    public interface IDaoFactory
    {
        IAccountDao GetAccountDao();
        ICreditHistoryDao GetCreditHistoryDao();
        ILoanDao GetLoanDao();
        ILoanApplicationDao GetLoanApplicationDao();
        IUserDao GetUserDao();
        IPersonDao GetPersonDao();
        IApplicantDao GetApplicantDao();
    }
```

```
    #region Inline interface declarations

    public interface IAccountDao : IDao<Account, int> { }
    public interface ILoanDao : IDao<Loan, int> { }
    public interface ILoanApplicationDao : IDao<LoanApplication, int> { }
    public interface ICreditHistoryDao : IDao<CreditHistory, int> { }
    public interface IUserDao : IDao<User, int> { }
    public interface IPersonDao : IDao<Person, string> { }
    public interface IApplicantDao : IDao<Applicant, int> { }

    #endregion
}
```

The first concrete implementation of the interfaces, as seen in Listing 10-17, can be observed in Listing 10-18. Here the `EFDaoFactory` exposes the EF DAO classes. This implementation is pretty straightforward: it exposes `GetENTITYDAO` methods that return new concrete DAOs as an interface. As you can see, the file is named `EF` because this implementation is EF specific.

Listing 10-18. *Concrete Implementation of DAOFactory*

```
namespace BoP.Data.EF
{
    /// <summary>
    /// Exposes access to LTS DAO classes.  This framework
    /// was adapted from Billy McCafferty's NHibernate Framework.
    ///
    /// This is the concrete implementation of IDaoFactory, which
    /// is exposed from the BoP.Core.DataInterfaces domain model
    /// </summary>
    public class EFDaoFactory : IDaoFactory
    {

        #region Inline DAO implementations

        public class AccountDao : AbstractEFDao<Account, int>, IAccountDao{ }

        #endregion

        #region IDaoFactory Members

        public IAccountDao GetAccountDao()
        {
            return new AccountDao();
        }
```

```
        public IPersonDao GetPersonDao()
        {
            return new PersonDao();
        }

        public ILoanApplicationDao GetLoanApplicationDao()
        {
            return new LoanApplicationDao();
        }

        public IUserDao GetUserDao()
        {
            return new UserDao();
        }

        #endregion

    }
}
```

You may have noticed that Listing 10-18 contains an inline implementation of the AccountDao class, which inherits from the AbstractEFDao and passes in the types needed for generic CRUD operations. The inline implementation is included because the AbstractEFDao contains all the functionality needed for now, and so it is not contained in its own file with extensions. As your model grows, this may need to be moved into its own file, similar to the PersonEFDao, which will be covered shortly.

Listing 10-19 shows the AbstractEFDao class containing the base implementation for your CRUD operations. This class takes advantage of the powerful functionality of generic types to create a multipurpose type-independent wrapper around the ObjectContext.

Starting at the top of the class, you can see that it inherits from the IDao interface, part of the BoP.Core.DataInterface namespace, which enforces the generic type T and the generic identifier IdT. In addition, the AbstractEFDao specifies an additional constraint on T so that it is enforced as a class (for example, where T:class). The class also contains generic implementation code for GetAll, Save, Delete, and SubmitChanges, plus a signature for GetById.

Listing 10-19. *The AbstractEFDao*

```
namespace BoP.Data.EF
{
    public class AbstractEFDao<T, IdT> : IDao<T, IdT> where T:class
    {
        EFSamplesEntities db = new EFSamplesEntities();

        public virtual T GetById(IdT id)
        {
            return default(T);

        }
```

```
        public virtual List<T> GetAll()
        {
            ObjectQuery<T> oq = db.CreateQuery<T>("[" + typeof(T).Name + "]");

            return oq.ToList<T>();
        }

        public virtual T Save(T entity)
        {
            db.AddObject(typeof(T).Name, entity as object);
            db.SaveChanges();
            return entity;
        }


        public virtual void Delete(T entity)
        {
            db.DeleteObject(entity as object);
            db.SaveChanges();

        }

        public virtual void CommitChanges()
        {
            db.SaveChanges();
        }
    }

    }
```

After you have the AbstractEFDao, you need to write some concrete code for your DAOs—specifically, Person and User. As you saw in Chapter 6, you need three methods in the PersonDao: GetById, GetByTaxId, and GetByExample. Listing 10-20 includes the PersonDao with these three methods. GetById uses the EntityKey to retrieve the StakeHolder and casts the returned Object to a Person. The GetByTaxId method uses LINQ to Entities to retrieve the First() Person type by the taxid provided. Finally, the GetByExample method uses LINQ and matches on all the criteria passed in to return a List of Person classes.

Listing 10-20. *PersonEFDao*

```
namespace BoP.Data.EF
{
    public class PersonEFDao
    {

        BoPObjectContext db = BoPObjectContextManager.Instance.GetContext();
```

```
        public override Person GetById(int id)
        {
            IEnumerable<KeyValuePair<string, object>> entityKeyValues =
                   new KeyValuePair<string, object>[] {
                   new KeyValuePair<string, object>("StakeHolderId", id)};


            EntityKey ek = new EntityKey("StakeHolder", entityKeyValues);
            object o = db.GetObjectByKey(ek);
            return (Person)o;

        }

        public Person GetByTaxId(string taxid)
        {

             Person sh = (from p in db.StakeHolder.OfType<Person>()
                          where p.TaxId == taxid
                          select p).First();

             return sh;

        }

        public List<Person> GetByExample(Person p)
        {

             List<Person> lp = (from s in db.StakeHolder.OfType<Person>()
                                where s.TaxId == p.TaxId ||
                                s.StakeHolderId == p.StakeHolderId ||
                                s.LastName == p.LastName ||
                                s.Gender == p.Gender ||
                                s.Email == p.Email ||
                                s.DOB == p.DOB ||
                                s.FirstName == p.FirstName
                                select s).ToList();
                                return lp;


        }

    }
}
```

Along with the Person DAO, you also need a similar User DAO to complete the functionality of the BoP application. Listing 10-21 shows the method GetByUserIdAndPassword(), which uses LINQ to Entities to retrieve the User by uid and pwd.

Listing 10-21. *UserEFDao*

```
BoPObjectContext db =
        BoPObjectContextManager.Instance.GetContext();

public User GetByUserIdAndPassword(string uid, string pwd)
{

    User u = (from p in db.User
              where p.UserId == uid &&
              p.Password == pwd
              select p).First();

    return u;

}
```

The next steps to complete the BoP application are to write some managers (workers) to encapsulate the business logic in your application and write some tests. While the code that you have seen thus far has had subtle differences between what you wrote in Chapter 6, the code here is identical and therefore is not shown.

As long as you remember that the clear demarcation between `BoP.Workers`, `BoP.Util`, `BoP.Data`, and `BoP.Core` is what has facilitated the reusability that you have seen in this chapter, and you use OOP patterns, you can create a framework for use with any ORM.

Summary

In this chapter, you learned that using repeatable patterns when building domain models enables significant reuse. This is exemplified by the fact that only minor changes to the model needed to take place from Chapter 6 to now in order to enable it for use with the EF. Additionally, you have learned that although EF does not support PI, you can work around EF's deficiencies via a few coding techniques and take advantage of its strengths.

In Chapter 11, you will learn how to take the models that you built for LTS and EF and use them in a true n-tier environment. You will explore the concept of DTOs and examine the disconnected ORM model by applying an ASP.NET façade to the model.

PART 5

Building on the Bank of Pluto Foundation

CHAPTER 11

N-Tier Architecture

In the previous 10 chapters, you learned about the patterns needed to work with ORM tools, the basics behind LTS and EF, and the core architecture behind building a reusable ORM foundation. One key area, however, remains: the web environment and the n-tier architecture applied to the LTS and EF foundations.

Why N-Tier?

There comes a time in the life of many software (web and other) applications when they outgrow their homes (memory, disk space, servers, and so forth) and require the ability to scale outward into multiple tiers. Although this phenomenon isn't limited to web applications, because this happens with rich clients too, the web is the focus of the discussion.

The web is the focus here because in most cases you will find yourself writing an application that needs to have a UI that is decoupled in a separate physical tier in the infrastructure. This is a common scenario because of the necessity of securing one's data behind firewalls by separating tiers into logical and physical layers.

There are many ways to split an application into layers, but only one is going to be covered in this text: Data Transfer Objects (DTOs). Although it is important to note that DTOs are not the only pattern for building a layered architecture, they are one of the most versatile and usable patterns with object-oriented programming (OOP) and thus are the focus here.

DTOs

Martin Fowler defines a *DTO* as "an object that carries data between processes in order to reduce the number of method calls" (`http://martinfowler.com/eaaCatalog/dataTransferObject.html`). Although academically correct, I like to think of a DTO more as a concept or technique than a concrete set of objects. If the sole purpose of a DTO is to be an object that can be serialized or marshaled across process boundaries through remoting or web services, which it is, then in my humble opinion there is no good reason not to use your domain objects as DTOs. Now, this idea is somewhat controversial because many pundits believe that a separate object/class should be created to encapsulate the DTO functionality, similar to a DAO. My personal belief is that your domain model should already be serializable, and therefore there is no need for a separate class for DTO functionality. With a little design and a few helper classes, you can create an elegant façade for marshaling objects across boundaries.

Speaking of marshaling, in terms of ORM, like everything else in software design, there are many ways to communicate across layers. For example, you can use remoting, web services, sockets, and more. Additionally, when you start talking about service orientation, there are many other facets to the discussion, all of which are interesting and worthwhile, but none of which are going to be discussed here. This chapter provides you with one technique to use web services with ORM to create a robust n-tiered architecture. There are many ways to write a distributed system, and many books about doing it; this is not one of those books.

Now that I have covered these caveats, it is time to design our DTO layer. Before you get into specific implementation details in LTS and EF, however, we should probably have a quick refresher on concurrency as it relates to database transactions. *Concurrency* is the act of multiple processes running at the same time with the possibility that these processes are interacting with each other. This scenario is common in the database world, when you have a multiuser environment and two threads that are trying to read or update the same row.

There are two techniques for handling concurrency in your database:

Pessimistic concurrency: The record is locked to avoid any concurrency issues.

Optimistic concurrency: A check occurs to see whether other transactions have changed values in the record prior to the update.

■ **Note** The term *optimistic* is used because the technique assumes that the possibility of a conflict/collision occurring is rare—thus optimistic.

Frankly, there isn't a good reason to have an in-depth discussion on pessimistic concurrency. It is what it is—lock the record so only one person can use it. In general, this design is not a bad one per se, but unfortunately pessimistic concurrency can result in time-outs and deadlocks in high-traffic situations. The pessimistic strategy is resource intensive and impacts performance; thus it is really necessary only in applications where data integrity is hypercritical—for example, a hospital application where lives are at stake.

Optimistic concurrency is where the real discussion exists. With optimistic concurrency, you have various strategies for handling data conflicts and integrity. These strategies fundamentally have to do with the way that the T-SQL `UPDATE` is crafted, which you will see later in this chapter by looking at the LTS and EF concurrency models. For now, realize that the following are the general strategies for handling optimistic concurrency. Additionally, understand that there is no one-size-fits-all solution when it comes to handling concurrency in your application. Only after a thorough analysis of the requirements should you select your strategy.

Check all fields: The `UPDATE` checks all fields in the row to ensure that nothing has changed.

Do nothing: The `UPDATE` does not check anything; instead it just performs the update.

Check only changed fields: The `UPDATE` checks only the values that have changed.

Timestamp check: The `UPDATE` checks the timestamp to determine whether the row has changed.

■ **Caution** Entire volumes have been written on concurrency and multithreading in databases and software. If you have never heard of optimistic or pessimistic concurrency, I highly recommend reading about them before moving on with this chapter. This text will not cover all concurrency scenarios in a database but will cover the general handling of concurrency in LTS and EF.

Layered LTS

Now that you have a general understanding of what a DTO is and how concurrency is important for maintaining data integrity, it is time to look at building a disconnected LTS application. Figure 11-1 shows the basic architecture of the disconnected web application. In this scenario, you have a layer of web services that expose your managers (that is, CRUD functions).

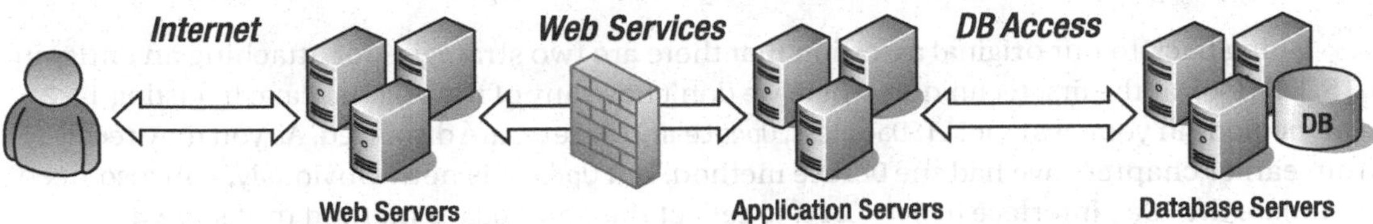

Figure 11-1. *Layered architecture*

As established earlier, rather than creating separate classes for DTOs, you will use your domain objects. In order to allow for your domain objects to be serialized, you must decorate each of your classes as serializable. Listing 11-1 shows an example of the Person class that is decorated with the [Serializable] attribute.

Listing 11-1. *A Serializable Class*

```
[Serializable]
public class Person: StakeHolder
```

■ **Note** The [Serializable] attribute is part of the core .NET Framework, specifically the System namespace, so no additional references are required.

After marking each of your domain classes as serializable, the next step is to dive into the LTS Attach method. The purpose of the Attach method, which is part of the System.Data.Linq.ITable interface, is to connect a disconnected entity to the change-tracking mechanism (for example, DataContext) so it can become part of the ORM solution again. Unlike EF, which you will see shortly, LTS does most of the heavy lifting so you are not required to call an explicit Detach method to disconnect an entity from the change tracker. The reason why you don't have to explicitly Detach when using LTS is that entities are automatically detached when they are serialized and deserialized, or, putting it another way, when your DataContext goes out of scope, the objects are no longer connected.

When it comes to LTS and a disconnected model, you have two approaches: either you have the original data before updates or you don't. This is important to understand because it affects the way that concurrency is handled in the application. Before we look at changing the AbstractLTSDao class to use the Attach method, let's first examine how concurrency is handled in LTS.

By default, LTS has the UpdateCheck attribute set to Always; thus every field is checked for optimistic concurrency violations. To change this, you need to explicitly set this attribute in your *column* mappings. The enumerations for the UpdateCheck attribute are as follows:

Always: The column is checked every time (default).

Never: The column is never checked.

When Changed: The column is checked only when it changes.

Going back to our original assertion that there are two strategies for attaching an entity in LTS, let's look at the first technique, where we don't have any of the original data. In Listing 11-2, two methods in your AbstractLTSDao class, Update and Delete, are displayed. As you may recall from earlier chapters, we had the Delete method, but Update is new. Obviously, you also need to update the IDao interface in BoP.Core, to reflect the new Update method (not shown).

As you can see in Listing 11-2, the Update method accepts two entities, newEntity and originalEntity, both of generic type T. No, I didn't forget that we are currently looking at scenario 1, where we don't have the original data. Instead of writing two methods, I thought I would solve both problems by allowing the consumer to pass in null for originalEntity if they didn't have it. As you can see, if the originalEntity is null, the Attach method is called with true to specify that the entity has been modified; otherwise, the originalEntity is passed into the Attach method. To clarify, when passing in the true parameter, you are telling LTS that the entity has changed and that it should do the work for you to infer the original data. Alternatively, when explicitly passing in the original entity as a parameter, you are saving the framework the extra step of inferring the original data.

Along with the new Update method, you also have a modified Delete method, which does an Attach on the entity, and then completes its DeleteOnSubmit call. In addition, you may have noticed in this example that the DataContext is no longer a singleton; instead it is a simple module variable. The reason for this change is that there are potential threading issues by using a singleton in this type of n-tier environment, and because AbstractLTSDao now supports a disconnected model, there isn't a good reason to hold a single instance to the DataContext.

Note In general, it is better to use a DataContext for a short period of time in n-tier environments. Because the DataContext uses connection pooling after the first initialization, there is no performance impact when creating it again; thus using it as a module-level variable within a method is a viable solution.

Listing 11-2. *AbstractLTSDao with Disconnected Support*

```
BoPDataContext db = new BoPDataContext();
public virtual T Update(T newEntity, T originalEntity)
{

    ITable tab = db.GetTable(newEntity.GetType().BaseType);
    if (originalEntity == null)
    {
        tab.Attach(newEntity, true);
    }
    else
    {
        tab.Attach(newEntity, originalEntity);
    }
        this.CommitChanges();
        return newEntity;

}

public virtual void Delete(T entity)
{

    ITable tab = db.GetTable(entity.GetType().BaseType);
    tab.Attach(entity);
    tab.DeleteOnSubmit(entity);
    this.CommitChanges();

}
```

You may have noticed in Listing 11-2 that instead of calling `SubmitChanges` on the `DataContext`, the methods are using the `CommitChanges` method. Listing 11-3 shows the `CommitChanges` method, which is obviously part of the `AbstractLTSDao` class. In this example, you have a `try…catch` block that is used to resolve concurrency conflicts by merging the values. Here, you use the `ConflictMode` enumeration and set it to `ContinueOnConflict` when calling the `DataContext.SubmitChanges` method. Next, you have a `catch` block that is trapping for `ChangeConflictException` errors, looping through the `ChangeConflicts` collection and resolving the conflict, and finally, `SubmitChanges` is called again but this time with the `FailOnFirstConflict` enumeration.

Listing 11-3. *Merging Values on Concurrency Conflict*

```
public virtual void CommitChanges()
{
    try
    {
        db.SubmitChanges(ConflictMode.ContinueOnConflict);
    }
```

```
    catch (ChangeConflictException e)
    {
        //Log Message (e.Message) to somewhere

        foreach (ObjectChangeConflict occ in db.ChangeConflicts)
        {
            occ.Resolve(RefreshMode.KeepChanges);
        }

    }

    db.SubmitChanges(ConflictMode.FailOnFirstConflict);
}
```

Although merging the values is always my preferred method of resolving concurrency conflicts (as in Listing 11-3), it is not your only option. Listing 11-4 shows another technique, which overwrites the values. As you can see, the code is similar, but instead of using `RefreshMode.KeepChanges`, the enumeration for the `Resolve` call is `KeepCurrentValues`. Additionally, in this example, because you are keeping the current values, there is no need for a second call to `SubmitChanges` as there is in Listing 11-3.

Listing 11-4. *Keep Current Value on Concurrency Conflict*

```
try
{
    db.SubmitChanges(ConflictMode.ContinueOnConflict);
}

catch (ChangeConflictException e)
{
    Console.WriteLine(e.Message);
    foreach (ObjectChangeConflict occ in db.ChangeConflicts)
    {
        //No database values are merged into current.
        occ.Resolve(RefreshMode.KeepCurrentValues);
    }
}
```

Your last option for resolving concurrency conflicts is to overwrite the current values. In Listing 11-5, you can see that the enumeration used with `Resolve` is `RefreshMode.OverwriteCurrentValues`. In this example, the strategy used is "the last one in wins."

Listing 11-5. *Last One In Wins on Conflict*

```
try
{
    db.SubmitChanges(ConflictMode.ContinueOnConflict);
}
```

```
catch (ChangeConflictException e)
{
    Console.WriteLine(e.Message);
    foreach (ObjectChangeConflict occ in db.ChangeConflicts)
    {
        // All database values overwrite current values.
        occ.Resolve(RefreshMode.OverwriteCurrentValues);
    }
}
```

■ **Tip** LTS by default assumes that you want to check every column in your table for optimistic concurrency violations; this can kill performance and can create very long SQL statements. Use the `UpdateCheck` attribute in your mapping to turn off optimistic concurrency checking on the fields that you don't care about.

Your next task in building the disconnected model is to expose some update functionality in your managers. In this example, you are going to create a new method in the `PersonManager` called `UpdatePerson` to use the new `Update` method in the DAO layer. Listing 11-6 shows the new `UpdatePerson` method, which accepts two `Person` objects, `newP` and `origP`, and then creates a `PersonDao` and calls `Update`. As you can see, this is a general-purpose manager method that is unaware of web services, disconnected state, and so forth.

Listing 11-6. *UpdatePerson Method in PersonManager*

```
public Person UpdatePerson(Person newP, Person origP)
{
    IServiceFactory serviceFactory = new ClassServiceFactory();
    IDaoFactory df = (IDaoFactory)serviceFactory.
                    FindByServiceName("BoP/Core/DataInterfaces/IDaoFactory");
    IPersonDao ipd = df.GetPersonDao();
    return ipd.Update(newP,origP);

}
```

After you have some manager functions, the next step is to expose this functionality through web services. Because we are writing this code in Visual Studio 2008, it makes sense that we expose this functionality as a Windows Communication Foundation (WCF) service instead of a classic `.asmx` service.

Before I spark a religious debate on web services, know that the purpose of these examples is to demonstrate how to build a disconnected architecture with LTS, not to provide best practices for WCF. There are plenty of books out there on WCF, SOA, and web services, but these topics are not covered here.

Listing 11-7 shows the WCF interface and implementation for the `GetPersonByTaxId` service and the `UpdatePerson` service. As you can see, in both examples you use the `ClassServiceFactory` to retrieve a `PersonManager`. In the `GetPersonByTaxId`, a string, `taxId`, is passed to the `GetPersonByTaxId` method in the `PersonManager` class. Similarly, in the `UpdatePerson` method, your parameters, in this case a new and an original entity, are being passed into the PersonManager, and in both cases a Person entity is returned.

In this example, I am allowing .NET/WCF to handle the serialization of the Person object graph for me. This technique of returning a complex custom type from a service is debatable because typically in this situation you would want finer-grained control over serialization and would choose to write your own serializer. However, to be concise, I have chosen to use the ServiceKnownType attribute in the WCF interface and allow the framework to handle the serialization for me.

Listing 11-7. *WCF Interface and Service*

```
namespace BoPServices
{
    [ServiceContract]
    public interface IManagerServices
    {
        [OperationContract]
        [ServiceKnownType(typeof(User))]
        Person GetPersonByTaxId(string taxId);

        [OperationContract]
        Person UpdatePerson(Person newP, Person oldP);
    }
}


namespace BoPServices
{
    public class ManagerServices : IManagerServices
    {
        IServiceFactory serviceFactory;

        //[ServiceKnownType("GetKnownEntityTypes", typeof(Person))]
        public Person GetPersonByTaxId(string taxId)
        {

            serviceFactory = new ClassServiceFactory();
            IPersonManager um = (IPersonManager)serviceFactory.
                        FindByServiceName("BoP/Core/Domain/IPersonManager");
            Person p = um.GetPersonByTaxId(taxId);
            return p;
        }

        public Person UpdatePerson(Person newPerson, Person originalPerson)
        {
```

```
            serviceFactory = new ClassServiceFactory();
            IPersonManager um = (IPersonManager)serviceFactory.
                        FindByServiceName("BoP/Core/Domain/IPersonManager");
            return um.UpdatePerson(newPerson, originalPerson);
        }

    }
}
```

After you have a web service or two that can be consumed to interact with your DAO/CRUD, you can write some code to actually do something. Listing 11-8 includes a simple example of a button event in an ASP.NET web page code-behind. In this example, you are creating a reference to the `ManagerServiceClient` (that is, your WCF service proxy), retrieving a `Person` entity with the `taxId` of 123-12-1234, updating the e-mail and passing it into `UpdatePerson` with `null` as the second parameter. Finally, the returned `Email` property on the returned `Person` is written out by using `Response.Write`, and the proxy connection is closed.

Listing 11-8. *Using the Web Services Layer*

```
protected void Button1_Click(object sender, EventArgs e)
{
    ManagerServicesClient msc = new ManagerServicesClient();
    Person pers = msc.GetPersonByTaxId("123-12-1234");
    pers.Email = "foofoo@bar.com";
    Response.Write(msc.UpdatePerson(pers, null).Email); ;
    msc.Close();
}
```

Executing the code, you might be expecting to see a happy web page at `foofoo@bar.com`. Unfortunately, that's not the case because an error occurs. The error, `System.InvalidOperationException`, is happening because you are supplying only the new values to LTS. LTS can attach an entity as modified without original state only if it declares a version member or does not have an update check policy. Because LTS by default checks for concurrency violations, an error occurs because LTS has no way of checking the original values. To use this technique, you have to turn off optimistic concurrency checking or add a version that you will see later in the chapter. Listing 11-9 shows a section of the `BoP.map` file that has been modified so that the `StakeHolders` fields have the `UpdateCheck` attribute set to `Never`.

Listing 11-9. *Disable Optimistic Concurrency Checks*

```
<Table Name="StakeHolders" Member="StakeHolders">
      <Type Name="BoP.Core.Domain.StakeHolder">
        <Column Name="StakeHolderType" Member="StakeHolderType"
             DbType="Int NOT NULL" IsDiscriminator="true" UpdateCheck="Never" />
        <Column Name="StakeHolderId" Member="StakeHolderId"
             DbType="Int NOT NULL IDENTITY" IsPrimaryKey="true"
             IsDbGenerated="true" AutoSync="OnInsert" UpdateCheck="Never" />
```

```
        <Association Name="FK_Roles_StakeHolders" Member="Roles"
            ThisKey="StakeHolderId" OtherKey="StakeHolderId"
            DeleteRule="CASCADE" IsUnique="true" />
        <Type Name="BoP.Core.Domain.Person" InheritanceCode="0"
            IsInheritanceDefault="True">
          <Column Name="FirstName" Member="FirstName"
               DbType="NVarChar(50)" CanBeNull="True" UpdateCheck="Never"/>
          <Column Name="LastName" Member="LastName"
               DbType="NVarChar(50)" CanBeNull="True" UpdateCheck="Never"/>
          <Column Name="Gender" Member="Gender" DbType="Char(1)"
                CanBeNull="True" UpdateCheck="Never"/>
          <Column Name="DOB" Member="DOB" DbType="DateTime" UpdateCheck="Never"/>
          <Column Name="Email" Member="Email" DbType="NVarChar(100) NOT NULL"
                CanBeNull="True" UpdateCheck="Never"/>
          <Column Name="TaxId" Member="TaxId" DbType="NVarChar(50)"
                CanBeNull="True" UpdateCheck="Never"/>
          <Association Name="FK_Accounts_StakeHolders" Member="StakeHolders"
               ThisKey="StakeHolderId" OtherKey="StakeHolderId"
               DeleteRule="CASCADE" />
        </Type>
      </Type>
    </Table>
```

After modifying your mapping file so optimistic concurrency is off, running the code works correctly and gives you your happy `foofoo@bar.com` web page. In Listing 11-10, you can see the SQL generated from your code in Listing 11-8. The first two statements are of course the `SELECT` statements to retrieve the `Person` from the `StakeHolders` and the `Roles` tables. The next statement is the `UPDATE` statement, which, as you can see, is updating all fields using the primary key. In this example, the `UPDATE` has no optimistic concurrency checking happening, thus this model is a "last one in wins" model.

Listing 11-10. *SQL Generated from Listing 11-8*

```
exec sp_executesql N'SELECT TOP (1) [t0].[StakeHolderType], [t0].[FirstName],
[t0].[LastName], [t0].[Gender], [t0].[DOB], [t0].[TaxId],
[t0].[Email], [t0].[StakeHolderId]
FROM [StakeHolders] AS [t0]
WHERE ([t0].[TaxId] = @p0) AND (1 = 1)',N'@p0 nvarchar(11)',@p0=N'123-12-1234'

exec sp_executesql N'SELECT [t0].[RoleType], [t0].[UserId], [t0].[Password],
[t0].[Active], [t0].[StakeHolderId]
FROM [Roles] AS [t0]
WHERE [t0].[StakeHolderId] = @x1',N'@x1 int',@x1=1

exec sp_executesql N'UPDATE [StakeHolders]
SET [FirstName] = @p2, [LastName] = @p3, [Gender] = @p4, [DOB] = @p5, [TaxId] = @p6,
[Email] = @p7, [StakeHolderType] = @p8
```

```
WHERE [StakeHolderId] = @p0',N'@p0 int,@p1 int,@p2 nvarchar(5),@p3 nvarchar(5),@p4
char(1),@p5 datetime,@p6 nvarchar(11),@p7 nvarchar(14),@p8
int',@p0=1,@p1=0,@p2=N'Admin',@p3=N'Admin',@p4='M',@p5=''1970-09-13
00:00:00:000'',@p6=N'123-12-1234',@p7=N'foofoo@bar.com',@p8=1
```

You have now seen the first scenario of updating an entity by using our disconnected scenario, sans optimistic concurrency. In the next scenario, you have the original values and enforce optimistic concurrency. To retain your original values, you need to have some sort of helper method to "clone" the original entity prior to making changes. Again, this is one of those scenarios in which there are many ways to achieve the net result, and again this text is not going to elucidate all of them.

Listing 11-11 includes one technique for cloning an entity. In this example, you have a generic `DTOHelper` class that has a public `Clone` method, which accepts a generic entity of type `T`. The `Clone` method uses reflection to create an instance of the object as type `T` and then continues by looping through said object's properties to get and set all available values.

Listing 11-11. *DTO Clone Method Using Reflection*

```
using System;
using System.Collections.Generic;
using System.Text;
using System.Reflection;

namespace BoP.Util
{
    public class DTOHelper<T>
    {
        public T Clone(T entity)
        {
            PropertyInfo[] pis = entity.GetType().GetProperties();

            object o = Activator.CreateInstance(typeof(T));

            foreach (PropertyInfo pi in pis)
            {
                o.GetType().GetProperty(pi.Name).
                    SetValue(o, pi.GetValue((object)entity, null),null);

            }
            return (T)o;

        }

    }
}
```

■Note Using reflection (as seen in Listing 11-11) is one technique for achieving a deep clone of a class in .NET. Some other examples include the use of the IClonable interface and serialization/deserialization of classes. There is never a one-size-fits-all solution for cloning (or anything else in software development), so base your decisions on your requirements and the solution that best meets those requirements.

Now that you have some code to do a deep clone, you can change your code to pass in a new and an original Person. Listing 11-12 shows the updated code, which "clones" origP by using the DTOHelper class seen in Listing 11-11. This example is identical to Listing 11-8, with the exception that the call to the UpdatePerson web service passes in the original entity instead of null.

Listing 11-12. *Pass in the Original Entity*

```
protected void Button1_Click(object sender, EventArgs e)
{
    ManagerServicesClient msc = new ManagerServicesClient();
    Person origP = msc.GetPersonByTaxId("123-12-1234");
    Person newP = new DTOHelper<Person>().Clone(origP);
    newP.Email = "foofoo@bar.com";
    Response.Write(msc.UpdatePerson(newP, origP).Email); ;
    msc.Close();

}
```

Executing the code in Listing 11-12, *without* reenabling optimistic concurrency checking, results in UPDATE SQL that is different from what you saw in Listing 11-10. The SQL code generated from this call can be seen in Listing 11-13. Here, because you have the original values, the statement is changing only the Email field, and because optimistic concurrency is disabled, the WHERE clause is based purely on the primary key field.

Listing 11-13. *UPDATE SQL with Previous Values*

```
exec sp_executesql N'UPDATE [StakeHolders]
SET [Email] = @p2
WHERE [StakeHolderId] = @p0',N'@p0 int,@p1 int,@p2
nvarchar(11)',@p0=1,@p1=0,@p2=N'foo@bar.com'
```

Let's see what happens when we turn optimistic concurrency checking back on. If you remember from Listing 11-9, the UpdateCheck attribute of the Column node controls the optimistic concurrency validation in LTS. In this case, rather than having every field checked for concurrency, let's check only the first and last names for concurrency violations. You can do this by changing the UpdateCheck value from Never to Always in the BoP.map file.

After changing the UpdateCheck value, recompile and run the code in Listing 11-12 again. The results of this test are displayed in Listing 11-14. In this example, you have the SQL that is being generated and that was captured from SQL Profiler. As you can see in this example, the FirstName and LastName fields are now included in the UPDATE statement.

Listing 11-14. *SQL with Optimistic Concurrency Checking on FirstName and LastName*

```
exec sp_executesql N'UPDATE [StakeHolders]
SET [Email] = @p4
WHERE ([StakeHolderId] = @p0) AND ([FirstName] = @p1) AND ([LastName] = @p2)',
N'@p0 int,@p1 nvarchar(5),@p2 nvarchar(5),@p3 int,@p4
nvarchar(14)',@p0=1,@p1=N'Admin',@p2=N'Admin',@p3=0,@p4=N'foofoo@bar.com'
```

The final technique for handling optimistic concurrency checking in LTS, and the one that is the easiest and most versatile to implement, is the use of a timestamp or version column in your database and mapping. To work with this example, you first need to add a field named `TimeStamp` to the `StakeHolders` table in the database with the database type of timestamp. For those of you not familiar with the timestamp data type, it is a T-SQL type that was introduced in SQL Server 2005. The sole purpose of this type is to provide a group of numbers that autoincrements every time a row in the table is changed. It is important to note that the TimeStamp field has nothing to do with date or time; it is just a binary field of autoincrementing numbers. If you are looking for a true date/time stamp, your best bet is to look up *T-SQL date time* on MSDN.

After you have added the new `TimeStamp` field to the `StakeHolders` table, you have to make a change to the `BoP.map` file along with a change to your `StakeHolder` class. Listing 11-15 shows both the updated mapping value and the C# property. As you can see, in this example the `Column` node is using the `IsVersion="True"` attribute, and the `DbType` is a `rowversion`, which tells LTS to use this column as version control. In addition, notice in the C# code, also in Listing 11-15, that the property returns type `System.Data.Linq.Binary` because the timestamp data type is a binary field.

Listing 11-15. *Using a Timestamp for Concurrency Checking*

```
<Column Name="TimeStamp" Member="TimeStamp" DbType="rowversion NOT NULL"
CanBeNull="False" IsDbGenerated="true" IsVersion="true" AutoSync="Always"/>

public System.Data.Linq.Binary TimeStamp
{
    get;
    set;
}
```

After the model and the mapping file have been updated, you can reexecute the code in Listing 11-12 to see what has changed. Listing 11-16 shows the SQL that is generated from the new configuration. Here you can see that you have an `UPDATE` statement with the `TimeStamp` field and an explicit `SELECT` to check the version of the `TimeStamp` field.

Listing 11-16. *SQL with TimeStamp Field*

```
exec sp_executesql N'UPDATE [StakeHolders]
SET [Email] = @p3
WHERE ([StakeHolderId] = @p0) AND ([TimeStamYp] = @p1)

SELECT [t1].[TimeStamp]
FROM [StakeHolders] AS [t1]
```

```
WHERE ((@@ROWCOUNT) > 0) AND ([t1].[StakeHolderId] = @p4)',N'@p0 int,
@p1 timestamp,@p2 int,@p3 nvarchar(11),
@p4 int',@p0=1,@p1=0x0000000000001391,@p2=0,@p3=N'foo@bar.com',@p4=1
```

Although the technique of using a TimeStamp field slightly corrupts your domain model, in general this technique is a good one to use. The TimeStamp field buys you a simple way to enforce a high-quality pattern of optimistic concurrency without having to write a lot of unnecessary code.

Layered EF

Now that you have a solid understanding of how to create a disconnected model with LTS, let's look at the same functionality with EF. Like LTS, EF implements an optimistic concurrency model. The difference is that by default your ObjectContext does *not* check for optimistic concurrency violations; you have to explicitly tell EF to check for concurrency violations through your metadata.

To specify concurrency checking, you use the ConcurrencyMode attribute in your .csdl file. For example, Listing 11-17 shows a condensed version of the EntityType Person, with the property FirstName, and the ConcurrencyMode set to Fixed. What this attribute does is tell EF to check for concurrency violations on the FirstName property.

Listing 11-17. *Condensed Person Metadata*

```
<EntityType Name="Person" BaseType="BoP.Core.Domain.StakeHolder">
   <Property Name="FirstName" Type="String"
         MaxLength="50" ConcurrencyMode="Fixed" />
. . .
  </EntityType>
```

■ **Note** Unlike in LTS, in EF you have only two concurrency options for the ConcurrencyMode attribute: Fixed and None.

Following the same pattern that you used for LTS, the approach for EF will be to create an Update method that can be used with or without the original entity. Starting off, you need to first create the Update method of the AbstractEFDao class that you developed in Chapter 10. As in LTS, you will also need to update the IDao interface so you have the correct contract for the AbstractEFDao class.

In Listing 11-18, you have the new Update method, which accepts two entities, newEntity and originalEntity, both of generic type T. Similar to LTS, the impetus here is to build out the entire solution (both with and without original values), thus the reason for creating a method with both of these parameters. As you can see, if the oldEntity is null, the AttachTo method is called. The AttachTo method takes the name of the EntitySet as the first parameter, and the entity being attached, as an object, as the second parameter. The framework then infers and populates the EntityKey. Because the AttachTo method has to attempt to infer the EntityKey, this method is more costly from a performance standpoint than the Attach method. After AttachTo is called, the new EntityKey is retrieved in order to retrieve the System.Data.Objects.ObjectStateEntry class, which is basically the EF state engine, in order to manually set the state of the entity as modified (for example, en.SetModified()). Finally, Refresh is called on the ObjectContext (we will be discussing this more in the next example) and outside of the if…else block, the CommitChanges method is called.

Caution The code in Listing 11-18, as with the rest of the book, is designed to work with Beta 3 of the Entity Framework. The fact that you have to do extra heavy lifting for disconnected entities and explicitly call Refresh, which executes a SELECT against the database to refresh the entity cache, is for all intents and purposes a design flaw. There is a strong probability that this code will change by RTM.

In the case where the oldEntity is supplied in Listing 11-18, the else block of code is executed. You first attempt to retrieve the EntityKey (that is, the key). If it is null, you basically follow the same code path as you would if the oldEntity were null. Alternatively, if the key is not null, you call the Attach method on the ObjectContext, which takes the oldEntity as the only parameter cast as System.Data.Objects.DataClasses.IEntityWithKey. Next, you call ApplyPropertyChanges, which applies the properties that have changed, and then call Refresh, SetModifed, and CommitChanges.

In addition, you may have noticed in this example that the ObjectContext is no longer a singleton; instead, it is a module-level variable that is declared with the using statement. The reason for this change is that there are potential threading issues with using a singleton in this type of n-tier environment, and because AbstractEFDao now supports a disconnected model, there isn't a good reason to hold a single instance to the ObjectContext. Also (and this can be applied to the LTS examples too), by declaring the BoPObjectContext with the using statement, you ensure that proper cleanup and disposal takes place. Connection leaks and memory leaks can occur in .NET too—make sure you code defensively.

Listing 11-18. *New Update Method for EF*

```
using BoPObjectContext = BoP.Data.BoPObjectContext;

BoPObjectContext db = new BoPObjectContext();

public virtual T Update(T newEntity, T oldEntity)
{

    EntityKey key;
    if (oldEntity == null)
    {
```

```
            db.AttachTo(typeof(T).BaseType.Name, newEntity as object);
            key = db.CreateEntityKey(typeof(T).BaseType.Name, newEntity);
            ObjectStateEntry en = db.ObjectStateManager.GetObjectStateEntry(key);
            en.SetModified();
            db.Refresh(RefreshMode.ClientWins, newEntity as object);

        }
        else
        {
            key = db.CreateEntityKey(typeof(T).BaseType.Name, oldEntity);
            if (key == null)
            {
                db.AttachTo(typeof(T).BaseType.Name, newEntity as object);
            }
            else
            {
                db.Attach(oldEntity as System.Data.Objects.DataClasses.IEntityWithKey);
                db.ApplyPropertyChanges(key.EntitySetName, newEntity as object);
            }

            ObjectStateEntry en = db.ObjectStateManager.GetObjectStateEntry(key);
            en.SetModified();
            db.Refresh(RefreshMode.ClientWins, oldEntity as object);

        }

        this.CommitChanges(newEntity as object);
        return newEntity;

    }
```

As with LTS, in EF the CRUD functionality stored in `AbstractEFDao` internally calls the `CommitChanges` method to save the changes to the `ObjectContext`. Listing 11-19 shows the code for the `CommitChanges` method. As you can see, the signature for `CommitChanges` has been changed to take an entity object as a parameter. Although not shown, because the signature has changed, the signature of the `IDao` interface also has to be updated.

Examining Listing 11-19, you can see that you have a `try…catch` block that first tries to save changes to your `ObjectContext` and then traps for `System.Data.Objects.OptimisticConcurrencyException`. If an `OptimisticConcurrencyException` occurs, a `Refresh` is executed on the `ObjectContext`, where the `RefreshMode` is `ClientWins` as you also saw in Listing 11-18. The `RefreshMode` is used to specify how changes get propagated. The first of your two `RefreshMode` options is `ClientWins`, where the original values stored in the object cache are replaced with the latest values from the store. The second option is `StoreWins`, which replaces all values in the cache with what is stored in the database. In general, I find that the `ClientWins` option is preferred because it helps to keep the values entered on the front from being lost. After the refresh is complete, `SaveChanges` is called on the `ObjectContext`, and in cases where the conflict can't be resolved, an error is thrown.

Listing 11-19. *CommitChanges*

```
public virtual void CommitChanges(object entity)
{
    try
    {
        // Try to save changes, which may cause a conflict.
        int num = db.SaveChanges();

        // Log Message
        Console.WriteLine("No conflicts. " +
                  num.ToString() + " updates saved.");
    }
    catch (System.Data.Objects.OptimisticConcurrencyException)
    {
        // Resolve the concurrently conflict by refreshing the
        // object context before re-saving changes.
        db.Refresh(RefreshMode.ClientWins, entity);

        // Save changes.
        db.SaveChanges();

        // Log Message
        Console.WriteLine("OptimisticConcurrencyException "
             + "handled and changes saved");
    }
    catch (Exception e)
    {
        throw (e);
    }

}
```

Similar to LTS, you will use WCF to serialize your model from one tier to another. This requires that your domain model be serializable. The difference between LTS and EF is that EF requires you to have far more custom interfaces and code implemented than LTS, thus requiring a slightly more advanced approach to serialization than LTS.

The only significant change from LTS to EF regarding serialization revolves around the `BaseEntity` class. This is the class with the implementation of `IEntityWithRelationships`, `IEntityWithChangeTracker`, and `IEntityWithKey`. The problem is that the `IEntityWithChangeTracker` implementation is not serializable, nor do you want to serialize it. An alternative to using the standard `[Serializable]` attribute, and technically the preferred WCF pattern way, is to use the `System.Runtime.Serialization.DataContractAttribute`. I say that this is the preferred method because it is part of .NET 3.0 (and up) and gives you more refined control over what is serialized (that is, your data contract) and what is not. The `DataContractAttribute` works in conjunction with the `DataMemberAttribute`. In Listing 11-20, you can see the `BaseEntity` class that is marked with the `DataContractAttribute`, and the two properties, ID and `EntityKey`, that are marked with the `DataMemberAttribute`. What this example demonstrates is that two of the methods in the class, `ID` and `EntityKey`, are serializable and are "data members" of the serialization contract.

Listing 11-20. *Data Attributes for Defining Serialization*

```
 [DataContract]
public abstract class BaseEntity<T> : IEntityWithRelationships,
                                IEntityWithChangeTracker, IEntityWithKey
{
    public BaseEntity()
    { }
    private T id = default(T);

    /// <summary>
    /// ID may be of type string, int, custom type, etc.
    /// Setter is protected to allow unit tests to set this
    /// property via reflection and to allow domain objects
    /// more flexibility in setting this for those objects with
    /// assigned IDs.
    /// </summary>
    ///

    [DataMember]
    public virtual T ID
    {
       get { return id; }
       set { id = value; }
    }

    // OTHER CODE REMOVED FOR READABILITY
    // PLEASE REFER TO CHAPTER 10 FOR MISSING CODE

    #region IEntityWithKey Members

    public void PropertyChanging(string propName)
    {
        if(propName.StartsWith("set_"))
                propName = propName.Replace("set_", string.Empty);
        if (_changeTracker != null)
        {
            _changeTracker.EntityMemberChanging(propName);

        }

    }
```

```
    public void PropertyChanged(string propName)
    {
        if (_changeTracker != null)
        {
            _changeTracker.EntityMemberChanged(propName);
        }
    }

    EntityKey _entityKey = null;
    [DataMember]
    System.Data.EntityKey IEntityWithKey.EntityKey
    {
        get
        {
            return _entityKey;
        }
        set
        {
            // Set the EntityKey property, if it is not set.
            // Report the change if the change tracker exists.
            if (_changeTracker != null)
            {
                _changeTracker.EntityMemberChanging("-EntityKey-");
                _entityKey = value;
                _changeTracker.EntityMemberChanged("-EntityKey-");
             }
             else
             {
                _entityKey = value;
             }

        }
   }

   #endregion
  }
}
```

■ **Note** Although the `DataContractAttribute` gives you finer-grained control over your object's serialization, there is nothing wrong with using `SerializableAttribute` as you have with the rest of the model (see Listing 11-1).

As with LTS, your next task in building the disconnected model is to expose some update functionality in your managers. The code for this example is identical to what you did in

Listing 11-6, where you have a method in the PersonManager called UpdatePerson that uses the new Update method in the DAO layer. Again, the new UpdatePerson method (see Listing 11-6) accepts two Person objects, newP and origP, and then creates a PersonDao and calls Update.

Along with the manager functionality, the WCF layer that you saw in Listing 11-7 and the button code seen in Listing 11-8 are also identical for EF. This, of course, is one of the biggest benefits for following reusable design patterns and OOP. In light of this, there is no reason to show you the same code that you saw in Listing 11-7 and Listing 11-8, so we are going to jump directly into the SQL that is being generated with EF.

Listing 11-21 shows the SQL that is generated from scenario 1 when you supply null for the original entity parameter to the UpdatePerson method.

Listing 11-21. *EF SQL sans Original Entity Values*

```
exec sp_executesql N'update [dbo].[Person]
set [FirstName] = @0, [LastName] = @1, [Gender] = @2, [DOB] = @3,
[Email] = @4, [TaxId] = @5
where ([StakeHolderId] = @6)
',N'@0 nvarchar(5),@1 nvarchar(5),@2 nvarchar(1),@3 datetime,@4 nvarchar(14),
@5 nvarchar(11),@6 int',@0=N'Admin',@1=N'Admin',@2=N'M',@3=''2001-07-13
00:00:00:000'',@4=N'foofoo@bar.com',@5=N'123-12-1234',@6=2
```

Let's see what happens when we pass in the original entity. Listing 11-22 provides the SQL that is generated by EF when you pass in the original entity.

Listing 11-22. *EF SQL with Original Entity*

```
exec sp_executesql N'update [dbo].[Person]
set [FirstName] = @0, [LastName] = @1, [Gender] = @2, [DOB] = @3,
 [Email] = @4, [TaxId] = @5 where ([StakeHolderId] = @6)
',N'@0 nvarchar(5),@1 nvarchar(5),@2 nvarchar(1),@3 datetime,@4 nvarchar(11),
@5 nvarchar(11),@6 int',@0=N'Admin',@1=N'Admin',@2=N'M',@3=''2001-07-13
00:00:00:000'',@4=N'foo@bar.com',@5=N'123-12-1234',@6=2
```

In the beginning of this section, I reviewed the optimistic concurrency options with EF. Let's see what happens when you add "fixed" concurrency settings to the FirstName and LastName fields in your CSDL file. After changing the ConcurrencyMode setting as seen in Listing 11-17, you can run the button code again. After executing the test code in this situation, something unexpected occurs: an error.

The following is the error that is raised when you try to run the button test code from Listing 11-12:

```
Schema specified is not valid. Errors: \r\nBoPDomain.csdl(3,4) : error 0145: Type
'BoP.Core.Domain.Person' is derived from the type 'BoP.Core.Domain.StakeHolder'
which is the type for EntitySet 'StakeHolder'. Type 'BoP.Core.Domain.Person' defines
new concurrency requirements which is not allowed for sub types of base EntitySet
types.
```

You can see from the error that because Person is a derived type, EF does not allow you to modify concurrency requirements. In my opinion, this is a design flaw with EF, and as this text is written against Beta 3 of EF, I hope this issue will be rectified prior to RTM. Fortunately, there are other ways to build the application with concurrency checking enabled.

As with LTS, you can use a timestamp column in your database to handle optimistic concurrency in your application. As in LTS, this is one of the easiest and most versatile ways to implement concurrency checking in your application. To work with this example, you first need to add a field named TimeStamp to the Person table in your database, with the database type of timestamp. As mentioned earlier in the chapter, the sole purpose of the timestamp type is to provide a group of numbers that autoincrement every time a row in the table is changed.

After you have added the new TimeStamp field to the Person table, you have to make a change to the BoPDomain.ssdl file. It is important to understand that you are making this change in your SSDL file only because it does not map back to a property, so no changes need to be made to your CSDL or MSL files. Listing 11-23 shows the change that needs to be made to the Person entity mapping in the SSDL file. As you can see, the code has been shortened for readability, but still shows the new TimeStamp property that is part of the Person table. Another interesting aspect of the XML seen in Listing 11-23 is the StoredGeneratedPattern attribute, which is set to Computed. Obviously, because SQL Server autogenerates the timestamp data, StoredGeneratedPattern has to be Computed, but it is important to note that your other option for this attribute is Identity.

Listing 11-23. *Using the TimeStamp Field from EF*

```
  <EntityType Name="Person">
...
      <Property Name="Timestamp" Type="timestamp" Nullable="false"
              StoreGeneratedPattern="Computed" />
  </EntityType>
```

The final piece of the puzzle is the SQL that is generated when you execute your button code with the TimeStamp field, as shown in Listing 11-24.

Listing 11-24. *SQL Generated from EF When Using a Timestamp Column*

```
exec sp_executesql N'update [dbo].[Person]
set [FirstName] = @0, [LastName] = @1, [Gender] = @2, [DOB] = @3,
 [Email] = @4, [TaxId] = @5 where ([StakeHolderId] = @6)
select [Timestamp] from [dbo].[Person]
where @@ROWCOUNT > 0 and [StakeHolderId] = @6',N'@0 nvarchar(5),@1 nvarchar(5),@2
 nvarchar(1),@3 datetime,@4 nvarchar(11),@5 nvarchar(11),@6
int',@0=N'Admin',@1=N'Admin',@2=N'M',
@3=''2001-07-13 00:00:00:000'',@4=N'foo@bar.com',@5=N'123-12-1234',@6=2
```

ASP.NET

There really isn't a compelling reason for me to examine all the possible UI patterns out there, because the fundamentals of what you have learned thus far are suitable for most, if not all, UI patterns. However, to round off your understanding and provide you with a more complete application, I want to take a look at the Model-View-Controller pattern.

The Model-View-Controller pattern is one of the oldest GUI architectures around. In fact, according to MSDN (`http://msdn2.microsoft.com/en-us/library/ms978748.aspx`), the *Model-View-Controller (MVC)* pattern separates the modeling of the domain, the presentation, and the actions based on user input into three separate classes:

Model: The model manages the behavior and data of the application domain, responds to requests for information about its state (usually from the view), and responds to instructions to change state (usually from the controller).

View: The view manages the display of information.

Controller: The controller interprets the mouse and keyboard inputs from the user, informing the model and/or the view to change as appropriate.

Now you may be wondering why I am not going deeper into UI development by using our newly created domain model. You may also be wondering why I'm not going into web forms, ASP.NET AJAX, Model-View-Presenter (MVP), template engines, and the like. Well, my opinion on this subject is simple: if you are reading this book, you probably already have knowledge about web forms, Hypertext Markup Language (HTML), ASP.NET, and so forth, so I can't really justify reviewing all this content.

On the other hand, odds are much better that you haven't seen the new ASP.NET MVC framework because it is still in preview at the time of this writing. Additionally, the MVC framework is not going to be nearly as known as the ubiquitous web form and UI model that everyone is accustomed to. Additionally, MVC is one of my favorite UI patterns because it is highly extensible, it creates clean separation between layers, and it is excellent for high-availability enterprise software.

Caution The ASP.NET MVC framework is in prerelease at the time of this writing. The name, code, and design may change by the time you read this.

The first thing that you need to do is download the ASP.NET 3.5 Extensions Preview from the Microsoft download site (`www.microsoft.com/downloads/`), and you additionally need to download the MVC Toolkit from the ASP.NET web site (`www.asp.net/downloads/3.5-extensions/`).

After you download and install the ASP.NET 3.5 Extensions Preview, and extract the MVC Toolkit (it's just an assembly that you reference), you are ready to go. For these examples, I am going to focus on EF, but you can also use the same techniques for LTS. To start, you need to add a new ASP.NET MVC web application project, whose template was installed with the Extensions Preview, to your `BoP` solution. Figure 11-2 shows the structure of what is created with the new MVC project template.

As seen in Figure 11-2, you have folders for controllers, models, and views. As you might expect, each of these folders is created so you can put your controllers, models, and views in them. However, as you'll see in this section, we are not going to put our model directly in the Models folder because our model is an already-defined structure. Along with the three folders, you also have a `Site.Master` master page, a cascading style sheet (`Site.css`), `HomeController.cs`, and a couple of `.aspx` pages (`About` and `Index`). For the most part, this template allows you to hit the ground running, and so that is what you will be doing shortly.

Figure 11-2. *ASP.NET MVC web application*

■ **Note** The ASP.NET MVC framework will likely have entire books written on it in the future. The purpose of this section is not to explore all aspects of the UI; rather the intention is to get you thinking about the different possibilities and techniques of using the code you developed in the previous ten chapters.

Before you write any code, it is important that you first understand a few basics about URL routing and the MVC framework. The MVC pattern in general is based on the concept of mapping URLs to controller classes, and so the ASP.NET MVC framework has implemented a powerful URL-mapping engine. The mapping engine allows for the setup and execution of routing rules and provides a mechanism to parse URL and form variables, as you will see in the coming examples. I wanted to mention this aspect because unless you have worked with the MVC pattern or a web framework such as Ruby on Rails, the concept of mapping a URL to a controller instead of a page or template (for example, ASPX, PHP, or JSP) may be foreign to you.

With the basics out of the way, let's write some code. The use case that we are going to be solving in this section is to provide an already-registered customer the ability to edit his profile and view his personal information. Listing 11-25 provides some stub code for a new controller called `ProfileController`. You are writing this stub code because you know what the problem is, but not all of the moving parts are apparent yet. In this example, we have references to `System` and `System.Web` (as you might expect to see in a web application). You also have `BoP.Core.Domain`, which gives you the ability to work with your domain model, and `System.Web.Mvc`, which gives you access to the base class `Controller` and to the `ControllerAction` attribute. Inheriting from controllers is not strictly required to use the MVC framework; however, the base class does have a number of helper methods that you will see later in this section, so you might as well use them. The `ControllerAction` attribute is just that, an action of your controller. In this example, you know that you are going to need to retrieve a customer profile (`CustomerProfile`) and update a customer profile (`UpdateProfile`). I like to think of these methods as your routing logic from view to view; however, at this point they are just stubs to which we will be adding the actual logic later. The last reference in this class is the `System.Web.Mvc.BindingHelpers`, which will be covered when we look at the implementation code.

Listing 11-25. *Profile Controller*

```
using System;
using System.Web;
using System.Web.Mvc;
using System.Web.Mvc.BindingHelpers;
using BoP.Core.Domain;

namespace BankOfPluto.Controllers
{
    public class ProfileController : Controller
    {
        [ControllerAction]
        public void CustomerProfile(string id)
        {}


        [ControllerAction]
        public void UpdateProfile()
        {}

    }
}
```

The next step in building the UI is to update the master page that comes with the MVC template. I am not an artist, and I respect my artist friends, so I am not going to even attempt to create a really sophisticated bank UI. Instead, we are going to use the existing `Site.Master` page and its existing CSS elements, with a few changes to the text and links for the examples. Figure 11-3 shows the default MVC site, and Figure 11-4 shows the updated site.

Figure 11-3. *Default MVC design*

Figure 11-4. *Updated design*

After viewing the significant artistic changes that I made from Figure 11-3 to Figure 11-4, I'm not going to bore you with the minor HTML changes. However, the addition of the link Edit Profile is important and worth looking at. Listing 11-26 shows the body of the `Site.Master` page. The most interesting aspect of this master page is the use of the inline `Html.ActionLink` code. To start with, HTML is a part of the `System.Web.Mvc.ViewMasterPage`, which your `Site.Master` page inherits from (not shown). This is one of many helper classes that are available to you, which you will see throughout this section. The purpose of this class is to emit HTML, and in this case to emit a link, but it is more than just a standard `href` link. The `ActionLink` method provides several overloads, but let's concentrate on the two overloads seen in this example:

- `ActionLink(string linkText, string actionName, string controllerName)`: This is the first example in Listing 11-26, where the first parameter is `About Us` (the text shown onscreen), the second parameter is the `ControllerAction` `About` (which can be seen in the appendix), and the third parameter is the controller name `Home`. It is important to note that this code is part of the default MVC template.

- `ActionLink(string linkText, object values)`: This is the second example in Listing 11-26, your custom code, where the text being displayed is Edit Profile, and the second parameter is a new object that is initialized with three properties: `Controller`, `Action`, and `id`.

At this point, you may be wondering why 123-12-1234 is hard coded in Listing 11-26. The reason for the hard coding is because we are trying to solve only the edit and list profile functionality, not the login functionality. Now, in a real application you would have a separate `LoginController` that did some routing and stored the customer ID, which would then be passed to our `Profile` controller, but for these examples, we are looking at a hard-coded scenario to meet the requirements.

Listing 11-26. *Master Page for the Site*

```
<body>

    <div id="inner">

        <div id="header">
            <h1>First Bank of Pluto</h1>
        </div>
```

```
        <div id="menu">

            <ul>
                <li><a href="~/" runat="server">Home</a></li>
                <li><%= Html.ActionLink("About Us", "About", "Home") %></li>
                <li><%= Html.ActionLink("Edit Profile", new
                    { Controller = "Profile", Action = "CustomerProfile",
                        id = "123-12-1234" })%></li>
            </ul>

        </div>

        <div id="maincontent">
            <asp:ContentPlaceHolder ID="MainContentPlaceHolder" runat="server">
            </asp:ContentPlaceHolder>
        </div>

    </div>

</body>
```

Before moving on to the next step, let's revisit our requirements for this scenario. I told you that we need to be able to list and edit a profile, but in Figure 11-4 the only link you have is Edit Profile. This is where routing comes in, so remember this when you implement the controller code. After a user clicks the Edit Profile link, she will be taken to an Edit view, and upon clicking the Save button, she will be taken to a List view. So the next step is to create our views.

In Figure 11-5, you can see that I have created a new folder under the Views directory called Profile. Because the MVC framework is using URL mapping for routing in the site, it is important that our Edit and List views are in the appropriate location for the engine to do its work.

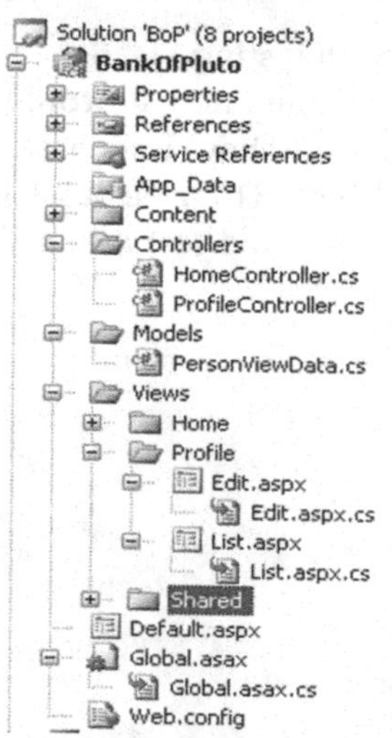

Figure 11-5. *A new Profile view directory*

Along with the new folder for Profile, you also have two new `.aspx` pages, Edit and List. I added both of these by adding a New Item to the project and selecting MVC View Content Page from my templates. You can see in Figure 11-6 that you have several new MVC templates installed, including the MVC View Content Page template.

Visual Studio installed templates

Web Form	Master Page
Web User Control	Web Content Form
MVC Controller Class	MVC View Content Page
MVC View Master Page	MVC View Page
MVC View User Control	ADO.NET Data Service
ADO.NET Entity Data Model	AJAX Client Behavior

Figure 11-6. *New MVC templates*

The new MVC template does a couple of things for you. Listing 11-27 shows the ASPX code, and the C# code-behind that was generated by the MVC View Content Page template for the Edit view. The ASPX code, seen first, creates the `asp:Content` pane for use with the `Site.Master` page. The C# code creates a partial class that inherits from `Sytem.Web.Mvc.ViewPage`, which is needed by the MVC framework.

Listing 11-27. *MVC View Content Template Output*

```
// ASPX CODE

<%@ Page Language="C#" MasterPageFile="~/Views/Shared/Site.Master"
AutoEventWireup="true" CodeBehind="Edit.aspx.cs"
Inherits="BankOfPluto.Views.Profile.Edit" Title="Untitled Page" %>
<asp:Content ID="Content1" ContentPlaceHolderID="MainContentPlaceHolder"
runat="server">
</asp:Content>

// CODE BEHIND
using System;
using System.Web;
using System.Web.Mvc;

namespace BankOfPluto.Views.Profile
{
    public partial class Edit : ViewPage
    {
    }
}
```

The first thing that you need to do to get this Edit view to do something is modify the code-behind. Listing 11-28 shows an updated Edit page code-behind. Here, you can see that I have made two changes: I added the `BoP.Core.Domain` reference, as well as changed the `ViewPage` so it has a generic type reference to the `Person` class. By providing the type to the `ViewPage`, we have access to a useful helper function, `ViewData`, which you will see next.

Listing 11-28. *Modified Code-Behind of the Edit View*

```
using System;
using System.Web;
using System.Web.Mvc;
using BoP.Core.Domain;

namespace BankOfPluto.Views.Profile
{
    public partial class Edit : ViewPage<Person>
    {
    }
}
```

Listing 11-29 shows the HTML and inline code that is between the asp:content control from Listing 11-27. Starting with the form tag, you have the Url.Action call in the action attribute of the tag. Url, as you may have guessed, is another helper class that is part of the MVC framework, specifically part of ViewPage. The purpose of Url.Action is to build a correctly qualified URL based on your Controller and ControllerAction attributes.

Continuing with the example, you have the Html helper, again part of the ViewPage base class. The first example is Html.Hidden("StakeHolderId", ViewData.StakeHolderId). Here, you are telling the Html helper to emit HTML input with the attribute of hidden, called StakeHolderId, with the value of ViewData.StakeHolderId. ViewData is of the type Person because it is created by the ViewPage with the values from the controller, which you will see shortly. In addition to the Hidden field, in this example you also have an HTML text box, and an HTML select, all of which are following a similar form of parameters (for example, name, value, or name, values, default). One exception is the TaxId field, which is using one of the HtmlTextBox overloads to pass in an initialized object with HTML attributes, Readonly and style. You may have noticed that the style is Webdings, the reason being that it is a ReadOnly HTML text box that looks just like a non-ReadOnly text box, so I needed some way to show you that the attributes are being applied at the end of the section when I do a screen print. What better way to demonstrate this than obfuscating the TaxId with Webdings!

Listing 11-29. *The ASPX Code for the Edit View*

```
<h2>Update your profile by editing the fields below
and clicking the Save button.</h2>


    <form action="<%= Url.Action(new { Action="UpdateProfile"}) %>" method="post">

        <table>
            <%=Html.Hidden("StakeHolderId", ViewData.StakeHolderId)%>
            <tr>
```

```
            <td>Tax Id (Not Editable -
                Please Contact Customer Service for changes):</td>
            <td><%= Html.TextBox("TaxId", ViewData.TaxId,
                new { ReadOnly = "true", style = "font-family: Webdings"
                    })%></td>
        </tr>
        <tr>
            <td>First Name:</td>
            <td><%= Html.TextBox("FirstName", ViewData.FirstName) %></td>
        </tr>

        <tr>
            <td>Last Name:</td>
            <td><%= Html.TextBox("LastName", ViewData.LastName) %></td>
        </tr>

        <tr>
            <td>Email:</td>
            <td><%= Html.TextBox("Email", ViewData.Email) %></td>
        </tr>
        <tr>
            <td>Gender:</td>
            <td><%= Html.Select("Gender", new string[] { "M", "F" },
                    ViewData.Gender)%></td>
        </tr>
        <tr>
            <td>Date of Birth:</td>
            <td><%= Html.TextBox("DOB", ViewData.DOB.Value.ToShortDateString())
                        %></td>
        </tr>

    </table>

    <p></p>

    <input type="submit" value="Save" />

</form>
```

I know that many of the seasoned ASP.NET developers are looking at Listing 11-29 saying, “Yuck, look at all that inline code. I thought we moved past that after classic ASP.” Although VS 2008 has made it easy to add inline code to your `.aspx` pages by supporting full IntelliSense and debugging in the editor, I tend to agree with the sentiment. With that said, let’s look at another method that ASP.NET developers are probably going to prefer—I know I do. Another technique of rendering views with the MVC framework is to use MVC View User Control, which is a template option that you can see in Figure 11-6.

For the List view, instead of creating another page filled with inline code, I am going to add a new MVC View User Control called `ProfileListControl.ascx` (not visually shown) to the project. The code for this can be seen in Listing 11-30. Here you have a fairly pedestrian .NET user control that uses an `asp:DataList` to create an HTML table of `Person` properties. Obviously, because this is a `DataList`, there is data binding happening, and you will see that next in the code-behind.

Listing 11-30. *ProfileListControl.ascx*

```
<%@ Control Language="C#" AutoEventWireup="true"
CodeBehind="ProfileListControl.ascx.cs"
Inherits="BankOfPluto.Views.Profile.ProfileListControl" %>
<%@ Import Namespace="BoP.Core.Domain" %>

<asp:DataList ID="profileDataList" runat="server">
<ItemTemplate>
        <table>
        <tr>
           <td><b>First Name:</b></td>
           <td><%# ((Person)(Container.DataItem)).FirstName %></td>
        </tr>
        <tr>
           <td><b>Last Name:</b></td>
           <td><%# ((Person)(Container.DataItem)).LastName %></td>
        </tr>
                <tr>
           <td><b>Email:</b></td>
           <td><%# ((Person)(Container.DataItem)).Email %></td>
        </tr>
                <tr>
           <td><b>Gender:</b></td>
           <td><%# ((Person)(Container.DataItem)).Gender %></td>
        </tr>
                <tr>
           <td><b>Date of Birth:</b></td>
           <td><%# ((Person)(Container.DataItem)).DOB %></td>
        </tr>
        </table>

</ItemTemplate>
</asp:DataList>
```

The C# code-behind is the most interesting aspect of the `ProfileListControl.ascx` file. Listing 11-31 shows the C# code for this control in all its glory. Similar to the `ViewPage` in the Edit view, you have the `ViewUserControl` base class that is taking a generic type `Person` parameter and giving you access to helper functionality like `ViewData`. In this example, you have a `List<Person>` being created and the `ViewData`, which is a `Person`, being added to the collection.

After the Person is added, the collection is set as the DataSource on the profileDataList control and the DataBind method is executed, enabling our code from Listing 11-29 to function.

Listing 11-31. *Code-Behind for ProfileUserControl*

```
using System;
using System.Web;
using System.Web.Mvc;
using BoP.Core.Domain;
using System.Web.UI.WebControls;
using System.Collections.Generic;

namespace BankOfPluto.Views.Profile
{
    public partial class ProfileListControl : System.Web.Mvc.ViewUserControl<Person>
    {

        protected DataList profileDataList;

        private void Page_Load(object sender, System.EventArgs e)
        {
            List<Person> lp = new List<Person>();
            lp.Add(ViewData);

            profileDataList.DataSource = lp;
            profileDataList.DataBind();

        }

    }
}
```

■ **Note** Although the examples in this section are passing in only a single Person variable to the View base classes (for example, ViewUserControl, ViewPage), you can also pass in collections of types, allowing you to manipulate and control aggregate data.

The ProfileListControl can be used like any other control, so all you need to do is add it directly to your Edit.aspx page. Listing 11-32 shows the Edit.aspx page with the new ProfileListControl added to it. Again, because it is a user control, it is a reusable widget, so no other code needs to be written.

Listing 11-32. *Using the ProfileListControl*

```
<%@ Page Language="C#" MasterPageFile="~/Views/Shared/Site.Master"
AutoEventWireup="true" CodeBehind="List.aspx.cs"
Inherits="BankOfPluto.Views.Profile.List" %>


<%@ Register src="ProfileListControl.ascx"
tagname="ProfileListControl" tagprefix="uc1" %>


<asp:Content ContentPlaceHolderID="MainContentPlaceHolder" runat="server">


    <form id="form1" runat="server">

    <uc1:ProfileListControl ID="ProfileListControl1" runat="server" />
    </form>

</asp:Content>
```

Now that you have the views, the next thing is to complete the controllers and connect to the model. Listing 11-33 shows the completed ProfileController code from Listing 11-25. The first thing you need to do for this example is add a service reference called localhost to the ManagerServicesClient that you created back in Listing 11-7. For the CustomerProfile method, you are instantiating a new ManagerServiceClient (as you saw earlier in the chapter), and you are retrieving a Person p by calling GetPersonByTaxId. Recall from Listing 11-26 that id is equal to 123-12-1234, which is the value that is passed into this ControllerAction. After the Person is retrieved, the connection is closed. This is WCF, so you need to explicitly close the connection, and RenderView is called. RenderView is one of those base class controller helper methods that I mentioned earlier in the chapter. This helper method takes the name of the view, Edit in this case, and an object of view data, your Person in this case. To summarize the process, CustomerProfile is called from the ActionLink that you saw in Site.Master, which in turn renders the Edit view whose ViewPage is of type Person, so the data from your GetPersonByTaxId is automatically passed into the page, thus enabling the ViewData functionality seen in Listing 11-29.

The UpdateProfile ControllerAction, unlike the CustomerProfile action, is executed when the form post from your Edit view occurs. In this example, you have the creation of a new Person p, and then you have something very cool, the use of extension method UdpateFrom in System.Web.Mvc.BindingHelpers. Extension methods are a new language feature in .NET 3.5 that enable developers to add new methods to CLR types without having to subclass or recompile the original type. I'm not going to go into too much depth on extension methods because you can find all sorts of details on MSDN, but I will say that all you need to do is add a reference to the assembly and the class with the extension method in the calling class (for example, ProfileController) and you have access to the static extension methods. In this case, you are using the UpdateFrom extension method, which is added to the Person p in order to populate Person p with the form data from your view.

After your Person is populated with the form data, a ManagerServiceClient is created and the UpdatePerson method is called. Finally, the helper method RenderView is executed with List and p as parameters. Similar to the CustomerProfile method, what UpdateProfile is doing is "controlling" or "routing" data from one view to another.

Listing 11-33. *Controller Implementation*

```
 [ControllerAction]
public void CustomerProfile(string id)
{
    localhost.ManagerServicesClient msc = new
          BankOfPluto.localhost.ManagerServicesClient();
    Person p = msc.GetPersonByTaxId(id);
    msc.Close();
    RenderView("Edit", p);
 }


 [ControllerAction]
 public void UpdateProfile()
 {
     Person p = new Person();
     p.UpdateFrom(Request.Form);
     localhost.ManagerServicesClient msc = new
          BankOfPluto.localhost.ManagerServicesClient();
     msc.UpdatePerson(p, null);
     msc.Close();
     RenderView("List", p);
  }
```

■ **Note** You probably have noticed that the Models directory has not been used in your project in these examples. Because we are in an n-tier environment with a complex model, placing the entire model in a web project is ill advised. However, it is important to note that in an environment where you aren't using web services for tiered communication, you can easily add you .dbml or .edmx files to the model directory. Additionally, as mentioned earlier in the chapter, you can shape the structure that gets passed into the ViewPage as needed, and an optimal place for this shaping code would be the model directory.

The final step is to run the code and see what happens. Figure 11-7 shows the Edit Profile view. As you might expect from the code, you have an edit screen for the Person entity with Webdings font for the TaxId and the rest of the data enumerated.

Figure 11-8 shows the List view that you created earlier in this chapter. As you may recall, this screen appears after you click the Save button in the Edit view. As you can see, you have fields for the Person entity as you created in Listing 11-30.

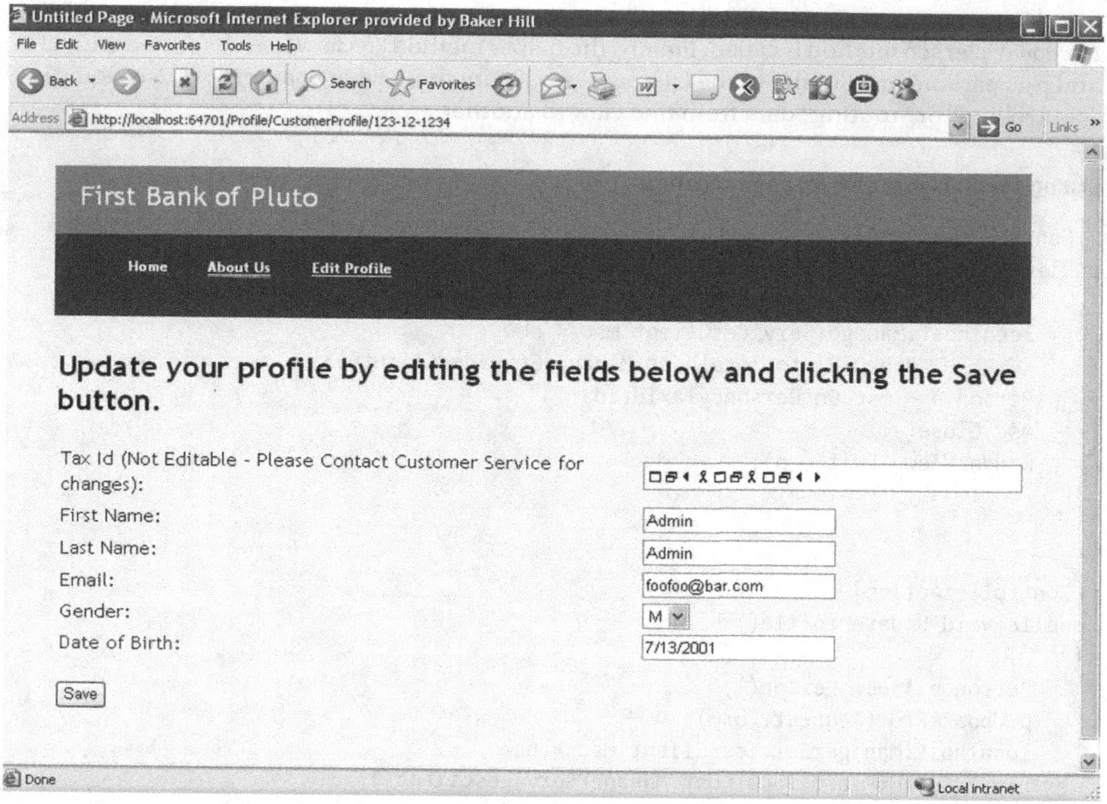

Figure 11-7. *The completed Edit view*

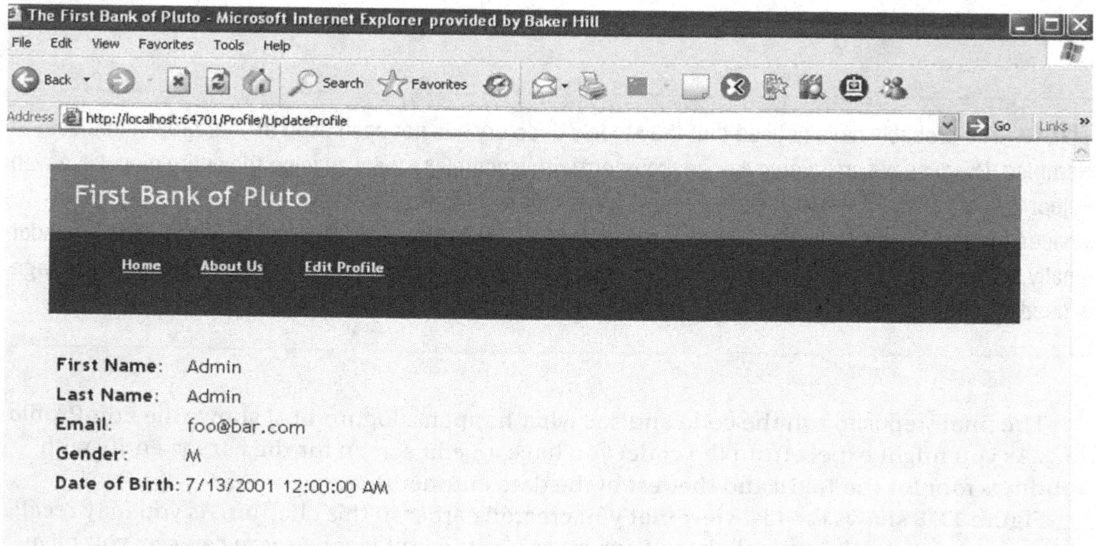

Figure 11-8. *The List view*

Summary

In this chapter, we covered a lot of ground, everything from DTOs to MVC. To sum up, it is critical in any software development that your design takes into account the possibility of n-tier deployment. To separate your application into multiple tiers, one tried and true pattern is to use DTOs for serialization. DTOs are simply a serialized entity in your domain model that can be dehydrated for use across multiple tiers.

In addition to your DTOs, concurrency is a critical aspect when working with ORM. LTS and EF both support an optimistic concurrency model; however, some configuration and design considerations exist. One simple method for handling concurrency with both of these tools is to use a timestamp or a version column in your tables.

The final topic covered in this chapter is the development of scalable UI architecture. Although many UI patterns exist, the MVC pattern is one that promotes the greatest separation of layers by mapping controllers to URLs. The ASP.NET MVC framework is a new extension release for .NET 3.5. The MVC framework is excellent for working with a robust domain model like the one you have developed in this book.

Chapter 12 is the last chapter of the book. In this chapter, you will learn about some of the differences between LTS and EF, some of my lessons learned while working with both tools, and some of the alternatives available to you.

CHAPTER 12

LINQ to SQL, the Entity Framework, and Your Other Options

Now that you have seen LTS and EF in action, it is time to look at the strengths and weaknesses of each of the tools, along with other ORM options that you have available to you as a .NET developer. This chapter examines some of the differences between the two ORM tools, the lessons I've learned while writing this book, and other .NET ORM tools that are available on the market.

LTS vs. EF

The general consensus when it comes to LTS is that it is best suited for rapid application development specifically against a Microsoft SQL Server database. This message is both espoused by Microsoft and is evident in the design of the software. For example, LTS really supports only a direct mapping of your database schema to your classes and is limited in some of its functionality. According to MSDN, LTS is "designed to provide strongly typed LINQ access for rapidly developed applications across the Microsoft SQL Server family of databases."

Alternatively, MSDN classifies EF as "designed to provide strongly typed LINQ access for applications requiring a more flexible object-relational mapping, across Microsoft SQL Server and third-party databases." Additionally, I classify EF as the enterprise solution because it separates its metadata into well-defined architectural layers. These layers are well suited for a large enterprise because they provide you with loose coupling and fine-grained control over the conceptual and physical models. In addition, whereas LTS is designed only as LINQ to SQL, EF presents many other constructs (for example, ESQL and provider independence) as well as LINQ to Entities.

The best way to examine the two products is to look at some of the differences in the functionality that they support. Much of the information in the rest of this section will be conclusions that you may have already drawn from reading the previous 11 chapters; however, along with comparing the products, the goal is also to present you with a list of best practices on when to use which tool.

Note Although EF provides various techniques for manipulating data, the following analysis focuses on EF as a whole, with special attention given to LINQ to Entities.

Functionality Differences

LTS is geared specifically at direct 1:1 mapping of .NET classes to SQL Server database tables. The goal in the design of LTS is clearly rapid development, where your database for the most part is mirrored in your domain model (that is, Table per Class), and foreign keys are exposed as strongly typed relationships. According to MSDN, the LTS APIs have been designed to "just work for common application scenarios."

Note All of the MSDN references in this chapter can be found at `http://msdn2.microsoft.com/en-us/library/cc161164.aspx`.

The simple design of LTS is evident not only in the API and the DML that gets generated for your CRUD operations, but also in the UI designer integrated in VS 2008. In Figure 12-1, you can see the simple design of the UI, which provides you with rudimentary functionality to manipulate your ORM solution. Whereas many ORM solutions provide you with a plethora of properties and options, LTS as seen in Figure 12-1 gives you the path of least resistance and handles nearly everything for you behind the scenes.

Along with the simple UI, LTS also offers Table per Hierarchy inheritance, the most straightforward form of inheritance in ORM. As you learned earlier in the book, this form of inheritance is supported through the use of a discriminator column in your database as well as the UI, as seen in Figure 12-2.

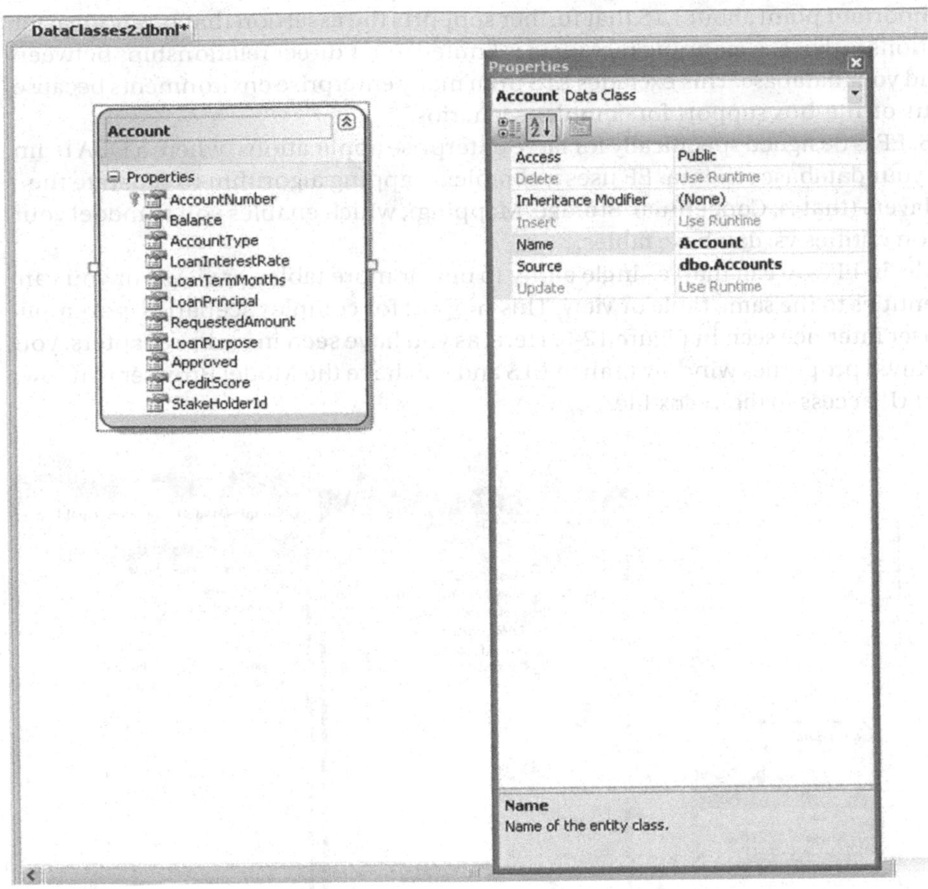

Figure 12-1. *LTS designer*

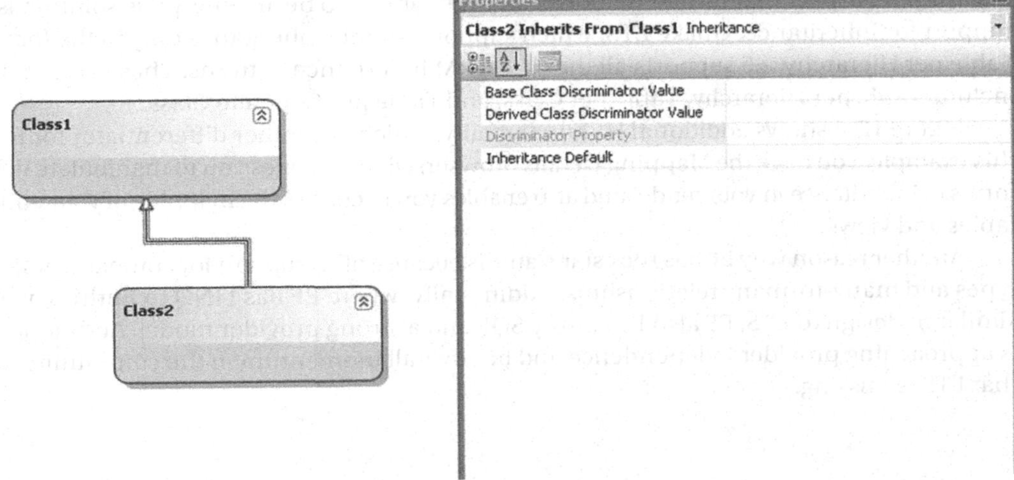

Figure 12-2. *Inheritance support in the LTS UI*

Another important point about LTS that further supports the assertion that LTS is ideal for simple applications is that the mapping metadata is limited to 1:1 direct relationships between your entities and your database. This excludes LTS from many enterprise environments because of its limited out-of-the-box support for complex scenarios.

Unlike LTS, EF is designed specifically for large enterprise applications, where a DBA team is in control of your database schema. EF uses a complex mapping algorithm to separate the metadata into layers (that is, Conceptual, Storage, Mapping), which enables you to model your domain based on entities vs. database tables.

For example, in EF you can map a single entity to one or more tables or views, or you can map multiple entities to the same table or view. This support for complex scenarios is exemplified by the EF user interface seen in Figure 12-3. Here, as you have seen in earlier chapters, you have a more defined properties window than in LTS and you have the Model Browser window, which gives you UI access to the `.edmx` file.

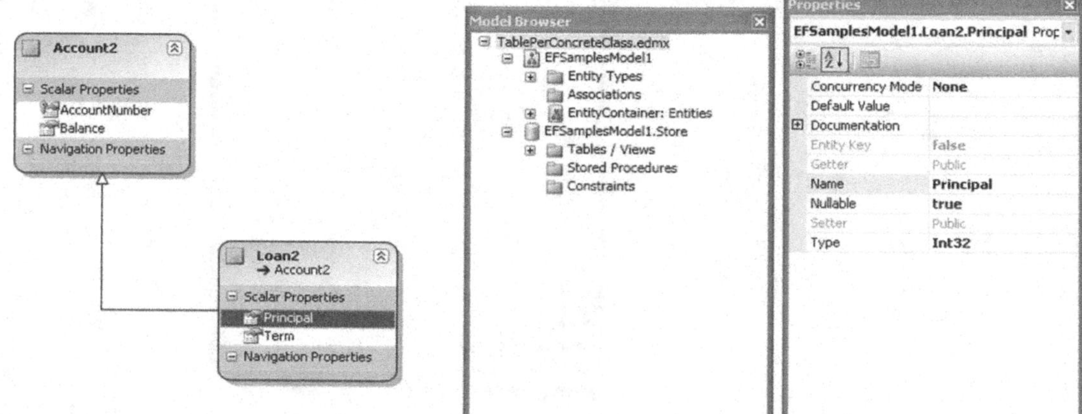

Figure 12-3. *EF Model Browser and Properties windows*

Another aspect that further demonstrates EF's ability to be an enterprise solution is its support for inheritance. Unlike LTS, which supports simple inheritance only in the form of Table per Hierarchy, EF supports all the core ORM inheritance patterns. These patterns include Table per Hierarchy, Table per Class, and Table per Concrete Class.

Figure 12-4 shows additional UI functionality, which is another differentiator for EF. In this example, you have the Mapping Details browser, which enables you to manipulate different forms of inheritance in your model and also enables you to control the mapping of your entities to tables and views.

Another reason why EF has rock star status is because of its support for complex composite types and many-to-many relationships. Additionally, where EF has LINQ to Entities, which is similar in design to LTS, EF also has Entity SQL and a strong provider model. Additionally, EF is approaching provider independence and has overall momentum in the community, things that LTS is missing.

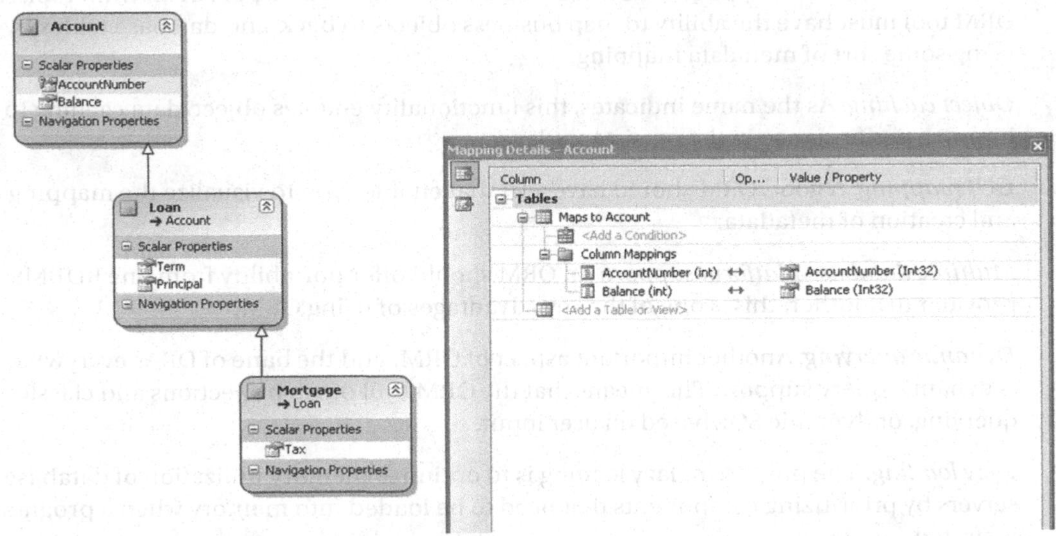

Figure 12-4. *The EF Mapping Details window*

Although LTS lacks some functionality for more complex scenarios, by using the patterns and practices learned in this text, you can easily adapt the use of LTS to any enterprise application. However, if you are looking for an ORM option that has everything you need out of the box for a complex n-tier application, you may want to start with EF.

My general opinion after writing this book is that both solutions have flaws. This has to be expected as these are, after all, Microsoft's first real go at ORM. I don't plan on dropping my third-party ORM tools from my solutions anytime soon; however, as Microsoft's products mature and as the community embraces ORM, I will likely be making the switch sometime in the future.

Alternatives

LTS and EF are far from the only games in town: ORM has been around for many years, so there is a robust and flourishing market of .NET tools available to you. The three alternatives that I want to briefly discuss are NHibernate, EntitySpaces, and LLBLGen Pro. You may be wondering how I came to this list, and why I left off such notable contenders as WilsonORMapper, DADO Solutions, Vanatec OpenAccess, and NPersist, not to mention all the code generators out there (for example, CodeSmith and DeKlarit). The answer is that I have only limited time and limited pages to devote to this, and these three products are the ones that I like because of price and usability. That's not to say that the other products on the market are not good, because many of them are, but I'm the author, so you are stuck with these three.

There is no possible way for me to cover all functional areas of these three ORM tools in this chapter, so instead of writing another book, I am going to focus on the qualities of a good ORM tool that I outlined in Chapter 1. To refresh your memory, the criteria are as follows:

Object-to-database mapping: This is the single most important aspect of an ORM tool. An ORM tool must have the ability to map business objects to back-end database tables by using some sort of metadata mapping.

Object caching: As the name indicates, this functionality enables object/data caching to improve performance in the persistence layer.

GUI mapping: A good ORM should have a UI that enables you to visualize the mapping and creation of metadata.

Multiple database platform support: An ORM should offer portability from one RDBMS provider to another; this is one of the key advantages of using ORM.

Dynamic querying: Another important aspect of ORM, and the bane of DBAs everywhere, is dynamic query support. This means that the ORM tool offers projections and classless querying, or dynamic SQL based on user input.

Lazy loading: The purpose of lazy loading is to optimize memory utilization of database servers by prioritizing components that need to be loaded into memory when a program is started.

Nonintrusive persistence: Nonintrusive persistence means that there is no need to extend or inherit from any function, class, interface, or anything else provider-specific.

Code generation: The purists will insist that there is no place for code generation in ORM, because a well-thought-out object model should be coded by hand. In my opinion, a successful ORM will optionally support some form of code generation.

Multiple object-oriented framework support: This is when a product offers compatibility with multiple object-oriented languages and development environments.

Stored procedure support: An ORM tool should support dynamic querying and stored procedures.

NHibernate

If there is a ubiquitous ORM tool in the .NET world, you could argue that NHibernate is it. NHibernate is a port of the highly successful Hibernate ORM in Java. NHibernate is an open source (free) ORM tool that gives you a persistent, ignorant, transparent framework for persistence. NHibernate uses metadata in a similar manner to LTS and EF and supports external XML mapping files and code attributes as the store for this metadata. Table 12-1 is an analysis of NHibernate based on the criteria that we established as qualities of a good ORM tool.

Table 12-1. *NHibernate Analysis*

Criteria	Analysis
Object-to-database mapping	NHibernate has full support for object-to-database mapping.
Object caching	NHibernate has a first-level cache where entities are stored, and an optional and configurable second-level cache where values of entities are stored across sessions.
GUI mapping	NHibernate does not have a packaged GUI. However, because it is open source, NHibernate has many third-party GUIs that work with the framework. Some examples include HQL Analyzer, MyGeneration, and CodeSmith, among many others.
Database independence	NHibernate supports the following databases: SQL Server, Oracle, Microsoft Access, Firebird, PostgreSQL, IBM DB2, MySQL, and SQLite.
Dynamic querying	The default behavior is for NHibernate to use dynamic querying, but they also provide a query language similar to ESQL called Hibernate Query Language (HQL) and support for inline SQL. Additionally, there is a community LINQ provider available, which will likely be included in a later release. Finally, NHibernate has full support for all types of associations and relationships (such as many-to-many).
Lazy loading	NHibernate supports optional lazy loading. By default this is disabled.
Nonintrusive persistence	NHibernate is one of the few ORM tools that support complete nonintrusive persistence.
Multiple object-oriented support	If anybody can claim this, NHibernate can. NHibernate is a port of a Java ORM and so the metadata is nearly identical, and NHibernate supports Mono (that is, .NET on Linux).
Stored procedure support	Yes, NHibernate supports stored procedures.

As you have seen throughout this book, my philosophy is to show you the metadata first and then show you the code. Listing 12-1 shows the XML metadata for the `Department` table in the `AdventureWorks` database. As you can see in this example, the mapping metadata is similar to EF and LTS in that it contains class details such as properties and types and database details such as table names, column names, and attributes about nullability.

Listing 12-1. *NHibernate Metadata Mapping Example*

```
<?xml version="1.0" encoding="utf-8" ?>
<hibernate-mapping xmlns="urn:nhibernate-mapping-2.0"
     assembly="AdventureWorks" namespace="AdventureWorks">
     <class name="Department" table="Department">
            <id name="Departmentid" column="DepartmentID"
                   type="Int16" unsaved-value="0">
                   <generator class="native"/>
            </id>
            <bag name="EmployeeDepartmentHistoryList" inverse="true"
                   lazy="true" >
                   <key column="DepartmentID" />
                   <one-to-many class="EmployeeDepartmentHistory" />
            </bag>
            <property column="Name" type="String" name="Name"
                   not-null="true" length="50" />
            <property column="GroupName" type="String" name="GroupName"
                   not-null="true" length="50" />
            <property column="ModifiedDate" type="DateTime"
                   name="ModifiedDate" not-null="true" />
     </class>
</hibernate-mapping>
```

Where there is mapping metadata, there is C# code. Listing 12-2 shows the C# class that would be associated with the metadata from Listing 12-1. This is a standard POCO class, as you have seen throughout the book.

Listing 12-2. *NHibernate Entity Class*

```
public class Department
{
       private short _departmentid;
       private IList<EmployeeDepartmentHistory>
              EmployeeDepartmentHistoryList;
       private string _name;
       private string _groupname;
       private DateTime _modifieddate;

       // Required by NHibernate
       public Department(){}

       public virtual short Departmentid
       {
              get
              { return _departmentid; }
```

```
        set
        { _departmentid = value; }
    }

    public virtual IList<EmployeeDepartmentHistory>
        EmployeeDepartmentHistoryList
    {
        get
        { return _EmployeeDepartmentHistoryList; }
        set
        { _EmployeeDepartmentHistoryList = value; }
    }

    public virtual string Name
    {
        get
        { return _name; }
        set
        { _name = value; }
    }

    public virtual string GroupName
    {
        get
        { return _groupname; }
        set
        { _groupname = value; }
    }

    public virtual DateTime ModifiedDate
    {
        get
        { return _modifieddate; }
        set
        { _modifieddate = value;}
    }
}
```

EntitySpaces

EntitySpaces is very different from NHibernate, LTS, and EF because the developers took a very code-generated approach to ORM. This approach has led to a very high-performing ORM tool because there is no reliance on external metadata mapping files. Instead, your mapping code is generated inline with your entities. Now, as you have learned over the previous 11 chapters, I am a strong proponent of a domain model that is independent of your data model, and yes, EntitySpaces goes against this; however, the ease of use and speed of this tool gives it a place at the table. Speaking of tables, Table 12-2 provides an analysis of EntitySpaces based on the criteria that we established as qualities of a good ORM tool.

Table 12-2. *EntitySpaces Analysis*

Criteria	Analysis
Object-to-database mapping	EntitySpaces provides full ORM support.
Object caching	The philosophy of the EntitySpaces designers is that caching leads to its own set of problems, so caching is not natively supported by EntitySpaces.
GUI mapping	EntitySpaces maps from the bottom up by using the MyGeneration code-generation tool as the GUI.
Database independence	EntitySpaces supports Microsoft SQL Server, SQL CE, Microsoft Access, Oracle, VistaDB, and PostgreSQL.
Dynamic querying	The DynamicQuery API is powerful in EntitySpaces because everything is parameterized and strongly typed, and subqueries are supported. EntitySpaces does not currently support LINQ as the query engine, but this may be included in a later release. Additionally, EntitySpaces supports all types of relationships and associations.
Lazy loading	EntitySpaces will generate a full hierarchical data model and supports all relationships and lazy loading in the model.
Nonintrusive persistence	EntitySpaces does not support nonintrusive persistence. All entities must inherit from an EntitySpaces base class.
Multiple object-oriented support	EntitySpaces has robust Mono support and supports both VB.NET and C#.
Stored procedure support	EntitySpaces has robust support for stored procedures, more so than most ORM tools. Switching from stored procedures to dynamic CRUD can be achieved with a configuration change, and none of the code is affected by this change.

EntitySpaces is modestly priced at $149 for a developer license and $499 for the source code. According to the EntitySpaces web site (`www.entityspaces.net/portal/Pricing/tabid/88/Default.aspx`), discounts are also available for bulk orders of the product. At this price point, EntitySpaces is quite affordable for most projects.

Before starting with EntitySpaces, you need to download MyGeneration, the open source, template-based code-generation tool (`www.mygenerationsoftware.com/portal/default.aspx`). As mentioned in Table 12-2, MyGeneration is the GUI for EntitySpaces. Figure 12-5 shows a screen shot of MyGeneration. As you can see, on the left side of the screen are many templates that can be used for code generation. In this example, I have expanded the EntitySpaces template directory, but also worth noting is that I have expanded the NHibernate template category. Using the code-generation templates is very intuitive, and so I am not going to show step-by-step examples of this. If you have been able to read this book, I assure you that you will be able to pick up MyGeneration and go with little or no assistance.

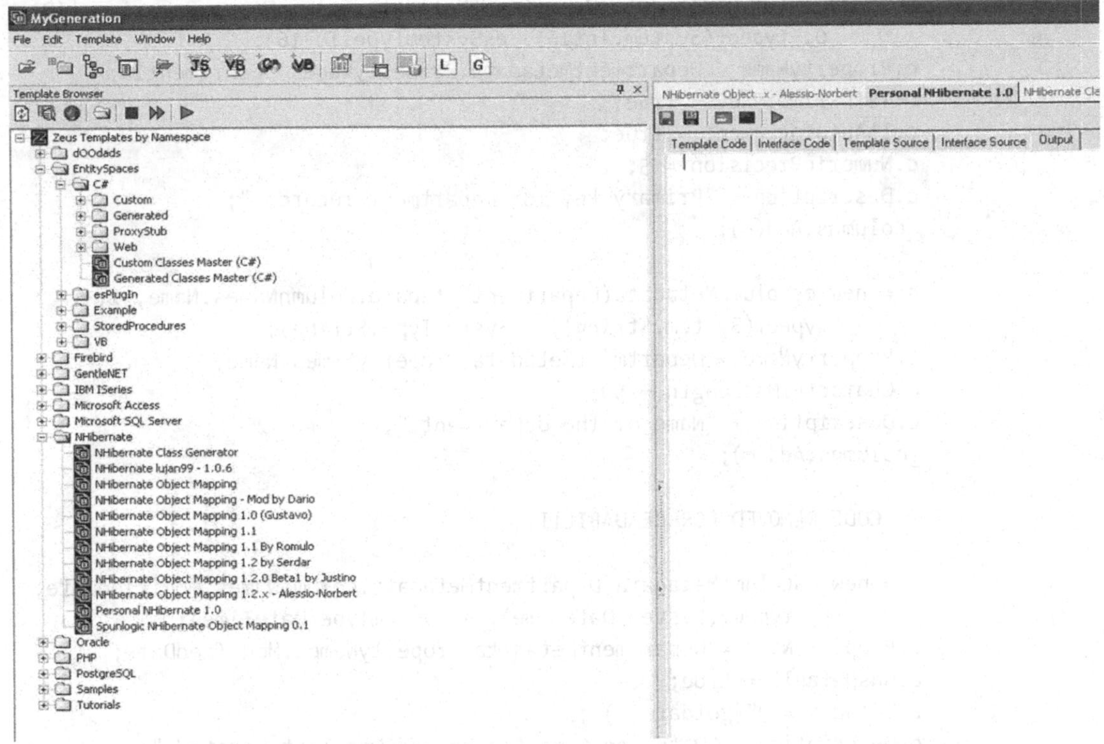

Figure 12-5. *MyGeneration, a free code-generation tool*

After you have generated the code for EntitySpaces (and again I am not going to go through all the details because you can go to the web site for help getting started), you basically have a complete data access layer. Listing 12-3 is an abridged version of the metadata used by EntitySpaces to work with a `Department` entity. As you can see, in this example a partial class called `DepartmentMetadata` is created to handle the mapping from entity to database. The constructor creates `esColumnMetadata` and a portion of the `esDefault` method, which builds the mapping used by the EntitySpaces engine.

Caution Listing 12-3 is not the complete set of metadata code used by EntitySpaces. This example is used to demonstrate only a few key areas of how EntitySpaces handles metadata mapping.

Listing 12-3. *Abridged Version of EntitySpaces DepartmentMetadata*

```
public partial class DepartmentMetadata : esMetadata, IMetadata
{

        protected DepartmentMetadata()
        {
                _columns = new esColumnMetadataCollection();
                esColumnMetadata c;
```

```
            c = new esColumnMetadata(DepartmentMetadata.ColumnNames.DepartmentID,
                  0, typeof(System.Int16), esSystemType.Int16);
            c.PropertyName = DepartmentMetadata.PropertyNames.DepartmentID;
            c.IsInPrimaryKey = true;
            c.IsAutoIncrement = true;
            c.NumericPrecision = 5;
            c.Description = "Primary key for Department records.";
            _columns.Add(c);

            c = new esColumnMetadata(DepartmentMetadata.ColumnNames.Name, 1,
                  typeof(System.String), esSystemType.String);
            c.PropertyName = DepartmentMetadata.PropertyNames.Name;
            c.CharacterMaxLength = 50;
            c.Description = "Name of the department.";
            _columns.Add(c);

            // CODE REMOVED FOR READABILITY

            c = new esColumnMetadata(DepartmentMetadata.ColumnNames.ModifiedDate,
                  3, typeof(System.DateTime), esSystemType.DateTime);
            c.PropertyName = DepartmentMetadata.PropertyNames.ModifiedDate;
            c.HasDefault = true;
            c.Default = @"(getdate())";
            c.Description = "Date and time the record was last updated.";
            _columns.Add(c);

      }

      private esProviderSpecificMetadata esDefault(string mapName)
      {
            if(!_providerMetadataMaps.ContainsKey(mapName))
            {
                  esProviderSpecificMetadata meta = new
                        esProviderSpecificMetadata();

                  meta.AddTypeMap("DepartmentID",
                        new esTypeMap("smallint", "System.Int16"));
                  meta.AddTypeMap("Name", new esTypeMap("nvarchar",
                        "System.String"));
                  meta.AddTypeMap("GroupName", new esTypeMap("nvarchar",
                        "System.String"));
                  meta.AddTypeMap("ModifiedDate", new esTypeMap("datetime",
                        "System.DateTime"));

                  //CODE REMOVED FOR READABILITY
```

```
                this._providerMetadataMaps["esDefault"] = meta;
        }

                return this._providerMetadataMaps["esDefault"];
        }
}
```

The last point that I want to make about EntitySpaces is about some of the other generated classes that get produced. Although you might expect a standard POCO class for `Department`, you actually end up with an abstract class called `esDepartment` that contains properties and helper methods, as seen in Listing 12-4. In this example, you have a get/set property that uses the `DepartmentMetadata` class (which you saw in Listing 12-3), and you have a method called `LoadByPrimaryKey`, which is used by the EntitySpaces framework and can be used to retrieve your entity. Following this pattern, the `Department` entity (not shown) inherits from the `esDepartment` class and thus becomes a data-aware smart object.

Listing 12-4. *Example Property and Helper Method in esDepartment Class*

```
virtual public System.Int16? DepartmentID
{
        get
        {
                return base.GetSystemInt16(
                        DepartmentMetadata.ColumnNames.DepartmentID);
        }
        set
        {
                if(base.SetSystemInt16(
                        DepartmentMetadata.ColumnNames.DepartmentID, value))
                {
                        this.MarkFieldAsModified(
                                DepartmentMetadata.ColumnNames.DepartmentID);
                }
        }
}

public virtual bool LoadByPrimaryKey
        (esSqlAccessType sqlAccessType, System.Int16 departmentID)
{
        if (sqlAccessType == esSqlAccessType.DynamicSQL)
                return LoadByPrimaryKeyDynamic(departmentID);
        else
                return LoadByPrimaryKeyStoredProcedure(departmentID);
}
```

LLBLGen Pro

First, I should say LLBLGen Pro is probably the grandfather of commercial .NET ORM tools and was developed by one of the experts on ORM, Frans Bouma. LLBLGen Pro is the child of LLBLGen, which was an ORM tool (now deprecated) designed specifically to use stored procedures. LLBLGen Pro, like EntitySpaces, uses code generation to build out a robust data access framework, based on ORM patterns. Similar to EntitySpaces, LLBLGen Pro doesn't support the POCO, or PI concept of ORM; instead LLBLGen Pro (like EntitySpaces) generates data-aware classes based on your relational model. Let's look at how LLBLGen Pro stacks up against our criteria in Table 12-3.

Table 12-3. *LLBLGen Pro Anlaysis*

Criteria	Analysis
Object-to-database mapping	LLBLGen Pro provides full ORM support.
Object caching	LLBLGen Pro does not use an in-memory object cache but does provide you with a mechanism for implementing this yourself.
GUI mapping	LLBLGen Pro has one of the best GUIs on the market.
Database independence	LLBLGen Pro supports Microsoft SQL Server, SQL Server CE, Microsoft Access, Oracle, VistaDB, PostgreSQL, DB2, and Sybase.
Dynamic querying	LLBLGen Pro supports highly optimized dynamic queries through its proprietary Dynamic Query Engine (DQE). LLBLGen Pro also has full support for all types of relationships and associations. Additionally, at the time of this writing, an unsupported LINQ provider is available, and a supported provider is on the roadmap to release a supported version in 2008.
Lazy loading	LLBLGen Pro has full support for lazy loading.
Nonintrusive persistence	LLBLGen Pro does not support nonintrusive persistence or POCO.
Multiple object-oriented support	LLBLGen Pro is supported on all versions of .NET but is not officially supported on Mono or other object-oriented frameworks.
Stored procedure support	Although the DQE is highly scalable, LLBLGen Pro also supports stored procedures.

In Table 12-3, I said that LLBLGen Pro has one of the best ORM GUIs on the market; let's take a closer look. In Figure 12-6, you have a screen shot of LLBLGen Pro. In this example, a project explorer contains your model. This screen shot doesn't really do the product justice, so I am going to narrate a few points about the tool. First, LLBLGen Pro has a robust template engine that can be used, like MyGeneration, for any number of tasks. Next, unlike MyGeneration, LLBLGen Pro uses a task-based approach to code generation, in which you have the ability to configure which tasks execute in which order based on a preset file (aptly named with a `.preset` file extension). Finally, out of the box LLBLGen Pro provides two template groups, or you might say architectures, for code generation: Self-Servicing and Adapter.

I am not going to go in depth on these two approaches because you can go to the web site (`www.llblgen.com/defaultgeneric.aspx`) and learn all about them, but I will give you a brief overview. The Self-Servicing template group generates all your entities with the necessary methods and interfaces required for persistence (that is, the persistence code is inline). Alternatively, the Adapter group generates entities that use a generated adapter, similar to the .NET `DataAdapter`, to handle persistence; the entities have no inline persistence code.

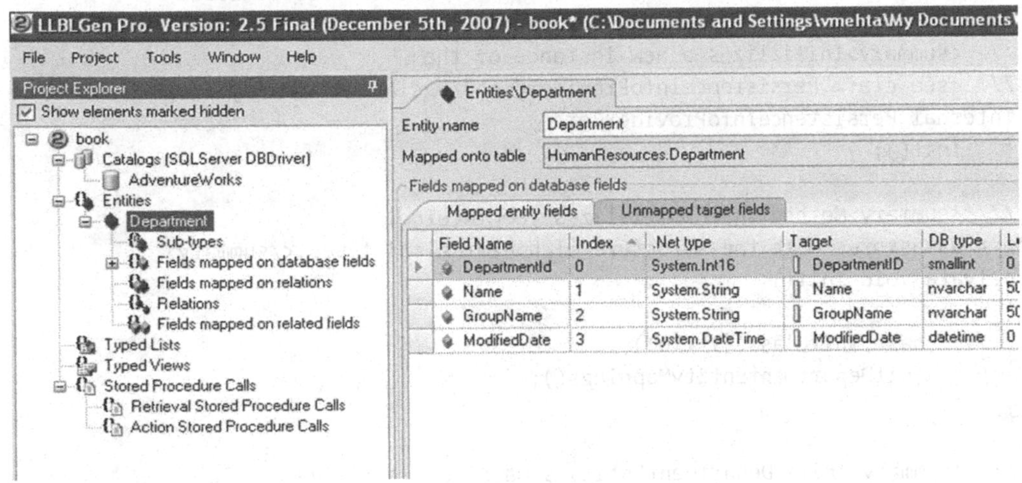

Figure 12-6. *LLBLGen Pro GUI*

■ Note The LLBLGen Pro examples seen in this chapter are all generated using the Self-Servicing template group.

Before we continue looking at the LLBLGen Pro entities and metadata, I should take a few sentences to talk about the cost of this product. LLBLGen Pro is developed in the Netherlands and so it is priced in euros. At the time of this writing, the price for a single developer license is 229 euros. It is important to note that the price, similar to EntitySpaces, drops as you purchase more licenses; however, with the current weak dollar, this does make this the most expensive of the alternatives. The good part is even at 229 euros, you are not going to be breaking the bank for any decent-size development project.

Continuing with the example, after connecting to the `AdventureWorks` database (as seen in Figure 12-6) and selecting the `Department` table for mapping, you can generate the data access framework. Listing 12-5 shows one of the classes that is generated. This class, `persistenceInfoProviderCore`, handles the metadata mapping in the framework. Here you can see that `AddElementMapping` is called on its base (`PersistenceInfoProviderBase`) to create the metadata used by ORM.

Caution The code shown in Listings 12-5 and 12-6 is used to demonstrate the basics of metadata mapping and entity generation in LLBLGen Pro. It is expected that there are classes that you won't be familiar with in these examples. If you would like to learn more about this product, I recommend visiting its web site (www.llblgen.com/pages/features.aspx).

Listing 12-5. *LLBLGenPro Metadata Mapping*

```
internal class PersistenceInfoProviderCore : PersistenceInfoProviderBase
{
       /// <summary>Initializes a new instance of the
       /// <see cref="PersistenceInfoProviderCore"/> class.</summary>
       internal PersistenceInfoProviderCore()
       {   Init(); }

       /// <summary>Method that initializes the internal
       /// datastores with the structure of hierarchical types.</summary>
       private void Init()
       {
              base.InitClass((1 + 0));
              InitDepartmentEntityMappings();
       }

       /// <summary>Inits DepartmentEntity's mappings</summary>
       private void InitDepartmentEntityMappings()
       {
              base.AddElementMapping( "DepartmentEntity", "AdventureWorks",
                     @"HumanResources", "Department", 4 );
              base.AddElementFieldMapping( "DepartmentEntity", "DepartmentId",
                     "DepartmentID", false, (int)SqlDbType.SmallInt, 0, 0, 5,
                      true, "SCOPE_IDENTITY()", null, typeof(System.Int16), 0 );
              base.AddElementFieldMapping( "DepartmentEntity", "Name", "Name",
                      false, (int)SqlDbType.NVarChar, 50, 0, 0, false, "", null,
                      typeof(System.String), 1 );
              base.AddElementFieldMapping( "DepartmentEntity", "GroupName",
                      "GroupName", false, (int)SqlDbType.NVarChar, 50, 0, 0, false,
                      "", null, typeof(System.String), 2 );
              base.AddElementFieldMapping( "DepartmentEntity", "ModifiedDate",
                      "ModifiedDate", false, (int)SqlDbType.DateTime, 0, 0, 0,
                      false, "", null, typeof(System.DateTime), 3 );
        }
}
```

The final topic I want to cover regarding LLBLGen Pro is the entity that is generated. Listing 12-6 shows an example of a property and a persistence/helper function found in the `DepartmentEntity` class. As you can see, the property for `DepartmentId` is using two methods (not shown), GetValue and SetValue, to encapsulate some ORM functionality. Additionally, in this example you have the FetchUsingPK method, which as its name indicates can be used to fetch the DepartmentEntity by primary key.

Listing 12-6. *Example Property and Helper Function in DepartmentEntity Class*

```
/// <summary> The DepartmentId property of the Entity Department<br/><br/>
/// </summary>
/// <remarks>Mapped on table field: "Department"."DepartmentID"<br/>
/// Table field type characteristics (type, precision, scale, length):
///          SmallInt, 5, 0, 0<br/>
/// Table field behavior characteristics (is nullable, is PK, is identity):
///          false, true, true</remarks>

public virtual System.Int16 DepartmentId
{
       get { return
                 (System.Int16)GetValue(
                 (int)DepartmentFieldIndex.DepartmentId, true);
           }
       set { SetValue((int)DepartmentFieldIndex.DepartmentId,
                           value, true);
           }
}

/// <summary> Fetches the contents of this entity from
///          the persistent storage using the primary key.</summary>
/// <param name="departmentId">PK value for Department
///          which data should be fetched into this Department object</param>
/// <returns>True if succeeded, false otherwise.</returns>
public bool FetchUsingPK(System.Int16 departmentId)
{
      return FetchUsingPK(departmentId, null, null, null);
}
```

Summary

In this chapter, you learned about some of the alternatives to using LTS or EF for ORM. Although in a lot of ways this chapter has not done these products justice, I hope that it has gotten you thinking about the different possibilities available when building your data access layer. While NHibernate follows a PI model, LLBLGen Pro and EntitySpaces take a different approach to ORM. I can honestly tell you that I have used all three products with great success in my solutions. What you need to take away from this chapter and this book is that there is no such thing as a one-size-fits-all ORM tool. There are too many variables when it comes to software development, and thus it is impossible to say, "I use only the so-and-so ORM tool." To conclude, I leave you with this thought: there is no tool on the market that is perfect in all situations. Only through good design can we achieve a level of perfection in software development.

Index

Numbers and Symbols

A

F

M

N

O

P

Q

R

S

T